Studies in

AFRICAN AMERICAN HISTORY AND CULTURE

edited by

GRAHAM RUSSELL HODGES

A GARLAND SERIES

African Americans in the Reconstruction Era

AFRICAN AMERICANS IN THE RECONSTRUCTION ERA

GAO CHUNCHANG

GARLAND PUBLISHING, Inc.
A MEMBER OF THE TAYLOR & FRANCIS GROUP
NEW YORK & LONDON / 2000

Published in 2000 by
Garland Publishing, Inc.
A member of the Taylor & Francis Group
29 West 35th Street
New York, NY 10001

10   9   8   7   6   5   4   3   2

Library of Congress Cataloging-in-Publication Data
Chunchang, Gao, 1966–.
    African Americans in the Reconstruction era / Gao Chunchang.
       p.   cm.—(Studies in African American history and culture)
    Includes bibliographical references (p.) and index.
    ISBN 0-8153-3596-2 (acid-free paper)
    1. Afro-Americans—History—1863–1877.   2. Reconstruction.
I. Title.   II. Series.
E185.2.G36   1999
973'.096073—dc21   99-35585
                                                                CIP

Printed on acid-free, 250-year-life paper
Manufactured in the United States of America

Contents

Series Editor's Preface

In the spring of 1998, I was privileged to serve as a Fulbright Senior Lecturer at the Foreign Affairs College in Beijing, China, and one of my duties was to visit and lecture at American Studies programs in China. At Nankai University in Tienjin, I met Li Jian-ming, professor of American Studies, and his student Gao Chunchang, who had just completed his doctoral dissertation on African Americans in the Reconstruction era. I was already familiar with Gao's work, because it had been listed as a recently finished dissertation in the *Journal of American History*. During my visit, Gao impressed me with his passionate interest in African American history, and I asked him for an abstract of his work in English. The careful analysis he presented in the abstract convinced me to seek a book contract with Garland Publishing for his dissertation.

On another visit to China, to the Overseas Chinese Institute at Ji Nan University in Guangzhou, I met and talked extensively with Wu Jin-ping, another graduate of Li's exciting program at Nankai. I was equally enthusiastic about Wu's dissertation on Frederick Douglass and secured a book contract for him. I was taken by these scholars' diligence and creativity in writing the American past, using the primary and secondary materials available to them. They worked on English translations of their dissertations, after which I polished their prose and Garland enlisted professional copyeditors to complete the conversion into English. The results are two books, Gao's *African Americans in the Reconstruction Era* and Wu's *Frederick Douglass and the Black Liberation Movement,* that provide American readers with fresh new analyses of our past through the eyes of scholars from the People's Republic of China. These books are, I think, the best kind of intellectual collaboration that can result from the collegial work of fellow international scholars, enhanced by the Fulbright fellowships. Administrators from the Fulbright agency often told new lecturers such as myself that the experience teaching abroad would transform our lives. Two years later, I can attest to the truth of that statement. I am grateful, too, that Garland Publishing has supported this positive international collaboration.

Graham Russell Hodges

Introduction

Is there discrimination against African Americans in American history? Some flatly deny its existence, and others resent the mere mention of this term. To some extent, the divergence of views is due to the different definitions of discrimination as well as the different identities of the persons concerned. In my opinion, discrimination against African Americans is a racial problem of differential social status caused by inborn ethnic factors rather than postnatal ones such as personal ability and achievements, and its existence is a continuous historical fact. Because of these inborn differences, blacks could not share equal opportunities or equal rights to participate in mainstream society, and in some cases they were even put into a conquered state. The extreme manifestation was slavery. In the light of slavery, we can describe the conquered state as follows:

- Politically, whites had fully deprived blacks of their personal rights, having exclusive, paramount, coercive power over blacks.
- In the economic sphere, whites continuously exercised extraeconomic exploitation and perpetual monopoly on black laborers. Blacks could not control their labor process or its fruits, let alone possess the means of production or freely compete in the labor market. As a factor of production, they were firmly fixed to their "place." The price of labor had little meaning to black themselves; it was only embodied among white owners. The most important quality of laborers was loyalty rather than efficiency; in other words, the factor of ability was covered with a thick layer of politics or ideology.

- Blacks' submissive social status was a basic character of the "peculiar system." Blacks were required to remain docile and obedient and follow the strict social etiquette. There was an invisible color line between the two races, though they might be physically close to each other. In an extreme sense, whites' coercive power even penetrated into the sexual sphere. Black females were not only exploited as laborers or machines for producing laborers, but also might become their masters' concubines, with their family rights rudely violated. At the same time, black men were regarded as untamed animals, and, as often as not, entered into whites' subconsciousness as a symbol of sexual aggression.
- Enjoying a monopoly on cultural tools such as religion, education, and the press, whites also could mold the prevalent criterion of social values. Blacks were put in an environment of coercive assimilation, and their spiritual world split into the contradictory "two souls"; in other words, blacks had to struggle between complete assimilation and their own self-consciousness. Meanwhile, whites created an embarrassing dilemma for themselves between the universal norms of conduct and their superiority complex, thereby being confronted with the same problem of how to harmonize their own "two souls."

Thus, breaching the barrier of discrimination against African Americans rested on changing the ethnic conquered state into a continuous dialogue between the two races, transforming whites' monopoly of public power into joint governance between the races, and translating the coercive relationship between the two races into a reciprocal contractual one according to universal norms of conduct. Reconstruction meant just this kind of attempt, and we can generalize its effects as follows:

- In the political aspect, Reconstruction amendments ensured blacks' civil rights, especially the right to vote. As a result, whites' exclusive power was to some extent changed into a reasonable authority and even into a state of condominium by the two races. The coercive enforcement of the amendments and other laws, however, gave rise to the complicated problem of the legality of Reconstruction governments.
- In the economic area, whites' monopoly on black laborers began to disintegrate, and laborers' free bargaining power arose. Blacks could determine the price of their labor, and the political

or ideological attribute of their economic ability was temperately reduced. While an employer could choose his employees, laborers also could choose their employers. On the one hand, laborers were continuously moving about; but on the other hand, employers united to boycott black initiatives, legally or illegally. As a result, a compromise mechanism gradually arose in agriculture; the sharecropping system came to the fore, and later rigidified.

• Racial relations deteriorated because of blacks' pursuit of their liberty and getting "out of their place." The invisible color line now became increasingly visible in churches, schools, railroads, hotels, and other public facilities. De facto segregation took shape and was further reflected in law. Since the distance between the two races was widened and blacks withdrew their labor, for instance, cases of miscegenation sharply decreased. Because white women now seemed to have the freedom to choose a black partner or face the menace of being assaulted by black men, however, the subject of defending racial purity took on more importance among white men. The rampant activities of the Ku Klux Klan reflected whites' dread of losing their white identity. In fact, racial relations were now in a state of warfare. All these conflicts helped to place the racial problem at the core of Reconstruction politics.

• On the issue of complete assimilation or self-consciousness, blacks eagerly absorbed the doctrine of whites' universal ideals; on the other hand, they could pursue their own self-realization, which had long been oppressed under slavery. Therefore, they were allowed to reconstruct the originally infantile "black souls" and keep some balance between utter assimilation and their particularism. At the same time, whites themselves were also faced with the difficult task of how to develop their cultural essence and eliminate its dross.

The analysis above lists only some aspects of the issue facing American blacks, without explaining the origins of blacks' special status. If the conquered state was the substance of discrimination against blacks, why were blacks chosen to be the sole object of enslavement? If blacks' bondage was due to their weak status, why were white indentured servants, among whom were convicts and captives, able to escape their initial predicament and merge into American society? In other words, why couldn't whites, who were preponderate in social power, integrate blacks into their developing universal norms of conduct?

Concerning the de facto deviation from the universal norms of conduct, racism performed its important selecting function, which to a large extent gave rise to the differential status of white and black. Without these racial differences exploited by racism, the problem of black discrimination would be immediately changed into a general problem such as the human rights problem, the labor problem, and so on. If bondage had involved the white race as well as the black race without racial distinction, for instance, there would have been no discrimination, despite the existence of slavery. The ideology of the dominant race was the key to understanding issues affecting black Americans, for it was always connected with the dominant power and could explain why some races were discriminated against or enslaved. Perhaps only in light of this angle can we best comprehend why racism formed the "the central theme of Southern history."[1] In a sense, this tragic flaw doomed the fate of Reconstruction and continued to be a troublesome disease in America.

Having established that racism has such significance, what about its origins, its development, and its relationship with political and economic factors? It is necessary then to summarize the historical debates on the relationship between slavery and racism.[2]

Regarding racism as an unfortunate result of slavery, many scholars hold that slavery was earlier than racism. In the early twentieth century, the first man studying this relationship was perhaps James C. Ballagh, who thought that the blacks first coming to Virginia were not "slaves in the strict sense of the term," because "they were under the protection of international law in maintaining their original status, and had they been citizens of a powerful civilized community they might have received it."[3] Blacks were nothing "but colony servants," and that there was "a disposition to recognize them as such seems apparent." Having observed that some blacks might receive wages and buy their freedom, and that their lengths of servitude often depended on their conversion to Christianity, Ballagh then drew his conclusion: "Servitude not only preceded slavery in the logical development of the principle of subjection, but it was the historic base upon which slavery, by the extension and addition of incidents, was constructed."[4]

Accepting Ballagh's argument without doubt, John H. Russell further expanded it to New England. By analyzing the lists of black names and presenting the evidence that blacks sued for their freedom and became landowners, Russell concluded that "since it is the fact that the white population in the colony in 1619 had not been familiar in England with a system of slavery or with a model of a slave code, and since they had developed in Virginia a system of servitude and were fortifying it by law, it is plausible that the Africans became servants in a condition similar to the status of white servants."[5]

Under the premise that slavery preceded racism, some scholars began to discuss the origins of slavery. George W. Williams listed four important factors that inevitably led to the enslavement of blacks: "the latitude, the products of the soil, the demand for labor, the custom of the indenture of white servants, were abundant reason why the Negro should be doomed to bondage for life."[6] Some historians focused their attention on land and the labor supply. Thomas J. Wertenbaker asserted that "it was this very superabundance of riches which in the end proved the curse of the South. It was the soil which brought on the South the curse of slavery. With land, rich land in almost unlimited quantities to be had at very low prices, the constant demand was for cheap labor."[7] R. S. Cotterill stressed the importance of labor stability. Because "permanency, not skill, was the quality that was most needed in a labor supply for the South . . . in Virginia and Maryland the settlers adopted slavery slowly and reluctantly as a thing alien to all his English experience and repulsive to his English ideals."[8] On the other hand, Clement Eaton emphasized that slavery was an inevitable result of the inexorable economic "laws," and thought that "the presence of plentiful and cheap land suitable for agriculture and the lack of labor bred slavery," as men would seldom work "for free wages when they can become independent farmers."[9]

In further developing the thesis of Ballagh and Russell, Oscar Handlin is a scholar worth mentioning. "An examination of the conditions and status of seventeenth-century labor," Handlin wrote, "will show that slavery was not there from the start, that it was not simply imitated from elsewhere, and it was not a response to any qualities in the Negro himself."[10] On the contrary, it was a result of European tradition responding to the American environment. At the beginning, blacks were similar to white servants in status. "These newcomers, like so many others, were accepted, bought, and held as kind of servants."[11] To attract more laborers to fill the need of an expanding economy, however, the colonists had to improve white servants' conditions and shortened their labor terms, while black laborers did not need such encouragement, for their coming was involuntary. In addition, "the rudeness of the Negroes' manner, the strangeness of their language, the difficulty of communicating to them English notions of morality and proper behavior occasioned sporadic laws to regulate their conduct."[12] Though he had abstracted the racial factor from the development of slavery, Handlin denied its importance: "until the 1660's the statutes on the Negroes were not at all unique."[13]

Yet some scholars maintained that blacks were slaves from the beginning. Originally, this opinion was advanced by slavery apologists in the nineteenth century, who emphasized the influence of international custom and blacks' biological characters. Partly because of their having been captured, transported, and sold, not unlike the millions of blacks enslaved in the West Indies prior to 1619, and partly because of their reputed inferior peculiarity, the first blacks who disembarked in Virginia and Maryland became slaves. "Measured by the size, weight, and capacity of the brain," declared George Sawyer, a member of the Louisiana bar, "they are inferior to the race of aborigines of America."[14] "The die is cast; nature has assigned the condition of the Negro race, and fixed the limits of their destiny."[15]

Other scholars accepted the argument that slavery was evident from the beginning, though they, unlike the apologists, had no political aim. "He was seized in Africa with slavery in mind," Avery Craven wrote in 1939. "He was sold outright in America. A few may have become indentured servants in the American colonies in the early period, but experience soon proved that system too liberal for Negroes raw out of Africa."[16]

Susie M. Ames held a similar view. There were indeed some blacks who were serving for specified terms, Ames conceded, but in most cases it was very difficult "to tell whether the 'indenture' was a voluntary surrender by the master of further service due him or merely the customary procedure."[17]

Wesley Frank Craven also thought that a "sharp distinction" existed between black laborers and white servants from the beginning. Though blacks' fate might vary with the attitudes of individual masters, Craven maintained, most of the "peculiar problems of slave discipline were adequately covered by an increasing elaborate servant code."[18]

The greatest challenge to Handlin's thesis came from Carl N. Degler. A major fault in Handlin's case, Degler pointed out, "is the difficulty in showing that the white servant's position was improving during and immediately after the 1660s."[19] Returning to the Ballagh-Russell thesis that black servants preceded and shaped slavery, Degler wrote that "if, instead of assuming that discrimination is a consequence of slavery, we work on the assumption that discrimination preceded slavery and thereby conditioned it."[20] The origins of the racial problem, he thought, lay in the discriminatory mood of the early seventeenth century, and "from the outset, as far as the available evidence tells us, the Negro was treated as an inferior to the white man, servant or free."[21] The biological, religious, and cultural differences and the widespread biases on the part of white settlers were the decisive factors in the development of slavery. Instead of regarding this process as an isolated case on the American mainland, Degler stressed that the settlers had enough opportunities to learn the relevant knowledge of slavery from the Spanish and Portuguese colonies and in fact performed it by themselves.[22]

Hence the thesis that slavery preceded racism was reversed. Winthrop Jordan, however, did not interest himself in this debate. Unwilling to allow himself to fall into the trap that either discrimination or slavery preceded the other, Jordan adopted an original approach. "Rather than slavery causing 'prejudice,' or vice versa, they seem rather to have generated each other. Both were, after all, twin aspects of a general debasement of the Negro. Both may have been equally cause and effect, constantly reacting upon each other, dynamically joining hands to hustle the Negro down the road to degradation."[23] Tracing the settlers' attitudes towards blacks, Jordan found that as early as the sixteenth century whites did show a strong aversion to blacks' racial characters, among which their religions, way of life, and especially their blackness were most distinguishing. "From the first," Jordan argued, "Englishmen tended to set Negroes over against themselves, to stress what they conceived to be radically contrasting qualities of color, religion, and style of life, as well as animality and a peculiarly potent sexuality."[24] Concerning the driving forces of slavery, Jordan considerably approved the factor of labor demand and said that "Negroes became slaves, partly because there were social and economic necessities in America which called for some sort of bound, controlled labor."[25] On the other hand, he held that "taken as a whole, the evidence reveals a process of debasement of which hereditary lifetime service was an important but not the only part,"[26] and the enslavement in Virginia and Maryland "points to less borrowing and to this kind of process: a mutually interactive growth of slavery and unfavorable assessment, with no cause for either which did not cause the other as well."[27]

In his study on this subject, *American Slavery 1619–1877*, Peter Kolchin also treated this question in a similar way: "Indeed, what we now know suggests that the most appropriate question is not whether slavery caused prejudice or prejudice caused slavery (a false choice, since the evidence sustains neither of these two conjectures) but rather how slavery and prejudice interacted to create the particular set of social relationships that existed in the English mainland colonies."[28] Unlike

Jordan, however, Kolchin thought the ideological factor had little influence on slavery, while he particularly underlined its economic origin. "The turn to Africa came not because [of] any ideological concerns but because the flow of indentured white labor seemed to be drying up."[29]

Undoubtedly, the scholarly debate about the origins of slavery and racism is pertinent to the black question, but it still has some inadequacies:

The Classification of Whites' Racial Notions. The first inadequacy of the debate about the origins of slavery and racism regards the classification of whites' racial notions. Was there any difference among them? In fact, George Fredrickson has probed into this subject, distinguishing between "the explicit and rationalized racism that can be discerned in nineteenth- and early twentieth-century thought and ideology and the implicit or societal racism that can be *inferred* from actual social relationships."[30] To Fredrickson, the question was "to what extent was America really born racist as a result of social, economic, and political developments which took place well after the colonists' initial contacts with Africans?"[31] Fredrickson's train of thought is of inspiring significance. I, however, would rather classify the so-called racism into two kinds: whites' self-consciousness and the racism that has combined whites' self-consciousness and their desire for conquest. Roughly speaking, whites' self-consciousness corresponds to the term "implicit racism," and the latter type, to "explicit racism." The evolutionary process of whites' racial notions perhaps can be generalized in a term of *ideologization*, which means how popular ideas become the foundation of the dominant power. In turn, the process of ideologization might reinforce the illusory nature of ideology, about which a modern scholar noted that ideology was nothing but the expression of the imaginary relationship between individuals and their actual existing conditions or common myth by which a society or an era recognizes itself.

The Socioeconomic Background to Racism. A second inadequacy is, Against what background did racism exert its influence and finish its evolutionary process?

First of all, economic force is still a basic factor. In a competitive environment, economic law requires that capital, labor, and other productive elements integrate in some way and to some extent. Hence arises the negative economic force, such as avarice and exploitation, as well as the positive one, including the pursuit of technological rationality and mutual cooperation. As Murry N. Rosebud put it, "Just as the peaceful cooperation vs. coercive exploitation or production vs. exploitation form the two fundamental and mutually repelling factors among men, human history, and especially economic history, may be regarded as a struggle between the two principles."[32] At the same time, there is also a law regarding the unity of opposites between men's social interests and their status. Therefore, while the economic necessities of resource deployment and the least transaction cost drove whites to include blacks in their physical world, the opposite of their interests or status helped whites to reject blacks ideologically. The crystallization of racial slavery was merely the outcome of this logic. In such a contradictory movement, racism was conspicuously significant as the bond among white people and the means by which the upper strata split possible alignments among lower class groups. Meanwhile, when the opportunity was ripe, the positive force of the economic law requiring technological rationality and fair dealing also might make a demand, just as Northern capitalism helped to abolish slavery in the Civil War era. Being connected to the split of whites' souls, therefore, capitalism as a value system corresponded to the development of discrimination against blacks *and* its solution.

Secondly, while the power conquest embodied in colonialism was the main means by which discrimination formed, the conquered state itself continuously produced the venom of racism. It was the flame and sword in the process of colonization that constituted the substance of the relationship between black and white. Compared with Native Americans, whose problem was just a question of unfinished conquest, the black problem was already a finished one. After all, most human countries were born from the process of conquest and exploitation rather than through social contracts, and someone even asserted that "in a substantial sense, the country was an outcome of the success made by a gang of bandits."[33] Concerning the conquered state of the African Americans it's no wonder that it began to be addressed under the special environments of the Civil War and under the coercive policies of Reconstruction governments.

Thirdly, neither the force of capital nor colonial subjugation can explain the oppressive nature of the black treatment, without the origins of status difference being touched. If blacks' treatment was not different from that of whites, as we mention earlier, there would be no discrimination even if some blacks were in bondage. Economic force and colonial conquest cannot perfectly explain the direction of whites' action, and this flaw may be remedied by the concept of racism.

In addition, the mutual irreducibility of the economic force, colonial conquest, and ideology should not be neglected. In other words, one factor should not be simply regarded as the cause or result of another factor; and the three factors mutually affect and condition one another, each having its own operational rules. Drawing support from Plato's famous metaphor, we may describe their mutual relationships as follows: the economic force is the drawing horse, the political factor the bearing cart, and ideology the driver.

The American Cultural and Democratic Framework. A third inadequacy of the debate about slavery and racism is that it pays insufficient attention to the American cultural and democratic framework through which issues affecting African Americans were gradually solved. As Margaret Just Butcher put it, "The right and most effective way to look at the Negro's relationship to American culture is to consider it not as an isolated race matter and minority group concern, but rather in the context of the whole of American culture."[34] The heart of the matter is the positive factor within American core values: the universal norms of conduct. To explore its contradictory relationships with whites' self-consciousness and with the economic and political background is very helpful to understand the other side of black issues.

As a matter of fact, Gunnar Myrdal has observed that on the one hand, American whites did their utmost to maintain an image as reasonable creatures; on the other hand, they irrationally delimited a clear line and excluded blacks once racial relations were involved. He regarded this contradictory phenomenon as "America's dilemma."[35] Once drawing much attention from academic circles, this thesis has been consolidated by a sample investigation conducted by some scholars.[36] In my view, this dilemma is nothing but the contradiction between the universal norms of conduct within American core values and whites' self-consciousness or racism. In other words, it is "white men's two souls," with "blacks' two souls" as its counterpart. Being linked with the preponderant power, white men's two souls were of special importance in the black question.

One inadequacy of Myrdal is, perhaps, that he has not pointed out the negative side of the core value, such as the desire for conquest and the power worship in Protestant Christianity, whose integration with whites' self-consciousness constituted the negative facet to white men' souls. It is necessary, then, to trace this evolutionary process. Certainly, the positive side of white men's souls also needs exploring, for it coincided with the healthy values of American society and was one valuable nutrient of the growth of black souls.

In addition, the inner conflicts of white men's souls stressed earlier generally took place against the background of the society as a whole. In the periods of the Civil War and Reconstruction, for instance, conflicts on the universal values formed the starting point to discuss racial problems. Conversely, an individual did not inevitably belong to this caste, but he had more possibility to enter a state of internal "moral freedom." "It does not necessarily follow from the logical contradiction," Ralph H. Turner wrote in the 1950s, "that most people in American society perceive any dilemma here. In fact, the overenthusiastic student of race relations may be distressed to find how many people and groups sincerely feel no disloyalty to democratic ideals in their support of segregation and discrimination."[37] W. J. Cash even asserted bluntly that the Southern whites had "no capacity for abstract analysis" and "critical distinctions."[38] Yet opposite examples did exist. For some individuals in the Revolutionary era, for example, the existence of inner conflicts was indeed true.

In sum, the universal norms of conduct not only are a yardstick of the formation of issues affecting blacks, but also have direct importance in solving them. In a society with pluralism as its goal, individuals must comply with the universal norms of conduct and should not adopt a different standard towards others. As Jurgen Habermas stressed, the rationalization of "intercouse acts" should be up to the common and universal criteria. Rather than impractical conceptions abstracted by theorists, the universal norms of conduct were firmly rooted in American historical realities and were in fact a powerful political and social force. As the positive side of whites' souls, it derived from whites' beliefs in "the higher law" and American mission, and later on was consolidated by the rationalism of the Enlightenment. As Logan Wilson and William Kolb have observed, the consensus of a society is always organized around a core of "ultimate values." "In our own society," they maintained, "we have developed such ultimate values as the dignity of the individual, equality of opportunity, the right of life, liberty, and the pursuit of happiness, and the growth of the free personality."[39] Since *culture* may be defined as the system of value and belief, and the gist of this book is to describe how the universal values were challenged and enacted in American history, it is clear that discrimination against blacks lies where a cultural fault line exists. In fact, the reverence for the universal norms of conduct and the deviation from them promoted by racism constituted white men's two souls. Other minor paradoxes, including blacks' contradiction between freedom and safety, the paradox of black power, the paradox of legality, and the contradiction between independence and coercion, were all based on the main paradox. We will examine them in light of the special background of Reconstruction and discuss them in detail.

For giving kindhearted aid and constructive counsel while I have been engaged in this work, I especially wish to thank Professors Zhan Youlun, Yang Shengmao, Lu Jingsheng, and Li Jianming of Nankai University, China. Without the strong, unselfish support from Professor Graham Russell Hodges of Colgate University, this volume would not have been published in America. He polished the manuscript and finished the index at the last writing stage. I am also indebted to many American scholars and publishers for the extensive quotations in this book. Surely, Garland Publishing and its two editors, Rebecca Wipfler and Richard Koss, deserve my respect, too. As for others whose names cannot be listed here individually, their help will long be engraved on my mind.

NOTES

1. Ulrich B. Phillips, "The Central Theme of Southern History," *American Historical Review.* October 1928, pp. 30–43.

2. The following discussion is mainly based on Joseph Boskin's work, *Into Slavery: Racial Decisions in the Virginia Colony.* Philadelphia: J. B. Lippincott, 1976, pp. 101–112.

3. James C. Ballagh, *A History of Slavery in Virginia.* Baltimore: John Hopkins Press, 1902, p. 28.

4. *ibid.,* pp. 31–32.

5. John H. Russell, *The Free Negro in Virginia, 1619–1865.* Baltimore: John Hopkins Press, 1913, p. 23.

6. George W. Williams, *History of the Negro Race in America, 1619–1880.* New York: George Putnam and Co., 1883, pp. 1, 120.

7. Thomas J. Wertenbaker, *The Old South.* New York: Charles Scribner's Sons, 1942, p. 5.

8. R. S. Cotterill, *The Old South.* Glendale, CA: Arthur R. Cook, 1939, p. 80.

9. Clement Eaton, *A History of the Old South.* New York: Macmillan, 1949, p. 45.

10. Oscar and Mary Handlin, "The Origins of the Southern Labor System," *William and Mary Quarterly,* 3rd ser., vol. 7. pp. 199–222.

11. *ibid.,* p. 203.

12. *ibid.,* p. 208.

13. *ibid.,* p. 209.

14. George Sawyer, *Southern Institutions, or An Inquiry into the Origins and Early Prevalence of Slavery and the Slave Trade, etc., in Defence of the Southern Institutions.* Philadelphia: J. B. Lippincott, 1859, p. 185.

15. *ibid.,* p. 201.

16. Avery Craven, *The Repressible Conflict.* Baton Rouge: Louisiana State University Press, 1939, p. 41.

17. Susie M. Ames, *Studies of the Virginia Eastern Shore.* New York: Russell and Russell, 1973, p. 104.

18. Wesley Frank Craven, *The Southern Colonies in the Seventeenth Century, 1607–1689.* Baton Rouge: Louisiana State University Press, 1949, pp. 217–219.

19. Carl N. Degler, "Slavery and the Genesis of American Race Prejudice," *Comparative Studies in History and Society.* Vol. 21, October 1959. Quoted from August Meier and Elliot Rudiwick, eds., *The Making of Black America: Essays in Negro Life and History.* New York: Atheneum, 1969, p. 93.

20. Carl N. Degler, *Out of Our Past.* New York: Harper & Row, 1959, p. 30.

21. Degler, "Slavery and the Genesis of American Race Prejudice," *op. cit.,* p. 94.

22. *ibid.,* p. 95.

23. Winthrop Jordan, "Modern Tensions and the Origins of American Slavery," *Journal of Southern History,* February 1962, p. 29.

24. Winthrop Jordan, *White over Black: American Attitudes towards the Negro, 1550–1812.* Chapel Hill: University of North Carolina Press, 1968, p. 43.

25. *ibid.,* p. 61.

26. *ibid.,* p. 80.

27. *ibid.,* p. 80.

28. Peter Kolchin, *American Slavery, 1869–1877.* London: The Penguin Group, 1993, p. 14.

29. *ibid.,* p. 14.

30. George Fredrickson, "Towards a Social Interpretation of the Development of American Racism," in Nathan I. Huggins, Martin Kilson, and Daniel M. Fox, eds., *Key Issues in the Afro-American Experience.* New York: Harcourt Brace Jovanovich, 1971, pp. 240–241.

31. *ibid.,* p. 242.

32. Terry M. Perlin, ed., *Contemporary Anarchism.* Brunswick, NJ: Transaction Books, 1979. Translated from the Chinese edition, Part Four.

33. *ibid.* Translated from the Chinese edition, Part Four.

34. Margaret Just Butcher, "The Negro's Role in American Society," quoted from Leland D. Baldwin, ed., *Ideas in Action: Documentary and Interpretive Readings in American History.* Vol. 3. New York: American Book Company, 1968, p. 57.

35. Gunnar Myrdal, *The American Dilemma: Negro Problem and Modern Democracy*. New York: Random House, 1962. Appendix, "The Mechanism of Rationalization."

36. Frank R. Westie, "The American Dilemma: An Empirical Test," in Norval D. Glenn and Charles M. Bonjean, eds., *Blacks in the United States*. San Francisco: Chandler Publishing Company, 1969, pp. 201–206.

37. Ralph H. Turner, "Value Conflict in Social Disorganization," *Sociology and Social Research*, 38 (1954), p. 304.

38. Keith McKean, *Cross Currents in the South,* quoted from Baldwin, *op. cit.,* p. 108.

39. Logan Wilson and William L. Kolb, *Sociological Analysis*. New York: Free Press, 1949, p. 513.

African Americans in the Reconstruction Era

CHAPTER 1

The Origins of Discrimination against African Americans

THE ORIGINS OF WHITES' SELF-CONSCIOUSNESS AND THE CORE VALUE

The self-consciousness of white men was not merely a result of their contact with blacks, but it was a self-identity long maintained in English culture. As birds of a feather flock together, its basis, of course, included their biological self-identity, which, at the same time, was mingled with their superiority complex concerning their cultural tradition. The white color, in fact, conveyed a special meaning to English people in the Elizabethan era. White was the ideal color of perfect human beauty, especially when it was complemented by red. English subjects praised their queen as follows:

> Her cheeke, her chinne, her neck, her nose,
> This was a lillye, that was a rose;
> Her bosome, sleeke as Paris plaster,
> Held upp twoo bowles of Alabaster.[40]

In England, white and black connoted utterly contrary messages, while red and yellow were generally inconsistent. Red was as likely to be compared to a rose as to blood, and yellow as the symbol of cowardice seemed to have little relationship to human beings.[41] Yet the usage of white and black was always consistent. The connotation of white was always highly positive in England. Being used in weddings and religious ceremonies, it represented purity, beauty, sincerity, goodness, kindness, intelligence, and courage, and angels always had a pair of white wings. On the contrary, black was the symbol of depravity and wickedness. As the contemporary *Oxford English Dictionary* explained, it meant

> Deeply stained with dirt; soiled, dirty, foul. Having dark or deadly purpose, malignant; pertaining to or involving death, deadly; baneful, disastrous, sinister. Foul, iniquitous, atrocious, horrible, wicked. Indicating disgrace, censure, liability to punishment, etc.[42]

When two different cultures come into contact with each other, the dominant one inevitably measures the inferior one by its own criteria. If "we recognize the fact," wrote Brewton Berry, "that conflict involves also those subtle, restrained forms of interaction wherein one seeks to reduce the status of one's opponent, and not to eliminate him entirely from the conflict, then perhaps it is true that conflict invariably occurs when unlike people meet." [43] Seeking dominant power over blacks in the era of colonial expansion, English culture provides such an example.

When they initially met blacks in West Africa, Englishmen immediately realized the marked racial and cultural differences between them and showed some disgust and curiosity.

Of the biological differences between them, the complexion of Africans was most impressive. Compared with the Portuguese and Spanish, Englishmen suddenly found themselves in contact with blacks, and the complexion of the Africans on the West Coast was much deeper than that of Moors in North Africa, with whom the Portuguese and Spanish had long had dealings. People were very uneasy about the possible mixture of the two races. Being so "discontented at the great number of 'Negars and blackamoors' which are crept into the realm" by 1601, Queen Elizabeth issued a proclamation for their transportation out of the country.[44]

Yet overseas exploration and plantations could not manage without blacks. How to treat this distinctive race? What did the presence of blacks mean? In such circumstances, Englishmen began to explore the origins of blackness. At first, they were satisfied with the version that the blackness of Africans was caused by their exposure to the hot sun, but they soon found that Native Americans in the same latitudes had no similar trait, and that blacks brought to the low latitudes made no change to their color. Therefore, some Englishmen resorted to the Bible to explain their innate nature. Jeremiah 13:23 said that "Can Ethiopians (or Nubians) change their skin / or leopards their spots? / Then also you can do good / who are accustomed to do evil." A modern writer believes that it was the "first recorded slur" against the black race.[45] Adopting this version as early as 1578, George Best, an Elizabethan voyager and geographer, declared that the blackness "proceedeth of some naturall infection of the first inhabitants of that country, and so all the whole progenie of them descended, are still polluted with the same blot of infection."[46] Furthermore, the Bible could give a seemingly satisfactory explanation about the origin of blackness and enslavement of Africans. Genesis 9 described that when his father Noah became drunk and lay uncovered in his tent, Ham did not evade him, whereas his two brothers, Shem and Japheth, took a garment, laid it on both their shoulders, and walked backward and covered the nakedness of their father. When Noah awoke from his wine, he blessed Shem and Japheth and cursed Ham and his son Canaan: "Cursed be Canaan; lowest of slaves shall he be to his brothers." He also said: "Blessed by the Lord my God be Shem; and let Canaan be his slave. May God make space for Japheth, be his slave." This story could be connected with slavery.

The Bible, however, did not mention here whether the descendants of Ham or Canaan were blacks or not. This was not found until the oral traditions of Jews were collected in the Babylonian Talmud from the second century to the sixth century A.D. One story related that God forbade anyone to have sexual relations while on the Ark and Ham disobeyed this command. Another legend was that Ham was cursed with blackness because he resented the fact that his father desired to have a fourth son. To prevent the birth of a rival heir, Ham was said to have castrated his father. Therefore, Ham was cursed by being black.[47] In the sixteenth century, Englishmen mixed the two legends. In 1577, George Best incisively and vividly developed this idea. Noah and his sons and their wives, he thought, were "white" and "by course of nature should have begotten white children. But the envie of our great and continuall enemie the wicked Spirite is such, that as hee coulde not suffer our olde father Adam to live in the felicite and Angelike state wherein he was first created so againe, finding at this flood none but a father and three sons living, hee so caused one of them to disobey his fathers commandment, that after him all his posteritie should bee accursed." The commandment was that they should behold God "with reverence and feare," and that "while they remained in the Arke, they should use continencie, and abstaine from carnall copulations with their wives which good instructions and exhortations notwithstanding his wicked sonne Cham disobeyed, and being perswaded that the first childe borne after the flood

should inherite all the dominations of the earth." To punish the "wicked
and detestable fact," God commanded that

> a sonne should bee born whose name was Chus, who not onely it
> selfe, but all his posteritie after him should bee so blacke and loath-
> some, that it might remain a spectacle of disobedience to all the
> worlde. And of this blacke and cursed Chus came all these blacke
> Moores which are in Africa.[48]

Here, Best willfully connected blackness with licentiousness, stubbornness, and the devil, and at the same time linked whites with the image of
God, piety, and self-restraint. Putting blackness and whiteness as two opposing extremes, this view vividly expressed the self-consciousness of
his white contemporaries.

Englishmen also realized that African natives had different aesthetic
standards. To Africans, the "horrid Curles" and "disfigured" lips and
noses described by whites were reckoned as "the Beauties of the Country."[49] Obviously, the aesthetic temperaments that connected with self-
consciousness were considerably relative, and different peoples with
different cultures might have different views. The problem was not the
existence of differences, but how to adopt a tolerant attitude towards a
people with a different culture. In the period of colonial expansion, however, the power of the strong cast aside the dignity of the weak, with the
aesthetic standard of the dominant race being consolidated in the social
systems; the tastes of the dominant race in turn continuously extended
the color line. The vicious circle was then formed.

Besides the biological differences between whites and blacks, the
cultural ones were also very important. In the opinion of Englishmen,
the heathenism and savageness of Africans was in sharp contrast to the
English Christian civilization in the process of commercial revolution.
Africans were distinctive in many ways: many counties had not yet
gotten rid of their tribalism; tribes were often in bloody warfare; and the
natives wore exotic clothes and ornaments, lived in simple and crude
houses, used seemingly queer languages, and believed in gods never
heard of. Having enormous curiosity about this new world, Englishmen
took great delight in talking about the cosmetic mutilation, polygamy, in-
fanticide, ritual murder, and alleged incest between human beings and
apes. This interest, however, was not only the psychology of curiosity, but
also a mirror of self-introspection. In England, an earthshaking change
took place in the sixteenth century, and the agricultural and commercial

revolution was developing indepth. The development of capitalism had not only created the enterprising spirit, but also spread the general mood of avarice and depravity. On the one hand, people were busy making fortunes, on the other hand, they were rather disturbed by the social atmosphere. Once in their field of vision, Africans became a reminder of self-restraint. The African reality was regarded as the antithesis of Christian civilization. How terrible a condition they would land themselves in if they departed from the course of God! It was a savage state that English people were absolutely unwilling to involve themselves in, and that they must constantly warn themselves to avoid. They understood that the inevitable price to maintain their own civilization and purity was perpetual vigilance over the invasion of foreign matter. When an island race that thought no end of himself went into the "wildness," the presence of a different culture strengthened the self-identity of English people.

Obviously, the biological and cultural elements were connected. While Englishmen made value judgments about the blackness of Africans, they measured the "savageness" and heathenism of Africans on the basis of the significance of racial traits. Compared with the blackness of Africans, the color of Native Americans had not shaken Englishmen deeply. While emphasizing the "savageness" or heathenism of Native Americans, Englishmen never allowed their racial traits to be the obstacle of conversion. So it was not strange that Thomas Jefferson later on suggested intermarriage between whites and Native Americans. Meanwhile, the seemingly incorrigible traits of blacks and the despair of whites never caused whites to seriously undertake the mission of converting blacks before the eighteenth century. In American thought, Native Americans became the symbol of conflict between savageness and civilization, whereas blacks became the evil spirit in whites' subconsciousness, and the semihuman and semibeast image of blacks was deeply rooted into whites' mind. Because blackness itself was so disgusting, it would be more serious if it was connected with savageness, licentiousness, and the "black devil." Using many metaphors in *Othello*, Shakespeare unremittingly hinted at the presence of this connection. Without mincing words, some contemporary critics even asserted that blacks were descended from apes, or that apes were the mongrels reproduced by blacks and other unknown beasts. When alleging that "promiscuous coition of men and animal took place, wherefore the regions of Africa produce for us so many monsters," Jean Bodin was not alone.[50]

While whites' self-consciousness was strengthened by their cultural contact with blacks, the attitudes of English people toward other white peoples explained the range of their self-identity. By the criterion of religion or nationality, Englishmen confidently placed themselves at the center of concentric circles, each of which successively contained Welshmen, Scots, Irish, and other peoples. Although the arrangement might vary with individuals and time, blacks were always placed at the outermost circle by whatever criterion was used and were thereby the chief object of enslavement.

The difference between Native Americans and Englishmen was so large that Englishmen might quietly enslave the former, for they were heathens, "savages," and "red men." Yet as a whole, their relationship with English colonists was not so much one of enslavement as one of opponent. Unlike blacks, they were not the unwilling uprooters and had the strong backing of a tribe or even a whole race. One result of this relation was that whites never enslaved Native Americans in large numbers as they pleased. On the contrary, the state that blacks were placed in was total conquest. How they were treated, to a large extent, depended on the economic, political, and psychological need of the dominating race. But Native Americans represented an unfinished conquest. When treating Native American prisoners, whites had to take account of the retaliatory danger of other Native Americans as well as the bellicose nature of the prisoners. No wonder that Native American slaves were so few and cheap that only blacks became the emblem of slavery, and that Native Americans became the symbol of whites' adventure in North America. Certainly, Native Americans and blacks also shared the same features, i.e., they were all "strangers" and "heathens," but on these points whites often paid fewer attentions to Native Americans than they did to blacks, which could explain the deepness of their biological self-identity.

To Englishmen, Welshmen, Scots, and Irish were different from themselves, too. They were all the conquered objects of England. Since Wales had been merged with England long before, and Scotland suffered a similar fate during the English Civil Wars, Englishmen could accept them with some condescension, although they were still regarded as "the best servants."[51] As to the Irish, the animosity of Englishmen was fairly strong, for they were both opponents in the battlefield and Catholics, or "papists" as Englishmen called them. Therefore, they were the "worst" servants. The Irish, however, had never been enslaved by the English, despite the cultural gap. After all, they were all Christians and had a common appearance, that is, the white color. This common ground became clearer when compared with the "strangers." As often as not, these attitudes of Englishmen might demonstrate how deep their self-consciousness depended on biological traits. The sharp differences on this point, in fact, had decided blacks' fate from the beginning.

In short, the appearance of blacks in the white field of vision strengthened whites' self-consciousness, and at the same time, whites experienced a self-orientating process in cultural contacts. The semi-human and semibeast image of blacks was in fact the reflection that whites observed in themselves while they tried to maintain their own purity and civilization.

Besides whites' self-consciousness, Englishmen also had their core value, which occupied an important position in issues regarding blacks. The fusion of whites' self-consciousness and the negative gene in the core value and the enhancement of the positive gene in the core value had in fact formed the basis of the contradiction later on between whites' self-consciousness and idealism.

The main element of the core value was the belief in "the higher law." Believing that there were established orders in everything, particularly in the natural world, was a characteristic aspect of Western culture ever since ancient Greece. Early in the time of sophism, the concept of natural law, which was higher than any man-made law, had been raised. In the opinion of the Stoics, the natural law was embodied in the concept of *logos*. On the one hand, the divine logos combined with Jewish belief in the transcendental and personified God; on the other hand, it was united with Romans' belief in the legal order. Thereafter it was transmitted to the Middle Ages through Christianity. Even the church of the Middle Ages often gave expression to this legal tradition. Theoretically, Thomas Aquinas generalized about the universe in a hierarchical system, which included the eternal law or divine law, the natural law, and the man-made law or common law. Thus when the Middle Ages were over, the belief in the divine law and natural law over the common law had become one part of public thought. The God of the Middle Ages still had some relativity. "As to the design of the government," said Aquinas, "God governs all thing immediately; whereas in its execution, he governs some things by means of others."[52] Yet the Reformation strengthened the image of God as the absolute ruler, and people were directly faced with the domination of God's rules.

Being over the common law, "the higher law" was also the basic source of the core value in North America. At the time when the first colonies were founded, it was almost universally agreed that the ultimate source of authority was God. The disputes were only how it came from God to man and how it was done by men on God's behalf. God had not only created the natural and man-made worlds, but also created the fundamental rules on which the motion and action of both depended. Because of the presence of the supreme rules, contacts among people had a universal norm of consultation. Their existence, therefore, was generally of positive significance for blacks. If people deviated from the direction and made special stipulation out of racial consideration, discrimination against blacks would arise; otherwise there would be none, even if enslavement existed in both races. Because of the presence of the universal rules, another result advantageous to blacks was that any secular power was limited, and even the authority of the master was not an exception. God, according to the Puritans, gave masters authority in order that they might use it "in furthering their Servants in a blameless behavior; and in restraining them from Sin." A master could not command his servant to do any evil act. If he did, "they must humbly refuse; for both the Masters and they are God's Servant, and they must not disobey Him to please Men."[53] If a master abused his power, he might be summoned by the court for interrogation, and would be under social moral pressure. "The Judeo-Christian religion," Harrop Freeman observed, "has always maintained the duty to obey God speaking through conscience as superior to any civil law. Touch where you will American thought and you will find this same emphasis on conscience."[54] "There is a higher law," proclaimed William Ellery Channing, "even Virtue, Rectitude, the voice of Conscience, the Will of God."[55] As to the salvation of souls, masters and slaves had equal opportunity. "All the Members in a Family," said Willard, "are therein equal, in that they have Souls equally capable of being saved or lost: And the Soul of a Slave is, in its nature, of as much worth as the Soul of his master."[56] As God's creatures, they were not only given some spiritual care, but were given some legal rights, as what was listed in *Massachusetts Body Of Liberties* of 1641.[57] Since it advocated selfless love and personal feelings, the Great Awakening later also strengthened the spirit of humanism.[58] Additionally, because it depended more on philosophy than on the Bible, it was rather easy for Puritanism to foster deism, which had more of the flavor of humanism.[59]

    The belief in "the higher law" was *potentially* disadvantageous for blacks, too. The reason was that, when incarnated into community laws, it still allowed the existence of hierarchy, and people's views of liberties had a concrete character. Since all authority originated from God rather than from people, the control of saints became the natural and reasonable conclusion, the people should submit themselves to the divine authority. Therefore, Governor Winthrop emphasized that "natural liberties" divorced from the hands of Saints were only "corrupt liberties."

> There is a twofold liberty, natural (I mean as our natural is now corrupt) and civil or federal. The first is common to man with beasts and other creatures. By this, man, as he stands in relation to man simply, hath liberty to do what he lists; it is a liberty to evil as well as to good. This liberty is incompatible and inconsistent with authority, and cannot endure the least restraint of the most just authority. The exercise and maintaining of this liberty makes men grow more evil, and in time to be worse than brute beasts. The other kind of liberty I call civil or federal, it may also be termed moral, in reference to the covenant between God and man, in the moral law, and the politic covenants and constitutions, amongst men themselves. This liberty is maintained and exercised in a way of subjection to authority; it is of the same kind of liberty wherewith Christ hath made us free.[60]

Not only was everyone restrained by authority, but different persons were restrained in different degrees and shared different "liberties." Evolving from the hierarchical orders of medieval England, the concept of liberties often referred to immunity from some duties and punishments. Everybody had his relevant rights and duties, and everyone could claim that he could occupy his appropriate position in the divine order of the cosmos or in the Great Chain of Being. In Massachusetts' codes of 1641, we may clearly see the remains of these ideas. Thereafter it was increasingly connected with the rights of property, which could be found in Thomas Jefferson's attitude towards freemen. So long as the concrete liberties had no racial flavor, and so long as the universal norms of conduct were carried out without any racial particularity, there would be harm to blacks. When in laws blacks were equated with beasts in the wildness and their ascending road was blocked for racial reasons, discrimination came to the fore.

Closely related to "the higher law" was whites' notion of mission. In the Old Testament, God made a covenant with the Hebrews, asking them to convert to Him and take on the concrete responsibility, including abiding by the Ten Commandments. Ever since Judeo monotheism did away with the mysterious elements of witchcraft in primitive religions, according to modern scholar Perter L. Berger, people had to shoulder the great duties that God vested with them.[61] The Reformation further eliminated the remaining elements of witchcraft from Catholicism, throwing people under the domination of an arbitrary God and into an unsafe world; and the notion of mission was thereby strengthened.[62] In the process of opening up North America, whites' expectations of the New World depended on their explanations of the will of God. They firmly believed that God's promise in Isaiah and Revelation to "make all things new" would be fulfilled in the end and show them admirable miracles. They were used to describing the setting in which they were making their new beginning as the "New World," "Wilderness," or "New Continent," so that they would always bear in mind God's promise. In their view, the Lord's overruling providence predetermined the course of history and would finish the uncommon cause in North America through their hands. On the one hand, the glory of God was shining over His obedient subjects, the believers were only passive; on the other hand, they had to prove the glory of God by their external action, and thus they were now on their own initiative. This connotation made Protestantism bear the strong character of secular expansion. So the English thought themselves an unparalleled nation, believing that they were an exceptional seed that would bear fruits in North America. "Get thee out of thy country into a land that I will show thee," "And all nations shall call you blessed."[63] Because of the vastness of the new continent, colonists could proceed boldly with their experiment. This made their mission here stronger than in England. As Daniel J. Boorstin put it, "Here at last men could devote their full energy to *applying* Christianity, not to clarifying doctrine but to building Zion."[64]

As for Puritanism in New England, its central creed was the Covenant of Grace. Initially God made the Covenant of Works with people, but the first ancestor of mankind gave way to temptation in the Garden of Eden and was no longer able to carry it out. Being merciful to miserable mankind, God sent His only son Jesus to bring the gospel to them. The death of Christ washed away human sin, and thereby God made with them the Covenant of Grace, which pointed the way to salvation and asked people to follow God's directions. As John Winthrop explained, Puritans would build on earth a community under God's laws. "Wee are a Company professing our selues fellow members of Christ," and "knitt together by this bond of loue. . . . For the worke wee haue in hand, it is by a mutuall consent through a special overruleing providence, . . . The end is to improue our liues to doe more seruice to the lord, . . . Thus stands the cause between God and vs, wee are entered into Covenant with him for this work." Their role would be "a City upon a

Hill" to demonstrate before "the eies of all people" what the result might be when a whole people was brought into the covenant with God.[65]

Yet New England was not alone in its belief that God had trusted Americans with a special mission. Although its rites and hierarchy were considered an "impurity," the Anglican creeds were very similar to Protestantism. As early as 1613, William Strachey insisted that God had kept America hidden for a purpose, that those who had established the small settlement in Virginia were but pursuing a course that God had foreseen and willed, and that God now was ready to carry out that course to its foreordained completion. Obviously it was an extended explanation of Protestant Predestination. When writing the history of Virginia in 1625, Samuel Purchas also regarded Virginia as the first wedge of English liberties into the oppressive world. Virginia's role was to "show how God had so managed the past that English colonization in the present was the fulfillment of his plan."[66]

As in "the higher law," there were two different directions in the notion of mission, too. The first direction, or the positive cultural gene of the mission, was spiritual liberty and the principle of equal opportunity. Since all men were sinful, and no one had any more value for salvation than anyone else, spiritual liberty recognized that men were equal before God. No matter how noble or rich a man was, he was negligible before the Almighty God, and only through redemption could he fulfill the hope of salvation; God kept an eye on everybody in the secular world, "for he makes his sun rise on the evil and on the good, and sends rain on the righteous and on the unrighteous" (Matthew 5:45). This positive character of mission and spiritual equality led to the egalitarian experience of primitive Christianity: "All who believed were together and had all things in common; they would sell their possessions and goods and distribute the proceeds to all, as any had weed" (Acts 2:44-45). Although the egalitarian practice lasted only briefly, the equalitarian tradition was not suspended completely. In America, the first attempt to oppose the enslavement of blacks benefited from the conviction that everyone was equal before God rather than the secular principle of equality. The typical example is the Quakers. Instead of advocating Predestination, Quakers stressed that God's grace was limitless, which was directly transformed into revelation in everybody's soul in the form of the Inner Light. The words of God, revealed alike by the Bible and by the Inner Light, declared everyone to be one family of mankind. It was morally wrong to make "slaves of them who bear the Image of God, viz. their fellow-Creature, man."

> Now, though they are black, we cannot conceive there is more liberty
> to have them slaves, as it is to have other white ones. There is a saying,
> that we should do to all men like as we will be done ourselves; making
> no difference of what generation, descent, or colour they are.[67]

This viewpoint of the Quakers led to their tense relationship with social reality, and in fact formed a religious basis for the antislavery movement.

The second direction was the desire for domination and conquest, which might be regarded as the negative cultural gene of mission. The appearance of Protestantism and Puritanism, in fact, was somewhat the process of pursuing survival or domination.[68] This experience must have affected their doctrines. In theory, the relationship between God and men was that of absolute domination vs. absolute deference. In the Protestants' eyes, God was an arbitrary and willful tyrant, and had His own way to punish some people forever by assigning them to hell without any reason. Puritanism only slightly alleviated this absolutism. In order to get rid of the sense of inner feebleness and powerlessness, believers were willing to submit to the tyrannical God. Since worldly authority derived from God, deference to God led to deference to secular authority. "Let every person be subject to the governing authorities; for there is no authority except from god, and those authorities that exist have been instituted by God." "Therefore one must be subject, not only because of wrath but also because of conscience" (Romans 13:1, 5). The requirement of deference to God and the secular authorities, however, might be easily transformed into that of deference to whites themselves, who proclaimed to be the chosen people. In fact, reflecting the residual worship of the Jewish war-God, Scripture also expressed the aspiration to conquer and dominate others. "Thy foot shall be dipped in the blood of thine enemies"; "I have this day set thee over the nations, to root out, and to pull down, to build and to plant"[69] "I will make my arrows drunk with blood, / and my sword shall devour flesh / with the blood of the slain and the captives, / from the long-haired enemy" (Deuteronomy 32:42). Once the conquest was finished, the relationship between master and slave became the overriding aspect of their lives, which was tolerated by the Bible. "Slaves, obey your earthly master with fear and trembling, in singleness of heart, as you obey Christ" (Ephesians 6:5). The psychology of domination vs. deference, according to Fromm, was in fact the reflection of the sadism-masochism complex.[70]

Living in a changing time, there was a profound sense of dislocation among the Protestants and particularly the Puritans. This strong anxiety led to both the inner control of the individual man and the outer control of "saints" among the community, corresponding to the themes of "anxiety" and "discipline" that Mitchell Walzer has advanced.[71] Although only some had confidence in their of having been elected, whites as a whole believed that they were "the salt of the earth." At the same time, other races might be easily regarded as the abandoned people and the conquered object. In reality, when colonists were in contact with blacks at the beginning, there was no intention of converting blacks to Christianity. On the contrary, but whites did not stop the attempt to convert Native Americans, despite the fact that they were the opponents on the battlefield.[72] Likewise, blacks were excluded from the educational plan. "As far as the blacks are concerned," wrote Cremin, "it appears that only a handful attended school along with the whites, and there is no evidence at all of the establishment of any all-black schools."[73] The conclusion was only that blacks were considered incorruptible.

The combination of whites' self-consciousness with different elements of the core value would have a different influence on the fate of blacks. The coordination of whites' self-consciousness and the positive element would open up a broader path for the development of American democracy, in which discrimination against blacks would continuously eliminate its disadvantageous elements and be gradually settled. The combination of whites' self-consciousness and the negative element of the core value would constitute the main ideological sources for discrimination against blacks. In the time of colonial expansion, this process was accelerated due to the lack of labor.

THE ORIGINS OF A POWER RELATIONSHIP: COLONIALISM AND THE LABOR SYSTEM IN NORTH AMERICA

Initially, the combination of whites' self-consciousness and the negative element of the core value benefited from the impulse of colonialism. In the English colonies of North America, the practice of enslaving the "strangers" ran parallel with the aforementioned process of combination. Both of them were mutually entangled and promoted. As a result, not only was black's status of bondage systematized, but also the sense of conquest was increasingly mixed into white men's souls. Because the oppression of black laborers took place against the larger background of exploiting white indentured servants, and there were no particular codes of slavery at that time, however, the existence of whites' self-consciousness and discriminatory acts seemed elusive.

Since the fifteenth century, the commercial economy of Western Europe developed very rapidly. Because there was no hard currency internationally recognized at that time, gold and silver became more and more important as the main means of payment in international trade. Yet the outflow of gold and silver from Western Europe was very serious, so the desire for gold became stronger and stronger, which was strengthened by the legendary richness of the Orient. The nobles, knights, clergymen, and navigators all had their "gold dreams," and the function of gold was even related to the regeneration of souls, as Christopher Columbus did. Propelled by the development of capitalism, overseas exploration and expansion made great strides. In the unbalanced international economy of the time, the development of capitalism "enticed" Eastern Europe into practicing serfdom again, and it revived slavery in the New Continent. Against this background, the slave trade thrived.

Initially, European tradesmen felt little need for African slaves, and only Portugal imported slaves to labor in its South. The commercial revolution brought about a large surplus of laborers and England was only worrying about this enormous social problem. When they came into contact with Africans, therefore, Europeans were mainly interested in bartering their industrial products for African ivory, gold, and spice. After the great geographic discovery, and especially after Columbus erected a continuous link between Europe and America, however, the door of a great labor market had been opened. After the failure to discover gold, the colonists turned to exploiting the land. Since the Native Americans were obstinate and unruly and unfamiliar with agricultural labor, Europeans turned their eyes to Africa.

Understandably, Europeans did not attribute the enslavement of Africans to their own invention. Tribal slavery prevailed in both Mali and Senegambia, the two countries of Western Africa. Through three commercial roads to North Africa, they exported slaves in exchange for salt and other goods. The southern countries and tribes afterwards also followed the former examples. Like slavery in any time, the slavery of Western Africa embodied the relationship of power domination, namely the conquest of one class or race over another. The essence of the power pattern could be seen from the origins of the slaves: there were men who were enslaved for encroaching on the interests of the ruling class through crimes or debts; as a result of war, captives might be manipulated by victors as they pleased; and the cases of born slaves could explain the entrenched and thorough nature of the dominating relationship. In Dahomean and Ashanti, slaves even could be sacrificed to the powerful royal ancestors, although their numbers were very few.

There was an important difference between West African and American slavery nevertheless. That is to say, slaves of West Africa had some legal rights. They could own their own properties and even other slaves; being eligible to swear in court, slaves could become a witness or one party of a suit; owing to the charity of their master, slaves might inherit the properties of their masters; while agricultural slaves were bound to the land, paying land rent and assumed corvee, home slaves were much like the members of a big family. In Ashanti, slaves could marry free people and even royalty; in Benin, they were permitted to earn enough to purchase their freedom; in Yorub and Hausa, rulers frequently choose slaves for high official position; and, among the Dahomeans, kings sometimes selected the son of a favorite slave wife to succeed them to the throne.[74] Unlike in America, slavery in West Africa did not draw a clear line between races; being mainly constituted of native slaves, it was not a highly exploitative system serving capitalism.[75] Although it had little influence on the forms of American slavery, slave traders undoubtedly knew of the existence of African slavery. Craven's version of events is reasonable. "He was seized in Africa with slavery in mind" and "he was sold outright in America."[76] As regards how he was treated after having been sold, it depended on the laws and personal wishes of his master.

European colonists inherited the dominating relationships of African slavery. Previously, they bought black slaves from African natives and then transported them to New World; when buying could not satisfy their appetite for squeezing more slaves into the ships, the shameless act of kidnapping slaves or free people began in the coastal areas. This was a particularly effective means in Angola and Congo. Since kidnappers must run great risks, Europeans found that it would be more advantageous to abet natives in warfare and then buy their captives. The avaricious coastal tribes thus gradually developed the system that reaped the spoils from hunting inland slaves or leasing trading posts. Once the greedy colonists and African natives worked hand in glove, the prelude to Africa's dark centuries began. Most slaves, historians generally acknowledge, were not captured by Europeans, but were Africans sold to them through some legal channels.[77] No matter what the forms of bondage in America, however, it bore direct relation to the evils of the slave trade and African weakness.

Following the examples set by the Spaniards and Portuguese, Englishmen joined the African slave trade. In 1588, the Guinea Company was founded and then involved in the slave trade. Before 1660, however, this trade was mainly manipulated by Dutch merchants. They were used to transporting "cargoes" to the West Indies, and only when there was a surplus would they go to Virginia and Maryland. In such a situation, the Chesapeake area received few slaves, and New England even less. Showing no strong wish for black labor at first, English colonists accepted it only when there seemed to be no other alternative.[78] In 1619, a Dutch tradesman transported twenty blacks to Virginia, who were the first black laborers imported by Virginia. Yet after forty-four years, there were only 1,500 blacks in this colony. After 1660, and especially after the Company of Royal Adventurers Trading to Africa (1662) and the Royal African Company (1672) were founded, English merchants plunged into the slave trade.[79]

Although blacks' coming was involuntary, and their services were bound for a lifetime, the real status of blacks was ambiguous due to the lack of contemporary materials and the fact that there were no ready-made laws about slavery in the colonies. Some people asserted that "until the 1660's the status on the Negroes were not at all unique,"[80] and others even thought the white colonists did not care about the racial difference at all.

Certainly there were few differences in the legal status of white servants and blacks. Before 1660, the Chesapeake colonies had not devised any particular law regarding slavery, and slaves, indentured servants, and free persons all shared the same legal rights and duties. Having no right to kill his black slaves for an offense, even a master must hand over the person concerned to the local magistrates according to due process.[81] Blacks must be provided with the same foods and clothes. They could sue and be sued, raise and trade livestock, earn some money, and sometimes buy their liberty. In some cases, they might be lucky enough to get a zealous Quaker for their master, from whom they might gain their liberty after several years' services. Quite a few free blacks accumulated substantial properties and even owned their own slaves.[82]

The similarities of legal status between black slaves and white servants make us guess at the influence of African slavery, but a more appropriate way is to analyze the background of the vagrancy legislation in England. Beginning in the fifteenth century with rapid development of the woolen industry, a large number of farmers were driven out off their land. Because the newborn industry could not fully absorb them and those who were accustomed to the agricultural rhythm could not easily adapt themselves to the strict disciplines of wage labor, many became beggars, thieves, and tramps. Worrying about those "without masters," persons who cared about social control and the moral mood helped these vagrants to cultivate a habit of deference and return to their appropriate places by compulsive means. Therefore, in the time of the Tudor and Stuart dynasties, English rulers gradually devised a legal framework for a labor system, which permitted some compulsion but not the state of complete loss of liberty. This vagrancy legislation vividly recorded a bloody chapter in which the state became involved in the economic sphere and forced the proletariat to sell their labor in the initial stage of capitalism.

In the seventeenth century, the law and tradition of involuntary service were inherited and transplanted to the New World. Vagrants, "ruffians" who refused to pay a fine decided by the court, persons incapable of paying their debt, and even those who had no fixed house all might be compelled to labor for a time without payment. The involuntary servants also included some stubborn children and unfaithful wives. Unwillingly breaking off relations with their children, parents might hand the young over to the authorities. Orphans and bastards also might be treated in the same way. Among white laborers sent to the New Continent, there were also some kidnapped children. Still others were Scotch captives. All the examples contained many elements of violence and the remains of serfdom. Involuntary servants, however, only made up a small proportion of white immigrants, most of whom were voluntary indentured servants. Nevertheless, the abuse of power was definitely not deficient in the latter's case. Edmund Morgan wrote that "Virginia was beginning to move towards a system of labor that treated men as things."[83] This description could be applied to white servants as well as blacks. In the initial stage of colonization in Virginia, the treatment of white servants was much worse than their counterparts in the homeland. "The servant had rights," wrote Lyon G. Tylor, "but while he was in servitude these rarely conflicted with the conception of him as property."[84] The deterioration in the status of white servants made them superficially similar to the involuntary black immigrants: all could be transferred and flogged, and all must absolutely obey the orders of their masters. The terms of their services sometimes had no definite limitation. Because of their similar legal status, the differences between them were covered up. As to the small number of involuntary white immigrants, their plight was even more similar to that of blacks.

Thus, the compulsive tradition and the remains of serfdom embodied in the vagrancy legislation of England, the violent means adopted in Africa, and the intrinsic power relationship of African slavery flowed together in the process of exploiting the New World. The differences of status between black slaves and white servants were then made ambiguous, de facto slavery at that time was placed in an illusive state, and it is easy to draw the wrong conclusion that whites' self-consciousness was of little importance or even nonexistent. We cannot say that there was no racial caste for the reason that blacks and whites were put in the same legal framework. On the contrary, the fact of racial caste was the basis on which the slave status of blacks was legitimatized.

WHITES' SELF-CONSCIOUSNESS
AND THE LEGALIZATION OF SLAVERY

Although black slaves and white servants had the same legal status in Chesapeake colonies before 1660, social customs allowed the existence of racial castes and had transplanted the racial discrimination of Englishmen.

Firstly, we can roughly see blacks' particular social status through the concept of "slave." The Company of Royal Adventurers once referred to their cargo as "Negers," "Negro-Servants," "Servants from Africa," "Negro Person," but sometimes as "slaves."[85] On the one hand, the concept of "servant" reflected the fact that the colonial laws had not definitely distinguished blacks and whites at that time; on the other hand, it should not be ignored that "servant" was a more generic term than "slaves," and the former might include the latter. Just as there might exist backward social elements in an advanced society, there existed the de facto slaves in the legal framework that stipulated equal status of white indentured servants, white involuntary immigrants, and black laborers. Furthermore, even if blacks were not called "slaves," it did not inevitably indicate that there was no de facto slavery. In fact, the concept of "slave" was generally applied to blacks and Native Americans, and almost never to whites. Only in a narrow sense was it applicable to whites themselves. In *Hamlet* (Act I, Scene 2), Hamlet sighed,"O what a rogue and peasant slave am I!"[86] Here it only could be explained as "despicable man." This usage is still common in modern English. Sometimes it might act as the synonym for a person of humble origin, as Sir Thomas More used it in 1551.[87]

The most distinct attribute of slavery was involuntary and lifetime bondage, which was not considered entirely suitable for whites. In reality, Englishmen had never misunderstood the nature of slavery. "Of all men which be destitute of libertie or freedome," wrote a commentator in 1590, "the slave is in greatest subjection, for a slave is that person which is in servitude or bondage to another, even against nature . . . Even his children are infected with the Leprosie of his father's bondage."[88] It was lifetime service, with the exception of a few non-lifetime "slaves" convicted by a court for a crime; it was hereditary, for bondage might be transferred to the next generation. As regards the power relationship embodied in slavery, Sir Edward Coke brilliantly explained that:

> it was ordained by [the] Constitution of Nations that he that was taken in Battle should remain Bond to his taker for ever, and he to do with him, all that should come of him, his Will and Pleasure, as with his Beast, or any other Cattle, to give, or to sell, or to kill.[89]

Thus captivity could fully explain the nature of slavery. It meant a person had lost the right to control his own life, and the captor could handle him like a hostage at will. Since warfare was generally waged among different peoples, it was legitimate only when treating another people as captives. In short, slavery was the antithesis of liberty, an involuntary conquered state, hereditary bondage, and one legal way of treating people considered "different." All these characteristics were connected with blacks, but had no, or few, links with whites themselves; there were only a few involuntary laborers among whites, with their terms being limited.

Besides the analysis of the concept of slave, the assessment of black status must be viewed in the context of the colonies. In the Chesapeake colonies, slavery underwent a slow, evolutionary process. Before the 1640s, blacks' bondage was not obvious, but the available evidence indicated that whites treated them in a different way. The censuses taken in Virginia in the 1620s generally omitted blacks' last names and placed them at the end of the lists. The census of 1624, for example, listed blacks as "one negar," "a Negors Woman" or just "negors," while whites had complete names, and where parts were missing other information was provided, such as "Symon, an Italien."[90] Another typical example demonstrating that blacks were regarded as inferior took place in Virginia in 1630. It was recorded that "Hugh Davis to be soundly whipt before an assembly of Negroes and others for abusing himself to the dishonor of God and shame of Christianity by defiling his body in lying with a Negro."[91] Since blacks did not belong to "Christianity," and mulattos were already considered as "abominable mixture," this incident proves that Davis was punished not only for his fornication, but also that whites wished to keep racial distance. It is noticeable that the object of punishment was a white man, which meant whites' sense of self-restraint was very strong. The usage of *Christianity* is also notable, applied exclusively to whites, implying that the acts of *non-Christians* might carry no weight with heathens, but Christians would never tolerate any similar crimes. One origin of the difference in treatment between whites and blacks perhaps came from the knowledge about the slave trade and the slave practices of the Spanish and Portuguese. In 1623, a voyager's book published in London indicated that Englishmen knew of the black as a slave in the South American colonies of Spain. The "black people who were sold unto the Spaniard for him to carry into the West Indies, to remaine as slaves, either in their Mines or in any other servile uses."[92]

Since the 1640s, there was evidence that blacks were not only regarded as inferior but also placed in powerless positions. In 1639, a Maryland statute declared that "all the Inhabitants of this Province being Christians (Slaves excepted) Shall have and enjoy all such rights liberties immunities privileges and free customs within this Province as any naturall born subject of England."[93] This statute showed an important character of the legalization of slavery: slaves were first excluded from the protection of laws, and then special laws about the status of slaves were enforced. In the initial stage of slavery, personal control was still enough to deal with the menace of slavery to social security and there was no urgent necessity to make special legislation. Since whites were born Christians, and blacks were regarded as heathens, the slaves mentioned in the laws could only be blacks and Native Americans. In the same year, another Maryland law stipulated that "all persons being Christians (Slaves excepted)" over eighteen who were imported without indentures would serve for four years, with the treatment of white servants being further consistent. As a result, the subtle difference between white indentured servants and the few involuntary white laborers vanished, and the difference between white and black laborers was clarified.

Just after the 1640s, the two important characters of slavery, durability and inheritance, became more and more obvious. In a case of punishment for seven runaway laborers in Virginia in 1640, the prime agent Christopher Miller, "a dutchman," was given the harshest treatment of all: thirty stripes, burning with an "R" on the cheek, a shackle placed on his leg for a year, and seven years of service for the colony upon completion of his time due to his master. The only other one to received the same punishment was the black Emanuel, but he did not receive any sentence of prolonged term.[94] It indicated that Emanuel was already serving his master for a lifetime. At the same time, Virginia county courts recorded the sales of slaves. In 1646 Francis Pott sold a black woman and boy to Stephen Charlton "to the use of him forever."[95]

Thus, between the 1640s and the 1660s, blacks in the Chesapeake colonies had been in a special position. The general trend was that the courts and social practice gradually admitted the differences between white indentured servants and blacks, and it became more and more difficult for blacks to escape from de facto slavery. Certainly, there were still a few blacks who became free persons after a period of faithful service, the mulattos released by their fathers, and some refugees who successfully escaped from capture. All constituted a steadily growing population of free blacks. Nevertheless, the limited growth of the free black population did not contradict the fact that the majority of blacks were fixed into slavery. On the contrary, it gave prominence to the evolutionary nature of slavery. In this process, the social practice of discrimination not only gradually deepened the inferior status of blacks, but also gained legal assistance. At first, the courts gradually admitted de facto bondage, and then the laws directly adopted the clauses that excluded blacks. As Paul C. Palmer pointed out, the laws of the first half century "seen more often to be describing any giving legal sanction to practices already in existence."[96]

The special legal status of blacks was established after the 1660s. In 1663, the Assembly of Maryland declared that "All negroes or other slaves within the province, and all negroes and other slaves to be hereafter imported into the province, shall serve durante vita; and all children born of any negro or other slave, shall be slaves as their fathers were for the term of their lives."[97] In order to clarify the ambiguity caused by mulattos, Virginia stipulated in 1662: "Be it therefore enacted and declared by this present grand assembly, that all children borne in this country shall be held bond or free only according to the condition of the mother."[98] The importance of this law was that it officially and legally defined the range of whites' biological self-identity. To exclude the possibility that blacks might get rid of bondage by converting to Christianity, the assembly of Virginia decided in 1667 that "it is enacted that the conferring of baptisme doth not alter the condition of the person as to his bondage or freedom."[99] The law of 1670 went further: "all servants not being Christians brought in by sea were declared slaves for life."[100] These statutes made it difficult for cultural identity to transcend biological differences, which in fact formed the basis of racial slavery.

As in the Chesapeake colonies, de facto slavery and racial castes existed before blacks' status was legalized in New England. In New England, slavery existed earlier than in the Chesapeake colonies, but the time of legalization was later. As early as 1639, a master in Boston Harbor sought to mate a black woman with another black, but she kicked her prospective lover out of the bed, saying that such behavior was "beyond her slavery."[101] The first legal code of Massachusetts, the Body of Liberties of 1641, declared that "There shall never be any bond slavery, villeinage, or captivity amongst us unless it be lawful captives taken in just wars, and such strangers as willingly sell themselves or are sold to us."[102] Obviously the "strangers" included blacks. Yet how about the white captives "taken in just wars"? John Cotton shows the range of whites' self-consciousness. In regard to the Scottish prisoners sent to New England, he wrote Cromwell in 1651 that "we have been desirous to make their yoke easy. They have not been sold for slaves to perpetual servitude, but for 6, or 7 or 8 years, as we do our owne."[103]

Blacks, however, had some rights. They could seek help from police to avoid illegal persecution. Even a master was willing to respect due process and resort to the court. For example, George Norton sued his slave for stealing wool in 1686. Blacks might undertake a lawsuit, and had the right to defense and give witness. They could also accumulated property. Before the 1680s, except for the military training measure,[104] it seemed that there were no laws applicable only to blacks.

In the 1680s, the process of legalization began in Massachusetts. In 1698, the phrase "Negro slave" appeared in its statutes.[105] As in the Chesapeake colonies, *black* had obtained the same meaning as *slave*. Racial slavery was fully established in both South and North.

In the evolutionary process of black status and slavery in the colonies, economic impetus was undoubtedly fundamental. One main motive of the colonists was to make a fortune, and many colonies were built by companies. The importation of slaves proceeded from the necessities of the Southern economy. The fertile and cheap land, the tobacco market, and the attactive prospects of becoming planters by cultivating the staple crop made the colonists overcome their instinctive aversions to "strangers" and bring blacks into their plan to open up North America. Therefore, blacks were compelled to come here as cheap and forced laborers from the beginning, and their future status would be gradually crystallized on this basis.

In the early seventeenth century, however, large plantations did not thrive for the lack of labor and the poverty of most white immigrants. In the Chesapeake colonies, at least 65 percent of landowners did not own any servant or slave. Therefore, the personal relationship between master and laborer was paramount, and the treatment of blacks had a strong individual color. Small plantations prevailed for a rather long period. After the Restoration in 1660, the Stuart monarchy promulgated a series of Navigation Acts, which stipulated that tobacco should only be transported to England or her colonies. The restrictions on the tobacco trade caused a serious drop in prices, and this lasted almost two decades. In this transformative stage, tobacco production on the small scale was confronted with a serious challenge. Large plantations had the advantage in controlling labor costs and bargaining over tobacco prices. So the drop in price propelled a change in the scale of production. Large plantations began to develop in the Chesapeake colonies and showed a tendency to expand. When the European market was restored in about 1680, the situation in which the underselling planters vied with each other to attract customers had taken shape. In such a situation, the pattern of labor control quietly changed. The personal relationship between master and slave was watered down by the economic necessity of larger numbers of slaves, and blacks were plunged deeper into an "unnatural" state. Strict discipline on the plantation, long labor hours, and absolute obedience to their masters all expedited the legalization of slavery.

At the same time, the social control of blacks became a problem. In Virginia, there had been only about 300 slaves in 1650; by 1670 there were 2,000 in a servant population of 8,000.[106] Such a development was enough to stimulate the planters and the authorities to fix the inferior status of blacks. The clarification of black status in turn strengthened whites' feeling of security and mitigated their fear of a large slave population. The formation of the Royal Company of Adventurers in 1662 and the Royal African Company in 1672 reflected the new economic reality, in which white Southerners were willing to import more blacks than before. Just when blacks became an integral element of the growing plantation economy, the masters and authorities felt it necessary to readjust the behavior of slaves. The rigorous discipline and despair over their fate would inevitably cause black resentment; while the population concentration might also stimulate riots. It was well understood that the fundamental object of the slave laws was to guard against blacks protest and keep racial order. "Slavery was instituted," explained Ulrich B. Phillips, "not merely to provide control of labor but also as a system of racial adjustment and social order."[107]

Furthermore, black control was connected with the problem of free persons. Since the representative assembly was summoned in Virginia in 1619, more and more prominent persons who had the ability to enact material gain but had little to do with the established social structure joined the ranks of the elite. After the promulgation of the Navigation Acts, however, the common people fell into dire straits, and social tensions were increased, climaxing in Bacon's uprising. Being anxious about the poor, the upper class was afraid that their increasing population might disrupt social order. So the terms of indentured servants were prolonged. Since blacks had been in the lowest position, usually had no contracts with their masters, and could not carry firearms or set up organizations, the real resistance and danger coming from them was much less than that from white servants. In this situation, to put particular restrictions on blacks was simple as well as necessary. Such a policy was unlikely to cause any protest from white communities; on the contrary, it might have the unexpected effect of splitting up opponents and consolidating the white line. In addition, the severe restrictions would not reduce the slave population and the production of tobacco, for black immigrants were involuntary.

It should not be neglected, however, that whites' self-consciousness had fulfilled a critical selective function in the process of enslavement. The assertion that enslavement was due to no ideological concerns cannot convince us. In fact, although Scots, Irish, and other white people were somewhat discriminated against, they were never held as "proper goods" like blacks. Race and cultural similarity made them go down the same road as Englishmen. As early as 1639, Maryland began to encourage naturalization of legal aliens, and all "Christians" might shared the same rights as those of Englishmen. In 1671, Virginia also made them enjoy "all such liberties, privileges, immunities whatsoever, as a nuturall borne Englishman is capable of."[108] No matter what cultural differences existed between Englishmen and Scots or Irish, they were above all white people. No matter how blacks tried to slough off their cultural differences, however, their biological traits could not be changed. To whites, the word *Christian* was of importance, which could both include all whites and serve as the appropriate reason for enslaving blacks. Because of their race, blacks could not be admitted as Christians even if they were baptized.

As late as 1705, the slave codes of Virginia continue to use this critical vocabulary. Once the continuous conversion of blacks obscured its contents, whites invented a substitute as the yardstick of their self-identity. While the enslavement of whites might incur an uneasy conscience and violent opposition from white communities, the enslavement of blacks had no similar consequences. It was this strong moral power of whites that allowed blacks to be the first and only candidates for enslavement.

Such an assessment of blacks was not confined to the Southern colonies. In New England, where the driving force of the plantation economy did not occur, whites' self-consciousness played a more active part in the evolution of slavery. As in the South, Yankees were disgusted at the presence of blacks, but there was no balancing power such as the need of staple crops for heavy labor. The anathema for the slave trade was so strong that some slave tradesmen such as John Saffin, John Usher, James Wetcomb, and Andrew Belcher had to import blacks secretly in 1681. While the popular worry was mainly based on the growing black population, zealous Quakers also had a practical consideration: the menace of blacks' uprising. To them, the abolition of slavery was both moral and practical.

In New England, the economic factor was entangled with discrimination against blacks in another way. Economic analysis showed no benefit in the presence of blacks. So the General Court of Massachusetts decided in 1702 to promote "the bring of White Servants and to put a period to Negroes being slaves."[109] The complaint about the disadvantage of blacks was more vividly embodied in an anonymous pamphlet in 1716. "Slaves are a great hindrance to the Peopling and Improving the Country," explained the author.[110] Blacks, the author thought, drained their owners of wealth and discouraged the population of indentured servants, who were the key to the economic growth of colonies. Now that the value of slaves as cheap labor was not worth much, and their behavior seemed improper (Massachusetts Governor Joseph Dudley said that blacks "are usually the worst servants"), the demand for laws to restrict their conduct became stronger.

Whether in Southern colonies or in Northern colonies, the fusion of whites' self-consciousness and their desire for conquest is worth mentioning. The fusion formed an important driving force in the process of enslavement, which in turn accelerated the process of fusion. This mutually promoting process was more obvious in New England.

From the beginning, white self-consciousness and the desire for conquest conditioned the relationship between colonists and blacks in different ways. On the one hand, whites' promises of justice, the fear of divine laws and God's commandments, and the worship of the golden rule overwhelmed their instinctive disgust for blacks, guaranteed the "liberties of foreigners and strangers," and even enacted that "No man shall exercise any tyranny or cruelty toward any brute creature";[111] on the other hand, their allegiance to Almighty Grace, their vigilance over the purity of the "chosen" race, and the fear of being contaminated by savageness or losing themselves, made whites imagine the state of human depravity and the danger of missing salvation. To avoid these, they must therefore resist internal and external evil by compulsory means, lest they fall into the trap of the Devil. From the beginning, this caused whites to keep blacks, the alleged posterity of the wicked Ham, at a distance. In the 1660s and 1670s, this facilitated the legalization of slavery in the Chesapeake colonies. In the North, these ideas proved potent. As several generations passed and as the society of New England became more complex in the 1680s and 1690s, the people's moral laxity became a focus of attention. Ministers warned endlessly that God was angry with the people; families, church, education, and other social institutions were all under scrutiny. They paid particular attention to blacks. In their opinion, the improper conduct of blacks was not only corrupting blacks themselves, but also threatening the self-restraint of whites. Whites continuously expressed the anxiety of losing self-control: without restraints, they would lose the most valuable thing, the means to construct a "city upon a hill." Thus the legalization of slavery began in New England. If racism was whites' discrimination against blacks and their attempt to control them, it embodied both the motivation to dominate others and the will to control the self. In other words, there were two contradictory impulses in the motivation of whites: one was the desire for conquest and domination, another the mission of equality; one was self-consciousness, another universal ideals; one was aggressive, another repressive; one was animosity and self-interest, another good wishes and justice; one was hate and detestation, another love and pity. Both mingled with each other, but the critical elements were whites' racial feelings and self-interests, which propelled whites to deviate from the route of universal norms. Here, whites' self-consciousness and desire for conquest and domination fused.

SLAVERY AND RACISM

Along with the evolution of slavery, whites' self-consciousness underwent a subtle change. As an element of racial discrimination in the initial stages, blacks' racial traits now became the principal criterion of whites' self-identity.

The process in which blacks' racial traits became conspicuous was realized in a way that negated the discriminated elements one by one. At first, whites' assessment of blacks was based on a series of characteristics rather than the sole factor of appearance. The whole cultural evaluation of blacks, including languages, customs, and morality, was as important as the biological element. As time went on, however, the cultural characteristics of blacks gradually vanished. In fact, from the time that he was captured and sold, the connection between the black and his African cultural roots was abruptly cut off. The slave had to separate from his family, acquaintances, and accustomed environments, and was deliberately placed together with those from different tribes. No matter what his original status was, he now fully lost his personal freedom and was put under the absolute control of others. The slave had to cast aside his native tongue and African tradition, and adapt himself to the rules established by whites. Due to this compulsory assimilation, whites seldom called black "savages" or "heathens"; they more frequently gave these titles to Native Americans. Perhaps to those whose process of conquest had been finished and who had been "tamed," these titles might mean whites' own dereliction of duty. Whites were accustomed to considering Native Americans as enemies, whereas blacks were considered as "our Negroes." Since blacks had to identify themselves with white culture, whites now had no reason to stress the "savage" characteristics of blacks. Here, the threat of violence was the critical element. In fact, the legalization of slavery was also a process of brainwashing. Blacks were forced to adapt themselves to the new environments, and the remains of African culture dwindled away nearly to nothing. Conspicuously, the process of assimilation came to a halt at this point, and their biological traits became more noticeable.

Correspondingly, the terms whites used to describe themselves changed. At first, whites relied on the term *Christian*. In the middle of the seventeenth century, the words *English* and *free persons* were also included. Taking the colonies as a whole, a new term of self-identification appeared after about 1680: *white*. In 1692, for example, a revised law of Maryland used *white* and *English* but dropped the term *Christian*. At the same time, the names of blacks were also revised. For most of the seventeenth century, whites often called blacks *Negroes* or *Negers*, which were replaced by *blacks* or *Africans* in the eighteenth century. This fact reflected that the racial characteristics of blacks attracted more and more attention. As the concern for "savageness" and "heathenism" decreased, visible racial characteristics occupied a more important position. In the end, race with blackness as its foremost character, was the primary criteria. As Reuter wrote, "When color differences coincide with difference in cultural levels, then color becomes symbolic and each individual is automatically classified by the racial uniform he wears."[112] In reality, blackness became the main reason for maintaining racial subordination at the end of the seventeenth century. When a "Spaniard" had petitioned the Massachusetts Council for freedom in 1709, "Capt. Teat alledg'd that all of that Color were Slaves."[113] In turn, the particular racial trait of blackness increasingly became the symbol of subordination, inferior intelligence, and immorality, which meant the faults of blacks' finite assimilation were due to blacks themselves rather than whites. Visible racial features formed the overwhelming basis and further made an impression far greater than what the actual racial differences were. The semantic content of *blackness* was thus continuously substantiated and went far beyond the biological fact itself.

After slavery was crystallized, not only was the link between subordination and racial features strengthened, but racism itself was nourished and endowed with new moral implications.

In the early eighteenth century, while the old colonies compiled systematic slave codes from the original slave laws, the newly established colonies followed the examples set by the former. Obviously, the main object of the slave codes was to protect the masters' property rights and the whole society from the menace of slave resistance and uprisings, and force blacks to serve white people more effectively. The boundless personal power of masters was confirmed. Slaves were forbidden to wander from their plantations without a "ticket." They were never allowed to congregate in large numbers and carry clubs or arms. Masters might inflict corporal punishment on their slaves without any legal prosecution. Authorized to arrest any black of suspicious acts, whites had duties to patrol the streets and protect the white community. If blacks committed a felony, the court, consisting of a Justice of the Peace and two slaveowners, would make whatever adjudication they deemed proper. Offenders might be whipped and occasionally burnt at the stake. On the one hand were the disciplinary laws intimidating slaves, on the other hand was the continuous use of the whip in daily lives. "It was the whip, or the fear of the whip, that made the system go," wrote Ostrander.

Good business sense might deter the planters from inflicting crippling punishments. Compassion might move him to moderate discipline at the cost of his profits. Skillful handling of slaves might reduce the necessity for corporal punishment to the minimum. The planter might even place the slave on a modified wage basis to give greater incentive. Nevertheless, the system remained one of involuntary servitude.[114]

The slave codes, however, were to control white behavior as well as to restrict blacks. While the laws warned blacks not to overstep their places, they also aimed to foster whites' spirit of vigilance and exhorted whites not to neglect the interests of the whole. To control blacks was not only regarded as the personal affair of slaveowners, but also connected with the future of the chosen, white people. "The slaveholding gentry," Jordan observed, "were coerced as individuals by the popularly elected legislatures toward maintenance of a private tyranny which was conceived to be in the community interest."[115] In such a situation, the punishments of blacks were both the exercise of slaveowners' authority and the performance of their duties; the discrimination of the white masses was both due to the necessity of defending the interests of the "superior" race and due to *natural* reasons. Once the system worked, discrimination against blacks became more and more strengthened, and in the end became part of a normal thought pattern among whites. In politics, to maintain racial supremacy had long been a self-evident aim and indispensable means. Personal avarice and desire for domination mingled with whites' duties and mission, as did personal feelings and the irrefutable *facts*. Practical crimes were cloaked in the beautiful garb of morality. The development of racism made it extraordinary difficult to get rid of evil, and made some whites continuously repent of the evil they had to tolerate. Once under attack from outside, however, they would immediately become very sensitive and aggressive on the issue of their morality.

At the same time, the existence of slavery provided an appropriate environment for absorbing and reforming of all sorts of racial theories. With the development of rationalism and social secularization in the eighteenth century, many persons no longer pondered over their position in God's plan for salvation, but became increasingly interested in themselves as natural creatures. In the context of overseas expansion, the physical differences among men absorbed heightened attention. Promoted by anthropologists, the Great Chain of Being concerning the proper order of human and animals again came to the fore.

The man who laid the foundation for classifying creatures was Carolus Linnaeus, a Swedish botanist. Puzzled by the delicate varieties of the species, he painstakingly explored natural laws and orders established by God behind the natural phenomena. In his *System of Nature* of 1735, Linnaeus created a system in which different species were ranked in proper order and every species had its own varieties. In his arrangement, man was closely adjacent to the ape. Although he had little interest in varieties within species, Linnaeus still divided mankind into four varieties: *Homo Europaeus, Homo Asiaticus, Homo Afer,* and *Homo Americanus.* In his view, these different races all belonged to the same level and had no substantial difference.

The method that Linnaeus ushered in was inherited by Georges Louis Leclerc Buffon. Paying most of his attention to the lower biological orders, his great work, *Natural History,* also addressed the variety of human races. To Buffon, the white race was the norm of human varieties, because white skin revealed the natural color of man. Based on this criterion, other races with varieties of color could be classified. Guessing that the blackness of Africans might derive from the tropical sun, Buffon concluded that human races were changeable. Although he thought that blacks had "little genius," Buffon denied the black race to be a different species and emphasized that "the unfortunate Negroes are endowed with excellent hearts, and possess the seeds of every human virtue."[116]

Another influential physiologist, Johann Friedrich Blumenbach, held a similar view. He traveled all over the world to collect specimens of crania, thereby establishing his position as the "father of craniology." To Blumenbach, the data of human body was so innumerable that any classification was relative. Nevertheless, he divided mankind into five varieties according to the forms of crania: Caucasian, Mongolian, Ethiopian, American, and Malay. It was Blumenbach who coined the word *Caucasian* as the synonym for the white race. The differences between human races, Blumenbach pointed out, were not as disparate as those between man and ape. Sometimes Blumenbach expounded against those who thought one race was superior to another. He was particular disgusted with those who ranked races according to their beauty. "If a toad could speak," he wrote, "and were asked which was the loveliest creature upon God's earth, it would say simpering, that modesty forbade it to give a real opinion on that point."[117]

The classifications of Linnaeus, Buffon, and Blumenbach only ranked the main species, and all refused to arrange the order of different races. Their study, however, stimulated the rise of another theory. Many persons were not satisfied with the description of a human web, but obstinately stuck to the explanation of the Great Chain of Being, an idea with its roots deep in the Middle Ages. Jordan described it wonderfully:

> The Chain of Being, as usually conceived, commenced with inanimate thing and ranged upwards through the lowest form of life, through the more intelligent animals until it reached man himself; from man it continued upward through the myriad ranks of heavenly creatures until it reached its pinnacle in God. By definition a chain was without gaps, the more so with the Great Chain forged by the Creator. Man, the middling creature on this scale, was carefully suspended between the heavenly and brute creation. As Edward Tyson had explained in the course of comparing simian and human anatomy, "*Man* is part a *Brute,* part an *Angel;* and is that *Link* in the *Creation,* that joyns them both together."[118]

In fact, Thomas Aquinas, the medieval master of scholasticism, had stated this theory centuries before. In his view, all creatures, including man, were the result of God's creation, but man was not the same type of creature as others. The flesh of man belonged to nature, and his natural and instinctive desires were much like those of other animals, whereas his soul came from the kingdom of heaven, and shared some divinity from God. Thus, man was the bridge between this world and the divine world, and was the entity of flesh and soul. Man himself also had his hierarchy, as a contemporary English writer vividly described:

> In this order angel is set over angel, rank upon rank in the kingdom of heaven; man is set over man, beast over beast, bird over bird, and fish over fish, on the earth, in the air and in the sea; so that there is no worm that crawls upon the ground, no bird that flies on high, no fish that swims in the depth, which the chain of this order does not bind in most harmonious concord.[119]

Inheriting the medieval tradition, the Chain of Being in the eighteenth century clearly expressed people's religious ideas about the cosmic and social orders. In America, it especially served to satisfy the ravenous appetite for the rationalization of racial subordination.

The Scriptures, however, emphasized that everyone was the descendant of Adam, placing the advocates of the Chain of Being in a dilemma between the continuity of the Chain and the admonitions of the Bible.

How could the difficulty be overcome? The advocates of the Chain of Being found that it might be readily solved by verifying the close relation between man and ape. By stressing the extent of the similarity between man and ape, not only was the classification of man possible, but the chains between man and animals became stronger. To those who were longing for the moral basis of slavery, it was indeed good news.

It was Peter Camper, a Dutch anatomist, who finally showed the ideal hierarchy of man on the basis of physical distinctions. In the 1770s, he developed the idea of the "facial angle" and found in his collection of skulls a regular gradation from apes, through blacks, to whites. "It is amusing to contemplate," he wrote, "an arrangement of these [skulls], placed in a regular succession: apes, orangs, negroes, the skull of an Hottentot, Madagascar, Celebese, Chinese, Moguller, Calmuck, and divers Europeans. It was in this manner that I arranged them upon a shelf in my cabinet."[120] This step-like gradation placed whites at the top of the ladder, and blacks were always next to apes. Although Camper denied that this proximity implied any inferiority of blacks, many whites did not restrain their passion as he did.

In America, while the Linnaean web was an independent method of classification, the Chain of Being prevailed for the last thirty years of the eighteenth century. Even the great thinker, Thomas Jefferson, was also deeply influenced by it. Although he once wrote that "All men are created equal" and did not approve of slavery, Jefferson was not an advocate of absolute equality, but only admitted the equality of opportunity in pursuit of life, liberty, and happiness. In his *Notes on Virginia* (1787), Jefferson clearly showed his racial views about blacks. Frank Shuffelton, editor of one of the most complete Jeffersonian bibliographies, commented that "no matter how much we admire him as an opponent of slavery, we must recognized his racism."[121] Regarding the racism Shuffelton mentioned, we should understand it in the context of whites' self-consciousness.

To Jefferson, "The first difference which strikes us is that of colour." "Are not the mixture of red and white," he asked,

> the expression of every passion by greater or less suffusions of colour in the one, preferable to that eternal monotony, which reigns in the countenances, that immovable veil of black that covers all the emotions of the other races? Add to these, flowing hair, a more elegant symmetry of form, their own judgment in favor of the whites, declared

by their preference of them. The circumstance of superior beauty, is thought worthy attention in the propagation of our horses, dogs, and other domestic animals; why not in that of man?[122]

Not only was blacks' appearance distinct, but their intelligence was even lower than that of Native Americans. "They are at least as brave, and more adventuresome," admitted Jefferson.

> But this may perhaps proceed from a want of fore thought, which prevents their seeing a danger till it be present . . . Comparing them by their faculties of memory, reason, and imagination, it appear to me, that in memory they are equal to the whites; in reason much inferior . . . In music they are more generally gifted than the whites with accurate ears for tune and time, and they have been found capable of imagining a small catch. Whether they will be equal to the composition of a more extensive run of melody, or of complicated harmony, is yet to be proved . . . Misery is often the parents of the most affecting touches in poetry. Among the blacks is misery enough, God knows, but no poetry." Jefferson asserted that black's lack of achievement was not due to the lack of opportunity, for "The Indians, with no advantages of this kind, will often carve figures on their pipes not destitute of design and merit."[123]

The part closely related to the Chain of Being in his thought, however, was not the comparison among blacks, whites, and Native Americans, but his emphasis on the animal tendencies of blacks. "In general, their existence appears to participate more of sensation than reflection," said Jefferson. "To this must be ascribed their disposition to sleep when abstracted from their diversions, and unemployed in labour. An animal whose body is at rest, and who does not reflect, must be disposed to sleep of course." Their grief is transient, and could soon divert their own attention. "They are more ardent after their female: but love seems with them to be more an eager desire, than a tender delicate mixture of sentiment and sensation." They especially cast greedy eyes on white women, "as uniformly as is the preference of the Orangutan for the black women over those of his own species."[124] Harping on the same string of the ancient legend, Jefferson here tried to bring to light sexual molestation, and established blacks' position between white men and the man-like apes. By this description, Jefferson expressed both the introspection of animal nature within whites themselves and his concern over the purity of the "superior" species. In fact, the worship of racial purity constituted the core of whites' self-consciousness. The biological differences and the resentment between the two races were so large, Jefferson concluded, that they could not peacefully live together after emancipation, and the inevitable convulsions would "probably never end but in the extermination of the one or the other race."[125] The only reasonable solution, Jefferson thought, was that blacks must be removed to remote countries lest miscegenation take place.

Although he adopted an empirical attitude to explain blacks' racial features, Jefferson overlooked the negative effects caused by racial oppression and then drew a conclusion disadvantageous to blacks. To tens of thousands of the white masses, these "facts" constituted the ironclad proofs of their racial beliefs, and daily realities constantly reminded them of the "truth" that blacks belonged to the inferior race: the humiliated sights on the auction platforms, the poor intellectual creativity, the twisted morality and characters, the miserable family lives, and so on. Compared with philosophers, common whites would rather use their intuition, perception, and experience. Beliefs were often stronger than arguments. It was easier to believe some of the strange tales and the propagation of agitators. The evil of Ham, the "beastly copulation or conjuncture" between blacks and apes, the juxtaposition of the man-like apes and the "lustful" "slave apes," and so on, all served to demonstrate the affinity of blacks and beasts. Du Bois observed that:

> The second thought streaming from the deathship and the curving river is the thought of the older South, the sincere and passionate belief that somewhere between men and cattle, God created a *tertium quid*, and called it a Negro, a clownish, simple creature, & times even lovable within its limitations, but straitly foreordained to walk within the Veil. To be sure, behind the thought lurks the afterthought, some of them with favoring chance might become men, but in sheer self-defence we dare not let them, and we build about them walls so high, and hang between them and the light a veil so thick, that they shall not even think of breaking through.[126]

Obviously, this was a vulgarized version of the Chain of Being. Whites sometimes considered the function of environments, but they would rather believe that blacks had made little progress in improving themselves. When turning to Africa, they found no ray of civilization there.

To begin with, the black people have no historic past. Never having evolved civilization of their own. Left to himself, he remained a savage, and in the past his only quickening has been where brown men have imposed their ideas and altered his blood. We must conclude that black Africa is unable to stand alone. The black man's numbers may increase prodigiously and acquire alien veneers, but the black man's nature will not change.[127]

Between the "inferior" reality of blacks and the racial ideas of whites, and between the oppression of whites and more "inferior" reality, there seemed to be a vicious circle. In promoting its formation, racial slavery, which made intrinsic discrimination more inveterately rooted in whites' souls, could not evade the blame.

THE DISTORTION OF IDEALISM

One singular phenomenon was that while whites' self-consciousness combined with their desire for conquest and domination, American idealism began to develop and expand. Idealism was later expanded by the addition of more and more rational elements. As to "the higher law," for example, the divine law gradually retreated into a secondary position, and the rational law or the natural law grew stronger and stronger; as to human nature, the empirical theory about *tabula rasa* and the Enlightenment's optimism stressing environments were gradually introduced. The American Revolution greatly strengthened these rational elements. Because of this great event, whites' self-consciousness came more and more into conflict with idealism. In the North, the contradiction was solved by abolishing slavery and gradually bringing blacks into the orbit of the universal principles. In the South, however, the contradiction was solved by distorting idealism. The power of idealism was so strong and irresistible that whites had to rely on blacks' "inferiority" as the fulcrum of their morality; if it was insufficient, they would not hesitate to emasculate the revolutionary nature of the ideal credos and resort to the negative aspects of Christian morality as their last defense of moral jurisdiction.

One origin of American democratic tenets was Christianity. From the beginning, religion itself had showed a tendency to support freedom. Although early churches in the colonies did not adopt a policy of religious freedom, many came to the New World to seek liberties not allowed in the Old World. Religious institutions were also continuously democratized, for example, the congregational system of the Puritans constantly appealed to the common people during the Great Awakening and the Revolution and in the process of moving to the frontier. Despite the existence of some contradictory sentences, the fundamental teachings of Protestant Christianity were democratic. As Calvinists, Puritans in New England did not strictly follow Calvin's aristocratic theory of Predestination; extrinsic signs of salvation seemed more important. According to Samuel Eliot Morison, Puritan clergy assumed that salvation lay within the reach of every person who made the effort; that "Christ helped those who helped themselves."[128] Although churches consisted only of visible saints, i.e., adults who had experienced regeneration, God included their "seed" in the grant whenever He extended the Covenant of Grace to His saints. Through the function of clergy who acted as "Ambassadors," the unregenerate sinners could be offered the "means" of conversion.[129] If an individual maintained his moral integrity, God was obligated to take his soul to Heaven. Peter Bulkeley (1583–1659) once expressed the mutuality of the covenant.[130] "The achievement of this theology," Perry Miller pointed out, "was that it did everything that could be done to confine the unconfinable God in human terms. It transformed the revealed Word from an exaction arbitrarily imposed by a conqueror into a treaty of mutual obligation."[131] This covenant provided individuals with sufficient space for their dynamic roles and theoretically gave everyone equal opportunity for upward mobility. Although some clergy like Cotton Mather stressed that blacks must remain patient and obedient, the teaching of spiritual equality before God was so basic that Christian doctrines theoretically excluded the possibility of advocating blacks' inferiority. As a matter of fact, many concepts of American democracy derived from the Christian faith: the mission of releasing the world from oppression was similar to the religious hope that the regenerate Christ would free the world from evil; the firm belief in the historical progress was in fact a secular version of the perfect realm of Millennialism; individualism emerged from the concept of gospel Protestantism that emphasized the free individual who had escaped from external restraint, while the Great Awakening transferred the emphasis from the divinely ordained disciplines to the free individual; the principle of brotherhood was more directly connected with the commandment of Christianity that "you shall love your neighbor as yourself" (Mark 12:31). In a sense, the course of American democracy was a result of constant secularization of democratic principles contained in Christianity; in other words, it was the fruit borne by the European tree of liberty that grew in the New Continent.

Concerning its rational origins, American creeds such as liberty and equality derived from the Enlightenment, especially the theory of natural rights in England. Because America derived from charters granted by English monarchs, the theory of social covenant based on natural rights had a very solid foundation. Once the colonies thought that the king had violated their rights and liberties, this theory then became a necessary and convenient instrument of protest. Greatly propagated in the Revolutionary era, the theory of natural rights was written into the Declaration of Independence: "We hold these truths to be self-evident, that all men are created equal, that they are endowed by their Creator with certain unalienable rights, that among these are life, liberty, and the pursuit of happiness."[132] Liberty and equality not only became the lofty ideals connected with the Revolution as closely as flesh and blood, but also provided an inexhaustible source that reformers drew upon later. "The Revolution," John Adams wrote, "was affected before the war commenced. The Revolution was in the minds and hearts of the people. This radical change in the principles, opinions, sentiments, and affections of the people, was the real American Revolution."[133] While the great historical event took place, the theory of natural rights mingled with complicated religious feelings. In the past, the divine laws of Puritans were the core of all the laws, because the presence of God was direct and continuous, and He was personified, whose activities covered the social and natural spheres. The God of the deists, on the other hand, was conceived as the impersonal first cause of the universe. Once the natural process had been started, God no longer interfered, but let it automatically abide by the natural laws He had given. Natural laws replaced the divine laws; the Covenant of Grace gave way to the secular social contract; and rationality became the chief guide of human affairs. Although God had not been entirely excluded (natural laws were still expressed in His name), God withdrew from human affairs into Himself, whose will was considered by some deists to be embodied in the revelation of nature rather than in the Bible. Some radicals, including Thomas Paine, even thought that Christianity and the Bible obscured the real God. Rationality was no longer a servant of religion, but became the beacon lighting people's way to liberty. The individuals under the light of rationality owned the limitless possibility of progress, and even a perfect Utopia on earth might be created. At the same time, since the concept of God was transferring from the personified Deity to the Creator of nature, man himself was also changing from an appendage of God to a natural species. All men, including blacks, would share some natural rights, not because of their religious belief or the status of a chosen people, but because of the simple fact that they were men and all men were the creatures of the Almighty. Thus, the increasing role of reason stimulated optimism and humanism about human nature and human capability. The great storm of thought fostered by the Revolution forced people to face the challenges posed by the position of blacks to American universal democratic values. In the Revolutionary era, Abolitionist feelings were so strong that the Continental Congress decided to prohibit the importation of slaves; before long, Northern states abolished slavery in succession. Once beliefs were reinforced by rationality, they released tremendous energies for social reform.

Under the pressure of democratic creeds, racists had to solve the problem of excluding blacks, for they were in an awkward dilemma between their promises and deeds. "How is it that we hear the loudest *yelps* for liberty," Old Samuel Johnson asked perplexedly, "among the drivers of negroes?"[134] The argument that the black was an inferior race was logically helpful to mitigate the moral problem. The unspoken words behind it were always that liberty and equality were the privileges of whites, which blacks had no qualifications to share. In other words, whites were not the hypocrites that said one thing and meant another, but they laid bare their limitation under the pressure of the black presence, i.e., the disparity between *what ought to be* and *what was*. When talking glibly about liberty and equality, they only gave consideration to themselves. Blacks were automatically excluded. Many whites turned a blind eye to what they saw: whenever blacks came to the fore, liberty and equality automatically stopped taking effect; once they were forced to face reality, whites would underline that "it is a white men's country." In a sense, the argument of racial inferiority serves as the last defense of whites, to which they never rashly resorted. In addition, their moral impulses also needed the argument of black inferiority to dissolve the conflicts in their own hearts. In other words, they must persuade themselves as well as others, and resist the internal perplexity as well as the external menace; and they must not merely prove that to tolerate some evil was for the greater good, but must go on to transform the evil into a good itself.

The moral predicament posed by the strong democratic creeds and the reality of racial oppression was most obviously embodied in the attitudes of Southern whites towards slavery. As Charles G. Sellers, Jr. put it, "The key to the tragedy of Southern history is the paradox of the slaveholding South's devotion to 'liberty.'"[135]

The experience of the Revolution made more discernible American devotion to liberty, as well as American idealism, which was now integrated with the patriotism of the new country. To Southern whites as well as other Americans, liberty was the lofty cause that the country had been striving for ever since its existence and was the great instrument to demonstrate its unusual mission to the world. The first inaugural speech of George Washington expressed the flourishing national spirit. "The preservation of the sacred fire of liberty and the destiny of the republican model of government," Washington declared, "are justly considered, perhaps, as *deeply*, as *finally*, staked on the experiment intrusted to the hands of the American people."[136]

Before the 1820s, the awkward situation caused by the reality of slaveholding and their devotion to liberty compelled Southern whites to adopt an attitude of moral apology. In the period of the Revolution, few persons dared praise slavery even in the far South. Many people realized that the enslavement of blacks was not only due to the necessity of the Southern economy, but due to their moral evaluation of blacks. The Revolution expedited the process in which Americans explored their consciences. They did not conceal their evils, admirably, but sincerely hoped to eliminate them. Before reaching the perfect realm, they would never feel comfortable and satisfied. Between the ideal and reality, there was after all a long distance. The most important thing was not the fact that they tolerated the evil, but their courage in facing that reality and the spirit of seeking purity. Despite being imperfect, they admitted, they were not incorrigible sinners either. This attitude was vividly illustrated in the letter written by Patrick Henry (1772), where he confessed that he had slaves because he was "drawn along by the general inconvenience of living here without them."

> I will not, I cannot, justify it. However culpable my conduct, I will so far pay my devoir to virtue as to own the excellence and rectitude of her precepts, and lament my want of conformity to them.[137]

Henry had to remain in the state of evil, for the evil could bring him more advantages; yet he must pay a price for the "necessary evil," continuous self-condemnation. Referring to slavery, Jefferson also anxiously warned: Whenever thinking of the justice of God, I would tremble with fear for my motherland; His justice will not be asleep forever.[138] It was, indeed, a "cruel confrontation" in whites' consciences. On slavery and black discrimination, Southern whites retreated from the rational world into the religious one. Being the very incarnation of absolute goodness, God was intrinsically complete and perfect. To create a faultless world,

He allowed the presence of some evils, which would set off the perfection of the world He had Created, just as the shaded part of a picture did the bright part. Since the existence of the ultimate goodness, the evils then might be tolerated and explained away. Thomas Aquinas, the medieval master of scholasticism, shared this moral opinion. In the American South, this moral opinion also gradually rose to the surface.

At the same time, however, the evil was after all, evil. Many persons were disturbed by its existence, perhaps because they had realized the price paid to maintain the evil and the challenge that its existence issued to whites. Southern statesmen in the Revolutionary period, including Washington, Jefferson, Monroe, and Adams, lamented the presence of slavery and condemned its inharmoniousness with national creeds. When discussing the difficult position that faced the universal norms of conduct, Jefferson was penetrating. To achieve fairness, he said, the laws must perform the reciprocal function of rights; without it, they were no more than rules of conduct based on violence rather than on conscience. Jefferson, the great planter who owned 185 slaves in 1774, devoted himself to purging the legal code of "principles inconsistent with Republicanism." Slavery, according to Jefferson, corroded the morality of whites.

> The whole commerce between master and slave is a perpetual exercise of the most boisterous passions, the most unremitting despotism on the one part, and degrading submissions on the other. The man must be a prodigy who can retain his manners and morals undepraved by such circumstance.[139]

At first, Jefferson proposed his emancipation schemes in the Virginia assembly; later on he failed to add the clause condemning, the slave trade into the Declaration of Independence. What embarrassed him, however, was that blacks were both men and property. Although he substituted the right to pursue happiness for the right to property in the Declaration, there is no reason to suspect that he would abandon the right to property. Therefore, the insoluble problem was that the compulsory expropriation of the ownership of slaves would lead to the appearance of a new kind of slavery. Another gloomy prospect was that while emancipation might increase racial tensions, the plan of overseas emigration was not practical at all. Jefferson's enthusiasm became fainter and fainter, and his emancipation schemes was put aside during the years from 1786 to 1790, leaving them to the "young men, grown up and growing up," who "have sucked in the principles of liberty, as it were, with their mother's milk."[140] The change in Jefferson's attitude dramatically illustrated white Southerners' dilemma.

Taking advantage of this dilemma, Northern Abolitionists continuously lashed out at the dignity of white Southerners and pushed them to the moral edge where they were at an impasse. With the invention of the cotton gin, slavery in the South also demonstrated a spurt of activity. From the 1820s onwards, white Southerners adopted an uncompromising stand. The debate in 1820 over the admission of Missouri as a slave state symbolized their change from moral apologists to undisguised defenders of slavery, and the moderate Virginia slave tradition gave way to the tough school of South Carolina.

First, slavery apologists vehemently denied the principle that all men were created equal. Tackling the Virginia school over the nonhistorical feature of the equality principle, Calhoun stressed that it had gone beyond biological and social reality. "Taking the proposition literally," Calhoun declared, "there is not a word of truth in it." Jefferson's careless acceptance of the dogma of romantic Frenchmen was indeed the origin of misfortune.

> It follows, from what has been stated, that it is a great and dangerous error to suppose that all people are equally entitled to liberty. It is a reward to be earned, not a blessing to be gratuitously lavished on all alike; a reward reserved for the intelligent, the patriotic, the virtuous and deserving; and not a boon to be bestowed on a people too ignorant, degraded and vicious, to be capable either of appreciating or of enjoying it.[141]

All the progress of human civilization, he asserted, depended on inequality among men. In the onward march of mankind, there had always existed, and must always exist, a front and a rear; if the order was upset, the harmonious laws of the cosmos would be disturbed, and the development of humanity obstructed.

> It is, in deed, this inequality of condition between the front and rear ranks, in the march of progress, which gives so strong an impulse to the former to maintain their position, and to the latter to press forward into their files. This gives to progress its great impulse. To force the front rank back to the rear, or attempt to push forward the rear into files with the front, by the interposition of the government, would put an end to the impulse, and effectually arrest the march of progress.[142]

The theory of natural rights also came under attack. Dr. Cooper of South Carolina emphasized that even according to the hypothesis of the primitive state, a man could not jump to the conclusion that all men were endowed with the same rights. Only power, either physical or spiritual, formed the natural law, which made animals subject to man and dominated relations between people at the same time. "The universal law of nature is force. By this law the lower animals are subdued to man, and the same law governs the relations between men." The so-called natural law and the natural rights claimed under such a law consisted merely of "systems fabricated by theoretical writers on a contemplation of what might usefully be acknowledged among men as binding on each other."[143] This distortion revealed the weakness of the natural law school, but the confusion of force and right was obviously a retrogression from Enlightenment principles and, in fact, led to the logic that might was right.

Even the most cherished principle, *liberty,* was derided by some people, among whom George Fitzhugh was a representative figure. In *Sociology for the South, or the Failure of Free Sosiety* (1854), Fitzhugh tried to cast away any philosophy on which the government might build. "Philosophy," he declared, "will blow up any government that is founded on it. If we would have our people normal and our institutions permanent, we should repudiate our political abstractions and adopt religious truths in their stead." In his opinion, liberty was not a positive good as many persons imagined, but the most hypocritical and foolish idea ever invented. "Sin," he asserted, "began with the desire for liberty and the attempt to attain it in the person of Satan and his fellow-angels." As civilization advanced, liberty receded. The idea of liberty was

> the most false and foolish that ever entered the human mind. The only free people in the world are the Digger Indians of the valley of New Holland. They know nothing of government, of society, of castes, classes, or of subordination of rank; each man digs for worms and climbs for birds' eggs on his own hook: they are perfectly free, famished and degraded.[144]

The presence of slavery made Southern whites deny the doctrines of equality and natural rights and even trample on liberty itself. It did not mean, however, that whites had completely abandoned rational laws, to which they subjected themselves *directly* and subjected blacks *indirectly,* namely through the hands of whites; they only removed the part connected with blacks and carried out a great reformation in democratic creeds according to the principle of "realism." To Calhoun, the foremost job that real democrats had to do was to penetrate the deep nature of democracy and eliminate its wrong hypotheses. Once popular in America, the philosophy of natural rights as a virus went deep into the core of Jacksonism. Now it was high time to expose and eliminate it. A theory that Calhoun was keen on was the exclusive nature of liberty. Liberty was not an inherent and indispensable right.

> On the contrary, its great praise, its proudest distinction is, that an all-wise Providence has reserved it, as the noblest and highest reward for the development of our faculties, moral and intellectual. A reward more appropriate than liberty could not be conferred on the deserving; nor a punishment inflicted on the undeserving more just, than to be subject to lawless and despotic rule. This dispensation seems to be the result of some fixed law; and every effort to disturb or defeat it, by attempting to elevate a people in the scale of liberty, above the point to which they are entitled to rise, must ever proved abortive, and end in disappointment.[145]

As a matter of fact, Calhoun was imposing limitation on the traditional concept of concrete liberties. Since the late Middle Ages, Englishmen gradually developed the concept of liberties. It was concrete and plural, and every individual struggled for his concrete liberties, whose meanings varied with their property and positions. Free persons in some cities, for example, had some specified liberties; once emigrating elsewhere, they would lose them. The concept of liberties often meant privilege or immunity from some duties. Even a king was not an absolute autocrat, and his liberties were limited. "The King," said Bracton, "is not subject to man, but is under God and the Law."[146] The rights or privileges shared by all Englishmen, such as the right to hold property and the right to sign a contract, were "the liberties of Englishmen." Although the social mobility and the political events since the commercial revolution had eroded the medieval hierarchy of privileges and duties, the idea of concrete liberties carried on as before. When they clashed with the king, what the colonies resorted to was also the "liberties of Englishmen" or the "rights of Englishmen." The concrete character of liberties could be seen from the rights Thomas Jefferson ticked off in the Declaration of Independence as having been denied by King George. As mentioned earlier, the liberty and equality many whites advocated were in fact white liberty and equality, which ceased to take effect as soon as blacks appeared.

Yet the stop was implicit. Under the pressure of universal liberty advocated by Abolitionists, Calhoun simply abandoned the idea of equality
and imposed conditions on the concept of liberty. In other words, the implication caused by slavery and whites' self-consciousness was now
made visible: Except for blacks, all men had liberties.

Following his train of thought, others explored the idea of concrete
liberties. To them, the problem was not that slavery had deprived blacks
of their liberties, but how it guaranteed blacks' appropriate liberties. One
writer argued that a man was born in a state of subjection and remained
in that state at least until he became an adult. Before that stage he had
"the right of such absolute control by others as that his will may retain its
self-acting power unimpaired."[147] Blacks were similar to children. Although the black was a person, he was not an adult; a child might grow
up, but the black would never be mature; both a black individual and the
whole race were "undeveloped," and "childish." If blacks could not
govern themselves, it was not unfair to govern them without their consent; blacks should be under guardianship forever, which would not
hamper the full development of their will. The white race, who abided by
the rules ordained by God and had self-restraint, were the ideal guardian.
As William C. Jarvis said, "Nothing can be plainer than that the barbar-
ian of the desert requires the restraint of a more powerful arm than the
[white] individual, whose passions and propensities are under the internal restraint of moral and religious sentiments."[148] The Reverend James
Thornwell, a leader of South Carolina's wealthy Presbyterians, called the
Southern system "regulated liberty," a discipline that opposed both "the
despotism of the masses on the one hand and the supremacy of a single
will on the other."[149] Based on this idea, some whites demanded that the
states protect the "rights" of slaves. The Reverend W. T. Hamilton of Mobile, Alabama, for example, denounced the failure to recognize slaves'
matrimony in law "an outrage to humanity and insult to God!"[150] Under
their pressure, many states passed the codes that guaranteed some "liberties" of blacks as well as masters' right to hold property, and all the
Southern states claimed that their laws protected slaves' right to life.
Some slaves managed to acquire their own property, though there was no
legal sanction.[151] Aside from these, there were almost no other rights.
Led by Mississippi Presbyterian James A. Lyon during the Confederacy,
some reformers proposed that no slaveholder be allowed to separate slave
children from their mothers, that the testimony of slaves be admissible,
and that slave religious assemblies be sanctioned by law. The movement was so strong that some achievements were gained.[152] Generally

speaking, however, these humanist reforms did not so much strike slavery as offer more reasons for the existence of slavery by increasing the "liberties" of slaves and restraining the cruelty of slavery. Perhaps the reforms made more people, including William Pinkney, not pause to "blush at the very name of Freedom," for it was in accordance with those very principles that "rights political and civil, may be qualified by the fundamental law, upon such inducements as the freemen of the country deem sufficient."[153]

Satisfied with the definite limitation proposed by Calhoun, others tried to find the historical tradition that held that liberty was monopolized by the Teutonic race. Francis Lieber, professor at the University of South Carolina, asserted that the "Anglican race" was the only one that had developed a system of restraints upon liberty, which were necessary if liberty itself was to survive. "We belong to the Anglican race," he went on, "which carried Anglican principles and liberty over the globe, because, wherever it moves, liberal institutions and common law full of manly rights and instinct with the principle of an expansive life accompany it."[154] Other races also had characteristic tendencies. The ancient Greeks had an "instinct" for aesthetics, and the Romans had one for "law." The modern "Gallican race," on the other hand, was easily influenced by mass appeals. As to blacks, they would never develop their abilities unless they were given social equality, but he himself opposed to such a solution. In his studies of the different fate of French Canada and the English colonies, Francis Parkman also found the importance of racial characteristics. "The Germanic race, and especially the Anglo-Saxon branch of it, is peculiarly masculine," Parkman said, "and, therefore, peculiarly fitted for self-government. It submits action habitually to the guidance of reason, and has the judicial faculty of seeing both sides of a question . . . The institutions of New England were utterly inapplicable to the population of New France, and the attempt to apply them would have nothing but mischief. Freedom is for those who are fit for it. The rest will lose it, or turn it to corruption."[155] The black race, Chancellor Harper of South Carolina added, represented a sordid, servile, laborious race, remarkably indifferent to personal liberty. They had been created to perform sordid, servile, and laborious work.[156]

Having settled the contradiction between democratic tenets and the reality of enslavement, Southern whites took further steps to prove that slavery was not "a necessary evil," but "a positive good" for the slave as well as society in general. Some authors even talked about "socialism" in a purified and dignified meaning. "By making the labor itself capital,"

Jenkins declared, "the conflict of interest, so evident in other labor systems, lost its foundation."[157] Thomas R. Dew, a professor at William and Mary College, insisted that by giving the superior few the leisure necessary to the progress of society, slavery had been the means by which civilization was created throughout history. As to divine sanction, Thornton Stringfellow, a Baptist minister of Culpeper County, Virginia, eloquently showed the abundant proofs in the Bible. The Old Testament contained accounts of dealings in slaves by the patriarchs of Israel, while in the New Testament, the Apostles demanded obedience to all secular ordinances, including those governing the relations of master and servant.[158] Slavery, John C. Calhoun asserted in the Senate in 1837, "is, instead of an evil, a good, a positive good." By this he did not mean to imply that slavery was always better than free labor relations, but simply that it was the best relation between the two races. "In few countries so much is left to the share of the laborer, and so little exacted from him, or more kind attention paid to him in sickness or infirmities of age."[159] He thought that "wage slavery" was more cruel and inhuman, while the condition of Southern slaves was greatly superior to that of poorhouse inmates in the more civilized portion of Europe. On the other hand, since the inferior class was excluded from politics, politics contained only the superior race and ablest men. Slavery then did not violate "the democratic principles, but was helpful to foster the real democratic spirit. All the white men then became gentlemen; Slavery was therefore the best guarantee to equality among the whites. It produced an unvarying level among them and did not even admit of inequality, by which one white man could domineer over another."[160] Consequently, moral and able persons voluntarily entered the cooperative relationship in accord with the public benefits, and inferiors were also under the conscientious guardianship of the society. This was once the dream of Greek democracy, on which the brilliant classical civilization was created. Now the ideal was regenerated in the American South. As Alexander Stephens put it, slavery was now becoming the foundation of the "new mansion" of the South.

Therefore, Southern whites not only emancipated themselves from their own moral affliction, but also sent blacks the "gospel" and "kindness" of whites. Having combined with the desire for conquest, whites' self-consciousness now became the spiritual mainstay of defending the "Southern civilization" in their controversy with Northerners. To blacks, whites' self-consciousness was not merely whites' exclusive self-identity, but also had become the philosophy encouraging the wolf to devour the lamb. Lincoln denounced slavery in such a way, "Wolves devour lambs, not because it is good for their own greedy maws, but because it [is] good for the lambs!!!"[161]

Based on racial tyranny, racism exhibited a strong syndrome of domination, conquest, and sadism. The belief that blacks belonged to an inferior race gave whites many practical advantages. It might explain that blacks were only fit to serve whites; it could prove the necessity of maintaining racial purity and preventing miscegenation; and it could explain away why blacks had no legal rights: no matter how we cared for our pets, we would not regard them as equal counterparts. Believing that blacks had small cranial capacities and simple brain structures, they were assured that blacks had no sufficient rationality and ability; believing that blacks were inherently lazy, they were convinced that blacks would not work without compulsion; they thought black women lacked the sense of chastity, so the fault of miscegenation was not due to white men, but derived from the temptation of the black devil; black men were at the same time considered libidinous, and this external danger reminded whites of the necessity of maintaining white women's purity and social control; and so on. For Southern whites, the evil reality became an origin of good, and in the end became good itself. Used to give service to practical interests, racial discrimination further formed the moral basis of slavery; in turn, the reality of racial oppression again produced a great variety of new racial theories. In a sense, black leader James Weldon Johnson hit the mark with a single comment: "the main difficulty of the race question does not lie so much in the actual condition of the blacks as it does in the mental attitude of the whites."[162]

Undoubtedly, the longest suffering victim of slavery and racial domination was the black slave. He had almost no civil liberty. If the right to life belonged to civil liberty, this protection was basically due to the consideration of guarding the property of the whole master class. Certainly, he might enjoy "moral freedom." However, what did "morality" mean under racial domination? It could mean only obedience, patience, or muddle-headedness. Doubtlessly, this "morality" was incompatible with real morality. So the practical predicament of morality made a slave show a dual personality. On the one hand, he had to submit to the reality of personal domination, muddle along from day to day, relax his soul, and thereby gain his "moral freedom" and become a "happy donkey" or "contented slave"; on the other hand, he was impatient and angry at his status of submission, hated social injustice, looked forward to real moral freedom and civil liberty, and thereby lost the "moral freedom" under the slavery. The extent of this "schizophrenia" varied with individuals and

with the time. At one end of the spectrum, he might be extruded through
the die of reality into a submissive wretch that had his "moral freedom,"
as the typical personality of "Samboo" described by Stanley Elkin or
Harriet B. Stowe's "Uncle Tom."

> No insult, no outrage, no suffering, could ruffle the Christianlike
> meekness of his spirit, or shake the steadfastness of his faith. Toward
> his merciless oppressors he cherished no animosity, and breathed noth-
> ing of retaliation. Like his Lord and Master, he was willing to be "led
> as a lamb to the slaughter," returning blessing for cursing, and anxious
> only for the salvation of his enemies.[163]

At the other end of the spectrum, he took the path of passive resistance
and even revolted. As Kenneth Stampp said, "slave resistance, whether
bold and persistent or mild and sporadic, created for all slaveholders a
serious problem of discipline . . . The record of the minority who waged
ceaseless and open warfare against their bondage makes an inspiring
chapter, also in the history of Americans of African descent."[164] The majority, however, were accustomed to using their skill for survival honed
in the harsh environment, and adopted opportunism and cynical attitudes
to face social reality. Neither did they resist the system in an extreme
way, nor did they allow the benefits to pass away. In vying for favors,
Frederick Douglass said, they "sought as diligently to please their overseers as the office and deceive the people."[165] Once having opportunities,
they would seek real freedom without any hesitation. Historian Bell I.
Wiley concluded in 1938:

> That disorder and unfaithfulness on the part of Negroes were far more
> common than post-war commentators have usually admitted. A corre-
> spondent of Senator Clay's wife wrote in 1863 from Selma, Alabama
> "the faithful slave is about played out. They are the most treacherous,
> brutal, and ungrateful race on the globe." This statement is doubtless
> extreme, but it is not farther from the truth than the encomiums of the
> slaves' loyalty and devotion which have been so universally circulated
> and accepted in the South.[166]

No matter how blacks reacted, it was definitely true that the majority
of blacks did not identify with the existing system. The law and discipline were awe-inspiring but not respectable, whose victims often received compassion rather than disgust from their companions. Due to the

conflict and confusion surrounding the criteria, it was hard for a black to abide by any criterion of morality, and, consequently, he only bore in mind the reality of force. He might be fearful when he stole the master's bacon, but he was never ashamed; he learned to turn a blind eye to what he saw and not to talk of the truth. Slavery and racism not only lashed the flesh of blacks, but also twisted their souls. The compulsory assimilation of slavery made blacks identify with whites' culture, among which was whites' universal idealism, but at the same time they had to defer to a special "morality." The two conflicting directions formed the basis of "blacks' two souls."

Blacks, however, were not the only victim of the moral dilemma. Although their appetite for racial superiority had been satisfied, whites paid a high price for their racism and the racial division. At the beginning, they admitted the evil of slavery and had no confusion regarding its morality, though they were embarrassed by the moral problem; later on they simply transformed the evil into good. However, they still subconsciously realized that this "good" was evil, otherwise why did they do their utmost to prove that the self-evident "good" was good? They abandoned some democratic creeds, only to find the ubiquity of the moral dilemma. Du Bois wrote that "Nor does the paradox and danger of this situation fail to interest and perplex the best conscience of the South. Deeply religious and intensely democratic as are the mass of whites, they feel acutely the false position in which the Negro problems place them."[167]

Just because whites tried to avoid the universal and just criterion regarding discrimination against blacks, they stressed their racist criterion of morality. As a result, racists themselves achieved their own "moral freedom."

Whites, however, saddled themselves with fear, suspicion, and unrest because of their infliction of fear on blacks. Worrying about black resistance, they regarded any collective activity of blacks as a potential menace. Consequently, the supervisory system became accepted practice, and such organizations as trade unions were merciless suppressed in the South. In order to strangle Abolitionism, they established a strict censorship system. As a result, whites themselves, especially poor whites, were isolated. Since their regime had lost legitimacy in black eyes, whites had to always be on the alert. "If they really believe there is danger from the Negro," Booker T. Washington said, "it must be because they do not intend to give him justice. Injustice always breeds fear."[168] "Yes," Thomas P. Bailey commented, "we Southerners need a freedom from suspicion, fear, anxiety, doubt, unrest, hate, contempt, disgust, and all the rest of the race-feeling-begotten brood of viperous emotions."[169] Both whites or blacks needed to reconstruct their respective "freedom from fear."

Slaveholders, who benefited most from slavery, became tyrannical because of their absolute power over slaves. Driven by a great need to maintain their hegemony, Steven M. Stowe thought, planters endowed Southern culture with assertive masculinity, with its concomitant commitment to the preservation of honor.[170] The Southern gentleman, according to Thomas Nelson Page, was imbued with "a certain pride based on self-respect and consciousness of power."[171] At the same time, since slaves were fully under their control, slaveholders sometimes felt a sense of responsibility for "their own blacks." Making the masters both emotional and tyrannical, therefore, racial slavery eroded the true democratic spirit. Holding power in his hands, a master was confident, firmly believed the perfection of his peculiar lifestyle, and was deeply resentful at any social change. He regarded white women as his exclusive domain; in the meantime, he did not care much about the racial line and carried on with black women. To mitigate his uneasy conscience and white women's disgust, he felt that

> the woman must be compensated, the revolting suspicion in the male that he might be slipping into bestiality got rid of, by glorifying her; the Yankee must be answered by proclaiming from the housetops that Southern Virtue so far from being inferior was superior, nor alone to the North's but to any on earth, and adducing Southern Womanhood in proof.[172]

Women might be protected by the gallant spirit, be released from the drudgery of chores, and enjoy the gaiety of social intercourse; yet she also paid a price for it, with the broader liberty and opportunity of self-realization lost.

> Open complaint about their lot was not the custom among Southern ladies; yet their contented acceptance of the home as the "sphere to which God had appointed them" was sometimes more apparent than real. Most Southern women would not have tried, or know how, to free themselves from the system which was supposed to be divinely ordained, but there is considerable evidence that many of them found the "sphere" very confining.[173]

Poor whites paid the highest price for maintaining racial order and slavery. Although they desired social change, poor whites were powerless, and as a class they were very concerned about how to keep blacks in the lowest position. Since slavery had reduced the competition between the races to the lowest extent and had kept the farthest distance between the two races, poor whites regarded slaveholders as the critical element in maintaining white supremacy. Conversely, the planter class lost no time in expanding their influence, but they had little interesting in improving the political and economic status of small farmers. They were willing to levy a poll tax rather than a property tax, thereby making the distribution of taxes unfair and the resources of public expenses insufficient. While planters could afford the expenses of private education, poor whites could not fully share the benefit of public education. Politically, poor whites were no longer limited by property qualifications, but they did not have any substantial political power. Skillfully manipulating local and state politics, planters nipped any harmful reforms in the bud. As for political conservatism, Deway W. Grantham wrote that

> Although only about one-fourth of the Southern families owned slaves in 1860, and few of those owned very many. Slavery nevertheless was the keystone in the arch of Southern society, the source of social stratification among white Southerners but paradoxically the solvent of strong class consciousness. There is no avoiding the fact, Louis Harts concludes, "that one of the crucial factors in the solidarity of the South was a democratic spirit enhanced by the slavery on which it rested."[174]

The eroded facet to the democratic spirit must also be pointed out. In the West, for example, the Mississippi constitution followed the form by then generally established in Southern states when it declared "That all freemen, when they form a social compact, are equal in rights," whereas the Indiana constitution still conformed to the direction of the Declaration of Independence:

> we declare, that all men are born equally free and independent, and have certain natural inherent, and unalienable rights; among which are the enjoying and defending of life and liberty, and of acquiring, possessing and protecting property and pursuing and obtaining happiness and safety.[175]

Before 1830, although the two-party system was born in the South, it was so immature that the competition between Whigs and Democrats was not so much important as that among the Democrats themselves. While the North and South could coexist peacefully, the two-party system might be barely maintained; once the crisis of disunion was impending, it was then no longer possible. On the eve of the Civil War, the two parties merged into one. The problem was the presence of a large black population in the South and whites' racism. Because of discrimination against blacks caused by racism, the great tragedy inevitably took place, and America had to continuously pay its debt, in the past and in the future.

Seen from the evolutionary process of whites' self-consciousness and slavery, we can get to the crux of issues affecting blacks. Driven by racism and self-interest, whites mobilized the whole legal and extra-legal power to dominate an allegedly inferior race; on the other side were the feeble status and the distorted lives of blacks. In such a seemingly inescapable deadlock, the only hope of blacks perhaps lay in the force of whites' idealism and the practical interests behind it. Emancipation and Reconstruction were just two positive results of the combination of idealism and practical interest. But without the striving of blacks themselves, certainly, the power of whites' idealism would never have played a leading role.

NOTES

40. Winthrop D. Jordan, "White over Black," quoted from Robert Marcus and David Burner, eds., *The American Scene: Varieties of American History.* Vol. I. New York: Appleton-Century-Crofts, 1974, p. 48.

41. David D. Anderson and Robert L. Wright, eds., *The Dark and Tangled Path: Race in America.* Boston: Heath, 1971.

42. Winthrop D. Jordan, *The White Men's Burden: Historical Origins of Racism in the United States.* New York: Oxford University Press, 1974, p. 6.

43. Brewton Berry, *Race and Ethnic Relations.* New York: Macmillan, 1958, p. 122.

44. Harold M. Hyman, *Into Slavery: Racial Relations in Virginia Colony.* Philadelphia & New York: J. B. Lippincott Company, 1976, p. 27.

45. Thomas F. Gossett, *Race: The History of an Idea in America.* Dallas, TX: Southern Methodist University Press, 1963, p. 5.

46. Jordan, *op. cit.,* p. 9.

47. *The Jewish Encyclopedia.* Vol. 3. New York, 1925, p. 186. Quoted from Gossett, *op. cit.,* p. 5.

48. Jordan, *op. cit.,* 23.

49. Winthrop D. Jordan, "White over Black," quoted from Robert Marcus and David Burner, eds., *The American Scene: Varieties of American History.* New York: Appleton-Century-Crofts, 1974, p. 49.

50. Jordan, *White Men's Burden,* p. 16.

51. *ibid.,* p. 48.

52. Helmut R. Niebuhr, *The Kingdom of God,* quoted from Ralph H. Gabriel, *The Course of American Democratic Thought: An Intellectual History Since 1815.* New York: The Ronald Press Company, 1940, p. 29.

53. Edmund S. Morgan, "Masters and Servants," in Marvin Meyers and J. R. Pole, eds., *The Meanings of American History: Interpretations of Events, Ideas, and Institutions,* New York: Scott, Foresman and Company, 1971, p. 34.

54. David R. Weber, *Civil Disobedience in America.* Ithaca, NY: Cornell University Press, 1978, p. 17.

55. Gabriel, *op. cit.,* p. 15.

56. Quoted from Morgan, *op. cit.,* p. 35.

57. Charles W. Dunn, ed., *American Political Theology: Historical Perspective and Theoretical Analysis.* New York: Praeger, 1984, pp. 21–23.

58. Harold J. Laski, *The American Democracy.* New York: Viking Press, 1948, p. 226.

59. Herbert W. Schneider, *A History of American Philosophy.* New York: Columbia University Press, 1963, p. 9.

60. *ibid.,* p. 10.

61. Perter L. Berger, *The Sacred Canopy: Elements of a Sociological Theory of Religion.* Garden City, NY: Doubleday and Company, Inc., 1969, pp. 115–121.

62. Max Weber, *The Protestant Ethic and the Spirit of Capitalism,* Trans. Talcott Parsous. New York: Charles Scribner's Sons, 1958, Chapter 4.

63. Leolan D. Baldwin, *Ideas in Action: Documentary and Interpretive Readings in American History.* New York: Random House, 1968, p. 24.

64. Daniel J. Boorstin, *The Americans: The Colonial Experience.* New York: Random House, 1958, p. 7.

65. John Winthrop, "Christian Charitie," in Frank Freidel, et al., eds., *Builders of American Institutions: Readings in United States History.* Vol. I. New York: Harper & Row, pp. 17–19.

66. Perry Miller, "Errand into the Wildness," quoted from Winthrop S. Hudson, *Religion in America.* New York: Scribner's, 1981, p. 27.

67. Jordan, *op. cit.,* pp. 92–93.

68. Ralph B. Perry, *Puritanism and Democracy.* New York: Vanguard Press, 1944, p. 70.

69. Quoted from Baldwin, *op. cit.,* p. 24.

70. Erich Fromm, *Escape from Freedom.* New York: Farrar & Rinehart, 1942, pp. 124–139, 141.

71. Howard H. Quint, *Main Problems in American History.* Vol. I. The Dorsey Press, 1978, p. 3.

72. Harold M. Hyman, *op. cit.,* pp. 6–10.

73. Lawrence A. Cremin, *American Education: The Colonial Experience, 1607–1783.* New York: Harper & Row, 1970, pp. 194–195.

74. August Meier and Elliot Rudiwick, *From Plantation to Ghetto.* New York: Hill and Wang, 1970, p. 27.

75. John Hope Franklin, *From Slavery to Freedom: A History of Negro Americans.* New York: Knopf, 1980, p. 30.

76. Avery Craven, *The Repressible Conflict.* Baton Rouge: Louisiana State University Press, 1939, p. 41.

77. William D. Piersen, *Black Legacy: America's Hidden Heritage.* Amherst: University of Massachusetts Press, 1993, p. 43.

78. Oscar Handlin, *Race and Nationality in American Life.* New York, 1957, p. 10.

79. Thad W. Tate, Jr., *The Negro in Eighteenth-Century Williamsburg.* Williamsburg, VA: Colonial Williamsburg, 1965, p. 23.

80. Oscar Handlin, *op. cit.,* p. 11.

81. Perter Kalm, "Servant and Slaves," in Vincent P. De Santis, ed., *American Past and Present.* Vol. I. Boston: Forum Press, 1968, p. 54.

82. James H. Brewer, "Negro Property Owners in Seventeenth Century Virginia," in August Meier and Elliot Rudiwick, eds., *The Making of Black America.* New York: Atheneum, 1969, pp. 201–205.

83. Edmond Morgan, "The First American Boom: Virginia, 1618–1630," *William and Mary Quarterly,* Vol. 28, p. 198.

84. Lyon G. Tylor, ed., *Narratives of Early Virginia.* New York: Scribner, 1907, pp. 278–279.

85. Carl N. Degler, "Slavery and the Genesis of American Race Prejudice," in August and Rudiwick, eds., *op. cit.,* p. 95; Handlin, *op. cit.,* p. 8.

86. Handlin, *op. cit.,* p. 7.

87. *ibid.,* p. 7.

88. Jordan, *op. cit.,* p. 31.

89. *ibid.,* p. 32.

90. Alden T. Vaughan, "Blacks in Virginia: A Note on the First Decade," *William and Mary Quarterly,* Vol. 39, p. 472.

91. Hyman, *op. cit.,* p. 39; Gossett, *op. cit.,* p. 30.

92. Degler, *op. cit.,* p. 96.

93. Jordan, *op. cit.,* p. 41.

94. Degler, *op. cit.,* p. 100.

95. Jordan, *op. cit.,* p. 42.

96. Paul C. Palmer, "Servant into Slave," *South Atlantic Quarterly,* Vol. 65, pp. 357–358.

97. Stanley M. Elkins, "Slavery: The Dynamics of Unopposed Capitalism," in Baldwin, *op. cit.,* p. 109.

98. Hyman, *op. cit.,* p. 44.

99. *ibid.,* p. 45.

100. Handlin, *op. cit.,* p. 13.

101. Degler, *op. cit.,* p. 105.

102. F. Champion, et al., eds., *The People Shall Judge: Readings in the Formation of American Policy.* Vol. I. Chicago: Unwin, 1949, p. 19.

103. George H. Moore, *Notes on the History of Slavery in Massachusetts,* quoted from Degler, *op. cit.,* p. 106.

104. Robert C. Twombly and Robert H. Moore, "Black Puritan: The Negro in Seventeenth Century Massachusetts," in Meier and Rudiwick, *op. cit.,* p. 121.

105. Degler, *op. cit.,* p. 106.

106. Stanley M. Elkins, *op. cit.,* p. 110.

107. Ulrich B. Phillips, *The Course of the South to Secession.* New York, 1939, p. 152.

108. Jordan, *op. cit.,* p. 47.

109. Robert C. Twombly and Robert M. Moore, *op. cit.* p. 122.

110. *ibid.,* p. 122.

111. F. C. Ward, *op. cit.,* p. 19.

112. Edward Byron Reuter, *The Mulatto in the United States.* New York: Negro University Press, 1969, p. 99.

113. Jordan, *op. cit.,* p. 52.

114. Gilman Ostrander, *The Rights of Man in America, 1606–1861.* Columbia: University of Missouri Press, 1969, p. 253.

115. Jordan, *op. cit.,* p. 61.

116. Gossett, *op. cit.,* p. 36.

117. *ibid.,* p. 39.

118. Jordan, *op. cit.,* pp. 100–101.

119. Ostrander, *op. cit.,* pp. 5–6.

120. Jordan, *op. cit.,* p. 103.

121. Alexander O. Boulton, "The American Paradox," *American Quarterly,* Vol. 47, 1995, p. 467.

122. Melvin Steinfield, *Our Racist Presidents: From Washington to Nixon.* Berkeley: University of California Press, 1972, pp. 20–21.

123. *ibid.,* pp. 20–22.

124. *ibid.*

125. *ibid.,* p. 20.

126. W. E. B. Du Bois, *The Souls of Black Folk.* New York: McClure, 1969, p. 122.

127. Gunnar Myrdal, *An American Dilemma: The Negro Problem and Modern Democracy.* New York, 1962, p. 99.

128. Ostrander, *op. cit.,* p. 37.

129. Perry Miller, "The Half-Way Covenant," in C. K. McFarland, ed., *Readings in Intellectual History.* New York: Random House, 1970, pp. 76, 78.

130. Peter Bulkeley, "The Gospel-Covenant," in Meyer C. Kern, ed., *Sources of the American Republic: A Documentary History of Politics, Society and Thoughts.* New York: Scott, Foresman and Company, 1967, pp. 65–68.

131. Perry Miller, "Errand into the Wildness," *op. cit.,* p. 100.

132. De Santis, *op. cit.,* p. 238.

133. Quoted in Ostrander, *op. cit.,* p. 100.

134. Gossett, *op. cit.,* p. 42.

135. Charles G. Sellers, Jr., *The Southerner as American.* Chapel Hill: University of North Carolina Press, 1960, p. 40.

136. Quoted from Baldwin, *op. cit.,* p. 60.

137. Quoted from Myrdal, *op. cit.,* p. 22.

138. Robert B., *American Perspective: The Dilemma of Individualism.* Translated from Chinese edition, p. 20. Beijing: People's Printing Co.

139. Alexander O. Boulton, *op. cit.,* p. 474.

140. Steinfield, *op. cit.,* pp. 38–40.

141. Vernon L. Parrington, *Main Currents in American Thought: The Romantic Revolution in America, 1800–1860.* New York: Harcourt Brace Jovanovich, 1954, p. 75.

142. *ibid.,* p. 75.

143. Charles Edward Merriam, *A History of American Political Theories.* New York: Macmillan, 1903, pp. 231–232.

144. *ibid.,* pp. 243–244.

145. Parrinton, *op. cit.,* p. 75.

146. Baldwin, *op. cit.,* p. 8.

147. Merriam, *op. cit.,* p. 233.

148. Gabriel, *op. cit.,* p. 19.

149. Bertram Wyatt-Brown, "Modernizing Southern Slavery: The Proslavery Argument Reinterpreted," in Kousser and McPerson, eds., *op. cit.,* p. 35.

150. *ibid.,* pp. 34–35.

151. Leon Schweninger, "Black Economic Reconstruction in the South," in Eric Anderson and Alfred A. Moss Jr., eds., *The Facts of Reconstruction: Essays*

in Honor of John Hope Franklin. Baton Rouge: Louisiana State University Press, 1991, p. 177.

152. Emory M. Thomas, *The Confederacy as a Revolutionary Experience.* Englewood Cliffs: Prentice-Hall, Inc., 1971, p. 127.

153. Ostrander, *op. cit.,* p. 258.

154. Gossett, *op. cit.,* p. 94.

155. *ibid.,* p. 95.

156. Ostrander, *op. cit.,* p. 260.

157. Myrdal, *op. cit.,* p. 442.

158. Thornton Stringfellow, "A Scriptural View of Slavery," in Eric L. McKitrick, ed., *Slavery Defended: The View of the Old South.* Englewood Cliffs: Prentice-Hall, Inc., 1963, pp. 86–98.

159. Richard Hofstadter, *The American Political Tradition and the Men Who Made It.* New York: Vintage Books, 1948, p. 101.

160. *ibid.,* p. 101.

161. David Anderson and Robert L. Wright, eds., *op. cit.,* p. 198.

162. Myrdal, *op. cit.,* p. 43.

163. George M. Fredrickson, ed., *William Lloyd Garrison.* Englewood Cliffs: Prentice-Hall, Inc., 1968, p. 57.

164. Kenneth Stampp, *The Peculiar Institution.* New York: Knopf, 1956, pp. 91–92.

165. *The Narrative of the Life of Frederick Douglass, An American Slave,* quoted from Stanley N. Katz, ed., *New Perspectives on the American Past, 1607–1877.* Boston: Heath, 1969, p. 353.

166. Bell I. Wiley, *Southern Negroes, 1861–1865.* New Haven, 1938, p. 83.

167. W. E. B. Du Bois, *op. cit.,* p. 207.

168. Myrdal, *op. cit.,* p. 43.

169. *ibid.,* p. 43.

170. *Review in American History,* Vol. 16, 1988, p. 24.

171. Charles S. Sydnor, "The Southerner and the Laws," in George B. Tindall, ed., *The Pursuit of Southern History: Presidential Addresses of the Southern Historical Association, 1935–1963.* Baton Rouge: Louisiana State University Press, 1964, p. 66.

172. W. J. Cash, quoted from Ostrander, *op. cit.,* p. 255.

173. Anne F. Scott, *The Southern Lady: From Pedestal to Politics, 1830–1930.* Chicago, 1970, p. 46.

174. Deway W. Grantham, *The Democratic South: The Economic and Social Revolution in the South Interpreted in the Light of History.* Athens: University of Georgia Press, 1963, p. 17.

175. Ostrander, *op. cit.,* pp. 265–266.

CHAPTER 2

Issues Affecting African Americans and African American Reconstruction

FREEDOM AND SAFETY: BLACKS' RESPONSE TO EMANCIPATION

In a sense, black Reconstruction began as early as the Emancipation Proclamation was published, because slaves were not entirely passive in their emancipation and freedom, and indeed they had stamped a deep brand on Reconstruction history by striving for the universal norms of conduct.

Freedom might be distinguished between "external freedom," which means that the restraints of the environment decrease to the lowest extent, and "internal freedom," which means the psychological state that has escaped ignorance, fear, and hate. Psychologically, freedom and safety are two kinds of needs, and the latter is more basic. They can be appropriately combined, providing that everyone abides by the universal norms of conduct, and that the basic rights of each person do not conflict with those of others. Having deprived blacks of their external freedom, however, slavery made the problem of freedom complicated. Because of the presence of the absolute power of their masters, slaves' behavior depended on the personal will of their master, and the basic necessities of life, including food, clothing, and shelter, and personal protection were all provided by their master. This was the most basic safety. If they could win their master' favor, blacks' safety might increase; the price was that blacks must be absolutely obedient and loyal. Any independent behavior, namely any act seeking external freedom, would incur anger or punishment from their master. Not only was the coefficient of safety reduced, but also the space of internal freedom narrowed. Thus, when freedom and safety could not both be gained, many blacks would rather sacrifice the former and hold back their thirst for real external and internal freedom, or were merely satisfied with the phantom visions of internal freedom; yet once the temptation of external freedom became stronger, and internal freedom might be built on a broader basis, many blacks bravely sought internal freedom based on external freedom.

In the period from the Emancipation Proclamation to full liberation, the system of authority was still confused. On the one hand, because of the proximity of the Union Army, the "hiring out" or "living out" of slaves, the absence of masters, and the confused situation, the absolute power of planters was reduced, and blacks had more opportunities to escape from bondage; on the other hand, the prospect of external freedom was still uncertain, and it was very dangerous for blacks to escape from slavery. The reality was that it was difficult to combine freedom and safety perfectly. The response of slaves to their impending emancipation vividly reflected their psychological conflicts between seeking freedom and safety.

On some plantations and especially on those where masters were maintaining normal control, slaves went on working as before, and there seemed no change taking place. As General Sherman's troops moved into South Carolina in early 1865, a planter observed little excitement among his slaves; as a matter of fact, they seemed "as silent as they had been in April 1861, when they heard from a distance the opening guns of the war." "Did those Negroes know that their freedom was so near?" he went on, "I cannot say, but if they did, they said nothing, only patiently waited to see what would come."[176]

The outward sign of calm, however, could not fully conceal the quiet change. Although slaves' mask of personality was still performing its function of self-protection in the transitional period, the proximity of the boom of guns led to different responses, including excitement, astonishment, expectation, and confusion. In eastern Virginia, an elderly slave "mammy" preparing the Sunday dinner greeted each blast of the cannon with a subdued "ride on, Massa Jesus."[177] When the Yankees approached, Sam Mitchell, a young slave of South Carolina, was in a state of stupefaction. "Son," his mother assured him, "dat ain't no t'under, dat Yankee come to gib you Freedom."[178] Being in high spirits, some slaves privately held dances. To many slaves, the coming of federal troops was nothing but the act of God's intervention, with the Yankees being cast as "Jesus's Aids," General Sherman as Moses, and Lincoln as "de Messiah." To relate what was happening to them with the divine will was their only way of understanding the marvelous event. "Us looked for the Yankees on dat place," a former South Carolina slave recalled, "like us look now for de Savior and de host of angels at de second comin'."[179]

The affairs on plantations were also affected. Although planters and overseers tried hard to maintain labor disciplines, their authority was challenged, and slaves increasingly showed their real selves. To slaves, the previous flattery and disguise now had little necessity. From the moment that Yankee soldiers were sighted in the vicinity, John H. Bill, a Tennessee planter, found that his slaves were no longer obedient. "My people seem Contented & happy, but not inclined to work. They say 'it is no use' the *Yankeys* will *take it all.*"[180] When the Union warships approached the Sea Islands in South Carolina, many whites went off to distant parts. Despite being under threats of violence and shooting, many slaves refused to follow their masters and hid themselves in marshes and woods. Resisting their master's commands to burn the cotton, still others took turns protecting it. Blacks' struggle for freedom in the old system was reaching a new stage.

On the plantations that masters did not directly control, the stubbornness and intractability of blacks were even more universal and obvious. Wartime necessity forced many slaveholders to go into battle, and they had to hand plantation affairs over to the old, women, and the young; at the same time, the flames of war made whites increasingly dependent on blacks to do all kinds of work. The decrease in supervision from whites and the increase in the role of blacks considerably reduced the core of slavery, namely, the master–slave bonds. Slaves slowed down their working speed, feigned compliance with the commands of mistresses and overseers, and allowed chores to go undone and weeds to grow. By making use of every means, including going slow, playing, and occasionally exercising violence, slaves shed a portion of their dependence. A mistress complained that "The negroes care no more for me than if I was an old free darkey and I get so mad sometimes that I think I don't care sometimes if Myers [the overseer] beats the last one of them to death. I can't stay with them another year alone."[181]

On a plantation in Alabama, slaves became "so bold" that the mistress notified her son that blacks had carried out a threat to kill the overseer. On the Millaudon plantation in Louisiana, "bad feelings" between the overseer and the slaves had prompted the absentee owner to pay a visit to his place. When the master tried to reprimand the "ringleader," the slave responded "with insolence." The master then flogged him with a whip. This time the slave responded by furiously charging Millaudon, and finally felled him with a stick. "This seemed to bring the negro to his senses, and he took refuge in his cabin; but he presently came out with a hatchet."[182] In the end, the rebellious slaves killed the overseer, and "the whole gang" of some 150 slaves left the plantation.

Being unsatisfied with their status of semi-independence in the old system, some slaves just ran away from the plantation, especially when this action had some certainty of success. Escape then became another important means of seeking freedom. Initially, quite a few blacks hid themselves in out-of-the-way places in the South. Among blacks a story was often told that the North and South fought over a bone (black people) like two dogs, whereas the "bone" had no business joining in the fray.[183] When Union troops approached, however, the "bone" regularly fled to them, hoping to be sheltered there and find the freedom longed for. Blacks got in touch with each other, secretly monitored the talks of whites, and shared the latest news with their companions. Once Union troops were approachable, they demonstrated their thirst for freedom by their feet. The outside temptation of freedom and the inside erosion of authority greatly accelerated the change in black conduct.

Runaway slaves included fieldhands, artisans, and servants, in all the Southern states. When the Union Army made its presence felt, the population of the slave quarters rapidly decreased. "They have shown no signs of insubordination," one Tennessee observer noted. "Down to the last moment they cut their maize and eat their corn-cake with their old docility then they suddenly disappear."[184] Compared with fieldhands, the servants, who had regular contacts with their master and had higher status, would rather seize the first chance to escape. It is worthy of attention that the most favored servants were often the first ones who left their master. Louis Manigault, a Georgia planter, said with deep sorrow that Hector was "a Negro We all of us esteemed highly," and "always spoiled both by my Father and Myself," but he was "the very first to murmur" and "give trouble" after the outbreak of the war. "This war has taught us the perfect impossibility of placing the least confidence in any Negro. In too numerous instances those we esteemed the most have been the first to desert us."[185] The desertion of the favorite servants particularly disturbed masters.

How to explain the seemingly implausible acts of "betrayal"? Being obviously superficial and sentimental, whites often attributed the anomalies to the so-called "African characters." The crux of the problem was the unnaturalness of the relationship between servant and master.

Even natural intimate acts were so distorted by external force that it was difficult to tell truth from falsehood. A servant was always at his master's beck and call and within the limits of the whole family's sight. To cope with the capricious attitudes of the master's family, he had to hold back his self-esteem, conceal his real feelings, learn to flatter the master and moderate his temper, and became a "good nigger." Therefore, a master was often misled by the false appearances of external harmony. Even when the master was a model of virtue, the sincerity of the loyalty of his servants was still doubtful. According to Wells Brown, beneficent treatment intensified slavest dissatisfaction with bondage much more than abuse did. The better treated the slave, Brown explained, the more miserable he felt, the more he appreciated freedom, and the more he detested the bondage that confined and restricted him.[186] Greatly distorting normal human relations, the power relationship in slavery cut a wide psychological gap between masters and slaves, of whom servants were particular typical. In such a situation, servants must learn the brilliant tactics of disguise, and loyalty was perhaps included among the necessary tactics. Their dealings with master made them have sounder judgment than fieldhands; the access to master made it easier for them to get accurate information about the war. Once realizing that the prospect of freedom was no longer illusive, a servant would seize the opportunity without hesitation. Thus arose a seemingly strange phenomenon: When freedom was impending, the most favorite and intelligent slaves, who were able to enjoy the "benefits" under slavery, were often the first to "betray" their master and taste the forbidden fruit of freedom.

Not all slaves, however, chose the road of resistance. A "faithful few" would rather entrust their fate to their master. To them, the master represented safety, while external freedom was uncertain and dangerous. Perhaps they understood that no matter what happened, they would still be in contact with whites in the future. In this uncertain period, to make a good impression on whites and avoid any possible revenge was a reliable investment. This motive was no doubt utilitarian, but there were indeed some who sincerely and wholeheartedly pledged loyalty to their master. The dependent character and grateful psychology formed in slavery were perhaps their real impetus. Since they had fully identified themselves with the system, it was possible for them to reach the state of internal freedom, though their bodies were kept in bondage. To save the family's silverware he had secreted, an elderly slave on a South Carolina plantation tried to impress the Yankee soldiers with how much he hated his "white folks" by slapping the master's children on the face. After the soldiers

went away, he "cried like a child afterwards because he 'had to hit Mas'
Horace's children.'"[187] On another plantation in this state, a young slave
went so far as to take her mistress' place to save her from rape.[188] In fact,
these sacrificial acts reflected the psychology of a sadomasochist, who
tries to get safety by inhibiting his ego and builds "symbiosis" with
others at the cost of losing himself. Even in the extreme examples of internal freedom, however, it was arbitrary to assert slaves fully abandoned
their hope of external freedom. They only held back this tendency to the
lowest extent. After observing the conduct of slaves in his region, Henry
W. Ravenel discovered two "exhibitions of character" he had never
anticipated. On many plantations "where there was really kind treatment
& mutual attachment," the coming of the Yankees suddenly shook the old
ties. At the same time, many slaves still resisted the temptation of freedom before them and remained, in his view, docile and submissive. With
blacks exhibiting such contradictory tendencies, his logical conclusion
was the utter impossibility of fathoming their loyalty.[189]

Once realizing that the external or internal freedom they had obtained was far from perfect, and that it was difficult for them to acquire
sufficient safety elsewhere, even runaway slaves would consider returning to their masters. The former plantation at least could provide them
with a familiar environment and the necessities of life, and there were
family members and friends to comfort them. If they thought that their
return would not invite serious punishment, they would go into action.
Having wandering for nearly eighteen months, Jack Savage, a runaway
slave of Georgia, returned to the old plantation, "looking half starved
and wretched in the extreme."[190] Before long he was sold in Savannah.
Explaining the reason for his return, another slave in this state complained that the Yankees did not respect him at all, and that he had to do
heavy work and suffer maltreatment.[191] Yet the act of returning did not
mean that a runaway slave had been satisfied with the usual routine on
the plantation, and he also faced the problem of obtaining his master's
confidence. Having gained some understanding of freedom through his
experience, a returned slave would often "act abnormally," and his anxious master usually took him under close supervision. This being the
case, a second escape might take place.

While slaves vacillated between safety and freedom and between
"loyalty" and "betrayal," the tendency to the latter was expedited once
the Union Army appeared. They no longer worried about danger in pursuit of freedom, for external freedom became a *fait accompli* to some
extent, and they could reconstruct a new personality in the harmonized

state between freedom and safety. The augmentation of the safety co-efficient benefited from the Union Army's removal of bondage from blacks and its limitations on planters' authority, but the safety coefficient still varied with the rationalizing extent of planters' authority. Yet no matter how the old dominating class thwarted changes, the new situation was after all not on a par with slavery. Therefore, the conduct of blacks now would further conform with their natural disposition and their inward pursuit.

Indeed, emancipation laid bare black characters. At all events, there were still "the faithful few" unwilling to leave. Watching the white flag of General Lee being hoisted, Fannie Berry, a house servant in Richmond, ran to the kitchen and exclaimed: "Mammy, don't you cook no mo.' You's free! You's free!" Then she ran to the henhouse: "Rooster, don't you crow no mo.' You's free! You's free! Ol'hen, don't you lay no mo' eggs. You's free! You's free!"[192] After the excitement, however, Berry went about her usual duties and allowed her mistress to hire her out, as if she did not understand the full implications of freedom. "I ain't never had no mother 'ceptin' only Mis' Patsey," a Florida freedwoman revealed, "an' I ain't never felt lak' a bond slave what's been pressed— dat's what dem soldiers say we all is."[193] Their dependence and their identification with slavery made them lose the pursuit of independence; though the outside world might destroy their shackles, they were enmeshed in a web of their own spinning. Being tamed birds in the cage, they did not intend to fly even with the door open.

No doubt the necessity of safety was still critical. As one slave said, "we couldn't do a thing without the white folks."[194] They viewed their master as "a perfect security from injury," and, to maintain this safety, blacks had to sacrifice their pursuit of freedom. To some blacks, freedom did not merit pursuing, and safety became their only spiritual sustenance. When freedom suddenly befell them, some blacks were as frightened as a stray dog. A former South Carolina slave recalled that on his plantation "some were sorry, some hurt, but a few were silent and glad." From the view of a Florida mistress, "some of them cried, some spoke gratefully, [and] only two looked surly and had nothing to say."[195] To "the faithful few," external freedom was not a good thing; it meant only uncertainty and insecurity. They were those who felt uneasy without ties. They were unprepared for unknown prospects and the outside world. Perhaps they were accustomed to their relations with their master and afraid of the disintegration of master–slave bonds. Therefore, the vexation they revealed did not inevitably mean hypocrisy or pretense. The old, sick, and disabled expressed their feelings more obviously. While admitting the freedom of these persons, some planters also extricated themselves from their relevant duties; consequently, what these blacks felt was not a feeling of release from bondage, but the mortification that they were deprived of their former protection and security. When Yankee soldiers told an elderly South Carolina slave that she no longer had a master or mistress, the woman responded as though she had been insulted: "I ain' no free nigger! I is got a marster an' mistiss! Dee right dar in de great house."[196] Subordinate relations seemed to have become one part of her life, whereas the emancipation would destroy the most important part of her. In some cases, some blacks even bitterly denounced those who deserted their master. Yet no matter how highly whites spoke of "the faithful few," the most "faithful" were often the old and weak, who of course had no opportunity to leave. Even in these cases, there were still some old persons privately glad at the freedom of their children; they maintained loyalty because they had no ability to realize their dream for external freedom and had to preserve what they could.

Clearly, the black loyalty praised by whites was somewhat exaggerated. The false appearance of "loyalty," admittedly, was to a large extent due to whites themselves. When freedmen were punished for their emphasis on external freedom, others would learn to act prudently. Even when blacks realized they had been freed, they would rather patiently wait the recognition of their master. When a North Carolina freedman was asked why he had not yet severed his ties with the woman who owned him, he responded that "my mistress never said anything to me that I was to have wages, nor yet that I was free; nor I never said anything to her. Ye see I left it to her honor to talk to me about it, because I was afraid she'd say I was insultin' to her and presumin', so I wouldn't speak first." Yet he had decided to leave her in due course and work "for myself."[197] Some blacks showed "sympathy" for their former masters' unfortunate experiences and even shed some crocodile tears. To them, "loyalty" only meant a crafty maneuver. Occasionally, the "loyalty" showed by blacks stemmed from the misunderstanding of whites. When sixteen-year-old Sallie Crane of Arkansas was sent to her mother by her mistress, her first thought was that she would be sold. "I cried because I thought they was carrying me to see my mother before they would send me to be sold in Louisiana."[198] Since whites tried to maintain blacks' loyalty by making freedom more dangerous and reducing the extent of safety, they allowed themselves to be fooled by the surface of things in the end.

While the character defects helped continue dependent relations between freedmen and their former masters, to stay where they were was not necessarily an obstacle to new constructive relations. The fact that blacks might search for freedom had put considerable pressure on planters. Forced to adjust their attitudes, they persuaded and even begged blacks to continue their service. With tears in his eyes, his head bowed, and his hands clasped behind his back, the Reverend Robert Turner, a farmer and storekeeper, told his newly freed slaves how much he admired each of them, appreciated their faithfulness, and hated to lose them.[199] Because labor control had been transferred to laborers themselves, emancipation imperceptibly raised blacks' social status. This newly obtained strength allowed blacks to make decisions favorable to themselves in their original place. In some cases, they could safely enjoy considerable freedom with nothing to do. Compared with the outside world, the former plantation was more familiar, safer, and even freer. After his brief sojourn, uncle Eph, a freedman of Virginia, had discovered the advantages of the old plantation. "I jes wanter see whut it feel lak tuh be free," he explained, "an' I wanter to go back to Ole Master's plantation whar I was born. I don' look de same dar, and I done see nuff uh freedom."[200] Since the former master on this plantation had taken a flexible stand on the transformation from slavery to freedom, and almost all former slaves remained here, the experience of uncle Eph made him the laughingstock of the plantation.

By and large, although some blacks remained on their former plantations, most freedmen decided to explore the outside world so that their newly obtained freedom could be proved. When her mistress asked whether she would stay in her usual place and work for wages, Patience Johnson, an ex-slave of South Carolina, flatly responded: "No miss. I must go, if I stay here I'll never know I am free."[201]

Long-term grievances were perhaps one motive behind their decision. Watching in horror as a freedman in Petersburg skinned a live catfish, the wife of a former slave trader asked how he could be so cruel. "Why, dis is de way dey used to do me," he answered, "and I's gwine to get even wid somebody."[202] In the confusing transitional period from slavery to freedom, in fact, many blacks participated in pillage and theft, squatted on the land, and even committed arson and murder. After Sherman had passed through Camden, South Carolina, a serious case of arson was narrowly averted, and "many other attempts at setting fire were discovered either just in time, or after some damage had been done both in Camden and the surrounding county keeping everyone in a constant state of anxiety and alarm."[203] As Emma graphically related, a planter reported killed was William Allen, "who was chopped to pieces in his barn."[204] Although blacks' acts of theft and looting to a large extent arose from the necessity of improving their living conditions, the spirit of revenge had some effect, as in the cases of arson and murder. "The conduct of the negroes in robbing our houses, store room, meat house, etc., and refusing to restore anything shows you think it right to steal from us, to spoil us, as the Israelites did the Egyptians."[205]

The typical slaves, however, did not let themselves be overwhelmed by vindictive passions, and further reconstructed their internal freedom to be rid of hate. In observing the black regiment commanded by him, Colonel Higginson was surprised at the absence of any feelings of affection or revenge toward their former masters and mistresses. A black sergeant collectedly pointed out to him the spot where whites had hanged his brother for leading a band of runaway slaves. "He spoke of it as a historic matter," Higginson recalled, "without any bearing on the present issue." Although his men tended to differentiate between various types of slaveholders, with some claiming to have had "kind" or "cruel" owners, emotion had no links with their hatred of the institution of slavery. "It was not the individuals," Higginson said, "but the ownership, of which they complained. That they saw to be a wrong which no special kindness could right."[206] For the most part, freedmen could forgive their former owners. A North Carolina man thought that they "felt for their masters and secretly sympathized with their ruin," and he specially noted what the local freedmen had written on a huge banner they unfurled at a recent celebration: "Respect for Former Owners!"[207] Yet this did not necessarily mean that they had utterly forgotten the past. Once working for "de meanest man on all de Easte'n sho'," Harry Jarvis fled the plantation early in the war, with a leg lost in the battle as a Union soldier. Being unexpectedly asked whether he had pardoned his former master, the glow immediately left Jarvis' face, and he dropped his head. After recovering his composure, he straightened himself and replied, "Yes, sah! I'se forgub him; de Lord *knows* I'se forgub him; but" and his eyes suddenly blazed "but I'd gib my oder leg to meet him in battle!"[208]

Due to psychological estrangement, blacks found that their pursuit of freedom needed the precondition of separation. As a symbol of bondage, former masters or mistresses reminded them of the old time. Blacks, a South Carolinian said, seemed "so eager to throw off the yoke of bondage they will suffer somewhat, before they will return to the plantations. It seems like a dream, dear Aunt, we are living in such times."[209] Even if a former master was a person of good will, freedmen still underscored the necessity of separation. "It ain't that I didn't love my Marster," Melvin Smith recalled, "but I jest likes to be free," and when he was told that he "didn't b'long to nobody no more," he immediately left his home plantation in South Carolina.[210] On a plantation in Virginia, emancipation enticed 109 out of 116 blacks away from their old homes. Despite having a high opinion of their former master, blacks did not lose their enthusiasm for leaving, even when they came to bid farewell to the former master, with tears in eyes, hands firmly clasped with each other.[211]

Yet not all freedmen said good-bye in such a polite way. Many quietly left without one word. Daniel was one favorite slave of Jefferson Thomas, a planter of Georgia, but he was the first servant to depart and did so at night "without saying anything to anyone." Betsy, another servant of Thomas, went out to pick up the newspaper, "as she was in the habit of doing every day." This time she never returned. Before her going, "she had taken her clothes out of the Ironing room under the pretense of washing them."[212] Abruptly throwing up their usual chores, some blacks left their master in the lurch. "Old Marry, the nurse, took the news quietly on Sat evening; said that none could be happy without prayer, and Monday by day light she took herself off, leaving the poor baby without a nurse."[213] Still others made impertinent remarks and posed in a despising way before leaving, hoping to provoke their master into a confrontation.[214] To blacks, this "rebellious character" was in reality a variety of dependence; in both cases the person concerned lacked the necessary sense of responsibility, which proved an obstacle to the development of a constructive relationship, let alone finding an internal freedom free of ignorance and hatred.

Certainly some blacks could appropriately deal with the relationship between freedom and responsibility. Quite a few slaves took account of the need of the plantation and packed their luggage only after the planter had arranged affairs. When David G. Harris made the announcement to his slaves, only one, Ann, left immediately, while "the others wisely concluded they would remain until New Years day."[215] While whites worried themselves about how to deal with the problem of the old and sick, blacks also felt awkward between looking after helpless whites and seeking freedom. "Marster was too old to wuk when dey sot us free," Nicey Kinney recalled, "so for a long time us jus' stay dar and run his place for him." "Mist'ess she jus' cried and cried," Elisha Doc Garey recalled of the death of his master. "She didn't want us to leave her, so us stayed on wid her a long time."[216] Others discovered that only after the death of their old master or mistress could they feel free to leave. A few blacks who had accumulated some property were even willing to subsidize their former masters in dire straits. A Georgia freedman, who amassed some savings from working in a sawmill and on his cotton lot, began to aid his former down-and-out mistress after the death of her husband. He supported her until the woman's death two years later, including paying the cost of her funeral.[217] In a sense, the nature of this conduct was different from that of the old loyalty. It was no longer shaped by compulsion, but was love and devotion based on self-respect, by which they were able to enter the moral realm of internal freedom. Undoubtedly, these acts were helpful to alleviate the throes arising from the birth of new racial relations and were good for blacks' images as well as their practical safety interest.

To whites, that "the faithful few" threw off their mask thereby to survive in the past hastened the parturition of new racial relations in an agonizing way. Under slavery, the disguising mask universally existed in the mentality of every slave, though the extent might differ. As time passed, some persons even voluntarily accepted it as one part of their spiritual lives, whereas most struggled between the utter freedom and the bondage of reality. When freedom did come, not only might the rebellious prisoners force open the door and have a breath of free air, but many seemingly "contented" persons in slavery now became hypercritical. The sails of imagination had been blown full, and the ideal shore seemed faintly visible. Just as the runaway slaves in wartime, servants were first to seize the opportunity, and the most "faithful" were often those who had the strongest desire to shake off the invisible mask and those who ran away the most quickly. For the former slaves, it was the release of feelings that had long hid in their heart of hearts, and it was the unprecedented reconstruction of distorted personalities. After the collapse of the power dike, the irresistible waves of true feelings rolled on incessantly. The lingering remembrance was always that

> *We wear the mask that grins and lies*
> *It hides our cheeks and shades our eyes,*
> *This debt we pay to human guile;*
> *With torn and bleeding hearts we smile,*
> *And mouth with myriad subtleties.*
>
> *Why should the world be overwise,*
> *In counting all our tears and sighs?*
> *Nay, let them only see us, while*
> *we wear the mask.*

We smile, but, O great Christ, our cries
To Thee from tortured souls arise.
We sing, but oh, the clay is vile
Beneath our feet, and long the mile;
But let the world dream otherwise,
We wear the mask.[218]

Now, a new dream indeed came. Blacks were determined to bid farewell to the past, break the old chains, and mold their utterly new selves. "Now they gradually threw off the mask," Booker T. Washington recalled, "and we were not afraid to let it be known that the 'freedom' in their songs meant freedom of the body in this world."[219] In 1865, the freedmen in Virginia sang impromptu:

Sun, you be here an' I'll be gone,
Sun, you be here an' I'll be gone,
Sun, you be here an' I'll be gone,
Bye, bye, don't grieve arter me,
Won't give you my place, not fo' your'n,
Bye, bye, don't grieve arter me,
'Cause you be here an' I'll be gone.[220]

"They know how a bird let out of a cage," a Virginia freedman explained. "You know how a bird that has been long in a cage will act when the door is opened; he makes a curious fluttering for a little while. It was just so with the colored people. They didn't know at first what to do with themselves. But they got sobered pretty soon."[221]

SELF-CONSCIOUSNESS AND ASSIMILATION: BLACKS' SOCIAL AND POLITICAL RECONSTRUCTION

Under slavery, the absolute domination of whites had severed the roots of African culture and made slaves familiar with the universal norms of conduct such as liberty and equality advocated by whites; at the same time, blacks had to conform to absolute submission and patience. In short, slavery precluded the full assimilation of blacks, who could not become complete Americans. When the mighty torrent of war and emancipation had burst the dam of slavery, what blacks hoped to do was to fulfill the long suppressed ideal creeds, namely to become equal participants in American society. The invisible veil, however, still impeded black ambition; their biological characters, their special experiences, and, of minor importance, the black subculture formed the basis of blacks' self-consciousness. As Du Bois put it, blacks wavered between the two.

> After the Egyptian and Indian, the Greek and Roman, the Teuton and Mongolian, the Negro is a sort of seventh son, born with a veil, and gifted with second-sight in this American world, a world which yields him no true self-consciousness, but only lets him see himself through the revelation of the other world. It is a peculiar sensation, this double-consciousness, this sense of always looking at one's self through the eyes of others, of measuring one's soul by the tape of a world that looks on in amused contempt and pity. One ever feels his tweness, an American, a Negro; two souls, two thoughts, two unreconciled strivings; two warring ideas in one dark body, whose dogged strength alone keeps it from being torn asunder.[222]

It is noteworthy that, while whites' self-consciousness combined with the desire for conquest facilitating the germination and growth of blacks' self-consciousness, the disintegration of whites' monopoly on the ideal creeds made blacks utterly inclined to this direction. The waves of assimilation were so turbulent that blacks' self-consciousness was submerged for a while.

Between the summer and fall of 1865, blacks in the whole South were on the move. Railway stations became crowded, men and women carrying big or small bags traveled on the county roads, and everywhere were hastily pitched camps. "Excitement rules the hour," Gertrude Thomas observed in May 1865. "No one appears to have a settled plan of action, the Negroes crowd the streets and loaf around the pumps and corners of the street. I see no evidence of disrespect on the part of the Negroes who are here from the adjoining plantations." [223] Regarding it as the revelries and impulses of a childish race, whites generally thought the black migration was due to their laziness. "Negroes generally very idle," a South Carolina planters commented, "wandering about the country enjoy their freedom, tho to my mind wonderfully civil, under the circumstances." [224] Another planter reached a similar conclusion: "They are just like a swarm of bees all buzzing about & not knowing where to settle." [225]

While blacks did want to have a taste of moving about, whites no doubt exaggerated the extent of blindness in migration. In reality, many freedmen had definite aims. To reconstruct their families was one of their priorities.

In wartime, thousands of slaves were removed from the areas menaced by the Union Army. In Texas, for example, there were 275,000 slaves in 1861. By 1865, the black population had risen to 400,000.[226] After freedom was approved, many black "refugees" longed for their old homes. Some hoped to return to their old plantations, and some the places where they were born. Yet their return was motivated by their nostalgia for the native places rather than loyalty to their former masters. Therefore, though what they returned to were the old places, they often chose a new employer. What they assiduously sought was a long checked innate sense of belonging, a lost self, and a spiritual asylum in a restless and hostile world. These feelings can be found in all the races on earth, just as naturally as whites cherished the Greek civilization, and as sincerely as Jews looked forward to Jerusalem after numerous calamities. The zeal was so high that a Freedmen's Bureau office in South Carolina was astonished. The blacks who had been removed to the up-country "were crazy to get back to their native flats of ague and country fever," while the "Highland darkeys who had drifted down to the seashore were sending urgent requests to be 'fotched home again.'"[227]

The zeal for reconstructing their families showed that slavery had not entirely destroyed blacks' idea of family. Since slavery did not recognize slaves' right to marriage, many families were broken up. When freedom suddenly came, blacks considered it as a good opportunity for healing the scar. They did not have to wait for the reunion in heaven, for emancipation made it possible for them to realize their dreams in this world. To William Curtis, a former Georgia slave whose father had been sold to a Virginia planter, "dat was de best thing about de war setting us free, he could come back to us."[228] Much of the movement was only local as husbands or wives used freedom to join their mates on neighboring plantations, or children hired out returned home. Now and then, a freedman who had been sold away to the Southwest in the 1830s crossed half a continent and half a lifetime to come again to the people and the land that had give him birth.[229] Family members engaged in these searches, a deeply impressed Freedmen's Bureau officer said, "with an ardor and faithfulness sufficient to vindicate the fidelity and affection of any race, the excited joys of the regathering being equaled only by the previous sorrows and pains of separation."[230] The movement of family reunion lasted for a long time, and by 1870 most blacks lived in families with both parents.[231]

Having testified to the authenticity of freedom, family reunion opened up a new field for blacks who were just released from bondage. Not only was the scar cut by the compulsory separation under slavery gradually healed, but those who were in a spiritual desert found in it a sweet and freshing spring. "In slavery I owns nothing' and never owns nothing,'" said Margrett Nillin, a former Texas slave. "In freedom I's own de home and raise de family. All dat cause me worryment and in slavery I has no worryment, but I takes de freedom." [232]

When blacks organized their families with full hope, what they followed was undoubtedly the current mode of the mainstream society. The sincerity of affection and the attachment to their families could be fully explained in the hardships of their journey. Slavery once severed their family ties, and now they held weddings one after another to demonstrate the end of the old era. "They take the white man's notions as they copy his manners, not for what they are but for the impression that's made by them on the world," a South Carolina woman commented on blacks' interests in solemnizing their marriages. "Now what [is] more common than to hear 'I must go with my wife,' not because they have investigated the matter and seen the right of the thing, but such is the view of the white and the view suits present circumstances, and is therefore adopted by the negro." [233] Bitterly ironic as the words might be, they point out a fact that the black race, who had just came to freedom and were still psychologically immature, copied indiscriminately the values of the mainstream society. In other aspects of the family organization, they also imitated white culture. Following the Victorian style, a man embarked on physical labor in the fields, kept general orientation of the whole family, and stressed his patriarchal position. In the Sea Islands, Lawra Towne, a Northern white teacher who devoted herself to black education, observed that "in slavery the woman was far more important, and was in every way held higher than the man." After emancipation, however, black leaders urged black men "to get the woman into their proper place, never to tell them anything of their concerns, etc., etc., and the notion of being bigger than women generally, is just now inflating the conceit of the males to an amazing degree." [234] The tasks of women were to rear their children, do housekeeping, and conserve morality. Voluntarily or from the emphasis of their husbands, many women withdrew from the field. "Most of the field labor is now performed by men," *De Bow's Review* reported in words that did not imply the editor's admiration, "the women regarding it as the duty of their husbands to support them in idleness." [235] Hating whites' sexual exploitation of black women under slavery, blacks were very wary of working under whites' supervision, and let their women withdraw from whites' kitchens as far as possible.[236] Having enjoyments and leisure, women were now keen on "playing the lady," despite freezing irony and burning satire from whites. "Rosetta, Lizzie's maid, passed me today when I was coming from church without speaking to me," a white woman complained. "She was really elegantly dressed, in King Street style."[237] Like whites, blacks also safeguarded the guardianship of their children. Before making a labor contract with whites, they often asserted their exclusive right on this issue. If possible, blacks would send their children to schools. Freedom enhanced blacks' sense of family and developed the patriarchal system; in other words, they were more and more like whites.

Black families, certainly, also had some exclusiveness. For example, black women often occupied a more important position than their white counterparts did in family lives. They had to care for garden lots, and worked as servants to increase their incomes. After the establishment of sharecropping, more and more black women returned to the fields.[238] In cities, it was the women rather than the men that had an easier time finding jobs. Some black men had to wander the streets, write themselves off as hopeless, and act recklessly. Complementary to the Victorian style, therefore, "black matriarchy" was spawned.[239] Some black families were still living under the shadows of slavery. The marriages imposed by former masters placed some blacks in a dilemma: How to chose between the de facto family and the beloved person, and how to choose one among his or her several mates? Nevertheless, the exclusiveness of black families was not merely the mixture of African tradition and remains of slavery, but to a large extent due to the unfortunate lives of a poor class in a male-dominated society.

Emancipation also allowed blacks to search freely for their consolation from God. In slavery, blacks could convert to Christianity, but black religion was regarded as an instrument of social control rather than the care of spirituality. What religious doctrines taught was to work diligently, obey God and master, and maintain a "pure" life. Worrying about possible black revolts, whites closely supervised blacks' every religious activity. In cities, churches built by the funds of free blacks legally belonged to white boards of directors. In white churches where blacks were accepted, slaves and free blacks obediently sat in the back seats. In the countryside, every state stipulated that any black should not preach the Gospel without whites on the scene, but black "exhorters" often secretly organized their congregations at night. With the coming of emancipation, black believers in cities rapidly seceded from white churches and organized their own segregated churches;[240] In rural areas, the former "invisible institution" now became visible. By 1866, independent black churches had been deeply rooted in the soil of South.[241]

One reason for black withdrawal was that whites refused to abandon their superior status in these biracial churches, while blacks could no longer endure its implication of humiliation and felt rather ill at ease to express themselves before whites. To blacks, the withdrawal from white churches was a positive affirmation of freedom, the silent revolt against racial domination, and a positive way of exploring themselves. An officer in the American Missionary Association observed that "the Ebony preacher who promises perfect independence from White control and direction carries the col[ore]d heart at once."[242] To blacks, who were bored with the requirement that they should be content with reality and obey their secular masters in order to gain admission to "the kingdom of heaven," the sermons of whites were not to the point at all.

> When the white preacher come he preach and pick up his Bible and claim he gittin the text right out from the good Book and he preach: "The Lord say, don't you niggers steal chickens from your missus. Don't you steal your masters' hawgs." That would be all he preach.[243]

Emancipation had not changed the attitudes of white churches. As late as the 1890s, they still avoid condemning slavery as an evil.[244] In addition, whites were fearful of the mixed churches based on racial equality, which would inevitably lead to the "mongrelization of the noble Anglo-Saxon race."[245] Thus, blacks decided to "preach to themselves."

At the same time, blacks would rather take on the spiritual work by themselves, although they praised the help given by Northern missionaries. It was not because black preachers were more eligible to act as the guides of heaven, but that they could at once shake off the great shame of belonging to "a white religion." To blacks, the condescension showed by some white missionaries in the salvation of "savageness" hurt their pride.[246] Only under "their own vine and fig tree," could blacks feel at ease and express themselves to their hearts' content. Therefore, they also refused to submit to the control of Yankees. According to blacks, "blood is always more potent than money."[247]

As with family structure, blacks' independent churches followed the model of the mainstream society. The physical secession from the white world had not led to an important reform of religious creeds or rites.

As white churches were named Trinity and St. Mark's, Mt. Zion, and St. John's, black churches had the same names. As there were bishops, presiding elders, ministers, and probationers in white churches, black churches had the same hierarchy. To whom the congregations prayed was the same Jesus, what they worshipped the same God, and what they believed the same value system of Protestantism that stressed self-help and spiritual salvation.

Black churches, however, had their own characteristics. Compared with the white religion, black religion was more flexible and less formal, more emotional and less intellectual. Henry M. Turner, a Northern visitor, observed that "Hell fire, brimstone, damnation, black smoke, hot lead, & c., appeared to be presented by the speaker as man's highest incentive to serve God, while the milder and yet more powerful message of Jesus was thoughtlessly passed by."[248] The black exhorter "Let a person get little animated, fall down and roll over awhile, kick a few shins, crawl under a dozen benches, spring upon his feet, then squeal and kiss (or buss) around for awhile, and the work is all done."[249] Yet blacks thought that passionate expression would make it easier for them to approach God.[250] As to their denominations, most black churches belonged to the Methodists and the Baptists. The Protestant Episcopal Church and the Presbyterian Church enjoyed no great popularity among the masses of Southern blacks because they were the former "master's churches."[251] The success of Methodism in reaching freedmen was largely due to the efforts of Northern missionaries and its Abolitionism tradition, but its popularity was much less than that of the Baptists. Interestingly, this was to a large extent because the Baptists were not as well organized as the Methodists. Every local church of Baptists was in reality independent. It set its own discipline, had its own sources of funds, and allowed its members to secede. Every ambitious black could find opportunities in a church, because the Baptist churches stressed the personality of leadership rather than formal education. Therefore, blacks' long-felt need for freedom was satisfied within the Baptist tradition: Any minor discord could become the reason for separation. Consequently, many new churches were spawned. Nevertheless, the particularism of black churches was not sufficient to form a distinctive religion, but was the result of combining white culture with blacks' attributes and hopes. As Francis B. Simkins wrote, "The radical changes in Negro religion which grew out of freedom were not in the direction of Africa, but rather in the direction of frontiers or backwoods America, with some imitations of Fifth Avenue standards of clerical correctness."[252]

Centering on families and churches and being completed by schools and benevolent societies, modern black communities gradually took shape. As regards their dwellings, many blacks in the countryside still lived in their former slave quarters, though what they chose might be on another plantation. At the same time, with the emergence of sharecropping, more and more blacks moved from former slave quarters and built simple huts on separate farms. This centrifugal tendency of residential sites is even discernible in the South today. By living in solitude, blacks published their own declaration of independence. In cities, free blacks had established some segregated black communities before the war.[253] Together with the hired-out slaves and some runaway slaves, free blacks lived in the peripheral zones of the South, such as the low-lying ground near contaminated streams, or the sites near flour mills, slaughterhouses, and funeral parlors.[254] Yet a certain number of blacks lived with whites as servants or employees.[255] After the emancipation, in order to sever dependent relations, numerous blacks deserted their old quarters and joined the ranks of free blacks. Another strong impetus for the peripheralization of residential sites was the floating population from the rural areas. Many freedmen regarded the cities as the outlet for freeing themselves from dull agricultural work and white violence, and hoped to use the well-equipped schools, churches, and relief centers. In cities, there were also the Freedmen's Bureau and the Union Army that might provide protection. Although the Freedmen's Bureau did its utmost to send them back, a considerable number of freedmen were detained. Thus, on the periphery of each city, there was a circular black residential belt. Noting that the freedmen's camps were broken up in 1866, for example, the *Republican Banner* of Nashville reminded its readers that "it was about this time that the classic localities of 'Black Center' and 'Hell's Half Acre' became known to fame."[256]

Churches were of central importance in black communities. They functioned not merely as places of worship, but as schoolhouses, lecture halls, meeting buildings, and entertainment centers. According to Du Bois, churches were "the first social institution fully controlled by black men in America."[257] Every local church was the epitome of a community. In the words of A. A. Taylor, the black historian, it was the "social center, the theater, the forum, and the general meeting house of the Negro community. To the church all Negroes ambitious for independent leadership had to look, inasmuch as other institutions touching the life of the Negro were controlled or directed by whites."[258] Being directly and regularly in contact with his congregation, preachers helped their congregations understand the concept of freedom and advised them how to elevate themselves. The *Atlanta Constitution* observed that "the colored man not only takes his spiritual information but also his special information from the pulpit of the church that he attends."[259] In a few places, the church even assumed the role of autonomous government, developing its own laws and rules. At one time or another, it functioned as a tribunal and settled disputes among its congregation. Sometimes it went further to get involved in politics, partly because it was difficult to make a clear distinction between political and religious problems. As one black journal asked, how could the church stand apart from politics when the issues in question were civil rights, the suffrage, education, and equal protection under the law?[260] In the aspect of belief, blacks also linked their religion with politics. They regarded slavery as the times of Paul (the time of obedience), whereas Reconstruction was the time of Isaiah (the times of great change). God had "scourged America with war for her injustice to the black men," dispatched Lincoln to bring the message of "universal freedom," and mystically brought him back before the full harvest. Because of the religious understanding of politics, no wonder that the political enthusiasm of blacks was so high in the period of Reconstruction. When one speaker at a meeting complained of preachers who spoke more "of politics than of Christ," for example, his voice was overwhelmed by shouts of "politics in Christ."[261]

The school was also an important instrument for blacks to explore the meaning of freedom. Aided by the Freedmen's Bureau, the benevolent societies, among which were particularly the American Missionary Association and the American Freedmen's and Union Commission, played a major role in educating freedmen during the early years after the war.[262] Between 1865 and 1866, blacks had taken steps to set up their own schools nevertheless. Some pioneers were free blacks, but among these early teachers there were also newly freed or escaped slaves who had managed to acquire some basic skills. Afterwards black teachers from the North began to take up the responsibility.[263] Blacks liked both the self-segregated schools and the teachers of their own race, though they were less eligible than their white counterparts. "There is jealousy of the superintendence of the white man in this matter," one Northern teacher made a comment, "what they desire is assistance without control."[264] Here schools faced the same problem the churches did, namely blacks had to waver between complete independence and whites' financial aid and other forms of encouragement.[265] As a matter of fact, the independence of schools was not so much as that of churches. Despite that, blacks still considered teachers as their community leaders. Like churches, schools also performed comprehensive functions. The teachers helped freedmen to make a contract, bring suit, or write a petition. Now and then the schools organized a trade fair, a ball, a lecture, or a picnic. Like churches, schools were also the places where political leaders steeled themselves. During the whole period of Reconstruction, at least seventy black teachers held posts in the states' legislatures.[266]

Another institution unifying the black community was the fraternal and benevolent societies of every hue. Before the war, free blacks had built many secret mutual aid societies. After emancipation, the number and scale were enlarged. Richmond, for example, had more than thirty secret societies by 1866.[267] Numerous funeral societies, debate societies, masonic lodges, drama societies, trade associations, prohibition societies, equal right leagues, and so on sprang up all over the vast rural and urban areas of the South. At first these organizations were often aided and supervised by churches and schools, but later on they became independent. With their main aim to lend the poor and the helpless a hand, the philanthropic societies established orphanages and employment agencies and raised aid funds. In West Virginia, black societies even provided aid for the white poor.[268] Similar welfare was also provided by the secret orders. Raleigh's Excelsior Lodge No. 21 of Colored Masons, for example, assisted its needy members, their widows and orphaned children.[269] Though their aims were slightly different, the benevolent societies and the secret orders organized the same activities, such as meetings, fairs, parades, excursions, and picnics, which took place almost entirely within the bounds of black communities.

All these institutions symbolized the unification of the black community. Their existence had both strengthened blacks' self-consciousness and encouraged their self-segregation. Many black leaders belonged to the antebellum free blacks, whose presence signified the unification between freedmen and free blacks and between Southern and Northern blacks. The process of unification went well particularly in the upper South, where the economic and cultural disparities between freedmen and free blacks were minor, and the latter could easily link up with freedmen through marriage and religion.[270] In the far South, however, mulattos had an ambiguous attitude towards freedmen. Hoping to make a good impression on their white folks, they once submitted requests to the Confederate authorities in wartime and offered their services to the Southern cause.[271] Afterwards they changed their position and defended the interests of freedmen through their mouthpiece, the *New Orleans Tribune*.

They welcomed emancipation, and bound themselves to the fate of freedmen on their own initiative. Thus the free and freed blacks could co-operate "to achieve common goals."[272] Free blacks, however, were also concerned with their own exclusiveness and cherished a subidentity within the black race. To some mulatto leaders, their black brothers at the bottom were no better than an embarrassing presence, or perhaps a burden on the whole race, because their ignorance and bad habits could be used by unfriendly whites to bring shame on their race. In some cases, the black elite often subdued the disobedient masses through the hands of whites. Nevertheless they could not escape from the framework of the color culture, either; racial characteristics formed the basis of blacks' self-consciousness. Here, complicated by the contradiction between free-dom and safety, the duality of union–division in the black community affected the black future. In the long run, it expedited the stratification of social groups, the concentration of power, and, perhaps, the formation of a black subculture.

Having discovered no suitable place in the order fixed by whites, blacks tried to find their feelings of safety and sense of self-belonging in their own race. In many aspects of life, such as family, church, school, and farm, blacks escaped as far as possible from whites to realize their full autonomy. Yet while they physically distanced themselves from whites, their lifestyle became more and more Americanized. It was by means of avoiding whites that they approached the universal ideals of whites. What they created was a copy of the society they broke away from. Originating in the uncertain period of war, this process was accel-erated when freedom became an inevitable fact. On the one hand, they tasted as much as they liked of the forbidden fruits of liberty cherished by Southern whites; on the other hand, the prospect of liberty became more concrete with the coming of Yankees. Just throwing off the chains of slavery, blacks became the main body seeking the meaning of liberty. In a sense, blacks had become what they would be long before Yankees decided what blacks should be: What blacks practiced was the white style and the universal ideals constrained under slavery. George A. Tren-holm, a planter in Georgia, did not go too far when evaluating slavery: "Sir, we have educated them. We took them barbarians, we return them Christianized and civilized to those from whom we received them; we paid for them, we return them without compensation. Our consciences are clear, our hands are clean."[273]

An index of their Americanization was the change in their conduct. In order to throw off the "mark of bondage" and confirm that they had become the owners of themselves, many blacks required that they be addressed as Mr., Mrs., or Miss and changed their names and surnames, thereby indicating their regeneration and their complete abandonment of the past. "When us black folks got set free," Alice Wilkins testified, "us'n change our names, so effen the white folks get together and change their minds and don't let us be free any more, then they have a hard time finding us."[274] Like whites, some blacks were now fond of keeping pets, going hunting, and taking a gamble, and refused to bow down and give way to whites on the pavement. Black women put on splendid attire, carried parasols, and wore "round hats, gloves and even lace veils."[275] What they did, however, was not merely imitate whites, but also use of the right to free expression. Like other Americans, they also stressed their rights to assembly and self-defense. After the war, blacks organized numerous parades and assemblies, most of which were celebrations of freedom itself. In July 1865, the director of the *New York Times* praised the stand of blacks in refusing to abandon their plans to celebrate Independence Day despite the protects of whites. "They may not get the vote or court rights in this way, but there are a hundred petty regulations of the slave period which can break to exert their influence. It is good that the white become accustomed to negro meetings."[276] In some cases, blacks who decided to defend their own rights joined together to take revenge on white criminals. In 1866, for example, a gang of armed blacks in South Carolina handed three white terrorists over to the county jail.[277]

Perhaps the pursuit of political rights could best express their high expectations for Americanization. While black communities took shape by means of contraction and self-segregation, the struggles for political rights meant blacks' positive and assertive assimilation into the mainstream society after their separation from whites and the formation of their true selves. Between the spring and summer of 1865, assemblies striving for political rights were very active, but their tone was considerable moderate. To avoid provoking Southern whites, blacks put emphasis on their loyalty to their district and only demanded the less disputable right of equality before the law rather than the franchise. Neither Africa nor the West Indies were places of asylum for American blacks, stressed James H. Harris, the black leader of Raleigh, North Carolina. The freedmen's right place was on Southern soil, and the only way to "receive what they had a right to claim" was to work faithfully and show "a patient and respectful demeanor."[278] Yet the moderate stand did not receive due rewards from the authorities, and some blacks began to stress their higher identity with the nation. "We are part and parcel of the great American body politic," Kentucky blacks solemnly declared. "We love our country and her institutions. We are proud of her greatness, her glory and her might. We are intensely American."[279] Citing inexhaustible grounds of argument from the Declaration of Independence, black delegates laid emphasis on their "unalienable rights" as Americans. Some blacks found that this attitude meant transferring their allegiance to the North and the Congress. "To the Loyal Citizens and Congress of the U.S.A.," a convention in Alexandria in August 1865 made such an appeal:

> we are "sheep in the amidst of wolves," and nothing but the military arm of the Government prevents us and all the *truly* loyal white men from being driven from the land of our birth. Do not then, we beseech you, give to one of these "wayward sisters" the rights they abandoned and forfeited when they rebelled until you have secured *our* rights by the aforementioned amendment to the Constitution.[280]

Hoping for equality as well as harmony, more people remained loyal to the district as well as the Union. Yet the tougher the attitudes of Southern whites were, the more blacks supported the North and the Congress.

To make their Americanization known, blacks tried to prove that they were more eligible for citizenship than the newcomers from Europe, with blackness disregarded. "We want to understand that we are no longer colored people, but Americans," declared John M. Langston.

> We have been called all manner of names. I have always called our people negroes. Perhaps you don't like it, I do. I want it to become synonymous with character. We are no longer negroes simply, no longer colored people simply, but a part of the great whole of the mighty American nation.[281]

In fact, many black leaders regarded themselves as the pioneers giving impetus to the great cause of diminishing the meaning of blackness. According to Williamson,

> It is a true, and intriguing, and a revealing paradox that if every Southern white person had deserted the South after the war, if the whites had left the task of rebuilding on that land entirely and exclusively to Negroes, that a perfectly Black Reconstruction would have been, in cultural terms, very white.[282]

At the same time, blacks also indistinctly realized their particularism and doubted whether this character would be an obstacle to their assimilation into mainstream society. George G. King, a former South Carolina slave, instinctively perceived that point. "The Master he says we are all free, but it don't mean we is white. And it don't mean we is equal. Just equal for to work and earn own living and not depend on him for no more meats and clothes."[283] Blacks' self-consciousness was more explicitly expressed by William H. Grey, the leader of the Arkansas freedmen's convention. Beneath an exterior and "seeming respect" made up of endless chants of "yes, sir, massa" and "no, sir, massa," blacks, Grey pointed out, had "a human soul, with a will and a purpose of its own."[284] Frustrated by whites' self-consciousness and racial domination, a few blacks, including Henry M. Turner, held that America had little to offer blacks save subordination.[285] To them, there was only one way out for blacks: return to Africa. Black identity should not be with America, but with Africa. So strong was their black self-consciousness that even American ideal values were suspected. To black masses, however, this pessimistic radicalism was not acceptable, not only because it was impracticable, but because they enthusiastically embraced American universal ideals. In this period full of hope, black people underestimated the counteracting force of whites' desire for conquest.

As a result, blacks as a whole wavered between the two opposite poles. While the introduction of whites' universal ideals contributed to their strong impetus to Americanization, whites' self-consciousness and their desire for conquest made blacks face the reality of being black. How to reconcile the seemingly conflicting directions, and how to maintain a balance between their pride as Americans and their respective racial consciousness? Blacks as well as whites had to take up the gauntlet thrown down by this question.

INDEPENDENCE AND COMPULSION:
BLACKS' ECONOMIC RECONSTRUCTION

In a sense, emancipation was also a revolution of economic relationships. It symbolized that planters had lost their power monopoly on the labor market, because slavery meant total power of an arbitrary master over his laborers, while freedom meant reasonable restrictions of the impersonal market on everybody. In theory, laborers had been emancipated from the despotic authority of their owners and might freely integrate themselves with other productive elements on their own initiative.

"The time has come when *the cash*, and not *the lash* commands labor," the *New Orleans Tribune* declared optimistically. "The blacks are no longer required to rise at four and work, work, work all day, till it is too dark to see; and then get up frequently during the night to wait upon the caprices of an indolent master or mistress to whom surfeiting forbids sleep."[286]

The impetus driving laborers, however, was not merely money, but the greatest hope they had, which, to blacks, meant the realization of land ownership. "The idea suggested itself of cutting the plantation up into numerous small farms, or rather patches," the *De Bow's Review* observed.

> It is no matter of surprise that this temptation proved irresistible. Every negro who procured one of these patches saw himself at once in the light of an independent planter, placed upon an equal footing with his former masters, and, looking into the future, beheld in himself a landed proprietor.[287]

In an agricultural society, indeed, land was the main resource for existence and the chief means of production; it was not only the key to riches and the guarantee of economic security, but also the prerequisite of independence and an important source of power; the possession of land could combine the identities of employer and employee, and laborers could fully enjoy the fruits of their labor. To the former slaves, who had suffered personal control for so long, the acquisition of land was the realization of freedom. As Vernon Lane Wharton put it, "Their very lives were entwined with the land and its cultivation; they lived in a society where respectability was based on ownership of the soil; and to them to be free was to farm their own ground."[288]

In fact, when the war still underway, the struggle for land ownership began. Recent research has made it clear that former slaves throughout the Americas sought after productive resources and tried to shape the character of their labor and the social relations in which their work was embedded.[289] "Everywhere," Eric Foner pointed out, "emancipation was succeeded by struggle for control of the scare resources of plantation economics, paramount among them, the labor of the former slaves themselves."[290] In places where planters had escaped, the newly freed slaves seized the opportunities and squatted on the abandoned lands. Early in 1863, the Union soldiers who raided the countryside around Jackson, Mississippi, told the slaves on a large plantation that they were free.

"The Federals went on their way but the Negroes measured off the land with a plowline, making a fair apportionment among themselves, and also divided the cotton and farm implements."[291] In many instances, they took possession of land near the battlefield in the lion's den. Along the North Carolina Coast, for example, when the Union Army had not captured enough grounds to "rest their tents upon," freedmen occupied lands outside the towns and on "No Man's Land" grew cotton and corn or made turpentine.[292] Even the return of their former masters could not cause the freedmen to surrender lands occupied by them. When Stephen Elliott returned to Beaufort, South Carolina, he found the freedmen "were delighted to see me, and treated me with overflowing affection." Yet they stressed the new relations and the accomplished fact. "They waited on me as before, gave me beautiful breakfasts and splendid dinners," Elliott said, "but they firmly and respectfully informed me: 'We own this land now. Put it out of your head that it will ever be yours again.'"[293] In some places, the freedmen's assertion led to a tense atmosphere. In southeastern Virginia, for example, freedmen settled on abandoned plantations, where they built cabins in which they dwelt until forcibly ejected.[294] Many blacks neither left their former plantations nor promised to work for whites. When Captain Thomas Pinckey returned to his plantation fronting the Santee River in South Carolina and asked the freedmen to work, they answered him impatiently: "O yes, we gwi wuk! We gwi wuk all right. We gwi wuk fuh ourse'ves. We ain' gwi wuk fuh no white man." If they refused to work for any white men, Pinckney asked them, where did they intend to go and how would they support themselves? "We ain' gwine nowhar," they declared. "We gwi wuk right here on de lan' whar we wuz bo'n an' whar belongs tuh us."[295] Radical as it seemingly was, the movement of squatting land did not violate the concept of private property at all. If whites did not think that their invasion of Indian land had violated the concept of private property, freedmen did not consider it illegal to capture land from rebels and oppressors. What they adopted was the style of the farmers on the frontier.

Many blacks thought it utterly proper and sensible to obtain a patch of land as reparation for their long-term hard labor. If they could not realize their dreams in the radical way of squatting on land, blacks were willing to place their hopes on the government. In the days of celebrating emancipation, freedmen imagined that "something extraordinary" would soon intervene to reshape the course of their lives. The notion of forty-acre lots and a mule "was no slight error, no trifling idea," a Freedmen's Bureau officer reported from Mississippi in 1865, "but a fixed and earned conviction as strong as any belief a man can ever have."[296] "Gib us our own land and we can take care ourselves," a Union officer quoted as the sentiment of the mass of country blacks in the spring of 1865, "but widout land, de ole massas can hire us or starve us, as dey please."[297] The expectations of land were so high that thousands of freedmen were unwilling to sign labor contracts in 1865. And in fact, this idea was firmly based in government practice. Before the war, there were quite a few laws encouraging the growth of small farmers. During the war, the passing of the Homestead Act of 1862 consolidated the concept of the independent farmer, and American government had a large quantity of abandoned land in hand according to the Confiscation Acts. The experiments of General Sherman in the Sea Islands and the coastal districts, the similar actions of General Grant in Davis Bend, and the establishment of the Freedmen's Bureau afterwards kindled freedmen's hopes of becoming independent farmers. The *New Orleans Tribune,* the mouthpiece of free blacks, also urged the government to divide the abandoned land into five-acre lots, and assign them to the "tillers of the soil" at a nominal price, so that freedmen would be "thoroughly imbued with that praiseworthy 'Yankee' idea, *that every man should own the land he tills, and head and hands he work with.*" "The division of the lands," the editor asserted, "is the only means by which a new, industrious and loyal population may be made settle in the South. Large estates will always be in the hands of an aristocracy. Small estates are the real element of democracy."[298] Although the development of politics in 1866 had made the Freedmen's Bureau give up the duel policy of building up independent farmers and free laborers, the freedmen's land dream still lingered for years.

When government land distribution did not work, the only way left was legal purchase. According to an estimate by *De Bow's Review,* land throughout the South in 1866 was selling at from 16 to 25 percent of its assessed prewar value, and, in December of that year, there were eighty-one plantations offered for sale in the alluvial region of Mississippi and Louisiana alone.[299] John Denett also mentioned the "devastating" prices of fertile land in Georgia.[300] Many states had a large number of public land for sale. In Mississippi, for example, there were more than three million acres of such land.[301] Yet the availability of land itself could not solve any problem automatically. Most freedmen were penniless; neither could they afford to buy the land and the necessary farm implements, nor could they successfully spend the first year without aid. In theory, however, the lack of funds was not an insurmountable obstacle to the purchase of land, and land itself was a guarantee of a land loan. But in the aftermath of the war, the financial market in the South was still in confusion, and the government had no interest in setting up a financial aid system. Even in the period of Radical Reconstruction, poor blacks found that they were not given such an opportunity. Perhaps the most serious problem was whites' animosity towards blacks' ambition to become independent farmers. A few blacks, including those who had an allowance for their military service and those who managed to obtain some incomes in the areas controlled by the Union Army, could indeed afford two or three hundred dollars to purchase a patch, but they often found themselves boycotted and even driven out by violence. Whitelaw Reid recorded whites' sentiment during his tour of the South soon after the war:

> The feeling against any ownership of the soil by Negroes is so strong that the man who should sell small tracts to them would be in actual personal danger. Every effort will be made to prevent Negroes from acquired land; even the renting of small tracts to them is held to be unpatriotic and unworthy of a good citizen.[302]

While upper-class whites were afraid of losing laborers and the integrity of the plantation, almost every white man opposed any action that encouraged blacks' social and economic equality. When social pressure was not enough to prevent white owners from selling land to blacks, violence was directed towards the black buyers. "As a general rule," one observer noted, "a man is very unpopular with his neighbors who will sell land to colored people; and then a colored man is in danger if he buys land. In Winston County [Mississippi] a dozen men were whipped, and the only charge against them was that they had bought land."[303] The violence, to be sure, did not entirely exclude the possibility of black purchase, but it greatly increased the risks run by the black buyers and the white sellers and thereby raised the prices of land. In fact, only a few blacks could get access to this narrow market. As a result, the proportion of acreage owned by blacks to that owned by whites was very low. As late as 1874, the acreage owned by blacks in Georgia only accounted for 1 percent of the total number.[304] And even those who fulfilled their land dream never rose above the barest subsistence level.[305]

Despite their great expectations of land, blacks had to choose above all between work and hunger. "What kin we do, sah?" a freedman in Virginia asked, "dey kin give us jes what dey choose. Man couldn't starve, nohow; got no place to go; we 'bleege to take what dey give us."[306] Although freedmen could control their own labor, the planter class owned the main means of production, and the great disparity in strength placed freedmen under the compulsion of the market. Furthermore, freedmen were also confronted with strong extra-economic compulsion from whites. Southern whites controlled local governments, and their vigilantes closely supervised every conduct of blacks.[307] Although it admitted freedmen's right to contract, the Freedmen's Bureau stressed that freedmen must contract with an employer, otherwise freedmen would be punished for vagrancy.[308] Thus, blacks had to seek to make their living within the narrow frame fixed by whites.

Yet this did not mean that blacks fully returned to their former level of labor. After all, emancipation provided them with the freedom to control their work lives, which made labor intensity and time lower than the standard in slavery. An agent of the U.S. Department of Agriculture estimated that the "effective labor" supply in 1867 was less than one-third the prewar level and quoted the opinion of "careful and experienced men" that it had fallen to one quarter the prewar level.[309] A Georgian lamented that "50 percent, more than 50 percent, of black labor has disappeared from the fields. The negroes are not dead, nor gone; but they have very much quit the fields."[310] In order to enjoy the fruits of their labor, blacks reduced their hours of labor. They valued life and leisure much more than labor itself. "Emancipation does confer real, actual liberty on negroes," conceded *De Bow's Review* in 1866. "Liberty which they know how to enjoy, in which they luxuriate, and which they mean to retain. The slave worked eight or nine hours a day; the negro freedmen will not average three hours a day."[311]

Besides decreasing their labor supply, blacks tried to protect their wives and children from the burden of labor. "The freedmen," a Georgia newspaper reported in 1869, "have almost universally withdrawn their women and children from the fields, putting the first at housework and the later at school."[312] The vacancies caused by the decrease in the labor supply had not been filled by white farmers, who were still working on their own farms and had no intention of joining the large body of laborers to mitigate the "labor shortage." "To work industriously and steadily, especially under directions from another man," Frederick L. Olmsted observed, "is, in the Southern tongue, to 'work like a nigger.'" Moreover, "the employment of whites in duties upon which slaves are ordinarily employed is felt to be not only humiliating to the whites employed, but also to the employer."[313]

The labor shortage created by blacks placed them in a more advantageous bargaining position, especially in the sparsely populated regions of Florida and the cotton-expanding Southwest. If a planter did not comply with the freedmen's requests, he often found that the laborers made their way elsewhere, and that other blacks also avoided this plantation. In Louisiana, a Northern observer was impressed with the fact that blacks were so rapidly learning their own power and worth. "They have a mine of strategy," he said, "to which the planter sooner or later yield."[314] Moving around was one of their main strategies. Although opportunities elsewhere were not necessarily better, the right to choose an employer put considerable pressure on planters. In Louisiana, when a delegation of fieldhands demanded the dismissal of a new overseer, who was obnoxious to the blacks because of his wielding the whip and using abusive language in addressing black women, the planter bluntly refused and ordered the hands back to work. Rather than go to the fields, the blacks returned to their cabins, got their luggage ready, and started down the road; yet they had not gone far before the planter promised them a voice in the selection of another overseer.[315] Any employer who had a reputation for his whip and deceit often lost all his laborers after the harvest, and the manpower was difficult to replenish. As a Florida planter said, "The Negroes have a kind of telegraph by which they know all about the treatment of the plantations for a great distance around."[316] Blacks' bargaining power, however, was not necessarily effective all the time. The crop failure of 1866, for example, seriously reduced their position. Since it alternated between drought and excessive rain, and plagues of insects were rampant, planters sustained heavy losses, with many breaking their promise of reward. "If Providence had smiled on this region in 1866 by giving it a reasonable crop," George Benham, a Northern planter, suggested with some exaggeration, "section politics, injustice to the negro and the newcomer, bitterness of heart, and hatred of the government would all have disappeared."[317]

What the black particularly loathed was the gang system generally adopted by plantations in the early years after the war. Having no experience in dealing with free labor and unwilling to give up traditional coercive methods, planters tried to revive the antebellum gang system, which was especially popular in the cotton and sugarcane regions. One character of the gang system was that the contract was signed between a planter and a group of freedmen. The contract signed by thirty-six wage laborers on the Peter B. Bacot plantation in South Carolina was typical:

The said servants agreed to perform the daily tasks hitherto usually allotted on said plantation, to wit: 125 to 150 rail; cutting grain 3 to 6 acres; ditching & banking 300 to 600 feet; hoeing cotton 70 to 300 rows an acre long; corn 4000 to 6000 hills. In all cases where tasks cannot be assessed, they agree to labor diligently ten hours a day.[318]

Laborers were liable to a fine for "absence, refusal or neglect," and persistent absence or misbehavior was punishable by forfeiture of any claim to wages at the end of year. Another character of the gang labor system was its close supervision. The whip and other corporal punishments were no longer stressed, but they did exist under some circumstances. The overseer was renamed "manager," "agent," or "superintendent," but his duties never changed. Laborers should be "obedient" and "dutiful," as a contract required on a plantation in Wake County, North Carolina. "That we will do our work faithfully and in good order, and will be respectful in our deportment to the Said Mial and family or superintendent."[319] As for the payment form under the gang system, it was generally in "standing wages." Based on the reward of an able-bodied man, the wages of other persons decreased successively according to their ability. Although many planters preferred to pay cash currency, the more popular practice in the early postwar years was to pay a share of the crop at the end of season because of the shortage of currency. Initially, the share of the crop offered to laborers in lieu of cash wage was very low. A. R. Lightfoot reported that in 1865 the fieldhands "were contented with share in the cotton and corn crops, ranging from an eighth to twelfth."[320] Receiving the share collectively, the hands then divided among themselves according to the contract.[321]

The gang system had many outward similarities with labor under slavery. Working in gangs on large agricultural units, living in former slave quarters, and being closely overseen, all made the freedmen suspect the certainty of freedom. They particularly kept a wary eye on the presence of overseers, some of whom changed their bad habits very little and still inflicted corporal punishments on workers. The change of name did not placate freedmen. As one observer put it, "it is easier to change an odious name than an odious character."[322] After the withdrawal of the overseer, blacks' discontent was often channeled towards the employer himself or a black foreman. Blacks, according to a contributor to the *Southern Cultivator* in 1869, were "anxious to rid themselves of all supervision on the part of the white race, and to look upon it as a sort of continued badge, or remembrance, of their former condition of servitude."[323] Blacks also complained about the postponement of payment to the end of the year, which meant "a free-extension of credit from the employee to employer, as well as a shifting of part of the risk of farming to the freedmen."[324] It also allowed employers to gain the initiative in disputes and gave them the critical explanatory right. Therefore, employers had many opportunities for fraud. In 1866, a year with a poor crop, the descriptions of frauds on the part of employers filled the reports of the Freedmen's Bureau. In addition, laborers stressed their right to participate in the decision-making process because of taking the risk of crop wages. Disputes between employer and employee took place endlessly.

Discontent with the gang system often led to resistance. Although payment was postponed to the end of the year, many laborers left plantations before the harvest to demonstrate their discontent. After the harvest, thousands of freedmen sought places elsewhere or refused to sign contracts, and this situation was precipitated by their persistent vision of land distribution. The leaving "in squads of five or ten at a time," for example, virtually sealed the fate of the rice industry in South Carolina.[325] Many planters complained that their hands did not "stick to a contract" and showed "obstinate arrogance." Even those who remained on plantations were dilatory in doing their work and now and again amused themselves by singing and sporting. "They did not prepare the lands according to custom but in the rudest & most slovenly manner," J. R. Cheves, a planter on the Sea Island, aired his grievance. More seriously, "finally taking umbrage at my presence among them, they assembled as a *Landsturm* [militia], surrounded my house & drowning my voice with violent, insolent & contemptuous denunciations declared that there was no master on the plantation."[326] What laborers demanded was the least supervision, the most independence, and the highest wages. Planters had to made some concessions to retain their laborers. One important tendency was that the gang system was gradually replaced by small-sized labor units, which were particularly popular on cotton plantations in 1866 and 1867. A planter generally divided his plantation into several pieces, and handed them over to the squads of a dozen or fewer laborers, who were directed for the most part by a black foreman and sometimes by a white overseer, though the proprietary right of land had not been subdivided at all.[327] By 1867, the gang system was disappearing from the cotton fields. "You do not see as large gangs together as of old times," commented an Alabama newspaper, "but more frequently squads of five or ten in a place."[328]

Yet the squads also proved to be a transitional form. Blacks preferred the tenancy system. In the first days of freedom, blacks had expressed their partiality for a rent farm. Zeal was so high that a planter phrased it "rent crazy."[329] As David Golightly Harris observed in 1866, "The negroes all seem disposed to rent land, & but few are willing to hire by the day, month or year."[330] As tenants, freedmen could work separately on their family farms, and their quarters might be removed from the former slave cabins to the rent farms, thereby freeing themselves from whites' supervision. Blacks particularly desired to pay a fixed rent, so that they could freely arrange their time and labor and gain the most profit. Worrying about freedmen's capability for independent management, however, planters generally believed that blacks would inevitably fail without white supervision. "The negro, left to himself, will barely do enough work to support existence."[331] Political and social considerations also prevented planters from giving up their guardianship. Hence a planter was unwilling to hire out the land unless he could control his laborers. As a compromise, a substitute type, i.e. sharecropping, arose.

The Freedmen's Bureau first commented on sharecropping in 1867. Reports from South Carolina, Florida, Texas, and other states all mentioned its increasing popularity. In Mississippi, a "majority" of black laborers were reported as working on share, and in the cotton district of Texas about one-half worked as sharecroppers.[332] As a matter of fact, most cotton plantations gave up the gang system after one or two experimental seasons. A contemporary report commented on blacks' insistence on sharecropping:

> It is regarded by the laborer as a higher form of contract, and is thereby more likely to secure labor especially in undesirable localities. It was this consideration led [to] the general adoption of the share contract. Then the colored laborer in the first flush of freedom seemed disposed to withdraw himself altogether from hire; while the farmer deluded by the high price of cotton, and accepting the theory that *any* labor was better than none at all, was prepared to make every concession.[333]

Signed between a planter and a black family, the share contract could give blacks more autonomy as well as more profit. Because they were paid a portion of the crop, freedmen who had skills and who were willing to work hard would be rewarded accordingly, while the gang system was not very sensitive to individual performance. The share received by laborers also showed an upward tendency. Low at the beginning, it now could reach one third and even one half of the year's crop.[334] At the same time, planters could not lose their shares even in the event of a poor crop. Another beneficial result planters obtained from the share-cropping system was the reduced cost of supervision. Blacks were left to their own devices, and many planters were no longer anxious about the initiative of black workers. The black sharecropper mobilized his whole family to work on his farm, and self-interest precluded him from ignoring the crop before the harvest. Planters were hence satisfied with labor stability under this system, which was a critical factor causing planters to make a concession to using it, especially when sharecropping could provide an income no lower than that under the gang system.

Thus the breakdown of the gang system was largely due to blacks' resistance to white supervision. The formation of sharecropping was not simply imposed by whites, but was a compromise between employer and laborer. Although blacks did not have the luck to own the land, their dream of being independent farmers came true to some extent. Admittedly, blacks did not anticipate that it would later evolve into debt peonage.

Even in the rice and cane regions, where the gang system remained, the continuous struggle of blacks also brought them considerable independence and more economic rewards. On the rice plantations, blacks learned quickly to put a money value upon their time and to require overtime pay for work beyond the normal quota. One planter complained that "If he goes to the house for an axe he is to be paid extra for it. It's well enough to pay a man for all he does, but who can carry on a farm in such a way as that?"[335] Planters found themselves obliged to allow freedmen to "work as they choose without any overseer," and even lamented that "the negro is virtually master of the soil."[336] On some rice plantations, including the Sea Island and the Cooper River Valley, South Carolina, there arose a widely practiced "two-day system," which demanded a laborer to work two days a week in return for his quarters, fuel, and five to seven acres of land allotment.[337] Additional labor was paid for in cash at the rate of fifty cents a day or task. On the cane plantations, planters also provided family plots for laborers and had to accept fewer days and hours of work. The diary of a planter in Louisiana reflected change: "Holy Friday. No work this morning the negroes being too pious to violate such holiness *by work*, but not too much so to go & harpoon fish in the high water. They however took up work at 2 o'clock as usual." And a week later: "Gave the negroes their land this morning."[338]

In these regions, the forms of payment changed somewhat, too. At first blacks preferred shares to cash wages. In the fall of 1866, a group of blacks in Sumter, South Carolina, refused to be paid in cash, cling-ing "to the preference for a moiety of the crops." One planter thought the reason was that blacks feared "Maybe it git lak Confeddick money."[339] By 1867, however, cash wages became popular on rice and cotton plantations, thanks to the influx of Northern funds and the dis-appearance of blacks' anxiety. On the whole, the payment became per-sonalized, and its intervals shorter and shorter. Sharply in contrast to the forms used under the original gang system, most laborers were paid daily, weekly, and monthly and contracted with employers individually instead of collectively by the end of Reconstruction.[340] In addition, due to laborers' continuous struggles for higher wages through their weapons of moving about and occasionally going on strikes, the sums of their wages also increased.[341]

The gang system and the family farm, sharecropping and the wage system, were all varieties of free labor in the South. Its different types of free labor varied with the disparity of strength between capital and labor, the characteristics of individual crops, the amount of funds, and so on. Although political and economic compulsion and whites' discrimination remained as they were, and precluded blacks from being fully incorpo-rated into the universal market system, these labor types were to a large extent based on voluntary terms. After all, emancipation represented the great discontinuity of history. In search of a more independent and high-quality life, freedmen fully utilized their bargaining power and deeply branded their influence on the postwar relationship between capital and labor. They had more opportunities to improve themselves and shape their own destinies. To a politically powerless and economically penni-less race that had just shook off the yoke of slavery, their achievements were undoubtedly substantial and impressive. As Peter Kolchin has noted, it was during the "short transition period" of Presidential Recon-struction that "many old modes of thought and behavior among blacks gave way to new ones."[342] Blacks had cultivated a spirit of self-respect and independence, and formed the basis of further changes. No matter how radical the political changes were during the period of Reconstruc-tion and Redemption, these fundamental fruits were retained to a con-siderable extent. It does not mean, to be sure, a significant reorganization of economic position or an important redistribution of wealth. Although they had smashed the trammels of the gang system, most freedmen remained landless, could not rid themselves of the inferior status of economic dependence, and could not elevate themselves as other poor whites did. Planters still firmly commanded most economic resources and enjoyed other privileges. To freedmen, dark clouds were still gathering and rolling, although there was a silver lining in the sky.

LIBERTY AND ORDER: THE UNION ARMY, THE FREEDMEN'S BUREAU, AND FREE LABOR

Liberty does not mean an unbridled state without restrictions, instead, it complements the principle of order. Where did the principle about order come from? As far as the Union Army and the Freedmen's Bureau were concerned, the beliefs of their officers and agents and their understanding of the official policies were critical factors. Was there any deviation from the universal principles in implementing the process? If the answer is affirmative, which factors led to this resistance? What about the effect of implementation? All these questions will be considered next.

In 1861 and 1862, when Union troops occupied the Mississippi Valley and the Sea Islands, South Carolina, a large number of refugees came swarming. According to John Eaton, "The arrival among us of those hordes was like the oncoming of cities."[343] How to define the status of these fugitives and how to help them settle became a pressing matter for the army.

In July 1861, General Benjamin Butler declared that the blacks who had been requisitioned by the Confederate army to be "contrabands" might be legally "confiscated." Based on the official policy that slaves were legal property, this order was a flexible, expedient measure and was confirmed by the first Confiscation Act passed by the Congress in August.[344] Yet it only solved the status of certain blacks, and the states of those who had not been used by the Confederacy for military purposes remained undecided. In July 1862, the second Confiscation Act declared that all slaves coming within the federal lines after serving a disloyal owner were captives of war and forever free.[345] Later on, the Emancipation Proclamation completed the repudiation of any claim on blacks in regions that military activities were being prosecuted. Thus the status of blacks was clarified gradually, laying a foundation for the next step.

At the same time, the second Confiscation Act stipulated that all cases concerning confiscated lands should be examined individually by the court, and the forfeiture of land should be limited to the owner himself and not extend to his progeny. Since the range of its implementation was narrow, most land commanded by the government was abandoned or untaxed land.[346] Because the war was defined first to wage against the rebellion and, afterwards, slavery, the land problem inevitably intertwined with the labor one. There was, however, little guidance from Washington. The two responsible departments, the Department of War and Department of the Treasury, both vied with each other for control over the affairs of freedmen and land, while freedmen themselves were to a large extent ignored and became a political football between the two departments. Hoping to fill the vacancy of power, benevolent societies and religious institutions were involved in wrangles over land and religion, and their resources and power were limited.[347] Until the establishment of the Freedmen's Bureau in April 1865, the confusion over authority had not been settled.[348] Henceforth the Department of War had responsibility for the affairs of freedmen. Without a doubt, the Freedmen's Bureau belonged to the military, but before its coalescence into the Union Army in 1867, the jurisdiction of both conflicted to some extent.[349] In such a situation, the policies towards freedmen were understandably in some confusion.

Some generals realized the urgency of the freedmen's needs and their long-term interests, and adopted measures to encourage their self-reliance and satisfy their desire for land. The most conspicuous experiment in economic independence was conducted in Vicksburg, Mississippi. About twenty-five miles below Vicksburg lay a large peninsula known as Palmyra or Davis Bend, on which there were six fertile plantations, including the great "Briarfield" and "Hurricane" estates of Joseph Davis and his brother Jefferson Davis, the president of the Confederacy.[350] Before the war, the Davis brothers performed an experiment in "model slavery," permitting the establishment of black community and promising considerable autonomy. Their attempt had made a favorable impression on blacks. After the war, a group of freedmen pressed for Jefferson's release from prison because "altho he tried hard to keep us all slaves some of us well know of many kindness he show his slaves on his plantain."[351] Yet when Joseph escaped from the Bend in 1862, slaves did not follow him, but burst open the door and divided the property among themselves. When the Union Army occupied Davis Bend, blacks had begun to manage the plantations. In a sense, the experiment of General Grant thereafter was not only an inherited reform from the Davis brothers, but was also a result of black pressure.

In July 1863, General Ulysses S. Grant began his plan to make the peninsula "a Negro paradise." By December of that year, over 600 freedmen had been arranged there and made the Bend an enclave from the outside world by cutting a canal across the neck that connected the area with the mainland.[352] In March 1864, U.S. Adjutant General Lorenzo

Thomas stated that "All of the property in the Palmyra Bend, Miss., except the Turner and Quitman plantations, is hereby reserved for Military purposes, on which will be established a 'Home Farm,' and to furnish land for freedmen, for their own cultivation." [353] The "Briarfield" and "Hurricane," whose lands were the heart of the Bend, were included. Hereafter "the bend with the exception of the Jeff Plantation" was leased to blacks, who had to organized themselves into "companies" of "from three to twenty-five hands that are able to do their share of the labor." For the sake of administrative convenience, the companies were divided into "colonies," for which a "Superintendent" was appointed, whose authority was to "see that every company in his colony work their ground in the proper manner," and to punish those who should "refuse or neglect to perform his share of the labor, or shall absent himself from the company without until willing to work for himself." [354] About 76 companies were established under the system, and over 2,500 acres of land were cultivated by the freedmen. Although army worms ran rampant in 1864, and five-sixths of the crops suffered a loss, most companies could make ends meet, and some even showed a profit of from five hundred to a thousand dollars, thanks to some extent to the high price of cotton. [355]

The military authorities were inspired with much confidence. In November 1864, General N. J. T. Dana issued an order to expand the plan. White investors were excluded, and hence Davis Bend became the exclusive land of freedmen. In the meantime, the return of Benjamin Montgomery, a former slave of Joseph and a black capitalist, energized the experiment. By early 1865, Davis Bend had become a famous example of black self-determination. It had its own government and elected its own officials such as sheriffs and judges. Scattering around each plantation, sheriffs could bring suits in court. The freedmen who committed crimes would be imposed a fine of up to one thousand dollars, the forfeiture of crop, a term of imprisonment, or forced labor. If they neglected their duties, sheriffs and judges also might be punished. Colonel John Eaton was much impressed with the "shrewdness of the colored judges," and found their execution "very remarkable." [356] As for production, 5,000 acres were divided among 181 companies in that year, involving 1,750 black people. [357] The "Home Farm" showed a profit of $25,929.80, and other plantations netted $159,200, which meant that the annual average income of 1,300 adults was slightly over one hundred and twenty dollars. [358]

Another experiment in autonomy on a moderate scale took place on the Sea Islands. On January 16, 1865, General William Tecumseh Sherman issued Special Field Order No. 15 with the purpose of parceling out land to the black refugees who accompanied his march through Georgia. The Sea Islands off the coast between Charleston, South Carolina, and Jacksonville, Florida, and all the rice plantations for a distance of thirty miles inland from the coast were arranged in an exclusively black reservation. The order defined that "three respectable negroes, heads of families" could come together to request the use of land. Once the request was confirmed, freedmen could claim their land and subdivide it among themselves, with no more than forty acres to each family. Yet Sherman only gave freedmen "possessory titles," and freedmen only had the right to work the land and to enjoy the fruits of their labor; they could not claim ownership. Because Sherman reserved the proprietary right of land, the order did not specify how long the freedmen could stay or whether and how they could buy it in the future.[359]

The performance of the special field order was entrusted to Brigadier General Rufus Saxton. As Inspector of Settlement and Plantations, and, after May 20, Freedmen's Bureau assistant commissioner for South Carolina and Georgia, Saxton vigorously supported blacks' request for land. Arranged by Saxton, forty thousand blacks settled down and began to work in peace and contentment. "the people," observed William H. Tiffany, the local agent, "not being driven by master or overseer, go to their work early and gladly, and the body shares the healthfulness of the mind."[360] The modes of production varied by region. In Ogeechee, blacks continued to cultivate the land "in concert." On the Sea Islands, however, freedmen individually worked their family plots, and showed more disgust at the "slave crop," that is, the Sea Island cotton, than their counterparts on the mainland did. Neither on the mainland or the Sea Islands, however, did blacks avoid market competition. As a matter of fact, in order to keep the sale of grain in hand, the Freedmen's Bureau had to place guards on the road to Savannah to stop freedmen on their way to the market. As a result of hard labor, most freedmen were well on their way to becoming self-supporting.[361]

Under Saxton's direction, these regions also established autonomous governments and mustered militias to protect the common good. In Ogeechee, for example, the local agent, Reverend William H. Tiffany, directly supervised the organization of government and the Ogeechee Home Guard. In May, the freedmen in St. Simons adopted a constitution and selected their officials. In St. Catherine and Ossabaw, T. G. Campbell, a free black, organized its institutions, including a militia with 275 men. Having their governments, freedmen were ready to accept the decisions of their leaders and to maintain community stability. The sense of responsibility and self-defense could be further shown in their actions resisting federal agents who later forced them to give up the land.[362] Certainly the sense of responsibility was not limited to dealing with outside threats. In St. Simons, for example, residents were required to labor on the island's road, and the black sheriffs and town guards had the authority to impose a penalty on those who refused to work. A confrontation led to an exchange of gunfire and to the death of one troublemaker. "I saw at a glance," Stephen Mayberry, a town commissioner, speaking in defense of this action, "that to maintain order, those men must at once be subdued, or all order was at an end."[363]

The experiments in Davis Bend and the Sea Islands indicated that freedmen could fully overcome their lack of education and experience and participate in the labor market according to the "natural law of supply and demand" stressed by white Northerners, provided that they were given some autonomy and the necessary resources, and that the government offered them essential direction and discipline and helped them to realize that freedom did not mean lawlessness. The true interests of freedmen lay in this dual policy of using both hard and soft tactics. Although it was very difficult to find a perfect intersection between autonomy and discipline, perhaps only this policy could help freedmen finish the transitional process from bondage to freedom. Autonomy without restraint might lead to disorder and unruliness, while unreasonable compulsion might strangle self-determination. Thus, the experiments in these two regions offered a valuable path to explore the paradox that C. Vann Woodward has advanced, the "paradox that lay at the heart of the problem of emancipations and reconstructions everywhere in the world," namely the problem of reconciling force with freedom, and liberty with necessity.[364]

By 1865, the Freedmen's Bureau commanded 850,000 acres of confiscated and abandoned land. Although its acreage was minimal if the whole population was taken into account, land reform could help freedmen to take a critical step in the transitional process of becoming independent farmers. Unfortunately, elsewhere there was no similar action encouraging freedmen in obtaining title to the land.[365] Most Americans scrupulously abided by the concept of private property, but Oliver Howard, Commissioner of the Freedmen's Bureau, had never abandoned the lofty aim of aiding freedmen. "He says he will give the freedmen *protection, land and schools,* as far and as fast as he can," a friend reported in March 1865.[366] As far as his jurisdiction was concerned, however, Howard did not have ultimate authority over the land. At most he could make an argument favorable to freedmen. During the summer of that year, Howard was involved in a fierce written wrangle with the president over the problem of confiscated and abandoned land. By September 12, the president had effectively nullified the section enabling the Bureau to distribute land to freedmen.[367] To understand this act more clearly, it is necessary to quote the entire section:

> The commissioner, under the direction of the President, shall have authority to set apart, for the use of loyal refugees and freedmen, such tracts of land within the insurrectionary states as shall have been abandoned, or to which the United States shall have acquired title by confiscation or sale, or otherwise, and to every male citizen, whether refugee or freedman, there shall be assigned not more than forty acres of such land, and the person to whom it was so assigned shall be protected in the use and enjoyment of the land for the term of three years. At the end of said term, or at any time during said term, the occupants of any parcels so assigned may purchase the land and receive such title thereto as the United States can convey.[368]

According to the Confiscated Act of 1862, land confiscation was only valid within the life of its former owner. Thus the two stipulations themselves contradicted each other. Yet the president was unwilling to confine himself to either of them. In the summer and fall, he granted a rash of pardons and ordered the restoration of land to the former Confederates. In the meantime, Howard issued Circular 13, urging local agents to parcel out the land to freedmen as quickly as possible. The president, however, soon required Howard to rescind his order. In September, Howard was forced to issue Circular 15, which ordered the restoration to pardoned owners of all land except for the small amount that had been sold under a court judgment.[369]

According to the pardon granted by the president in March 20, 1865, Joseph Davis was finally restored to full use and enjoyment of his lands on January 1, 1867, with rent paid to him from the effective date of his pardon.[370] Yet the restoration of land in the Sea Islands did not go as well. In October 1865, Howard paid a private visit to the Sea Islands and tried to persuade freedmen to give up the land they had been cultivating. His announcement was greeted with complicated looks of dismay and shouts of "No! No!" The occasion was so confused that Howard could barely finish his speech.[371] Perhaps moved by this experience, Howard spared no effort to support Captain Ketchum, the officer in charge of restoration, who played for time as slowly as possible in the hope that Congress would eventually confirm the freedmen's possessory titles, although Howard himself had issued orders that recognized the right of pardoned planters to petition for the restoration of their lands.[372] At the same time, General Saxton, who still had authority over the granted land on the Sea Islands, continued to doubt the legality of Howard's Circular 15. The vexed planters lodged a complaint with the president. Consequently, Johnson ordered Saxton removed in early 1866. By these actions, the president "changed radically the character of the Bureau."[373] Under the circumstances, Davis Tillson, assistant Commissioner of the Bureau, had not entirely satisfied Johnson's expectations.[374] If the resistance from blacks was taken into account, it is no wonder that the blacks in the Sea Islands retained their ownership of land more successfully than their brothers elsewhere in the South. The postbellum census showed the ownership of land among blacks to be higher in the Sea Islands than elsewhere in the country.[375]

Because of the negative attitude of the president and the traditional concepts of private property and laissez-faire, the policy concerning the ownership of land did not carry much weight in the experiments of the Union Army and the Freedmen's Bureau, and the population affected was limited. The heart of their policy was to create a free labor market centering on agricultural wage workers, and allow blacks to participate without racial difference.

In the spring of 1862, Union troops captured New Orleans and soon occupied the cane regions of Louisiana. Considering it as the first step toward full freedom, a flood of black refugees sought shelter with the Union Army and desired land distribution. Many planters of the state, however, were Whigs and Unionists, whose plantations completely depended on compulsory labor. Since their lands could not be taken, and it would not work to supersede blacks for other laborers, military officers generally stressed the necessity of stability and production. Yet they disagreed with each other on how to reform the labor system. Among them some contented themselves with the old way, simply sending back blacks to their former masters. Others, however, saw in Louisiana an opportunity to test the virtues of free labor.[376] As it was rather difficult to tell "loyal" planters from "disloyal" ones, General Benjamin F. Butler, commander of the Department of the Gulf, required refugees to do menial jobs under military supervision or work on sugar plantations for loyal slaveholders who promised to pay wages to slaves. In addition, some refugees were sent to the confiscated land leased by Northern investors. As for those who refused to work, the military police had authority to impose punishments.[377] Although some laborers were never paid, some were subjected to corporal punishment, and blacks were still slaves by law, Butler's plan still meant the beginning of free labor.

General Nathaniel Banks, Butler's successor, continued the experiment in free labor. In 1863, Banks met with a group of "loyal" planters and frankly told them that any theory and discrimination based on the old system were out of date, and that they must adapt themselves to the new order of free labor. On the one hand, he pointed out that a contract between planters and the government must be made, in which slaves would be bound for a year to work for low payments, adequate rations and just treatment; on the other hand, he insisted that blacks should stop vagrancy and indolence and provide "continuous and faithful service, respectful deportment, correct discipline, and perfect subordination."[378] Once employed, a black would not be allowed to leave the plantation without permission, and half of his wage would be withheld until the end of harvest. Anyone who refused to work or showed "indolence, insolence, and disobedience " would forfeit his payment or have to work without any payment. To mitigate increasing criticism, Banks drafted new regulations in early 1864, which allowed blacks to select an employer, slightly raised the wage standard, and required the allocation of an acre of land to each first-class hand with a family.

Banks's system, as Banks himself put it, was "the first step in the transition from slave to free labor."[379] Based on the starting point of equal status under the law, the contract system meant that employer and employee had reciprocal rights and duties, and did not convey complete dependence of one side on another. It symbolized a new cooperative relationship and a reasonable compromise between employee and employer. Despite its ploy to win support from planters by using the army to restore plantation discipline and maintain stability in the labor market, the value of Banks's system, to blacks, lay in its recognition of paid labor and its protection of basic rights. The prohibition of corporal punishment and the supremacy of the contract were in fact concrete negations of the absolute authority of planters.

Banks's system, however, imposed rigid restrictions on blacks' freedom of action, and did not tolerate their right to refuse given jobs. As the *New Orleans Tribune* criticized, the army was performing the function of patrols under slavery, and its compulsion had in fact made liberty a "mitigated bondage."[380] In addition, the term of contracts was as long as one year, and the disparity in strength between employer and employee great, all driving blacks into a predicament. These factors were not the main concerns of the army. More than anything, officers interested themselves in fostering blacks' diligence in work instead of depending on the government. In their opinion, to provide special protection for those who were able to work would strangle personal initiative and encourage the bad habit of indolence among blacks. Although their worry was not entirely unreasonable, the liberty permitted by military officers was transitional, and the idea that blacks would not work on their own initiative was rooted in this system. In addressing the relation between liberty and compulsion and between change and stability, the Union Army laid particular emphasis on the latter.

After the Union Army occupied Vicksburg and controlled the Mississippi Valley, Banks's system was introduced into the vast cotton region. According to General Grant's Special Order No. 15, John Eaton initially devised a labor form in which the government commanded production and sale and black laborers were paid wages. Unfortunately, it ended in failure due to the attack of Confederate guerrilla bands.[381] In the spring of 1863, Adjutant General Lorenzo Thomas again drew up another scheme, which allowed Northern investors to lease plantations in the Mississippi Valley, provided that they abided by conditions set by the army. Investors might use the horses, mules, and equipment found on the plantations, and each bale of cotton was only taxed two cents. Meanwhile, the freedmen were paid low wages ranging from two and one-half to five dollars per month according to sex and age. The cost of clothing and other supplies, except for rations and shelters, was to be deducted from their wages.[382] Thomas required that blacks choose between working under military supervision and entering a contract with an investor or loyal planter. Coming largely from the group of "sharks" following the army, many lessees had as little regard for black rights as the most brutal slaveholder. "The desire of gain alone prompts them," one observer testified, "and they care little whether they made it out of the blood of those they employ or from the soil."[383] Thus, slaveholders might keep an eye on the long-term interests of their investment in slaves, while Northern investors aiming at short-term speculation had no scruples. Thomas's lease plan then incurred widespread criticism, among which the most effective was made by James Yeatman of the Western Sanitary Commission. The censure of Yeatman, however, played eventually into the hands of the Department of the Treasury, which temporarily controlled the lease system in the winter of 1863–1864. Soon the Treasury began to carry out reforms demanded by Yeatman, affording wages ranging from ten to twenty-five dollars per month, requiring the lessees to improve residential conditions, and supplying blacks with garden lots.[384] After Thomas's appeal to the president, however, most of the Treasury's authority on this issue was terminated and reforms were suspended.

The Freedmen's Bureau followed the compulsory policy of wage labor adopted by the Union Army after its establishment. Since the Bureau was an independent division of the Department of War, whose officers and agents were generally serviceman, the Bureau carried out its policy in coordination with the army. In places where there was no Freedmen's Bureau agent, the commanding officer of the nearest detachment would assume the duties of the Bureau as well as his troop assignment.[385] Like the army, the Freedmen's Bureau held that the interests of the whole South and the freedmen rested on economic success, and paid attention to sending freedmen to plantations. General Howard ordered his Assistant Commissioner in February 1866 to "continue to use every possible effort to reduce any accumulations of people in the different cities and villages."[386] A large number of "vagrants" were sent back to the countryside, and compelled to enter a contract. Those who would not accept a job, the Freedmen's Bureau declared, would be forced to labor on plantations without pay.[387] This policy ultimately led to the disintegration of most camps in cities and towns. Although the Bureau required that both planter and laborer abide by a contract, many agents thought that their mission was to press freedmen for work and to punish them for their violation of a contract. Those who did not respect the contract were also punished by hard labor without compensation.[388] "Doing justice," an observer reported, "seems to mean seeing that the blacks don't break contract and compelling them to submit cheerfully if the whites do."[389] As for the "two evils" it had to contend against, namely, "cruelty on the part of the employer and shirking on the part of the negroes," the Bureau seemed more hostile to blacks' reluctance to labor. Local agents also detested freedmen's indulgence in "fine cigars" and useless dress or ornaments.[390] Interested in restricting them as local whites did, they often treated freedmen harshly in military tribunals. In Raleigh, North Carolina, for example, the penalty for a black who was convicted of stealing a lot of bacon was that he "exhibited himself, as many have done before him, near Turners corner, suspended by the thumbs to a lamp post. A card affixed to his back, marked Abram stole meat, informed all passerby of the reason for his punishment."[391] In Atlanta and Montgomery, blacks had a special curfew and had to carry special passes. In Richmond, an officer told a group of blacks, who tried to exact the arrears of payment from their former master, that he would send them to prison if they did not stop their accusation.[392] Also practicing the convict system, the Freedmen's Bureau dispatched blacks convicted of crimes to hard labor while whites could pay fines. Being more or less corrupted by their power, some local agents acted in collusion with Southern whites. Lured by the promise of profit, many were ready to discipline blacks to satisfy the planters. Lieutenant H. Smith, the agent at Jackson, Mississippi, was described as a "popinjay," for he soundly berated the freedmen to gain the favor of the young ladies of the place.[393]

Generally speaking, however, the establishment of the Freedmen's Bureau made the army more effectively protect the interests of freedmen. In places where the local authorities did not treat blacks fairly, their protection was particularly important. When the army and the Bureau arrived, the atrocities committed on blacks stopped, the system of paid labor was brought into operation, and due process in court could not be suspended; once they departed, the circumstances became the same as before.[394] Having the backing of the army, the Freedmen's Bureau spared no effort in putting the contract system into operation and imbued planters with the concept of paid labor. Planters were not required by law to submit their contracts to the Freedmen's Bureau, but local agents often pressed their supervision on planters. Some agents canceled contract clauses regulating daily conduct of blacks, prohibited any maltreatment of laborers, and insisted that a worker who had to leave a plantation before the end of the season should receive appropriate payment. In 1865 and 1866, the Freedmen's Bureau sought to ensure a wage of between eight and ten dollars per month.[395] In Mississippi, garden lots were required by the Bureau to supply to laborers in proportion to their respective sizes of families, and their wages were protected by a lien on the crops on the land cultivated by them.[396] In Texas, the housing conditions of laborers gained the special attention of the Bureau. Also in Mississippi, the Freedmen's Bureau declared that the ban on leasing land to blacks was invalid.[397] In July 1865, Secretary of War Stanton informed Southern commanders to stop pass requirements and inhibited the army from obstructing in any way the blacks' freedom of movement. At the same time, discriminatory vagrancy laws in some cities were annulled.[398] The movement of laborers caused by these measures had overcome the inherent faults of Banks's system, and would soon release blacks' potential bargaining power and further advance their liberty in the near future.

In order to protect the interests of freedmen and maintain social order, the Freedmen's Bureau asserted that it had jurisdiction over

Southern affairs under military occupation and set up Bureau courts to settle disputes between employer and employee. Most officers of the Bureau stressed the principles of equality under the law and due process, protected the laborers' right to participate in market competition without racial distinctions, and declared that the cases involving freedmen would be tried in the Bureau courts until the civil courts allowed black testimony and fair treatment.[399] In addition to the Bureau courts, there were also military tribunals. Thus the jurisdiction of each court tended to overlap, and now and then a ruling in one tribunal was overturned by another.[400] Under normal conditions, however, local agents of the Bureau individually adjudicated a wide variety of complaints and in some regions established three-man courts to hear individual contract disputes, with planter, freedmen, and the Bureau each choosing a member.[401] Insisting that it had no intention of giving freedmen any special privileges, the Freedmen's Bureau was not to interfere in any way in civil courts that had granted freedmen the rights as a man and a free laborer. Howard himself thought that any treatment that discriminated in favor of blacks would be ultimately harmful to them. After civil courts had admitted blacks' testimony, the Freedmen's Bureau generally gave up its interference at the end of 1866, and only acted as a deterrent force to guard against the possible transgression of civil courts. In Mississippi, for example, Colonel Thomas announced that there was no Bureau court from now on in this state as early as October 1865.[402] Since blacks could sue and be sued in civil courts, admittedly, their interests were guaranteed in some cases. Many disputes involving the small sum of debt to laborers were successfully settled out of court, for whites preferred to pay rather than condescend to confront blacks as equals in court.[403] But the discriminatory treatment of law had only been concealed; blacks could barely obtain equal justice from civil courts. Furthermore, poverty often hindered blacks from employing a lawyer, and those who lived in remote areas had to trudge a long distance to lodge a complaint.

Therefore, the Bureau's policy on free labor was in some confusion, with each agent acting respectively according to his own reason. On the one hand were the radical experiments in land reform, on the other hand were forced labor and the convict system. There were ardent supporters of black causes as well as indifferent bystanders and prejudiced persons who only cared for whites' interests. Corruption and conflicts of duties complicated the policy confusion. As a matter of fact, the complication of the Bureau's policy reflected its contradiction between recovering the

Southern economy and protecting black interests, between protecting black liberty and establishing a new order, and between propelling change and maintaining relative stability, mirrored in the different choices of each agent of the Bureau.

Yet the concepts of free labor, equality before the law, and due process were never shaken. The agents generally believed that if these rights were guaranteed, laborers would seek their self-interests of their own accord and ultimately enter into the competitive market governed by the law of supply and demand. "To the establishment of these principles [which govern free labor]," said General Robert K. Scott, the Bureau's chief officer in South Carolina, "the Bureau is committed."[404] "This," asserted Wager Swayne, the Bureau's assistant commissioner in Alabama, "is more and better than all laws."[405] If whites treated blacks fairly, stressed William E. Strong, inspector general in Texas, freedmen would work hard.[406] These ideas were understood by William Gannett at Port Royal, South Carolina, exactly in the same way. "Let all the natural laws of labor, wages, competition, &c come into play and the sooner will habits of responsibility, industry, self-dependence & manliness be developed."[407] Sparing no pains, the Freedmen's Bureau tried to integrate "the higher laws" into the newly born labor system in the South. Liberty did not merely mean the escape from the fetters of absolute personal authority, but also the devotion to rational rules and the cultivation of moral self-restraint.

Thus, the Bureau's policy showed duality. As for improving the freedmen's external environment, the Bureau tried to help them break away from irrational restrictions and rationalize competitive conditions; at the same time, the Bureau seemingly paid more attention to reforming freedmen's habits and fostering economic rationality like frugality and diligence. This was the internal goal devised by the Bureau to introduce market principles.

The Bureau placed particular emphasis on education, for it seemed to perform a dual function, in that it could encourage the material ambitions of freedmen and instill in them a sense of responsibility. What the Bureau counted on was the conservative role of education to reconcile liberty with order. In a field report to President Johnson, Carl Schurz summarized this principle as the Bureau understood it: "The education of the lower orders is the only reliable basis of the civilization as well as of the prosperity of a people." Moreover, it was "the true ground upon which the efficiency and the successes of free labor society grows," and it was an instrument of making the freedman "an intelligent co-operator in the general movement of society."[408] Based on these ideas, the Bureau put a great deal of time and effort into education, although its responsibility for education had not been specified at first.

Education, to Howard himself, was the basis upon which all endeavors to aid freedmen rested. Under his direction, local agents made efforts with Northern benevolent societies to improve the educational conditions of freedmen. Generally speaking, the Bureau committed itself to build the facilities for study and afforded rations and quarters to Northern teachers, while the societies assumed the responsibilities of recruiting Northern teachers and providing their salaries and activity funds. According to the statistics of the Freedmen's Bureau, there were 975 schools "regularly organized" under its supervision in 1866, with enrollments totaling about 90,000 black students. Including "many schools not regularly reported," the Bureau estimated that "there are now 150,000 freedmen and the children who are earnestly occupied in the study of books."[409] Financed by a separate black poll tax and supplemented by tuition charges, Texas and Florida established a public school system that included blacks.[410]

Like the Freedmen's Bureau, the benevolent societies intended to cure freedmen of the sequelae of slavery, to enhance their independence, and "to plant a genuine republicanism in the southern States" by means of education.[411] Once the work was done, the dual goals of the freedmen's economic and social interests might be realized, and social burdens and conflicts avoided. They guessed that the long-term effects of bondage had made freedmen apathetic, immoral, and dependent. As Lydia M. Child, a veteran Abolitionist who devoted herself to black education in the South, put it, "I doubt whether we *can* treat our colored brethren *exactly* as we would if they were white, though it is desirable to do so. But we have kept their minds in a state of infancy, and children *must* be treated with more patience and forbearance than grown people."[412] Thinking that their bad habits resulted from slavery rather than racial characteristics, most educators tried to tap the potentialities of the freedman and accord him "an opportunity for development before his capacity for development can be known."[413] The Bureau and the societies did their utmost to integrate freedmen into a larger social order.

The relief activities of the Freedmen's Bureau similarly embodied its internal aim. Howard himself considered public assistance to the poor "abnormal to our system of government," and thought that giving "unearned" land or even seed corn to freedmen could easily forge new chains for a new kind of dependence.[414] "A man who can work has no right to support by government," asserted a Mississippi Bureau agent. "No really respectable person wishes to be supported by others." "A man could scarcely be called free," remarked a Tennessee Bureau official, "who is the recipient of public charity."[415] In most cases, the Freedmen's Bureau confined its relief to children, the aged, and those unable to work. Having issued over 23 million rations, of which two thirds were sent to blacks, Howard resolutely ordered the end to relief in the fall of 1866.[416]

Undoubtedly, the achievements of the Freedmen's Bureau in fulfilling its internal aims, among which was to spread Northern values among freedmen, cannot be denied. Regarding its external aim, the effect was not so remarkable because of the existence of whites' deep-rooted prejudice. Although it had afforded the most fundamental liberty by which blacks could advance, the Bureau was incapable of overcoming and reforming the racial ideas of Southern whites. If he found his economic ambition to be continuously frustrated, and if he found it easier and safer to stay at the bottom, a black would drift with the tide and even resign himself to his backwardness. The limitation imposed on the achievements of the external aim greatly hindered the transition of the internal aim. Here, as a feeble contender fighting against his strong opponent, the Freedmen's Bureau with limited functions was doomed to setback and failure from the beginning. All the same, the Freedmen's Bureau still marked that this nation had assumed the new responsibility of universal norms of conduct and began her unprecedented exploration of them, despite its limitations.

NOTES

176. Leon F. Litwack, *Been in the Storm so Long: The Aftermath of Slavery.* New York: Random House, 1979, p. 107.

177. *ibid.,* p. 109.

178. *ibid.*

179. *ibid.,* p. 122.

180. *ibid.,* p. 109.

181. Bell I. Wiley, *Southern Slaves, 1861–1865.* New Haven: Yale University Press, 1938, p. 52.

182. Litwack, *op. cit.,* pp. 145–146.

183. Emory M. Thomas, *The Confederacy as a Revolutionary Experience.* Englewood Cliffs: Prentice-Hall, Inc., 1971, p. 124.

184. Henry Y. Thompson, *An Englishman in the American Civil War.* New York: Pantheon, 1971, p. 94.

185. Litwack, *op. cit.,* p. 106.

186. Gilbert Osofsky, ed., *The Slave Narratives of Henry Bibb, William Wells Brown, and Solomon Northup.* New York: Harper & Row, 1969, p. 212.

187. Litwack, *op. cit.,* p. 150.

188. *ibid.,* p. 151.

189. Arney R. Childs, *The Private Journal of Henry William Ravenel, 1859–1887.* Columbia: University of South Carolina Press, 1947, p. 221.

190. Litwack, *op. cit.,* p. 105.

191. J. Carlyle Sitterson, *Sugar Country.* Lexington: University of Kentucky Press, 1953, p. 211.

192. Litwack, *op. cit.,* pp. 171–172.

193. *ibid.,* p. 214.

194. *ibid.,* p. 216.

195. *ibid.,* p. 212.

196. Myrta L. Avery, *Dixie after the War.* New York: Harper & Brothers, 1906, p. 183.

197. John R. Dennett, *The South as It Is, 1865–1866,* ed. Henry M. Cristman. New York: Macmillan, 1965, pp. 121–122.

198. Litwack, *op. cit.,* p. 213.

199. *ibid.,* p. 190.

200. M. L. Avary, *op. cit.,* p. 185.

201. William W. Ball, *The State That Forgot: South Carolina's Surrender to Democracy.* Indianapolis: Bobbs-Merrill, 1932, p. 128.

202. Litwack, *op. cit.,* p. 199.

203. Joel Williamson, "The Meaning of Freedom," in Seth M. Scheiner and Tilden G. Edelstein, eds., *The Black Americans: Interpretive Readings.* New York: Holt, Rinehart & Winston, 1971, p. 237.

204. *ibid.,* p. 239.

205. J. H. Easterby, ed., *The South Carolina Rice Plantation,* quoted from Litwack, *op. cit.,* p. 142.

206. Thomas W. Higginson, *Army Life in a Black Regiment,* quoted from Litwack, *op. cit.,* pp. 199–120.

207. Hope S. Chamberlain, *Old Days in Chapel Hill,* quoted from Litwack, *op. cit.,* p. 201.

208. Litwack, *op. cit.,* p. 205.

209. *ibid.,* p. 296.

210. *ibid.,* p. 298.

211. J. R. Dennett, *op. cit.,* pp. 13–14.

212. Litwack, *op. cit.,* p. 294.

213. Joel Williamson, *op. cit.,* p. 222.

214. Litwack, *op. cit.,* p. 296.

215. Joel Williamson, *op. cit.,* p. 223.

216. Litwack, *op. cit.,* p. 330.

217. *ibid.,* p. 202.

218. Rodney P. Carlisle, *Prologue to Liberation: A History of Black People in America.* New Brunswick, NJ: Rutgers University, 1972, p. 149.

219. Booker T. Washington, *Up from Slavery: An Autobiography.* New York: A. L. Bunt, 1902, pp. 19–20.

220. Charles L. Perdue, Jr., et al., eds., *Wheels in the Wheat: Interview with Virginia Exslaves,* quoted from Litwack, *op. cit.,* p. 292.

221. J. Trowbridge, *The South,* quoted from Litwack, *op. cit.,* p. 223.

222. W. E. B. Du Bois, *The Souls of Black Folk.* New York: McClure, 1969, p. 45.

223. Litwack, *op. cit.,* p. 293.

224. Joel Williamson, *op. cit.,* p. 231.

225. *ibid.,* p. 228.

226. William Richter, *The Army in Texas During Reconstruction, 1865–1870.* College Station: Texas A & M University Press, 1987, p. 33.

227. John W. De Forest, *A Union Officer in the Reconstruction,* quoted from Litwack, *op. cit.,* p. 307.

228. Litwack, *op. cit.,* p. 229.

229. Joel Williamson, *The Crucible of Race: Black–White Relations in the American South Since Emancipation.* New York: Oxford University Press, 1984, p. 45.

230. Litwack, *op. cit.,* p. 230.

231. Eric Foner, *Reconstruction: America's Unfinished Revolution, 1863–1877.* New York: Harper & Row, 1988, p. 84.

232. Litwack, *op. cit.,* p. 230.

233. *ibid.,* p. 241.

234. Rupert Holland, ed., *Letters and Diary of Laura M. Towne,* quoted from Litwack, *op. cit.,* p. 245.

235. Roger Ransom and Richard Sutch, *One Kind of Freedom: The Economic Consequences of Emancipation.* New York: Cambridge University Press, 1977, p. 55.

236. Foner, *op. cit.,* p. 86.

237. Joel Williamson, "The Meaning of Freedom," p. 237.

238. Foner, *op. cit.,* p. 86.

239. Williamson, *The Crucible of Race,* p. 59.

240. Foner, *op. cit.,* p. 90.

241. William Montgomery, *Under Their Own Vine and Fig Tree: The African-Americans' Church in the South, 1865–1900.* Baton Rouge: Louisiana State University Press, 1993, p. 96.

242. Litwack, *op. cit.,* p. 464.

243. *ibid.,* p. 464.

244. Foner, *op. cit.,* p. 89.

245. John Lee Eighmy, "The Baptist and Slavery: An Examination of the Origins and Benefits of Segregation," in Norval D. Glenn and Charles M. Bonjean, eds., *Blacks in the United States.* San Francisco: Chandler Publishing Company, 1969, p. 299.

246. Robert Cruden, *Negro in Reconstruction.* Englewood Cliffs: Prentice-Hall Inc., 1969, pp. 76, 80.

247. Ralph E. Morrow, *Northern Methodism and Reconstruction.* East Lansing: Michigan State University Press, 1956, p. 136

248. Litwack, *op. cit.,* p. 458.

249. *ibid.,* p. 458.

250. The rapid exposure and development of the "invisible institution" directly benefited from its informal character.

251. Montgomery, *op. cit.,* p. 126.

252. Francis B. Simkins, "New Viewpoints of Southern Reconstruction," *Journal of Southern History,* 21, February 1939, quoted from Gerald N. Grob and George Athan Billias, eds., *Interpretations of American History: Patterns and Perspectives.* New York, 1972, p. 517.

253. C. Vann Woodward, *The Strange Career of Jim Crow.* New York: Oxford University Press, 1968, pp. 13–14.

254. Howard N. Rabionowitz, *Race Relations in the Urban South, 1865–1890.* New York: Oxford University Press, 1978, p. 98.

255. Rabinowitz, *op. cit.,* p. 97; Woodward, *op. cit.,* pp. 14–15.

256. Rabinowitz, *op. cit.,* p. 100.

257. W. E. B. Du Bois, "Reconstruction and Its Benefits," in Robert D. Marcus, ed., *The American Scence.* New York: Appleton-Century-Crofts, p. 398.

258. Cruden, *op. cit.,* p. 79.

259. Rabinowitz, *op. cit.,* p. 198.

260. Litwack, *op. cit.,* p. 470.

261. Foner, *op. cit.,* p. 94.

262. Rabinowitz, *op. cit.,* p. 153.

263. Litwack, *op. cit.,* p. 494.

264. Foner, *op. cit.,* p. 99.

265. Cruden, *op. cit.*, p. 84; Rabinowitz, *op. cit.*, p. 199.

266. Foner, *op. cit.*, p. 100.

267. Rabinowitz, *op. cit.*, p. 227.

268. Foner, *op. cit.*, p. 96.

269. Rabinowitz, *op. cit.*, p. 227.

270. Foner, *op. cit.*, p. 100.

271. Joel Williamson, *New People: Miscegenation and Mulattos in the United States*. New York: Free Press, 1980, p. 76; E. M. Thomas, *op. cit.*, p. 120.

272. Blassingame, *Black New Orleans*, quoted from Eric Anderson and Alfred A. Moss, Jr., eds., *The Facts of Reconstruction: Essays in Honor of* John *Hope Franklin*. Baton Rouge: Louisiana State University Press, 1991, p. 48.

273. Litwack, *op. cit.*, p. 189.

274. Julius Lester, *To Be a Slave*, quoted from Litwack, *op. cit.*, 249.

275. Joel Williamson, "The Meaning of Freedom," p. 234.

276. *ibid.*, p. 235.

277. Foner, *op. cit.*, p. 121.

278. Litwack, *op. cit.*, p. 504.

279. *ibid.*, p. 517.

280. *Proceeding of the Convention of the Colored People of Virginia, Held in the City of Alexandria, August 2, 3, 4, 5, 1865*, quoted from Richard W. Leopold, Arthur S. Link, and Stanley Coben, eds., *Problems in American History*. Vol. I. Englewood Cliffs: Prentice-Hall, Inc., 1972, p. 529.

281. Litwack, *op. cit.*, p. 539.

282. Williamson, *The Crucible of Race*, p. 50.

283. George P. Rawick, ed., *American Slaves*, quoted from Litwack, *op. cit.*, p. 224.

284. Litwack, *op. cit.*, p. 518.

285. Cruden, *op. cit.*, p. 159.

286. *New Orleans Tribune*, November 21, 1865, quoted from Litwack, *op. cit.*, p. 388.

287. Ransom and Sutch, *op. cit.*, p. 81.

288. Vernon Lane Wharton, *The Negro in Mississippi, 1865–1890*. New York: Harper & Row, 1947, p. 59.

289. Rebecca J. Scott, "Defining the Boundaries of Freedom in the Word of Cane," *American Historical Review*, Vol. 99, 1994, p. 71.

290. Eric Foner, *Nothing But Freedom*, quoted from Anderson and Moss, eds., *op. cit.*, p. 45.

291. James S. Allen, Reconstruction: *The Battle for Democracy*. New York: International, 1937, p. 43.

292. *ibid.*, p. 44.

293. Ben Ames Williams, ed., *A Diary from Dixie,* quoted from Litwack, *op. cit.,* p. 206.

294. Allen, *op. cit.,* p. 44.

295. Litwack, *op. cit.,* p. 208.

296. *ibid.,* p. 399.

297. Reid, *After the War,* quoted from Joel Williamson, "The Meaning of Freedom," p. 240.

298. August Meier, "Negroes in the First and Second Reconstruction of the South," in S. M. Scheiner and T. G. Edelstein, eds., *op. cit.,* p. 246.

299. Ransom and Sutch, *op. cit.,* p. 81.

300. Henry M. Christman, *op. cit.,* p. 564.

301. Wharton, *op. cit.,* p. 60.

302. William H. Harris, *The Harder We Run: Black Workers Since the Civil War.* New York: Oxford University Press, 1982, p. 9.

303. Ransom and Sutch, *op. cit.,* p. 87.

304. *ibid.,* p. 85.

305. Loren Schweninger, "Black Economic Reconstruction in the South," in Anderson and Moss, eds., *op. cit.,* p. 180

306. Litwack, *op. cit.,* p. 443.

307. Wharton, *op. cit.,* pp. 217–218.

308. James Currie, *Enclave: Vicksburg and Her Plantations, 1863–1870.* Oxford: University of Mississippi, 1980, p. 150.

309. Ransom and Sutch, *op. cit.,* p. 46.

310. *ibid.,* p. 46.

311. *ibid.,* p. 55.

312. Foner, *Reconstruction,* p. 85.

313. William E. Dodd, *The Cotton Kingdom.* New Haven: Yale University Press, 1919, p. 87.

314. Litwack, *op. cit.,* p. 393.

315. *ibid.,* p. 393.

316. *ibid.,* p. 437.

317. Currie, *op. cit.,* p. 157.

318. Joel Williamson, "New Patterns in Economics," in Irwin Unger, David Brody, and Paul Goodman, eds., *The American Past: A Social Record.* Waltham, MA: D. C. Heath, 1971, p. 194.

319. Ransom and Sutch, *op. cit.,* p. 58.

320. *ibid.,* p. 60.

321. Joel Williamson, *op. cit.,* p. 195.

322. Litwack, *op. cit.,* p. 410.

323. Ransom and Sutch, *op. cit.,* p. 66.

324. Foner, *op. cit.*, p. 172.

325. Litwack, *op. cit.*, p. 431.

326. Paul A. Cimbala, "The Freedmen's Bureau, the Freedmen, and Sherman's Grant in Reconstruction Georgia, 1865–1867," *Journal of Southern History*, Vol. 55, 1989, pp. 621–622.

327. Ransom and Sutch, *op. cit.*, p. 78.

328. Foner, *op. cit.*, p. 173.

329. Williamson, *The Crucible of Race*, p. 46.

330. Joel Williamson, "New Patterns in Economics," p. 192.

331. Ransom and Sutch, *op. cit.*, p. 94.

332. *ibid.*, p. 68.

333. *ibid.*, p. 67.

334. Foner, *op. cit.*, p. 173.

335. Thomas C. Holt, "An Empire over the Mind: Emancipation, Race, and Ideology in the British West Indies and the American South," in J. M. Kousser and J. M. McPerson, eds., *op. cit.*, p. 300.

336. Foner, *op. cit.*, p. 175.

337. Williamson, *op. cit.*, p. 196.

338. R. J. Scott, *op. cit.*, p. 75.

339. Williamson, *op. cit.*, p. 196.

340. *ibid.*, p. 197.

341. Scott, *op. cit.*, p. 76.

342. Peter Kolchin, *First Freedom: The Responses of Alabama's Blacks to Emancipation and Reconstruction.* Westport, CT: Greenwood, 1977.

343. Wharton, *op. cit.*, p. 28.

344. Du Bois, *op. cit.*, p. 55.

345. Wharton, *op. cit.*, p. 25.

346. LaWanda Cox, "The Promise of Land for the Freedmen," *Mississippi Valley Historical Review*, No. 3 (1958), p. 419.

347. Cruden, *op. cit.*, p. 10.

348. Meier and Rudiwick, *From Plantation to Ghetto.* New York: Hill and Wang, 1970, p. 150.

349. Barry A. Crouch, *The Freedmen's Bureau and Black Texans.* Austin: University of Texas Press, 1992, p. 7.

350. Wharton, *op. cit.*, p. 39.

351. Foner, *op. cit.*, p. 59.

352. Wharton, *op. cit.*, p. 64.

353. Currie, *op. cit.*, p. 92.

354. *ibid.*, p. 93.

355. Wharton, *op. cit.*, p. 39.

356. Currie, *op. cit.*, p. 102.

357. Rodney P. Carlisle, *Prologue to Liberation*. New Brunswick, NJ: Rutgers University Press, 1972, p. 130.

358. Currie, *op. cit.*, p. 114.

359. Cimbala, *op. cit.*, p. 599; Carlisle, *op. cit.*, p. 131.

360. Cimbala, *op. cit.*, p. 603.

361. *ibid.*, pp. 605–606.

362. Litwack, *op. cit.*, p. 406.

363. Cimbala, *op. cit.*, p. 603.

364. Quoted from Thomas C. Holt, *op. cit.*, p. 285.

365. Meier and Rudiwick, *op. cit.*, p. 152.

366. Foner, *op. cit.*, p. 159.

367. Cimbala, *op. cit.*, p. 607.

368. Cruden, *op. cit.*, p. 12.

369. Foner, *op. cit.*, p. 159.

370. Currie, *op. cit.*, p. 121.

371. Litwack, *op. cit.*, p. 405.

372. Cimbala, *op. cit.*, p. 609.

373. Foner, *op. cit.*, p. 161.

374. Cimbala, *op. cit.*, p. 613.

375. Carlisle, *op. cit.*, p. 132.

376. Scott, *op. cit.*, p. 72.

377. *ibid.*, p. 73.

378. Litwack, *op. cit.*, p. 377.

379. Foner, *op. cit.*, p. 55.

380. Litwack, *op. cit.*, p. 29.

381. Wharton, *op. cit.*, p. 29.

382. *ibid.*, p. 33.

383. *ibid.*

384. *ibid.*, p. 36.

385. Richter, *op. cit.*, p. 33.

386. Rabinowitz, *op. cit.*, p. 21.

387. Wharton, *op. cit.*, p. 75.

388. Cimbala, *op. cit.*, p. 621.

389. Litwack, *op. cit.*, p. 419.

390. Foner, *op. cit.*, p. 157.

391. Rabinowitz, *op. cit.*, p. 32.

392. *ibid.*, p. 33.

393. Wharton, *op. cit.*, p. 77.

394. Richter, *op. cit.*, p. 37.

395. Ransom and Sutch, *op. cit.,* p. 60.

396. Wharton, *op. cit.,* p. 75.

397. William C. Harris, "The Reconstruction of the Commonwealth," in Richard A. Melemore, ed., *A History of Mississippi,* Vol. I, Jackson: University Press of Mississippi, 1973, p. 550.

398. Foner, *op. cit.,* p. 155.

399. Wharton, *op. cit.,* p. 76.

400. Richter, *op. cit.,* p. 44.

401. Foner, *op. cit.,* p. 149.

402. Wharton, *op. cit.,* p. 77.

403. Rabinowitz, *op. cit.,* p. 33.

404. Foner, *op. cit.,* p. 155.

405. *ibid.,* p. 167.

406. Richter, *op. cit.,* p. 37.

407. Thomas Holt, *op. cit.,* pp. 287–288.

408. *ibid.,* p. 296.

409. Ransom and Sutch, *op. cit.,* p. 24.

410. Foner, *op. cit.,* p. 207.

411. *ibid.,* p. 147.

412. Litwack, *op. cit.,* p. 477.

413. *ibid.,* p. 478.

414. Cimbala, *op. cit.,* p. 613; Foner, *op. cit.,* p. 152.

415. Paul D. Phillips, *A History of the Freedmen's Bureau in Tennessee,* quoted from Foner, *op. cit.,* p. 152.

416. Foner, *op. cit.,* p. 152.

CHAPTER 3

Issues Affecting African Americans and White Reconstruction

CLUTCHING AT OLD AUTHORITY: SOUTHERN WHITES' RECONSTRUCTION

The consequences of the war were disastrous for white Southerners. The toll in the battlefield brought unbroken agony to many families. About one million men had served the Confederate cause, of whom 258,000 died, another 150,000 were disabled, and countless people suffered the lingering pains of wounds or disease.[417] The ratio of men to women was out of proportion. In Georgia alone, for instance, the 1870 census counted 36,000 more women than men.[418]

Material losses were just as great, especially for planters, merchants, and lawyers, the elite that once controlled Southern power. Emancipation resulted in the sudden "disappearance" of slave capital, which mounted to two billion dollars, though for blacks or the whole South this was just the shift of labor capital. Black's withdrawal from the fields perhaps led to almost the same loss of the estate. According to the official agricultural census, land value decreased from 55 percent in Georgia to 70 percent in Louisiana.[419] The nullification of bonds and debts, of which over $1.5 billion in Confederate currency and $700 million in public bonds could never be recovered caused the South to sink into poverty.[420] In the war the Confederacy confiscated property owned by Northerners, and asked Southern debtors to pay the Confederate Treasury. Now white Southerners had to once again pay debts to the rightful creditors. White Southerners also paid their share of the two million dollars to the federal government in the form of direct taxes during the war.[421] In addition, the high tariff opposed by Southerners for so long increased to 47 percent during the war, and continued to increase thereafter.[422] When the federal troops arrived in Georgia, North Carolina, and Virginia, countless railroads, bridges, cities, and houses were crushed to ruins.[423]

For white Southerners, their psychological frustration was even harder to bear. Having a strong sense of honor and dignity, they firmly believed the justice of their cause. Their stubbornness could sometimes turn to arrogance or conceit. Yet with the triumph of the federal cause, their great expectations changed to dismay, which was mixed with unrestrained excitement and harshness. "Touch it not, unfold it never," Abram J. Ryan bitterly wrote of "The Conquered banner," "let it drop there, furled forever, / For its peoples' hopes are dead." "I forget my humiliation for awhile in sleep," a Richmond man said in melancholy, "but the memory of every bereavement comes back heavily, like a sullen sea surge, on awakening, flooding and submerging my soul with anguish. The idolized expectation of a separate nationality, of a social life and literature and civilization of our own, together with a gospel guarded against the contamination of New England infidelity, all this has perished, and I feel like seaweed on a desert's shore."[424] Southern whites' mentality was on the verge of spiritual bankruptcy. Even so, white Southerners were still unreconciled to their new position. Always accustomed to a leading role in national affairs since the colonial period, these states were now under the rule of the bayonet, and their bitterness was difficult for outsiders to comprehend fully. Until 1870, the Reverend Robert Lewis Dabey could still say, "I do not forgive, I try not forgive. What! forgive those people, who have invaded our country, burned our cities, destroyed our homes, slain our young men, and spread desolation and ruin over our land! No, I do not forgive them."[425]

Against this background of psychological anxiety, blacks became a symbol of failure and humiliation. Regarded as the root of trouble, blacks were allegedly utilized and manipulated by the Yankees to achieve their "vicious ends." So any "indocile" acts of blacks would be identified as contempt for white men, and anger at Yankees was immediately shifted to them. Imamiti Motomobu said: "When being under the unpleasant attack from someone else, or detesting ourselves, we would kick off the pebbles under our feet, and even stalk off with the crawling worms crushed."[426] Especially sensitive to Northerners' "manipulatin" of blacks, Southern whites stressed Northerners' instigation and harmful demonstration to blacks. To resist Yankees' invasion and contamination, it was very necessary to absolutely control blacks. It was a token of their last dignity, a exclusive domain that outsiders were not entitled to, and the last fort for Southern whites to defend to death. "Any one who thinks that the war is over," Samuel G. Swain commented after a hunting trip north of Vicksburg, "should go through the country between the Yazoo and Mississippi rivers. The southern people are determined to drive northern people out of the country. All the northern men planting in that part of the country bar thier [sic] doors night and have thier firearms where they can lay thier hands on them at any moment."[427] White Southerners, Schurz said, were determined to get rid of any Northern interference and demonstrate to the world what Southerners were made of, and were not hesitant to fight another war. "They are 'not conquered but only overpowered.' They are only smothered for a time."[428]

In Southern whites' opinion, even worse was the great social and economic turmoil resulting from emancipation. Convulsed with the lingering fear of social reform, the whole South worried about how to control the freedmen. When visiting the South in the aftermath of the war, many Northern journalists found that Southern whites seemed to be haunted by only one idea and one idea only. "Everybody," one tourist reported, "talks about the negro at all hours of the day and under all circumstances. One might in truth say using the elegant language of opposition (racist Democrat) orators in Congress that the people have got nigger on the brain."[429]

At the first moment of the disintegration of slavery, many a white was at a loss. Since they could no longer control blacks' conduct at will, they got bogged down in endless despair, which was no weaker than the fear of doomsday. "Miss Polly died right after the surrender," a former Virginia slave recalled. "She was so hurt that all the negroes was going to be free. She died hollering 'yankee!' She was so mad that she just died."[430] Billy Fannely, whose brother had been killed at the front, downheartedly returned to his home, only to find his slaves freed and most leaving the plantation. He seemed numbed by the reality. One day his mother found him lying in a shed, his throat alashed, and beside him a razor and a note which revealed that he died because he did not care to live "cause de nigger free."[431]

According to psychologist Erich Fromm's analysis of sadism and masochism,[432] slaveholders, as sadists, could not separate themselves from their dominating object: blacks. They needed those who were ruled by them and could not make do without them for any time. They psychologically depended on their dependence. Only when having controlled someone else were they satisfied with a sense of security, strength, and power. Because of their domination of others, some "affectionate feelings" might well up in their hearts, and then the next logic might emerge: they actually "loved" their slaves because they were dominating them. In reality, the paternalism growing on Southern soil was a mirror of this mentality. They could provide some care, petty favors, or economic sops, but never the right to seek liberty and independence. Having mitigated the cruelty of slavery, paternalism simply added some humanist elements to the peculiar institution under the prerequisite of absolute rule. When blacks actually had opportunities and courage to ask for their rights, the psychological shock to whites was particularly strong. Left with an illusion of being conquered, they could not smoothly adjust to the new reality. When the news of Confederate failure reached Mary Darby, daughter of a prominent South Carolina family, she staggered to a table, sat down, and wept aloud. "Now," she screamed, "we belong to Negroes and Yankees."[433] They could not imagine their circumstances without slaves' services. "Nobody that hasn't experienced it knows anything about our suffering," a young South Carolina planter sighed, "we are discouraged: we have nothing left to begin with. I never did a day's work in my life, and don't know how to begin."[434] Southern whites keenly regarded the disintegration of slavery and the Confederacy and the arrival of Northern troops as the shameful yoke that harnessed them. Either they had to tolerate the insolence of their former slaves or appeal to their Northern "masters" for judgment, one white man resentfully wrote, "as if we were slaves ourselves and that is just what they are trying to make of us. Oh, it is abominable!"[435] "The most discouraging feature," General Hatch reported in 1866,

> was the utter helplessness of the white community in the face of the terrible problem. According to Sidney Andrews, 'the Negro, as bad as his condition is,' said he, 'seems to me, on the whole to accommodate himself more easily than the white to the changed situation.' I should say that the question at issue in the South is not 'what shall be done with the Negro?' but 'what shall be done with the whites?' The blacks manage to live comfortably for the most part and help each other; but the white, accustomed to having all their affairs managed by an aristocracy that was then ruined, seemed powerless.[436]

Yet once they overcame their temporary perplexity and determined to rid themselves of their powerless state, Southern whites desperately clutched at what they had relied on in the past, namely, the control of blacks, striking back with all their might.

Not all planters, however, looked at the end of the old system pessimistically. Many planters thought that the "peculiar institution" had tied them to inextricable burdens. When blacks were no longer slaves, quite a few whites felt relieved to get rid of the heavy responsibilities of livelihood and the uneasiness about black's potential protests. Upon freeing their slaves, a Virginia woman declared that "I was glad and thankful on my own account when slavery ended and I ceased to belong, body and soul, to my negroes."[437] Cornelia Spencer, a prominent resident of Chapel Hill, hailed emancipation for the benefits it would bestow upon all whites. Slavery, she insisted, had been "an awful dray" on the proper development of the South. "And because I love the white man better than I do the black, I am glad they are free."[438] Another high-minded Virginian, Henry A. White, praised God daily for having relieved him of the "negrodom or niggerdom" of slavery. Yet he claimed to feel some compassion for the real victim. "He is now a freedman but without a friend. But he is a freedman. I am now free of responsibility for his care and comfort, and, I repeat I am content."[439] Emancipation not only provided blacks with personal freedom, but also gave the same spiritual freedom to some responsible whites. But it was quite rare that they could admit that at the time.

No matter what they thought about emancipation, whites had not dramatically changed their pro-slavery opinions. Being angry or confused at current affairs, many indulged in nostalgia for "the good old days," and deplored the disappearance of "the happy and faithful nigger." The *Constitution* was most preoccupied by the living memory of the "old darkey." When an old black named Aaron Harper died in Atlanta, the *Constitution* described him as a "faithful good negro, who won the esteem and confidence of all who knew him by his unfailing devotion to duty. He was punctual as a clock, always reliable and trusty."[440] Obviously, what whites needed was lackeys rather than equal co-operators; they highly praised slavery, just because it guaranteed white men's domination and supremacy. When they felt content with the situation, they naturally thought slaves were also content. One Virginian said: "I have seen slavery in every Southern State, and I am convinced that for the slave it is the best condition in every way that has been devised."[441] Once discontented, however, they would point out how miserable freedmen were. Still in the state of moral freedom, whites did not intend regret the fact that they had enslaved another race for hundreds of years. Thus there is no reason to suspect any hypocrisy or self-deception in the "strong conviction" of Henry W. Ravenel "that the old relation of master & slave, had received the divine sanction & was the best condition in which the two races could live together for mutual benefit."[442] They did not hope to introspect and apologize. "Sir," George A. Trenholm proudly told the chamber of commerce of Augusta, Georgia, "we have educated them. We took them barbarians, we returned them christianized and civilized to those from whom we received; we paid for them, we return them without compensation. Our consciences are clear, our hands are clean."[443]

Whites had not changed their basic idea that blacks were semi-human and semibeasts. They believed that when blacks began to seek their liberty and became "indocile," their beast nature would become stronger. After the war, the tender feelings of paternalism subsided and hate began to grow vigorously. A Georgia white man said:

> Before, they considered him as a gentle animal that they would take care of for his services; at least that was my feeling and I think it was the feeling generally among the people where I was raised. Now, in place of that kindly feeling of the master, there is a feeling of bitterness, a feeling that the negro is a sort of instinctive enemy of ours. And I do not think that feeling leaves the mind in a condition to treat him as kindly as the white man would be treated under similar circumstances.[444]

Slavery was not only an economic system, but also a means of social control, in which docile laborers were provided for the plantation economy, and whites' domination and their sense of security were ensured. If the disintegration of slavery had to be accepted as a fact, a substitute system must be found.

In the long history of slavery, domination or sadism had become routine among Southern whites. Emancipation did not change this, but was aggravated by white men's uneasiness. Carl Schurz summed the matter up:

> wherever I go—the street, the shop, the house, the hotel, or the steamboat—I hear the people talk in such a way as to indicate that they are yet unable to conceive of the Negro as possessing any rights at all. Men who are honorable in their dealings with their white neighbors, will cheat a Negro without feeling a single twinge of their honor. To kill a Negro, they do not deem murder; to debauch a Negro woman, they do not think fornication; to take the property away from a Negro, they do not consider robbery. The people boast that when they get freedmen's affairs in their own hands, to use their own expressions, the niggers will catch hell.[445]

In fact, the idea that blacks served the white race was particularly popular after the war. As New Orleans liberal writer George W. Cable pointed out, "He still served, we still ruled, all need of holding him in private bondage was disproved. Emancipation had destroyed private, but it had not disturbed, subjugation. The ex-slave was not a free man; he was only a free Negro."[446] "The whites," Schurz said, "esteem the blacks their property by natural right, and however much they admit that the individual relations of masters and slaves have been destroyed by the war and by the President's emancipation proclamation, they still have an ingrained feeling that the blacks at large belong to the whites at large."[447] If personal domination had became impractical, whites now yearned for the social control of blacks.

The idea that blacks belonged to every white to some extent bridged the prewar differences between slaveholder and farmer, and it was possible to transform the pro-slavery sentiments of the latter into support for the planter class. Although a poor white's livelihood was no better, or even worse, than that of a slave, he was after all a white man and was free. After emancipation, there was only one difference left, and poor whites might be confronted with competition from blacks. Hence stressing racial differences, consolidating white men's self-consciousness, and maintaining racial supremacy became a practical choice. Thus poor whites could not see their common interests with blacks as a lower class dominated politically and exploited economically by the upper groups. During the war, poor whites strongly opposed the conscription and tax policy of the Confederacy. Many deserted battlefronts and squatted in the abandoned land as blacks did. In Mississippi, "refugees from the hills are flocking in & setting all the vacant places."[448] Many poor whites expressed their hope for reform. A fifty-year-old poor white named Elijah of Virginia said optimistically: "I reckon thar's go'n' to be a better chance for the poo' man after this. The Union be in' held together was the greatest thing that could have happened for us."[449] While looking forward to social change, they nevertheless did not want to unite with blacks. At the same time, it was difficult for them to achieve something in isolation. Racism had driven a wedge between the two low strata. Elijah said in addition: "I'm no friend to the niggers. They ought all to be druv out of the county."[450] Making use of the poor whites' dilemma, the planter class astutely divided and demoralized the potential allies, and when necessary, even aided poor whites to retain their loyalty. In the face of the alien black element, poor whites and planters temporally united out of the racial consideration. This fact testifies to the conclusion that in a multiracial society, the consciousness of the status group is very likely to undermine the basis of class consciousness and class struggle.

Another expression of the desire for domination was that whites generally thought they had the privilege of punishing blacks. If blacks were out of their "place," it was regarded as whites' duty to lash them or inflict other physical punishments on them. "They can't be governed except with the whip," one planter declared. "Now on my plantation there wasn't much whipping, say, once a fortnight; but the negroes knew they would be whipped if they didn't behave themselves, and the fear of the lash kept them in good order."[451] Before the war, this "privilege" was limited to the slaveholding families and overseers, and, as the property of their masters, blacks were thus provided with some protection. After emancipation, however, this "privilege" was virtually extended to every white man, and the function of violence was socialized. A Mississippi official pointed out in 1871,

> As a slave, the negro was protected on account of his value; humanity went hand in hand with the interest of the owner to secure his protection, to prevent his being overworked, underfed, insufficiently clothed, or abused, or neglected when sick. But as a free man, he was deprived of all the protection which had been given to him by his value as property; he was reduced to something like the condition of a stray dog.[452]

The number of murders and personal injuries increased unexpectedly after emancipation. Many whites wished to test the prophecy as soon as possible that emancipation would lead the black race to extinction. Having experienced the initial painful shock, whites began to vent their grievances.

The disappearance of property status, however, was not the main reason for the steady escalation of violence. To resist black's independence and self-respect in home, church, field, personal behavior, and other spheres, and to make sure that blacks were in a conquered state, was the main reason for the deteriorating situation. Not intending to pursue their own supremacy, blacks were only aiming at equality before the law. Though whites privately admitted this fact, most did not try to accept or imagine the prospect that the blacks' liberty was the same as that of white men. As a Georgia editor put it,

> The different races of man, like different coins at a mint, were stamped at their true value by the Almighty in the beginning. No contact with each other, no amount of legislation or education, can convert the

negro into a white man. Until that can be done, until you can take the kinks out of his wool and make his skull thinner, until all these things and abundantly more have been done, the negro cannot claim equality with the white race.[453]

Any conduct deviating from prewar racial etiquette would provoke violent reaction. The very natural and ordinary behavior of blacks was often considered "arrogant" and "indocile," and even trifles might cause whites to burst with rage. "Now," Schurz commented,

> under the new order of things, a great many are wearing veils. This is an outrage which cannot be submitted to; the white ladies of the neighborhood agree in being indignant beyond measure. Some of them declared that whenever they meet a colored woman wearing a veil, they will tear the veil from the face.[454]

One North Carolina planter complained bitterly to a Union officer that a black soldier had "bowed to me and said good morning," insisting blacks must never address whites unless spoken to first. In Texas, a black was murdered because he "did not remove his hat," and another met the same fate because he "wouldn't give up his whiskey flask."[455] In Virginia, a white men shot a black veteran after overhearing him "boast" of his service in the Union Army.[456] In Tennessee, "an old nigger" working in a sawmill "got his head split open with an axe" for having "sassed" a white man.[457]

When blacks emphasized that their liberties would not allow encroachment by others, whites produced an atmosphere of terror for the sake of social control. Trying to leave the plantation, asking for higher salaries or better working conditions, not working in the expected way, and resisting white men's punishment could provoke disaster. "The fact is," a Freedmen's Bureau officer in North Carolina reported, "it's the first notion with a great many of these people, if a Negro says anything or does anything that they don't like, to take a gun and put a bullet into him, or a charge of shot."[458] In Georgia, freedman James Jeter was beaten "for claiming the right of whipping his own child instead of allowing his employer and former master to do so."[459] In North Carolina, a white woman killed a black mother who had tried to rescue her child from a severe beating. In Alabama, a planter found himself embroiled in a controversy with one of his former slaves over the ownership of a horse left behind by the Yankees. The evidence clearly favored the freedman's claim, but the planter threatened him with death: "A nigger has no use for a horse like that, I just put my Spencer to Sip's head, and told him if he pestered me any more about the horse, I'd kill him."[460] In Clarendon, South Carolina, six freedmen left the plantation to express their discontent with the overseer. The overseer and his neighbors used hounds to besiege them, with one being shot dead, and the others hanged.[461]

Shooting and whipping were only two ordinary punishments. Whites invented many cruel torments in the name of restraining blacks' savagery and depravity. Various atrocities were committed, including mutilating arms and legs, cutting off ears, pulling out the viscera, castrating men, roasting "criminals" on the stake, drowning offenders in the river, and the brutal rape of black females. A Freedmen's Bureau officer reported that in Mississippi "the negro was murdered, beheaded, skinned, and his skin nailed to the barn."[462] In Caldwell County, Texas, it became common each morning to see blacks hanging from trees by their necks, thumbs, or toes. Although "gentleman" and "ladies" tended to deplore the excesses, many remained aloof and indifferent. "This class is ashamed of such outrages," said a Freedmen's Bureau officer, "but it does not prevent them, and it does not take them to heart and I could name a dozen cases of murder committed on the colored people by young men of these first families."[463]

Some violence on blacks was inflicted by individuals, but much was well organized, anticipating the Klan-type groups that would spread so quickly during Congressional Reconstruction. During the war, many affairs were in a state of anarchy, with the civil law practically abandoned, and guerrilla bands haunting here and there. Having grown up in these disorganized years, thousands of idle young men and boys found themselves unable or unwilling to attend school or secure employment in the initial years after the war. They sauntered up and down, always longing for some exciting incidents to break the monotony of their existence. It is estimated that at least two-thirds of the racial conflicts in this period were instigated or carried out by these young men and boys.[464]

The same difficult adjustment was required for Confederate veterans. Contrasted with the warm welcomes given to Northern demobilized soldiers, their Southern counterparts faced a confused world. To these veterans familiar with collective massacres in the battlefields, it was easy to join the restless forces. In the circumstances, it had become the regular practice to carry a pistol in one's belt as a necessary ornament. Big cities partially avoided this practice, but in towns and villages almost everyone wore one. Frontier customs were revived, including personal vengeance and the duel. Awe-inspiring vigilantes supervised the "unruly" freedmen, returning them to their former masters. These phenomena were especially popular in frontier states such as Arkansas, Mississippi, and Texas, but the Atlantic coast areas, where communities were established a century before, were also influenced. Gradually, these vigilantes organized secret societies in nearly every county with the avowed purpose of compelling blacks to their place. The old control system characterized by its personal authority was now socialized. As a Freedmen's Bureau officer in Mississippi reported, "The fear of a class of citizens calling themselves regulators, in some localities, is so great that peaceable citizens who are disposed to restore order and quiet are afraid to give the necessary information to secure the punishment of these men. These regulators shoot freedmen without provocation, drive them from plantations without pay, and commit other crimes."[465] In addition to the "regulators," there were also so-called "reformers," "moderators," "rangers," and "nigger killers." Any freedman who violated racial customs would be flogged or killed. If Union soldiers temporarily prevented retaliation, violators were warned that the Yankees would not be there to shield them forever.[466] A Southern banker offered this advice to the Yankees: "never in this country interfere in behalf of a nigger." [467]

In order to mobilize the white masses to take coordinated action and realize their common interests, whites often made use of the rumor of black insurrection and created a mounting wave of terror. With the approach of Christmas in 1865, the rumor that blacks were prepared for a general insurrection spread throughout many Southern states. Influenced by the general fear, Mississippi Governor Benjamin Humphreys ordered the state militia to patrol roads and search black cabins for arms.[468] Even the President was disturbed, ordering Major General James B. Steedmen to "keep a vigilant watch upon this subject and at once suppress any and all moves of an insurrectionary character."[469] Although no evidence was found, similar incidents occurred in South Carolina and Georgia, and the same rumor spread in 1866 and 1867. "No man lives now at his ease," a resident of Rockingham, North Carolina, confessed. "When he lies down at night, although his door and windows are locked and bolted, he put his gun and pistol, in readiness, not knowing at what hour he may be called upon to use them."[470] On the one hand, this worry betrayed whites' "blackphobia"; on the other hand, the possibility of propaganda could not be ruled out. For example, according to Clinton B. Fisk, a black man shooting squirrels in the woods inspired the rumor that hundreds of armed blacks were intending to "rise en masse and kill of the white people." [471] All the same, the important function of rumor could not be denied. If blacks were a menace, then to let them know their place was decisive. In other words, it was important to arouse whites' vigilant consciousness and maintain the spirit of racial solidarity. Then insurrection was a necessary means to the end of white supremacy rather than a practical action of blacks. Through the rumor whites might convey a sign that the situation had been out of control, and that all whites should gather together under their common banner. Just like a real outside menace, a fabricated one could also consolidate the white race, with their status differences transcended. By channeling the animosity towards a feeble object, a new militant spirit was born.

The same function was performed by the Southern "super taboo" racial amalgamation. The fear of surprise uprisings was a result of injustice inflicted on blacks, while the fear of miscegenation was the inner phobia of whites' self-consciousness about losing themselves. It was the deepest anxiety, an impassable psychological barrier, and the fierce reaction to the provocation of sexual monopoly in a world dominated by white males. If a black was really considered as a higher beast "like a dark, a chicken, or a mule," whites understandably never wanted to see the dreadful prospect of "the mongrelization of the race." In that event, one Southern Carolinian declared, "we shall become a race of mulattoes, another Mexico; we shall be ruled out from the family of white nations. It a matter of life and death with the Southern people to keep their blood pure." [472] They believed that racial miscegenation would inevitably give rise to an race even inferior to blacks themselves, and the mulattos would not live long, just as a mule hybridized by horse and donkey would soon become extinct because it could not reproduce any offspring or would bear inferior ones. [473] If blacks wanted to build mixed schools, the logic followed was that "to the ignorant and brutal young Negro, it signifies but one thing: the privilege of cohabiting with white women." [474] Even in segregated schools, the social relations between black students and their white teachers, who were usually unmarried white women, was considered shocking. [475] The inevitable progression was allegedly that incidental contact at school would lead to social contact outside, which in turn would give rise to mixed marriages and inferior children. Although most mulattos were the offspring of white masters and their female slaves, white people often turned a blind eye to this fact, for this conduct was considered the privilege of white males. White men were concerned with the purity of their white women, their sexual monopoly on white women, and not limitations on white men themselves.

The corresponding theme was the menace posed by black males. Thus the endless fear of mixed marriage was mingled with the myth of black rape. The legend about the supersexual capabilities of blacks still circulated among Southern white people. With emancipation having removed restraints on blacks, the alleged black men's covetousness of white women now became an active fear. This threat presented a more dreadful picture than mixed marriage did, and the excitement of Southern whites on this question was great. In actual fact, because the end of slavery decreased contact between the races, cases of miscegenation became less and less. An exception was that in some areas, the number of white women who accepted blacks as their partners increased slightly as a result of the high death-toll of white males in the war.[476] Cases involving black rape were still rarer. As the astute observer William J. Cash remarked, a Southern white woman had less chance of being raped by a Negro than that of being struck by lightning.[477] To the allegation that black males were drooling with envy over the daughters and sisters of white men, Henry M. Turner retorted,

> What do we want with their daughters and sisters? We have as much beauty as they. Look at our ladies, do you want more beauty than they? The difficulty heretofore has been, our ladies were not always at our own disposal. All we ask of the white men is to let our ladies alone, and they need not fear us.[478]

The problem was that white people sincerely believed or encouraged themselves to believe in the increasing cases of black assault. If this kind of accident actually occurred, whites would indulge in unbridled propaganda and magnify the true danger. If a black was suspected of this conduct, he would not be let off easily. As a matter of fact, extremely cruel tortures like mutilation of sex organs and lynching were meted out in the name of defending the purity of white women. A black of Vktibbeha County, Mississippi, for instance, was suspected of the rape of a white woman in 1865. Upon the receipt of a payment of two hundred dollars, the captain of a Federal troop stationed in the county allowed the black to be run to death by hounds.[479] The struggle against "racial amalgamation" on the one hand reflected the inner anxiety of white people, on the other hand, it effectively performed the dual function of personal conformity and social control. By this means, the upper class could both divert the attention of a lower strata thirsty for social reform and intimidate blacks discontented with the status quo.

Compared with ordinary whites, planters retained great influence over social affairs, though their number was small. The war had sapped their vitality and brought about changes in social status, and some planters could not manage to survive in the new environment. But the large estates remained, with a growing tendency to consolidation. Concerning the increase in the concentration of landownership in Louisiana, Roger Shugg pointed out that

> Between 1860 and 1870 there was nearly a threefold increase in the number of [large landholdings] while the number of [owner-operated] farms decreased. The tendency of the larger properties to outstrip the smaller was strong between 1860 and 1873, and was only partially counteracted in the later years of reconstruction.[480]

As land was the most important source of power as well as the most important capital in an agricultural society, the planter class retained their prestige as before. Generally speaking, almost every white had his strong self-consciousness, but those having the strongest motivation for racial hatred ought to be those whose interests had the most conflict with those of blacks. In reality, it was the Southern upper class in the black belt that depended on the dependence of blacks more than any other classes did. They had the necessary influence and ruling experiences as well as the practical aim of controlling blacks. At the same time, though the lower strata had a tendency to animosity, they were mostly scattered in the mountain areas and strongly looked forward to change. To suppress this poor class, it was necessary to advocate white superiority and to intensify the vigilant consciousness of whites.

Like other whites, the planters' foremost priority was to maintain white supremacy, which coincided with another basic aim of keeping a faithful labor class. Although they had yielded to the contract system, planters tried to reconstruct their authority over freedmen within this new framework. Laborers must render "perfect obedience" to the employer and remain "hardworking and faithful." On the Heyward plantation in South Carolina, laborers had to recognize the "lawful authority" of the employer and his agents, and agree to conduct themselves "in such manner as to gain the good will of those to whom we must always look for protection."[481] Some employers even required laborers to obey orders "strictly as my slaves" and address them as "master." Most contracts prohibited blacks from possessing "deadly weapons," or "ardent spirits." In some cases, freedmen had to submit to punishment for contract violations, with "our employer being the judge whether we are to be punished or turned off."[482] Employers were usually stipulated as the arbitrators of labor disputes, having the right to forfeit all or parts of wage or crop share. They generally had the right to enter black cabins at any time, and might prohibit freedmen from receiving visitors, holding meetings, or leaving the plantation. If the question of supremacy was settled, they fully understood, everything else would go well.

Most contracts did not specify corporal punishment for offenses, otherwise a Bureau official would disallow the agreement. In fact, however, it was still practiced rather generally. A planter summarized the viewpoint of his class clearly:

> Northern laborers are like other men, [but] southern laborers are nothing but niggers, and you can't make anything else out of them. They're not controlled by the same motives as white men, and unless you have power to compel them they'll only work when they can't beg or steal enough to keep from starving.[483]

Planters always thought that freedmen would not work on their own initiative. "I have come to the conclusion," said a Louisiana sugar planter, "that the great secret of our success was the great motives power contained in that little instrument."[484] In addition to corporal punishment, planters also allied themselves to cut wages and limit labor mobility. The habitual practice was to list the names of disobedient laborers in newspapers and then boycott them when making a contract. When the freedmen in Fredericksburg, Virginia, defected in large numbers and demanded higher wages, white residents responded by agreeing among themselves not to employ any of them. After one white broke the pact, "the gentlemen of the town" warned him immediately that he was establishing a dangerous precedent and violating the laws of Virginia, and that his action would mark him as a traitor to the state.[485]

Planters soon realized that their capability for labor control to a large extent depended on whites' monopoly on the land, the most important economic resource at that time. Even if a few freedmen became independent farmers, the strict discipline on plantations might be badly corroded. Just as free blacks had been for slaves before the war, the successive freedmen were the external temptation for an immobile and obedient employee. The threat to planters' control over employment would in turn weaken the superior status of white men. As William H. Trescot said, "It will be utterly impossible for the owner to find laborers that will work contentedly for wages alongside of these free colonies."[486] What planters wished for was to dispel the freedmen's idea "up to the ladder," take away a straw to clutch at, and force them to surrender without a struggle. To destroy the freedmen's capacity for independence, planters united to prevent freedmen from buying and leasing land. They also made use of the poor white's fear of competition, agitating them to adopt "necessary" violence. Blacks therefore had to stay at their lowest place and "content" themselves with their labor status.

In short, a tendency of white Reconstruction after the war was that, since the former system of absolute personal authority was disintegrating, and the white men's superior status was challenged, the white elite had to take up the gauntlet to adjust themselves to the reality and build a tight social system of impersonal authority by fully making use of economic means, mobilizing all sorts of social forces, and maintaining the white line on the basis of white self-consciousness. In order to maintain the racial conquered state, they stopped at nothing and tried to create the impression that black liberty would lead to danger. At the same time, however, they needed blacks economically and psychologically. So long as blacks remained obedient and "contented" with the conquered state, whites might leave them some space for existence and even provide them with some protection; in other words, some tender feelings might be poured into the container of absolute authority. This contradictory mentality based on whites' self-consciousness and the dual tactic of wielding threats and promises constituted the basis of blacks' contradictory choice between freedom and safety. As a result, blacks were tied in invisible fetters.

LOCAL AUTONOMY AND AFRICAN
AMERICAN CIVIL RIGHTS

According to the official view, Reconstruction issues were not black issues or civil rights issues, but the Constitutional ones caused by the states trying to secede from the United States. The fundamental aim of the war was consistently defined as follows: "this war is not waged [for the] purpose of overthrowing or interfering with the established institution of those states, but to maintain the states unimpaired; and that as soon as these objects are accomplished the war ought to cease."[487] To promote liberty and equality, however, had obviously become the practical aim of the war. When peace had come, how to deal with the basic goal of federal restoration and the moral goal that derived from the former was still a thorny matter. Congress and the president's emphases deeply affected the process of Reconstruction.

For President Johnson, who was just coming to power, there were few places for blacks in the process of Southern Reconstruction in spite of his ambiguous stand at first. Radical Senator Ben Wade once praised him: "Johnson, we have faith in you. By the gods, there will be no trouble now in running the government."[488] Concerning Southern secessionists, the president consistently stressed, "Treason must be made infamous and traitors must be impoverished."[489] Even on the sensitive matter of black suffrage, Radicals were still filled with exultation. According to Charles Sumner, at a private meeting the president said, "on this question [suffrage] there is no difference between us; you and I are alike."[490] When walking away that evening, Sumner assured himself that the battle of his life would be crowned with success. Writing to Lieber on May 2, 1865, he quoted Johnson as saying that "colored persons are to have the right to suffrage; that no state can be precipitated into the Union; that rebel states must go through a term of probation. All this he had said to me before. Ten days ago Chief Justice [Salmon Chase] and myself visited him in the evening to speak of these things. I was charmed by his sympathy, which was entirely different from his predecessor's."[491]

The Radicals pinned great hopes on Johnson until May 1865. In fact, however, Johnson had never promised black political equality to the Radicals. In antebellum Tennessee, he had never been famous for having an antislavery standpoint. In reality he identified with this peculiar institution and owned five slaves. Yet he was not satisfied with slavery, for could it lead to miscegenation and its benefit was monopolized by slaveholding oligarchies rather than Southern common people. He once said: "I wish to God every head of a family in the United States had one slave to take the drudgery and menial service off this family."[492] As a benevolent master, he occasionally spoke sarcastically about the black: "You won't get rid of the Negro except by holding him in slavery."[493] At the 36th Congress, he vehemently presented his view that if Abolitionists freed slaves and let them loose on the South, "the non-slaveholder would join with the slave-owner and extirpate them," and "If one should be more ready to join than another it would be myself."[494] As the military governor in Tennessee, however, he observed that the war would end slavery and gradually adopted a realistic attitude towards its death, hoping that this development would eliminate an unstable factor from the country. On June 10, he declared, "I am for emancipation for two reasons: First, because it is right in itself; and second, because in the emancipation of the slaves, we break down an odious and dangerous aristocracy."[495] When charged with advocating racial equality, he provided the following explanation: "Damn the Negroes, I am fighting those traitorous aristocrats, their masters."[496] Like other Southern whites, he never tried to include blacks in his democratic tenets. As a Southern constituent said, "I have grounds to fear President Johnson may hold almost unconquerable prejudices against the African race."[497]

Though he might have had no personal prejudice, Johnson did not intend to confer franchise to blacks directly for fear of infuriating Southern whites. As a white Southerner, he was especially familiar with the racial sentiments of the South. He once said,

> While I say that I am a friend of the colored man, I do not want to adopt
> a policy that I believe will end in a contest between the races, which
> if persisted in will result in the extermination of one or the other.
> God forbid that I should be engaged in such a work![498]

So he persistently thought that emigration or separate black communities were the best solution for black emancipation. Afterwards he realized this plan was impractical and agreed to begin a experiment of "integration and assimilation." But at present, he only wanted "to begin the work of preparation."[499]

Such being the case, why did the Radicals misunderstand Johnson? This can be partly attributed to his weakness of character, and partly to the carelessness of the Radicals. Despite his unbending natural disposition, Johnson always spoke so ambiguously as to be barely intelligible before making a decision, and even those he disagreed with were easily under the impression that the president supported them. Gideon Wells, Johnson's Secretary of the Navy, observed that "it has been the misfortune, the weakness, the great error of the President to delay, hesitate before acting."[500] Once taking a firm stand, however, no one could be firmer than he, with his action characterized by rigidity and loyalty to his paramount principles. This fault was further aggravated by his poor communication abilities. Unsociable and eccentric, Johnson had few confidential friends. Gideon Wells accurately pointed out that "he has no confidants and seeks none," and his major decisions appeared to have been made without consultation with "anyone whatever."[501] His predecessor, Lincoln, on the other hand, would never make such a mistake, and he pressed the rightness of his view and worked behind the scenes to seek the necessary support. In the first months after he attained power,

Johnson was not quite sure how to deal with Southern affairs, and he did not intend to drive away any possible ally. So it was understandable that he spoke evasively. At the same time, as a representative rising from the lower classes in the mountain area, Johnson was still hostile to the planter class, and this stand was the basis on which the Radicals identified with him. Yet the Radicals overestimated Johnson's promises. For Johnson, even if he could provide all sorts of "possible facilities," Reconstruction could be done only by Southerners themselves. He said he was not willing to execute any "tyrannical" power.[502]

Here the problem of federalism was involved. To Johnson, the paramount goal of Reconstruction was to restore Southern states to the Union as soon as possible, to which all other questions were subordinate. As a defender of states' rights, Johnson consistently believed in limited federal government and the strict structure of the Constitution, and felt extremely anxious about the expansion of federal power during the war. His strong federalism made him dare to fly his own colors in the crisis of secession, but his loyalty to the Union did not contrast with his respect for state rights, which did not include the right to secession. What he loved was a unified federation that had the least federal power and protected the states' rights. In order to achieve this aim, he did not spare any necessary use of federal power, as he proved in Tennessee when he was a military governor. He declared: "Suppose you do violate law, if by so doing you restore the law and the constitution, your conscience will approve your course, and all the people will say, amen!"[503]

On the problem of Southern Reconstruction, Johnson was also confronted with the paradox of power brought by the war. On the one hand, he was eager to restore the normal balance of power; on the other hand, he had to continue using the unusual presidential power under the state of emergency. If he did put forward some requirements for Southern restoration, did it mean that the seceded states had sacrificed some accustomed rights? How was the result of the war to be guaranteed? The second choice was obviously impractical, and the sensible way only questioned how far the Union exercised its authority and who should do it, the president or Congress. The president believed that it was within his war powers as commander-in-chief of the army and navy. Based on this presumption, he could establish any appropriate law and then withdraw it as he saw fit. A fact favorable to the president was that the Congress was adjourned, and the president could list prerequisites at his own will. Yet while he did so, Johnson tried to touch on lightly the *fact* of violation done by him. Unable to secede from the Union, according to his explanation in 1861, the states were indestructible and still existed, and could not give up their autonomous rights.[504] In his report about the status of Southern states in December, this viewpoint was stressed again. Johnson here held that a state could not secede, but by their attempt to secede, states "placed themselves in a condition where their vitality was impaired, but not extinguished their functions suspended, but not destroyed."[505] Johnson had never directly declared whether or not he had power to impose conditions, and he only did so without publicity, avoiding any impression of his exercising "tyrannical" power and any action Congress might oppose.

Turning to Lincoln's cabinet to learn what plan his predecessor had made, Johnson knew that Secretary of War Stanton had proposed an occupation program. On the day after the assassination, April 16, the cabinet briefly discussed the revised plan. At night, a few influential Republicans, including Stanton, exchanged their opinions over the program. Everyone agreed that military occupation could not last forever, but they disagreed on how to restore local governments. With the help of his friends, Stanton designated the duties of the military governors as organizing the elections for constitutional conventions. Once the constitutions were changed, Southern states would elect their officials under the new constitutions. Then they debated about who should be allowed to elect the delegates to constitutional conventions. After long hours of dispute, Stanton proposed that all men, including blacks, be allowed to participate. On May 9, Johnson submitted Stanton's program to the cabinet, and black suffrage soon became the main portion of dissension. After several days' arguments, the members of the cabinet were evenly split on this problem (their most important member, Secretary of State Seward, was absent).

Johnson did not say a word in the whole process. Yet on the day the cabinet cast the vote, he recognized the four governments Lincoln had formed in Arkansas, Louisiana, Tennessee, and Virginia, with none adopting black suffrage. The logic conclusion of this action was that Johnson attributed suffrage as the exclusive rights of Southern states. Since these states were recognized by his predecessor, however, his view was still not clear and definite.

On May 29, Johnson issued two proclamations embodying his plan for Reconstruction. The Amnesty Proclamation followed Lincoln's wartime policy of offering amnesty to those who might take an oath to the Constitution of the United States, the Union of the states, and emancipation. The proclamation listed fourteen kinds of persons who would have to apply directly to Johnson for a presidential pardon. The North

Carolina Proclamation outlined the process by which this state could establish its government. He chose William H. Holden as the provisional governor of the state, whose duty was to arrange a constitutional convention, "for the purpose of altering or amending the constitution thereof," with the authority to "enable such loyal people of the State of North Carolina to restore said State to its constitutional relation to the Federal Government and to present such a republican form of State government."[506] Any person who had not been pardoned under the Amnesty Proclamation could not be allowed to elect delegates to the constitution convention, and the qualifications of electors were decided according to the stipulations existing before 1861. Thus, Johnson roughly adopted the Stanton pragram, with one critical exception: only whites could vote by ballot. If Johnson's stand was still ambiguous when recognizing the four state governments established by Lincoln, the North Carolina Proclamation definitely excluded blacks from the first step of reorganizing the governments.

All the same, there was still a cloud of suspicion over whether or not the president intended to impose black suffrage on the constitutional conventions. When receiving a white delegation from South Carolina in June, Johnson disclosed that he worried that former slaveholders would manipulate the vote to cope with poor whites if black suffrage was practiced.

> Let us speak plainly on this subject. I, too am a Southern man, have owned slaves, bought slaves, but never sold one. You and I understand this better; we know our friends are mistaken, and I tell you that I don't want you to have the control of these negro votes against the vote of this poor white man. I repeat our friends here are mistaken, as you and I know as to where the control of negro vote would fall. When they come to talk about the elective franchise, I say let each State judge for itself. I am for free government; for emancipation; and am for emancipating the white man as well as the black man.[507]

No doubt, this standpoint was a refurbished version of his former opinion that "The colored man and his master combined kept [the poor white] in slavery by depriving him of a fair participation in the labor and productions of the rich land of the country."[508] Nevertheless, provided that black suffrage was controlled by white Southerners themselves, Johnson seemed not adamantly opposed to it, in spite of his lack of moral enthusiasm. In this month, Secretary of the Navy Gideon Wells reassured

Charles Sumner that there was not "on the part of the President or his advisers any opposition to most liberal extension of the elective franchises."[509] Wells, however, was later reported in a local newspaper in Connecticut as having expressed that "President Johnson is opposed to negro suffrage, as he is opposed to forcing negro voting upon the South."[510] The Republicans in this state was shocked and asked Wells to clarify the fact, but Wells avoided making a reply.

On August 14, the first constitutional convention under the Johnson plan was convened in Jackson, Mississippi, and the president's attitude was becoming clear. The next day, he wired provisional governor W. L. Sharkey to add the emancipation article to the new state constitution and recognize the Thirteenth Amendment. Then he went on:

> If you could extend the elective franchise to all persons of color who can read the Constitution of the United States in English and write their names, and to all persons of color who own real estate valued at not less than two hundred and forty dollars, and pay taxes thereon, you would completely disarm the adversary and set an example the other states will follow. I hope and trust your convention will do this, and, as a consequence, the Radicals, who are wild upon Negro franchise, will be completely foiled in their attempt to keep the Southern States from renewing their relations to the Union by not accepting their senators and representatives.[511]

From the way in which he spoke about the matter, it could be gathered that black franchise was not a demand of the president, but the most suitable tactic the South might adopt. This stand arose neither out of any moral concern, nor as an fruit of Union victory that transcended state rights. On August 20, Sharkey wired back that the convention would abolish slavery, but the right to witness and suffrage perhaps would be left to the state legislatures. "I am much gratified to hear of your proceedings being so favorable," President Johnson replied with satisfaction the next day, without mentioning black suffrage at all.[512]

In the report about the status of Southern states in December, Johnson still stressed the historical and legal bases of the states' control of suffrage. But under this prerequisite, Johnson soon showed his new flexibility. On January 28, 1866, when meeting with his supporter, Republican Senator James Dixon, the president mentioned the Constitutional amendment that the Reconstruction Committee was considering. Johnson thought that any amendment at present was dubious and unnecessary and would diminish respect for the Constitution itself. If any amendment was to be made, he knew of none better than the simple proposal that representation be based on the number of voters, whose qualifications depended on the direct taxation of property. Such an amendment "would remove from Congress all issues in reference to the political equality of the races," and leave the states to the absolute determination of "qualification of their own voters with regard to color."[513] Thus, Johnson involuntarily approved an amendment proposal that would put white Southerners in a difficult dilemma between reduced representation and the extended franchise. What embarrassed the president was that an amendment submitted by Samuel Shellabarger along the lines suggested by Johnson garnered only twenty-nine votes in the House.[514] Though he was not absolutely opposed to congressional power imposing conditions, Johnson's concessions were very limited. When Republicans sought other proposals, his original wavering attitude became uncompromising.

On the issue of black testimony in court, Johnson also provided advice, fortunately being more definite than on the suffrage question. On August 16, 1865, the newly elected governor of Mississippi Benjamin G. Humphreys wired the president that the legislature seemed to be willing to admit black testimony, provided that the Union Army withdrew. In addition, they were also worried that one concession was inevitably followed by another, whereupon the new governor asked what promises he could make to allay their fears. The president replied the next day:

> There can be no other or greater assurance given than has heretofore been on the part of the people of Mississippi or the Legislature, other than a loyal compliance with the laws and Constitution of the United States, and the adoption of such measures giving protection to all freedmen, or freemen, in person and property without regard to colors, as will entitle them to resume all their constitutional relations in the Federal Union.[515]

While he refused to promise to withdraw the army, Johnson emphasized that his words were friendly advice rather than a command. On the advice of President Johnson, provisional governor Sharkey declared in September that black testimony must be admitted in all cases involving black interests.[516] The legislators, however, hesitated to specify this right in legislation even in places where black testimony had already been accepted. Despite his pressure in the case of Mississippi, the president responded delicately when confronted with Southern protests. In Alabama, provisional governor Lewis E. Parsons and Bureau officer Wager Swayne all tried to formulate a systematic law allowing black testimony. In September, Parsons asked the president twice for advice only to receive no reply. Only when the constitutional convention was adjourned did Johnson send a congratulatory telegram. In November, Tennessee gave out similar appeals, and this time the president expressed his view that "black testimony would save infinite trouble," so great was "the enthusiasm you have kindled among the people." On December 9, he said again, "the subject of negro testimony, in all cases where they are parties, would be conclusive."[517]

On these questions, Johnson tried to avoid making the impression of forcing conditions on Southerners. When receiving a black delegation in February 1866, Johnson expounded again the basis of his policies. He underlined that the imposition of black suffrage would violate the principles of white autonomy, and asked, "Do you deny that first great principle of the right of the people to govern themselves? Will you resort to an arbitrary power, and say a majority of the people shall receive a state of things they are opposed to?"[518] Bypassing his own racism, Johnson's grievance touched the complicated nature of black issues. The helplessness blacks and the widespread racism of whites made it extremely difficult to realize racial equality, which required that blacks be specially protected and whites specially constrained. But these actions would contradict the principle of federalism and majority rule. As Johnson put it, it was "whether we shall not let the people in the States decide the matter for themselves."[519] Furthermore, since black people were discriminated against because of class as well as race, the realization of racial equality would inevitably be followed by great social changes, and social changes would inevitably bring about radical reactions from whites and "a war of races," therefore leaving Johnson's plan in a vulnerable position. If a commonwealth excluded a large number of citizens from participating in its affairs, however, how would American democratic creeds be fulfilled? If the people had the right to decide their own affairs, was it reasonable that blacks were dependent on others to decide their affairs? Johnson had little courage and willingness to face these problems. He took the easy way and supported white autonomy. Though he was beyond reproach in his use of presidential power, Johnson underestimated the moral potential stimulated by the war, and let slip the opportunities for use of his administrative power, at least by seeking a better balance between federalism and idealism in a changing situation.

Johnson still used the "arbitrary power" on a critical point concerning the black interests. When the constitutional convention of Mississippi was convoked in the summer of 1865, Johnson stated that the abolition of slavery was an absolute requirement the South must concede.[520] When the constitutional conventions of other states were summoned in the fall, Johnson suggested again that the recognition of the Thirteenth Amendment was one condition of their restoration.[521] Although slavery had been irredeemably killed and Southern whites had to face this fact, they were still afraid that this Amendment empowered the Congress to interfere in the status of freedmen. The president was especially careful on this point. Despite his willingness to recognize the perpetuity of freedom, Johnson was vigilant about any possible expansion of congressional power. Even though he had not personally clarified the suspicion created by the Thirteenth Amendment, his secretary of state, William H. Seward, replied to Southern inquiries in a letter on November 6 to B. J. Perry, the provisional governor of South Carolina. "The objection you mention to the last clause of the constitutional amendment is regarded as querulous and unreasonable, because that clause is really restraining in its effect, instead of enlarging the power of Congress."[522] Therefore, South Carolina recognized the amendment on the condition that Congress had no power to interfere in the status of freedmen. Mississippi, Alabama, and Florida also had similar prerequisites.[523] Southerners went much further than the president did as regards resisting the interference of congressional power.

To encourage Southerners to guarantee the minimum rights connected with freedom, and at the same time to avoid the definite recognition of black citizens' status, Johnson circumscribed his policy concerning blacks, the gist of which is embodied in his talk of January 1864:

> The Negro will be thrown upon society, governed by the same laws that govern communities, and be compelled to fall back upon his own resources, as all other human beings are. Political freedom means liberty to work, and at the same time enjoy the products of one's labor. If he can rise by his own energies, in the name of God, let him rise. In saying this, I do not argue that the Negro race is equal to the Anglo-Saxon. If the Negro is better fitted for the inferior condition of society, the laws of nature will assign him there![524]

White Southerners had to admit black's personal freedom, their right to property, and their right to existence related to emancipation, but the right to testimony and limited suffrage depended on white Southerners' own willingness. When confronted with the contradiction between local autonomy and civil rights and between the fundamental war goal and the moral one, Johnson chose the former. Generally speaking, blacks' civil rights did not occupy any important place in Johnson's Reconstruction plan. Except for the supreme goal federal restoration, Johnson's personal objectives, to which black issues were subordinate, were to punish the planter class and establish a political force loyal to him.

Some scholars studying Reconstruction doubt whether Johnson's aim in Reconstruction was to punish the planter class, without satisfactorily explaining why he changed his tune on that matter. In my opinion, this was an integral part of his personal dual objective. What Johnson concerned himself with was that "white men alone must manage the South" and which white men would do so. To punish the planter class was the base on which Radicals temporarily cooperated with him, but they separated and went their own way as soon as they realized that there was no place for blacks in his plan. Meanwhile, Johnson had always defined himself as a spokesman for the Southern yeomanry, and it was normally difficult for him to change that stand. For most of his political career, Johnson consistently waved flags and shouted battle cries for the welfare of the yeomen. In Tennessee, his most successful political action was to demand a public school system based on taxation. In national politics, as a Senator he made unremitting efforts to submit homestead proposals and acquire Western land for white laborers, in the hope of creating an independent farmer class of large numbers. In this campaign, he often presented his view vehemently: "I do not look upon the growth of cities and the accumulation of population around the cities as being the most desirable objects in this country . . . Let us try to prevent their further accumulation. I want no miserable city rabble on the one hand; I want no pampered, bloated, corrupt aristocracy on the other; I want the middle portion of society to be built up and sustained."[525] On the one hand, he was opposed to the power monopoly of the planter class, thinking that this class had put yeomen in a miserable condition by exploiting public resources and blacks and by dragging them into the trouble of secession and war; on the other hand, he could not accept Northern financial monopoly, either, for he was disgusted with any form of "aristocracy." As a spokesman for the common people, he believed that a democratic regime must transcend the monopoly of the few and work for the welfare of the whole people. All his words and deeds were based on his populism. Upon coming to power, he found that history had provided him with a golden opportunity to foster the "middle portion of the society" and resist the expansion of oligarchy, by which he could realize his lifelong dream for reform. He revised the Reconstruction plan of his predecessor, and in fact stealthily substituted his objective for that of Lincoln. In the Amnesty Proclamation of May 29, the upper classes of the Confederacy were required to turn over a new leaf; otherwise they would exert no influence in the politics of Reconstruction. He spoke of the need to "punish and impoverish" the antebellum leaders of the South, break down their "social power," and remunerate the Unionists for wartime losses from the property of the "wealthy traitors."[526] "A new set of men," he insisted, "who are to vitalize and develop the Union feeling in the South" must be "brought forward,"[527] and the "great plantations must be seized and divided into small farms, and sold to honest, industrious men."[528] However, the Southern yeomen could not get rid of the control of the antebellum elite, despite their wishes for reform. By the end of 1865, under the Presidential Reconstruction plan, former Confederate leaders manipulated elections and staged a comeback. Was it suitable to admit his ideal objective had been frustrated and invite Congress to revise the process of restoration? Johnson decided to take a firm stand and maintain his dignity. Besides, Johnson increasingly found that the control of blacks could not spare the elite. From now on, his devotion to "the good of the whole human race" and "the laws of nature"[529] began to prevail in his idealism. In the initial stage, amnesties were granted rather carefully. When he found no route to retreat, however, President Johnson began to widen the scope of amnesty, and rushed to complete it before Congress convened. No longer did he cry out for punishing the rebels, but emphasized that the South had accepted the result of the war. At the same time, Johnson stopped his plan for confiscation, with his attorney general declaring that the Confiscation Act of 1862 was effective only in wartime. Johnson also revised his policy of punishing white Southerners, but there was no reason to suspect the sincerity of his initial words. He only readjusted his views to the changing reality, leaving aside blacks both at the beginning and at the end.

Whatever his ideal objective might be, Johnson was a practical statesman rather than an innocent idealist. If he could easily give up his ideal object, it was because another realistic aim was more attractive, i.e., to build up his personal influence in the South. If he could not achieve more, Johnson would rather choose this.

The death of Lincoln, who was a strong national leader, created a power vacuum, which greatly affected the political situation. As a man rising to the supreme administrative power by accident, Johnson's top priority was to foster an impression as a strong statesman. At the beginning, he was chosen by Lincoln as his campaign partner only for his symbolic function of unification and not for his representation of any major interests. To make matters worse, he embarrassed Republicans because of his drunkenness at the inaugural ceremony. Charles Sumner even felt that "the Senate should call upon him to resign."[530] The weakness of his position spurred him to build up stable supporting forces in both South and North. The power of amnesty and the choice of provisional governors were the two sharp weapons to implement his plan. A clause specifying a charge of twenty thousand dollars is especially worth mentioning. If they hoped to rally their forces, the old elite must seek special pardons from the president. This elaborate design, different from that of his predecessor, was intended to put Southerners into a trap. When Southern delegates came to beg for amnesties, it was a natural to promise political loyalty, which greatly satisfied his desire for power and his vanity. The memory of abject poverty in his early years, the political scars made on the political background, and the freezing irony and burning satire the elite gave him wounded his pride and strengthened his ardent wish for dignity. Nothing could soothe his pain more than the loyalty and respect of his old enemies. As early as June 5, 1865, Carl Schurz pointed out that

> during the summer the White House had been fairly besieged by Southern men and women of high social standing who had told the President that the only element of trouble in the South consisted of a lot of fanatical abolitionists who excited the Negroes with all sorts of dangerous notions, and that all would be well if he would only restore the Southern States' government as quickly as possible, according to his own plan as laid down in his North Carolina proclamation, and that he was a great man to whom they looked up as their savior. Now it was thought that Mr. Johnson, the plebeian who before the war had been treated with undisguised contempt by the slave-holding aristocracy, could not withstand the subtle flattery of the same aristocracy when they flocked around him as humble suppliants cajoling his vanity.[531]

At such an enchanting time, the president, who was "as dedicated a hater of the negroes as the rebels from whom he had separated,"[532] became increasingly close to the South, increasingly like a noble man defending state rights with elegant manners instead of an angry common man who loudly appealed to the public. Johnson, a hostile Republican congress-man would comment in 1866, "is no poor white trash now."[533]

A dilemma facing Johnson in establishing a political following was that since there was virtually no Southern Republican partly before the war, he had to win round the moderate Democrats, especially former Whigs and Unionists, and at the same time he must retain support of the Republican majority in the North. Without the former, Reconstruction would be a fantastic castle in the air, unless a new Republican party was built by black votes. That was, however, a minefield Johnson did not dare approach, for his racism, federalism, and political considerations of win-ning over a following could not allow him to do so. Without the latter, Johnson would desert the party which sent him to power, and earned himself the infamy of "Tylerization." How to reconcile these two con-tradictory choices? In his cabinet, the strategic perspective of Secretary of State William Seward shaped the president. In order to consolidate the Republican political position on a new basis of national unification and help the party surmount regional limitation, the conservative Repub-licans, among whom were mainly Seward and his consultant Thurlow Weed, designed an alignment that centered on conservative and moder-ate Republicans, united with local Democrats, and meanwhile isolated the Radical Republicans and copperhead Democrats. There still was, however, a Blair family who vied with Seward to establish a transdistrict conservative party. Relying on their great influence in the Democratic party and the South, the Blairs tried to establish a national conservative party that centered on Unionist Democrats and former Whigs and also absorbed conservative Republicans, urging Johnson to "dispense with the support of the Radicals."[534] Johnson adopted this strategy of alliance, but he did not intend to bear any burden. What he expected was to be-come the head of a conservative party that would revolve around presi-dential policy and include most Republicans and Democrats, and to easily win the next general election. The New York *World*, which was very supportive of the president, regarded Johnson as the indisputable leader in the evolution of the conservative party, which had two "coat-tails," of which Republicans might follow one and Democrats another; Johnson might count on the whole party, only "except the Chase-Sumner faction who don't belong to the people."[535] "The whole party," the *World*'s co-owner, Samuel L. M. Barlow commented, "is today a John-son party."[536] The inevitable result of this strategy was that he must exclude the support of Radicals in the North to win over the South. The concrete action taken to effect his was to express kindness to the South on the Freedmen's Bureau Bill and the Civil Rights Bill, and take the offensive towards the Radicals. When criticizing the Radicals, Johnson, unfortunately, did not fully take into account the requirements of moderates, and was rather insensitive to the change of Northern public sentiments. He was confident that the impending middle elections of Congress would consolidate his strength; perhaps he thought the Democratic party having resumed its vitality might be acted as his last card: the potential votes of the South and the strength of the Democratic party in the North would substantially form a majority disparity. After emancipation, the black population was no longer counted as three-fifths, and the number of Southern congressmen would increase by at least fifteen. Based on the number of congressmen, the number of Southern electors in the Electoral College would similarly increase by about one-third. If blacks remained excluded from the ballot box, the Democratic party would immediately control the political fate of the country. That was what the Republicans worried about, and was also what Johnson might use. He did not have to depend fully on the Republican party. Thus Johnson resolutely put a bet on his political fate.

Therefore, it seemed that blacks' fate could only be handled by Southern whites under the plan of Presidential Reconstruction. The principle of white autonomy had scored a temporary success. Despite its radical change in appearance, the presidential plan had its consistency. That is to say, on black issues, Constitution and state rights were always preferred to civil rights, and presidential authority was attributed more importance than congressional power. If the punishment of the upper class and reform ideals were unfavorable to the said principles and the consolidation of presidential power, Johnson would rather abandon them. Consequently, the enemies who once despised him now began to praise him. A planter of South Carolina, Henry W. Ravenel, said: "How hard it is to know really the character of a public man. I had always heard of [President Johnson] as a demagogue and pot house politician in Tennessee of the lowest order. I freely acknowledge that my first impressions of him [were] erroneous. [He] has placed himself in opposition to the radicals and by his acts and influence has shielded the South from vindictive policy."[537] Not allowing his plan to impair his position in the Republican party, Lincoln had once dropped a hint that it was merely tentative, and said that he was unwilling "to be inflexibly committed to any single plan of restoration."[538] So adamantly did Johnson adhere to his principles of "the good of the whole human race" and uphold his authority, however, that he put himself in an opposition to the Congress, and in the end lost his influence to a considerable extent.

The dilemma confronting Johnson between civil rights and local autonomy reflected the privileged nature of American democracy in the nineteenth century. White men, and especially Southern white men, were the dominant force in mainstream society. Their supreme status was maintained by the political system and all sorts of voluntary organizations. To a certain extent this situation was in accordance with democratic principles, for democratic principles were practised only within mainstream society. To realize racial justice, however, it was necessary to substitute universal democratic principals for the limited ones. This change would inevitably be carried out under compulsion, and it was impossible to break through within the South itself, because persistent racism and black weakness had decided the complicated nature of the great change, and whites' temperate tolerant self-consciousness could not be fostered in a short time. So the black civil rights question was itself concerned with the reform of American democratic institutions. This solution, which Johnson did his best to avoid, was admittedly difficult for him to settle and was also the root of his failure, for the North and Congress intended to exert the victor's power and impose their own majority will on the South.

THE NEW CONTROL SYSTEM

To face the challenge created by the disintegration of absolute personal authority, Southern whites went through a readjustment period. Since the grassroots effort to reconstruct the old authority could barely provide them with a feeling of serenity, however, whites eagerly hoped to consolidate their gains by official policies, caring little whether it would irritate the North or not. The laissez-faire policy of the president gave them an opportunity, and they decided not to let it pass by.

The famous scholar Thomas B. Alexander, studying the Whig party, held that Southern Whigs had truly experienced an opportunity to restore their party and lead a moderate Reconstruction after the war.[539] Because they had dragged the South into the war, Democrats were low-spirited and self-abased at that time. The *Hinds County Gazette* in Mississippi observed that "They wore sack-cloth. They heaped several bushel of ashes on their heads. They took back seats, muffling in broken accents, 'we made a great mistake in secession.'"[540] In the meantime, the former Whigs, who had involuntarily followed in secession, now began to revive and intended to set about their political reorganization. When the president decided to build up the conservative party, the sign of its resuscitation became much clearer. Among the provisional governors chosen by the president were William H. Holden, the Democratic leader of the small farmers in the hill-country area of North Carolina, and Lewis Parsons, a former rich Whig from Alabama, both of whom had given great impetus to the restoration of peace during the war. In Texas and Florida, Johnson also named men who had never sworn any kind of allegiance to the Confederacy or who had been opposed to secession.[541] This policy had encouraged both the small-farmers in hill counties and the former Whigs to participate in politics, and, consequently, there was a change in the political structure of the South.

The election results of the constitutional conventions in the summer of 1865 reflected this change. Few high Confederate officials or wealthy men had yet received individual amnesties, and the discredited mainstays of secession did not seek election. Understandably, over two-thirds of those elected had opposed secession in 1860.[542] The former Whigs were especially conspicuous, many of whom had held office before the war. While the top level of antebellum secessionists were excluded, the professional constitution of the delegates did not show too many differences from their antecedents. Despite having no formal organization, Whigs to a large extent influenced the process of the constitutional conventions. To cooperate on the presidential strategy, they tried to form "a great party, irresistible in its power, and sufficiently efficacious and strong to control the next Presidential election, to defeat the Radicals, and to place some conservative Northern man in the presidential chair of the United States."[543] This party would conditionally approve the Thirteenth Amendment, involuntarily pronounce the secession ordinances null and void, and acquiesce in repudiation of all debts contracted by the Confederacy. Generally speaking, the constitutional conventions demonstrated the triumph of the moderates. At the same time, seizing the opportunities created by the Confederate failure, the delegates of hill counties pushed forward their long-desired reforms in the political structure. With the support of Governor Perry and the president, South Carolina abolished property qualifications for membership in the legislature and revised the outdated system of representation that required state officials and presidential electors to be chosen by the legislature. In Alabama, the convention adopted the "white basis" of legislators, the fond dream that the upcountry district had jealously craved. The campaign to reduce the influence of the plantation region, however, was less successful in other states. Since the entire black population was counted, the power of plantation counties became even stronger in Georgia.[544]

Whenever the black issue was raised, however, the political alignment immediately became ambiguous.[545] Neither Whigs nor Democrats, and neither plantation counties nor hill counties, were interested in protection of black rights. On the contrary, they all concerned themselves with ensuring white supremacy. The planters especially took care over the control of black labor, for the former ruling class had a peculiar stake in black failure.[546] Although a handful delegates suggested extending suffrage to literate blacks, this voice was very faint even among the unconditional Unionists.[547] The upcountry whites suspected that planters would control the black vote, while planters were afraid of a laborer class whose bargaining power was increasing. A Mississippi delegate expressed his creed that " 'tis natur's law that the superior race must rule and rule they will."[548]

After Johnson's conditions were satisfied, the South began to elect its legislators, governors, and congressmen under the new constitutions in the fall of 1865. In most states, the former Unionist Whigs were in the majority. Of seven governors elected in 1865, six were Whigs. They also controlled legislatures and congressional delegations. In the Upper South, including Arkansas, Tennessee, and Virginia, the strengthen of Unionists was even stronger, for these states had experienced wartime Reconstruction. In the far South, former Whigs also dominated the elections, but service to the Confederacy emerged as a virtual prerequisite for success.[549] The new governors here quickly collaborated with the former Confederate elements, appointed them as officials at different levels, and cooperated with them to deal with the desperate Unionists. As a result, the former Confederate hard-liners regained some of their power.[550]

The new legislatures soon seized upon the problem of freedmen. The vast majority of their members agreed that freedmen must be kept under restraint; they only disagreed as to what extent and in which way. As to the aim of restraint, Mississippi Governor Benjamin Humphreys expressed it clearly. Several hundred thousand Negroes, he related, had been turned loose upon society, and the state must assume guardianship over them. They might be allowed to rise as high in the scale of civilization as they could, but the social and political supremacy of the white race must be maintained. The purity and progress of both races demanded that racial castes be preserved and intermarriage forbidden. Then he turned to the economic problem:

To work is the law of God. The cultivation of the great staples of the South require continuous labor from January to January. The planter cannot venture upon their cultivation unless the laborer is compelled to comply with his contract and if he attempts to escape he should be returned to his employer. By such a system of labor, the welfare and happiness of the African may be secured and our homes again become the abode of plenty.[551]

Although the "Black Codes" in Southern states varied in their provisions, the fundamental principles were very much the same. To frustrate the Radicals, the moderates emphasized that the constitutional conventions had taken over the responsibility to freedmen, and it was necessary for the elected governments to fulfill this duty. Otherwise, "the work of reconstruction will stop," the *Meridian Clarion* warned, "and our delegation to Congress will be refused admission."[552] So the Black Codes partially recognized the new reality and admitted blacks' basic rights as human beings. Blacks' rights to marriage and childbearing were legalized, which might be conducive to the stability of their families. Yet intermarriage was generally forbidden, and Mississippi regarded it as a felony:

That it shall not be lawful for any freedmen, free negro, or mulatto to intermarry with any white person; nor for any white person to intermarry with any freedman, free negro, or mulatto; and any person who shall so intermarry shall be deemed guilty of felony and, on conviction thereof, shall be confined in the state penitentiary for life.[553]

Blacks might own, inherit, buy, and sell property, and only in Mississippi had the ownership of land been definitely excluded. As laborers, blacks were exempted from working on the weekend and at night and from gratuitous violence and unsuitable food. Their wages and work terms must be defined in contract, too.[554] The Black Codes also awarded blacks the right to sue or be sued. They could provide testimonies, but this right was confined to cases involving black disputes. They could not sit on a jury. Yet in some states, blacks might act as a witness in whites' litigations, provided the two parties agreed to it.[555] Thus, Black Codes only permitted justice among blacks themselves, and blacks could not expect to be given justice between black and white in court. When the Black Codes of South Carolina were published in 1866, H. Melville Myyers explained the nature of the laws in the preface. The black race, he declared, at all times had "been excluded, as a separate class, from all civilized governments and the family of nations," for it was "doomed by a mysterious and Divine ordination." Though the war had settled the matter of slavery, it did not mean that blacks were to be regarded as citizens. They were only to be "equal before the law in the possession and enjoyment of all their rights of personal liberty and property."[556]

In the economic aspect, what the Black Codes most cared about was to ensure the social control of a docile labor class. To counteract the unfavorable effect of black leisure, some states required every black to show written certification of "lawful employment," otherwise he would be imprisoned or fined as a vagrant. If he could not pay the fine, he might be leased to the employer who provided the most money to carry out forced labor, or be sent to work gratuitously on public projects. Vagrancy might be inflicted on any black who could not make a living, did not support his family, or had no fixed dwelling, and on the peddlers and thespians without licenses, fortune-tellers, beggars, drunkards, hunters, prostitutes, gamblers, and thieves.[557] Mississippi even included men who could not pay a newly designed pauper tax and those who attended an illegal assembly in vagrancy.[558] By means of the vagrancy laws and the convict lease system, blacks' bargaining power was greatly reduced, and blacks were increasingly becoming the victims of a system that sought cheap labor, fines, and social stability. In 1867, Texas blacks constituted about one-third of the convicts confined to the state penitentiary and nearly 90 percent of those leased out for railroad labor.[559]

The Black Codes required that blacks strictly abide by contracts. Blacks must sign one-year contracts and work every day from sunrise to sunset, and could not leave the plantation or entertain a guest without permission. In Mississippi, blacks forfeited their wages if they left their job halfway through their term. As under slavery, every person and official might arrest a runaway black.[560] Etiquette was also stipulated by law. Laborers were required to deport themselves in a respectful manner, and time-wasting and fraudulent illness were strictly forbidden. The Louisiana codes employed the language a master might have used in his instruction to the overseer:

> Bad work shall not be allowed. Failing to obey reasonable order, neglect of duty, and leaving home without permission will be deemed disobedience; impudence, swearing, or indecent language to, or in the presence of the employer, his family, or agent, or quarreling and fighting with one another shall be deemed disobedience.[561]

The Alabama codes defined as a vagrant "any runaway, stubborn servant or child" and any laborer "who loiters away his time" or fails to comply with the terms of his employment.[562] Black violators of their contracts might be flogged, shackled, or fined, or be forced to labor without compensation for one year. To counteract the withdrawal of black women from field labor, Louisiana and Texas mandated that contracts "shall embrace the labor of all members of the family able to work."[563] The Florida codes considered the collective negotiation of labor price as one kind of vagrancy.

Correspondingly, the Black Codes stipulated the rights and responsibilities of employers. The Louisiana codes mandated that all disputes between an employer and his laborers "shall be settled by the former."[564] Seeking to reduce the influence of blacks' competitive power, virtually all the Southern states passed "anti-enticement" measures. Mississippi, for example, enacted that any person who "would persuade or attempt to persuade, entice, or cause any freedman, free Negro, or mulatto to desert from the legal employment of any person," or "knowingly give or sell to any such deserting freedman, free Negro, or mulatto, any food, raiment, or other thing," shall be guilty of a misdemeanor and be fined, or be sentenced to the country jail.[565] Some states, including South Carolina, prohibited employers from driving out old freedmen. Yet these measures were hints that the old paternalism was still present. A fact that reminds us of its substance was that this state defined the two parties in a labor contract as "servants" and "masters."[566]

Another measure to maintain the authority of employers was the apprenticeship law, which permitted judges to bind to the guardianship of white employers the black orphans or those whose parents were considered unable to support them, without the consent of their parents. Some states, including Mississippi, limited the apprenticeship law to blacks.[567] At that time, admittedly, these laws were popular in America and Europe, and even Lincoln once mentioned the possibility of an apprenticeship law.[568] The aim of the Southern apprenticeship law, however, was not to train the young in a skill, but mainly to provide cheap labor for white employers. Under the jurisdiction of Southern authorities, former owners might easily get black children back in their hands.[569] In some cases, the courts even classified adults as "apprentices." One-tenth of the apprentices in a county of North Carolina, for example, exceeded the age of sixteen, including an "orphan" working at a turpentine mill and supporting his wife and child.[570] By using arbitrary power, Southern courts separated black families and supported the interests of whites.

The Black Codes placed many restrictions on blacks who tried to leave agricultural labor. To discourage those who aspired to be artisans, merchants, or shopkeepers, and those who had already held such professions, the South Carolina codes prohibited blacks from pursuing any employment except for agriculture labor or domestic service unless they obtained a special license and a certification from a local judge about their skill, fitness, and "good moral character." The application fee was as high as one hundred dollars, and the license was "good for one year only."[571] The Mississippi codes also required that any freedman engaged in an irregular job or work carry a license issued by local authorities, which might be revoked for any reason at any time.

Blacks were also prevented from renting or leasing any land or tenement excepting in incorporated cities or towns.[572] The local authorities might virtually place any obstacle on blacks' procurement of real estate. In addition, the South passed fence laws, which applied only to the black belt, requiring livestock owners to fence in their animals. Thus, landless blacks were deprived of the right to freely graze livestock. Similarly, hunting and fishing were also limited.[573] By these measures, blacks' income sources were reduced, and they had to be content with their place as agricultural laborers.

The Black Codes also spared no pains to restrict blacks' other rights and suppress their "crimes." For instance, Southern states placed strict restrictions on their mobility. The police regulations of St. Landry Parish, Louisiana, ordained that "no negro shall be allowed to pass within the limits of said parish without special permit in writing from his employer," and "every negro who shall be found absent from the residence of his employer after ten o'clock at night shall be compelled to work five days on the public road, or suffer corporeal punishment."[574] Almost every state prohibited blacks from carrying arms. In Florida, for example, violators would be pilloried for an hour, or be lashed to thirty nine. The Mississippi codes also stipulated that no black "shall keep or carry firearms of any kind, or any ammunition, dirk, or bowie knife," and no white person "shall sell, lend, or give to any freedman, free Negro, or mulatto, any firearms, dirk, or bowie knife, or ammunition."[575] Blacks' right to assembly was rigidly restrained. Also in St. Landry Parish, Louisiana, it was ordained that "no public meetings or congregations of negroes shall be allowed" after sunset, and in daytime "no negro shall be permitted to preach, exhort, or otherwise declaim to congregation of colored people, without a special permission in writing from the president of the policy jury."[576] Blacks had to be careful about all sorts of their behavior. The Penal Code of Mississippi ordained that any black should be punished who was

> committing riots, routes, affrays, trespasses, malicious mischief, cruel treatment to animals, seditious speeches, insulting gestures, language, or acts, or assaults on any person, disturbance of the peace, exercising the function of a minister of the Gospel without a license from some regularly organized church, vending spirituous or intoxicating liquors, or committing any other misdemeanor.[577]

Not only was the range of crimes widened, but many minor offenses would also be severely punished without mercy. In Virginia and Georgia, to steal a horse or mule was made a capital crime.[578] Florida forbade any "colored and white person respectively from intruding upon each other's public assemblies, religious or other, or public vehicle set apart for their exclusive use, under punishment of pillory or strips, or both."[579] As for felonies, the punishments allowed no ambiguity. In South Carolina, the capital sentence might be imposed on blacks guilty of

> willful homicide, assault upon a white woman, impersonating her husband for carnal purpose, raising an insurrection, stealing a horse, a mule, or baled cotton, and house-breaking. For crimes not demanding death, Negroes might be confined at hard labor, whipped, or transported.[580]

Blacks that had been sentenced fell into the trap of the convict lease system. Thus, the laws became an ingenious instrument of maintaining social control and obtaining cheap black labor.

Aimed at reducing blacks' competitive power in the labor market and manipulating labor for white advantage, the Black Codes were both the immediate response to the economic problems after the war and the legal expression of white superiority and their desire for social control. Although the Codes had drawn on the experience of the supervisory precedents practiced by the Union Army and the Freedmen's Bureau as well as experience of free blacks in the South and the North, the principles that the Codes adhered to and those of the army and Bureau were poles apart. Some Codes undisguisedly adopted a double racial standard, defiantly despising the principle of equality before the law. This was especially typical in Mississippi and South Carolina. Federal officials had to cancel some clauses with naked prejudice, but they did not touch them if these clauses did not clearly show racial differences. In places where the Bureau refused to interfere or freedmen found it difficult to bring accusations, however, the original clauses remained intact. Such being the case, the appearance of the Black Codes epitomized the transformation of social control in the South. In other words, the former dependent relationship characterized by its absolute personal authority was now transmuted into the impersonal right-duty relationship based on legal compulsion. The authority originally exerted by planters was gradually transferred to the hands of local authorities. In this regard the interference of states in the labor market was most obvious. As a Southerner put it, "Teach the negro that if he goes to work, keeps his place, and behaves himself, he will be protected by our white laws."[581]

Under Presidential Reconstruction, not only was legislation exclusively arranged by whites, but the enforcement of law was monopolized by them also. Since blacks in fact had not participated in the judicial system, whites could easily explain and make judgment in favor of their fellows. Because lawyers, judges, and jurors were white citizens without exception, it was hard for blacks to obtain fair adjudication even if the laws themselves contained no discriminatory clauses. The main instrument restricting blacks' behavior, the vagrancy law, outwardly made no distinction, but judicial authorities might decide whether or not it was applicable to whites. As Alabama planter and Democratic politician John W. Du Bois bluntly remarked, "the vagrant contemplated was the plantation negro."[582] Though black testimony was accepted, blacks had no right to speak in adjudication. Thus it was no surprise that "the verdicts are always for the white men and against the colored man."[583] Local sheriffs and justices of the peace similarly composed of whites were reluctant to prosecute any white accused of crimes against blacks, for this action would be "unpopular" and dangerous. When such cases were brought to court, "it seldom results in anything but acquittal of criminal."[584]

At the time of Presidential Reconstruction, the Southern police system was a closed one, and no blacks were included. To whites, the police force was the first line of defense against blacks and an important instrument of social control. Whites were unwilling to face a black law enforcement official who had legal authority over them. Whites were both the members of state militias and urban police forces, among whom were some white immigrants and Confederate veterans. In fact, the Codes in explicit terms forbade blacks to serve in any military organization.[585] Almost all militiamen patrolled the black belts. By ransacking blacks' homes, abusing those who refused to sign agricultural contracts, and arresting the so-called vagrants, these militiamen continually spread terror among the black population. In their view, blacks constituted a criminal class and were their main problem. As a result, the number of blacks who were chained and thrown into prison was much higher than that of whites.

At the same time, the policy of excluding or segregating blacks in public facilities began to take shape. In the Presidential Reconstruction era, the first batch of segregation laws was born. Before the war, blacks as servants often appeared in public vehicles with their masters, and few received comments and reproaches. Yet once they were freedmen, whites' strong abhorrence was immediately aroused. When a black couple tried to go aboard a steamboat on the Mississippi River, the captain refused to grant a stateroom to them. One passenger explained the reason as follows: "How would you feel to know that your wife was sleeping in the next room to a niggar and his wife?"[586] The railways immediately adopted the conventions of refusing blacks in the "ladies" cars; on the smaller railways which had no classification of cars, blacks were driven to the old cars, freight cars, or open platforms, though they had paid full fare. The laws of Mississippi, Florida, and Texas simply gave legality to de facto segregation. The law of Mississippi in November 1865, for example, made it illegal for an employer of any railroad in the state to allow "any freedman, negro, or mulatto, to ride in any first class passenger cars, set apart, or used by, and for white persons."[587] An exception was that the law was not applicable to blacks traveling with their masters or mistresses in their capacity as nurses. It is also to be noted that whites might voluntarily choose second-class cars. Even though this law was only applied to railroads, its principle was immediately followed by passenger boats, theaters and other public facilities, and abided by other states that had not stipulated these practices in explicit terms. In most cases, hotels, bars, and other entertainment places were regarded as private enterprises, and state authorities refused to intervene in their exclusion of blacks. In addition, most state or city authorities barred blacks from poor relief, orphanages, parks, schools, and other public facilities, excusing themselves by saying that the Freedmen's Bureau should provide whatever services blacks required.[588] Nevertheless, Georgia decreed that black and white patients in the "Lunatic Asylum" be kept separate; in Richmond, Virginia, blacks and whites applied for "destitute rations" at separate places; and in Texas and Florida, segregated black schools were also established.[589]

At the time of Presidential Reconstruction, the main tendency of Southern public policy was becoming clear. First-class facilities were set aside for the exclusive use of whites, while poor facilities might be shared by both races. Segregated facilities were respectively allocated to each race, and blacks received the inferior ones both in quality and in quantity or were even completely excluded. In either case, the racial line was evident, and it is to be noted that the segregation laws were just a prelude to de jure segregation in effect at the end of the nineteenth century.

Thus, with the vagrancy laws, contract laws, and penal codes as its driveshaft, with an exclusive force monopolized by whites as its operational instrument, and coordinated by the mechanism of grassroots social mobilization, a new control system was meticulously constructed after the disintegration of slavery. As Du Bois noted, whites "build about them walls so high, and hang between them and the light a veil so thick, that they shall not even think of breaking through."[590]

However, it is hard to say that the system would encounter no challenge. To whites, the consolidation of social control revealed less of their strength as the increase in their feelings of insecurity. In reality, blacks' determination to seek their liberty constituted the main challenge. As in slavery, this new control system could not completely eliminate the potential or apparent intensity of conflict from racial relations. At the same time, the military occupation continued, and the Northern media was watching every act of the South. What the South had done, including the appearance of Black Codes, would to a large extent decide the politic fate of Presidential Reconstruction. Insightful Southern men were rather disturbed by the recklessness of the legislatures. The editor of the Columbus *Sentinel* bemoaned the fact that the legislature of Mississippi had been controlled by "a hard and shallow-headed majority, that were far more anxious to make capital at home than to propitiate the powers at Washington. They were as complete a set of political Goths as were ever turned loose to work destruction upon a State."[591] "We showed our hand too soon," a planter in this state conceded regrettably, "we ought to have waited till the troops were withdrawn, and our representatives admitted to Congress; then we could have had everything our own way."[592] Anxiously seeking social control, white Southerners had to face the threat of Northern interference as well as the challenge from blacks. It was not that they had not perceived this danger, but that they so intensely watched over the latter that they simply cast aside the former. It seemed "little short of madness" for white Southerners, said Daniel E. Goodloe, a North Carolina–born Abolitionist, to believe "the triumphant North would tolerate this new slave code."[593]

Drawn into the center of the conflict were the black soldiers. Since black soldiers were connected with federal military authority, they were on the edges of the social control mechanism. In the opinion of white Southerners, these eighty thousand black soldiers were the greatest menace to social order, and must be eliminated. To begin with, these soldiers were the most "indocile" blacks. Governor Benjamin Humphreys of Mississippi thought that "everyone is afraid of the Negro soldiers. They crowd everybody off the sidewalks, and shoot and kill us, and protect the freedmen in their indolence and acts of crime."[594] These soldiers advocated blacks' possession of land and civil rights, advised freedmen to leave the plantation, organized debate societies and political meetings, and attempted to travel in segregated public vehicles reserved for whites. Southern whites found it difficult to accept the fact that their former docile slaves were transformed into rebellious elements. "How the war has demoralized the cussed brutes!" sighed a Confederate veteran.[595] Secondly, the presence of black soldiers was also a symbol of Southern failure and humiliation. Wearing federal uniforms and shouldering glossy muskets, black soldiers continuously reminded white Southerners of their conquered state. Through them, in the white Southerners' view, the triumphant North deliberately punished the indomitable Southerners. Relying on military authority, black soldiers sometimes intervened in disputes on plantations, rebuked whites in city streets, released black suspects, and arrested whites. "It is very hard," a Confederate veteran said angrily, "to see a white man taken under guard by one of those black scoundrels."[596] If they found local courts did not intend to punish white criminals, black soldiers might occasionally take extra-legal revenge and clash with the civil authorities. In Victoria, Texas, several black soldiers seized an alleged white murder, and then lynched him.[597] And thirdly, black soldiers were considered to be dangerous examples for other blacks. They plucked up freedmen's courage, made them unsatisfied with present labor conditions, and expedited their withdrawal from field labor. Their authority over whites gave freedmen a new understanding of power. The black soldiers who were mixed with whites in public facilities violated Southern custom. By their behavior, the white Southerners believed, these "diabolical savages" had turned "a quiet, contented, & happy people" into "dissatisfied, unruly, madmen intoxicated with the fume of licentiousness, ready for any acts of outrage."[598]

On the other hand, many acts considered impermissible by whites were thought to be legitimate among blacks. Because of this, whites could only give vent to their rage in the extralegal way. Many atrocities committed by whites were induced by the presence of black soldiers. When two privates from the 80th U.S. Colored Infantry went for a drink of water near Jefferson, Texas, the deputy town marshal, Jack Pillips, swung his double-barreled shotgun into position and blasted the two soldiers at point-blank range. As the dying black infantrymen writhed in pain on the bloody ground, he then calmly blew their brains out.[599] In Savannah, a white man brutally raped a black woman, vowing vengeance on the families of men who had served in the "God damned Yankee army."[600] If blacks insisted on a fair punishment, the conflict would escalate and sometimes led to race riots. The accident that took place in Memphis in early May 1866 illustrated the white men's attitudes towards black soldiers.

After the capture of Memphis by the Union troops in 1862, the city soon became a gathering place for black refugees as well as a shelter for thousands of blacks seeking protection from their former masters. At the end of the war, when black Union troops were used to patrol the city, tension was immediately heightened. White policemen, who were mostly Irish, often arrested black soldiers for the slightest offense, and then treated them with extreme brutality. On May 1st, the trouble began when Memphis police attempted to arrest a discharged black soldier. The forcible release of the prisoner triggered pent-up emotions and skirmishes between the two authorities. The Union Army commander worried that the situation might be deteriorating and ordered the black soldiers back to the fort. All temporarily seemed quiet. In that night and the next two days and nights, however, white police and civilians looted and terrorized the new black community. Forty-six blacks were dead, 285 had been victimized in one way or another, six black women were raped, and over 100 houses, schools, and hospitals of the Freedmen's Bureau were burned. Yet no arrest was ever made for murder, rape, theft, or arson, although many rioters were well known to the victims, who later identified them to a congressional committee.[601]

The Memphis riot was undoubtedly a nightmare for blacks, and whites felt satisfied with its frightening effect on social control. "The late riots in our city," the local newspaper declared, "have satisfied all of one thing: that the Southern men will not be ruled by the negro. The negroes now know, to their sorrow, that it is best not to arouse the fury of the white man."[602] Bloody as it was, this tragedy demonstrated how obstinate the white racism was that intended to maintain black subordination, and how far whites would go if they were allowed.

The Memphis riot and the New Orleans riot, which was induced by the attempt of the legislature to introduce political change, illustrated the intensity of Southern determination to resist any change in racial pattern, and greatly aroused public indignation in the North. "The hands of rebels are again red with loyal blood," the *New York Tribune* declared.[603] If the South fell into the hands of rebels, they asked, would the fruits of victory gain nought? If Reconstruction only meant the birth of another kind of slavery, how would the moral aim stimulated by the war be guaranteed? That Southern whites were too impatient to wait eventually enhanced the strength of radicalism and led to the interference of Union forces. From this point of view, the failure of Presidential Reconstruction was not so much the mistake of presidential policy itself as the inevitable result of Southern whites' political gamble and the mischief inspired by their racism.

NOTES

417. I. A. Newby, *The South: A History.* New York: Holt, Rinehart & Winston, 1978, p. 235.

418. *ibid.,* p. 235; Joel Williamson, *New People: Miscegenation and Mulattos in the United South.* New York: Oxford University Press, 1980, p. 89.

419. Roger L. Ransom and Richard Sutch, *One Kind of Freedom: The Economic Consequences of Emancipation.* New York: Cambridge University Press, 1977, p. 51.

420. Michael L. Benedict, *The Fruits of Victory: Alternatives in Restoring the Union, 1865–1877.* New York: University Press of America, 1986, p. 4.

421. Albert Moore, "One Hundred Years of Reconstruction," in Gerald N. Grob and George A. Billias, *Interpretations of American History: Patterns and Perspectives.* New York: Oxford University Press, 1972, p. 499.

422. Jack M. Bloom, *Class, Race, and Civil Rights Movement.* Bloomington and Indianapolis: Indiana University Press, 1987, p. 21.

423. Arthur S. Link and Stanley Coben, *The Democratic Heritage: A History of the U.S.A.* Los Angeles: Krieger, 1971, pp. 266–267.

424. Newby, *op. cit.,* p. 236.

425. *ibid.,* p. 237.

426. Imamiti Motomobu, *About Love.* Beijing, China: Sanlian, 1987, p. 179.

427. James T. Currie, *Enclave: Vicksburg and Her Plantations, 1863–1870.* Oxford: University of Mississippi, 1980, p. 153.

428. Thomas Bailey, *The American Spirit.* Lexington: University of Kentucky Press, 1973, p. 461.

429. Sidney Andrews, *The South Since the Civil War.* Boston: Ayer, 1969, p. 22.

430. Leon F. Litwack, *Been in the Storm So Long.* New York, Knopf, 1979, p. 194.

431. *ibid.*, p. 194.

432. Erich Fromm, *Escape from Freedom.* New York: Farrar & Rinehart, 1942, pp. 78, 126, 131, 141.

433. Ben A. Wiliams, ed., *A Diary from Dixie.* Boston: Ticknor & Fields, 1949, p. 520.

434. Litwack, *op. cit.,* p. 178.

435. *ibid.,* p. 178.

436. W. E. B. Du Bois, *Black Reconstruction in America, 1860–1880.* Cleveland: World Publications, 1964, p. 143.

437. Litwack, *op. cit.,* p. 196.

438. Hope S. Chamberlain, *Old Days in Chapel Hill.* Chapel Hill: University of North Carolina Press, 1926, p. 130.

439. A. A. Taylor, *The Negro in the Reconstruction of Virginia,* quoted in Litwack, *op. cit.,* p. 196.

440. Howard N. Rabinowitz, *Race Relations in the Urban South, 1865–1890.* New York: Oxford University Press, 1978, p. 29.

441. Litwack, *op. cit.,* p. 188.

442. Arney R. Childs, ed., *The Private Journal of Henry William Ravel, 1859–1887.* Columbia, SC: University of South Carolina Press, 1947, p. 219.

443. Litwack, *op. cit.,* p. 189.

444. Allen W. Trelease, *White Terror: The Ku Klux Klan Conspiracy and Southern Reconstruction.* New York: Harper & Row, 1971.

445. Du Bois, *op. cit.,* p. 136.

446. Arvin Turner, ed., *The Negro Question.* New York: World Publishers, 1958, p. 138.

447. *ibid.,* p. 136.

448. Stephen V. Ash, "Poor Whites in the Occupied South, 1861–1865," *Journal of Southern History,* Vol. 57, 1991, p. 52.

449. *ibid.,* p. 60.

450. *ibid.,* p. 61.

451. Benedict, *op. cit.,* p. 83; Litwack, *op. cit.,* p. 371.

452. Trelease, *op. cit.,* p. 124.

453. Litwack, *op. cit.,* p. 223.

454. Bailey, *op. cit.,* p. 463.

455. Eric Foner, *Reconstruction: America's Unfinished Revolution, 1863–1877.* New York: Harper & Row, 1988, p.120.

456. Litwack, *op. cit.,* p. 278.

457. *ibid.,* p. 278.

458. *ibid.,* p. 277.

459. Foner, *op. cit.,* p. 120.

460. John R. Dennet, *The South as It Is, 1865–1866.* Ed. Henry M. Christman, New York: Sheed and Ward, 1965, p. 194.

461. *ibid.,* p. 223.

462. Litwack, *op. cit.,* p. 277.

463. *ibid.,* p. 280.

464. Vernon Lane Wharton, *The Negro in Mississippi.* New York: Harper & Row, 1965, p. 218.

465. Trelese, *op. cit.*

466. William L. Richter, *The Army in Texas During Reconstruction, 1865–1870.* Texas A & M University Press, 1987, p. 34.

467. Foner, *op. cit.,* p. 121.

468. Wharton, *op. cit.,* p. 218; Paul H. Bergerson, ed., *The Papers of Andrew Johnson,* Vol. 8. Knoxville: University of Tennessee Press, 1989, p. 667.

469. Bergerson, *op. cit.,* p. 646.

470. Litwack, *op. cit.,* p. 554.

471. Foner, *op. cit.,* p. 121.

472. David Macrae, *The Americans at Home,* quoted from Trelease, *op. cit.*

473. Joel Williamson, *The Crucible of Race: Black-White Relations in the American South Since Emancipation.* New York: Oxford University Press, 1984, p. 32.

474. Walter Lord, "Mississippi: The Past That Would Not Die," in Stephen B. Oates, ed., *Portrait of America.* Vol. I. Boston: Houghton Mifflin Company, 1978, p. 38.

475. Richter, *op. cit.,* p. 42.

476. Williamson, *New People,* p. 89.

477. Lord, *op. cit.,* p. 38.

478. Litwack, *op. cit.,* p. 267.

479. Wharton, *op. cit.,* p. 224.

480. Roger Shugg, *Origins of Class Struggle in Louisiana.* Louisiana Baton Rouge: Louisiana State University Press, 1939, p. 241.

481. Duncan L. Heyward, *Seed from Madagascar,* quoted from Litwack, *op. cit.,* p. 409.

482. Litwack, *op. cit.,* p. 409.

483. Thomas C. Holt, "An Empire over the Mind: Emancipation, Race, and Ideology in the British West and the American South," in J. Morgan Kousser and James M. McPerson, eds., *Region, Race, and Reconstruction: Essays in Honor of C. Vann Woodward.* New York: Oxford University Press, 1982, p. 298.

484. Foner, *op. cit.*, p. 132.

485. Katherine M. Jones, ed., *Heroines of Dixie: Confederate Women Tell Their Story of the War,* quoted from Litwack, *op. cit.*, p. 395.

486. Foner, *op. cit.*, p. 134.

487. C. Vann Woodword, *The Burden of Southern History.* Baton Rouge: Louisiana State University Press, 1993, p. 71.

488. Kenneth M. Stampp, *The Era of Reconstruction, 1865–1877.* New York: Alfred A. Knopf & Random House, 1965, p. 52.

489. Richard B. Morris and William Greenleaf, *The History of a Nation.* Vol. V. Chicago: Aldine, 1969, p. 17.

490. Du Bois, *op. cit.*, p. 249.

491. *ibid.*, p. 250.

492. Stampp, *op. cit.*, p. 56.

493. Du Bois, *op. cit.*, p. 242.

494. *ibid.*, p. 243.

495. *ibid.*, p. 245.

496. *ibid.*, p. 246.

497. Foner, *op. cit.*, p. 179.

498. Melvin Steinfield, ed., *Our Racist Presidents: From Washington to Nixon.* Berkeley: University of California Press, 1972, p. 150.

499. *ibid.*, pp. 150–152.

500. Stampp, *op. cit.*, p. 60.

501. Foner, *op. cit.*, p. 177.

502. Steinfield, *op. cit.*, p. 152.

503. LaWanda Cox and John H. Cox, *Politics, Principles, and Prejudice, 1865–1866.* New York: Free Press, 1963, p. 98.

504. Foner, *op. cit.*, p. 179; Raymond G. Gettell, *History of American Political Thought,* New York: The Century Co., 1928, p. 376.

505. Cox, *op. cit.*, p. 136.

506. Benedict, *op. cit.*, pp. 87–89.

507. Bergerson, *op. cit.*, p. 282.

508. Foner, *op. cit.*, p. 181.

509. Cox, *op. cit.*, p. 155.

510. *ibid.*, p. 155.

511. Du Bois, *op. cit.*, p. 258.

512. Bergerson, *op. cit.*, p. 635.

513. Cox, *op. cit.*, p. 161.

514. Earl Maltz, *Civil Rights, the Constitution, and Congress, 1863–1869.* Lawrence: University Press of Kansas, 1990, p. 51.

515. Cox, *op. cit.*, p. 158.

516. Wharton, *op. cit.*, p. 134.
517. Cox, *op. cit.*, p. 168.
518. Steinfield, *op. cit.*, p. 151.
519. *ibid.*, p. 151.
520. Wharton, *op. cit.*, p. 131.
521. Benedict, *op. cit.*, p. 15.
522. Cox, *op. cit.*, p. 170.
523. Wharton, *op. cit.*, pp. 132–133.
524. Du Bois, *op. cit.*, p. 244.
525. Stampp, *op. cit.*, p. 56.
526. Foner, *op. cit.*, p. 183.
527. Stampp, *op. cit.*, p. 65.
528. Du Bois, *op. cit.*, p. 245.
529. Steinfield, *op. cit.*, p. 152.
530. David Donald, "Why They Impeached Andrew Johnson," in Oates, ed., *op. cit.*, p. 4.
531. Du Bois, *op. cit.*, p. 255.
532. Stampp, *op. cit.*, p. 56.
533. Foner, *op. cit.*, p. 191.
534. *ibid.*, p. 218.
535. Cox, *op. cit.*, p. 89.
536. Foner, *op. cit.*, p. 217.
537. Stampp, *op. cit.*, p.69.
538. *ibid.*, p. 40.
539. Dewey w. Grantham, *The Democratic South: The Economic and Social Revolution in the South Interpreted in the Light of History.* Athens: University of Georgia Press, 1963, p. 19.
540. *ibid.*, p. 20.
541. Benedict, *op. cit.*, p. 15.
542. Foner, *op. cit.*, p. 193.
543. Wharton, *op. cit.*, p. 133.
544. Foner, *op. cit.*, p. 195.
545. William C. Harris, "The Reconstruction of Commonwealth, 1865–1870," in Richard A. Melemore, ed., *A History of Mississippi.* Jackson: University Press of Mississippi, 1973, p. 547.
546. Litwack, *op. cit.*, p. 362.
547. Foner, *op. cit.*, pp. 192, 195.
548. *ibid.*, p. 195.
549. *ibid.*, p. 196.

550. Robert S. Alexander, "Presidential Reconstruction: Ideology and Change," in Eric Anderson and Alfred A Moss, Jr., eds., *The Facts of Reconstruction: Essays in Honor of John Hope Franklin.* Baton Rouge: Louisiana State University Press, 1991, p. 40.

551. Wharton, *op. cit.,* p. 83.

552. W. C. Harris, *op. cit.,* p. 547.

553. F. Champion Ward, et al., eds., *The People Shall Judge: Readings in the Formation of American Policy.* Vol. I, Chicago: University of Chicago Press, 1949, p. 778.

554. Du Bois, *op. cit.,* p. 169.

555. *ibid.,* p. 176.

556. Thomas F. Gossett, *Race: The History of an Idea in America.* Dallas, TX: Southern Methodist University Press, 1963, p. 256.

557. Du Bois, *op. cit.,* p. 175.

558. F. C. Ward, et al., eds., *op. cit.,* pp. 782–783.

559. Foner, *op. cit.,* p. 205.

560. F. C. Ward, et al., eds., *op. cit.,* p. 779.

561. Litwack, *op. cit.,* p. 367.

562. *ibid.,* p. 367.

563. Foner, *op. cit.,* p. 200.

564. *ibid.,* p. 201.

565. F. C. Ward, et al., eds., *op. cit.,* pp. 779–780.

566. Du Bois, *op. cit.,* p. 170.

567. F. C. Ward, et al., eds., *op. cit.,* p. 780.

568. Stampp, *op. cit.,* p. 47.

569. Wharton, *op. cit.,* p. 84.

570. Foner, *op. cit.,* p. 201.

571. Benedict, *op. cit.,* p. 91.

572. Wharton, *op. cit.,* p. 87.

573. Foner, *op. cit.,* p. 203.

574. Benedict, *op. cit.,* p. 90.

575. F. C. Ward, et al., eds., *op. cit.,* p. 783.

576. Benedict, *op. cit.,* pp. 90–91.

577. F. C. Ward, et al., eds., *op. cit.,* p. 783.

578. Foner, *op. cit.,* p. 202.

579. Du Bois, *op. cit.,* p. 172.

580. *ibid.,* p. 176.

581. Whitelaw Reid, *After the War: A Southern Tour,* quoted from Litwack, *op. cit.,* p. 366.

582. James K. Green, ed., *Alabama's Tragic Decade,* quoted from Foner, *op. cit.,* p. 201.

583. Foner, *op. cit.,* p. 204.

584. *ibid.,* p. 204.

585. Gossett, *op. cit.,* p. 256.

586. Litwack, *op. cit.,* p. 265.

587. Wharton, *op. cit.,* p. 230.

588. Foner, *op. cit.,* p. 207; Rabinowitz, *op. cit.,* p. 332.

589. Litwack, *op. cit.,* p. 263.

590. W. E. B. Du Bois, *The Souls of Black Folk.* New York: McClure, 1969, p. 122.

591. Wharton, *op. cit.,* pp. 89–90.

592. Litwack, *op. cit.,* p. 368.

593. Foner, *op. cit.,* p. 209.

594. Litwack, *op. cit.,* pp. 267–268.

595. *ibid.,* p. 268.

596. Foner, *op. cit.,* p. 81.

597. Charles W. Ramsdell, *Reconstruction in Texas.* Austin: University of Texas Press, 1910, p. 130.

598. Litwack, *op. cit.,* p. 269.

599. Richter, *op. cit.,* p. 32.

600. Litwack, *op. cit.,* 280.

601. Altina L. Waller, "Community, Class and Race in the Memphis Riot of 1866," in Kenneth L. Kusmer, ed., *The Civil War and Reconstruction, 1861–1867.* New York: Oxford University Press, 1991, pp. 25–26.

602. Litwack, *op. cit.,* p. 281.

603. Allen W. Trelease, *Reconstruction: The Great Experiment.* New York: Harper & Row, 1971, p. 66.

CHAPTER 4

African American Issues and Congressional Reconstruction

PRAGMATISM AND IDEALISM: CIVIL RIGHTS, THE CONSTITUTION, AND CONGRESS

Deeply rooted in the beliefs of Southern whites, Southern racism, on which the racial control system was firmly built, was so strong that blacks were unable to upset the status quo. Blacks could not shake off their fetters without help from the outside. While discrimination against blacks derived from the whites' souls, the impetus for emancipation also came from their souls, in their devotion to the universal ideals. Since Southern whites had excluded the part contradicting the slaveholding reality from the universal ideals, and there was no sign of change in the visible future, the responsibility for emancipation fell onto the shoulders of Northerners: the special circumstances created by the war allowed this idea to become a reality.

Indeed, Northern whites showed considerable discrimination against blacks. Even Republicans who took a firm stand on slavery equally opposed absolute equality between the two races. Yet racial discrimination in North and South had differences in degrees: the existence of whites' self-consciousness did not hinder Northern whites from recognizing some black rights, and it did not mean their absolute conquest over blacks. While they might be estranged from blacks in their personal feelings, Northern whites, once the formal relationship between individuals and the nation or states was involved, were willing to recognize their equal rights, including right of due process and the right to freely participate in a free labor–based society. The majority of Republicans insisted that each person had some minimum natural rights, whatever his condition or attributes might be. Blacks, Abraham Lincoln stressed, were entitled to equality with whites in certain respects:

> There is no reason in the world why the negro is not entitled to all the rights enumerated in the *Declaration of Independence*, the right to life, liberty, and the pursuit of happiness. I hold that he is as much entitled to these as the white man in the right to eat the bread, without the leave of anybody else which his own hands earns, *he is my equal and the equal of Judge Douglass, and the equal of every living man*.[604]

When touching on the fundamental rights of blacks, the antebellum Republicans placed emphasis on blacks' legal rights as men rather than as property. As an eminent Republican put it, with respect to natural rights, the rights to life, liberty, and property, "It is a question of manhood, not of color."[605]

Constituting their starting point in promoting racial justice, this basic position of Republicans on black issues was eventually embodied in the Fourteenth Amendment to the Constitution. Propelled by Republicans, most Northern states in fact set about protecting black freedom within their jurisdictions as early as the antebellum period. In *Commonwealth v. Aves* (1836), Chief Justice Lemuel Shaw ruled that any slave brought into Massachusetts would immediately become free. By 1860, every Northern state except for Indiana, Illinois, New Jersey, and California followed this decision, and every Northern state except for Minnesota and Oregon had enacted some sort of "personal liberty laws," which were used to impede the return of fugitive slaves and protect blacks from kidnapping. All blacks, free or fugitive, were invested with the rights to counsel, jury trial, and habeas corpus.[606] Although he was not allowed to sit on the jury, a black might receive equal protection under the law and give witness against whites.[607] When forced to choose between racism and due process, white Northerners generally chose the latter. By 1860, most Northern states appropriated tax dollars for black education, showing their comparatively enlightened attitudes towards blacks' right to education. Blacks could not be bought or sold, or separated from their families, or legally forced to work without pay. Blacks could buy and sell property, contract with employers, build their own churches, form an association, and present a petition.[608] At the minimum level, white Northerners and especially the Republicans admitted that blacks were on equal terms with whites. Historian John Hope Franklin commented that for the black man

> the essential difference between the South and the North and West was that in the latter sections he had more of the law on his side and could therefore resist encroachment on his rights. Northern Negroes could organize and fight for what they believed to be their rights, and there was a substantial group of white citizens who gave them both moral and material support.[609]

Even on the sensitive issue of the franchise, there were some Republicans who firmly stood by blacks. These persons were often called "Radicals," for the franchise was generally considered as a privilege that had gone beyond the principle of equality before the law. Yet the Radicals, including Charles Sumner from Massachusetts and Salmon P. Chase from Ohio, would rather classify it as a basic right. The majority of Republicans, however, remained undecided in this regard, because the advocacy of this right would lead to political disaster. They were more willing to place blacks under the protection of the privilege and immunity clause of Article II of the Constitution the comity clause, and avoided directly calling them citizens.[610] Even so, there was a sizable minority that did favor this extension of basic rights and made a sustained effort at the state level in the 1850s. Despite their failure, the attempt itself indicated that some Republicans would rather risk their political prospects than give up their moral beliefs. Since it was state legislatures instead of voters themselves that had the right to approve amendments to the Constitution, later on it proved more successful for them to amend the federal Constitution than some state constitutions.[611]

The Civil War was an important evolutionary stage in Republican attitudes towards civil rights. The extraordinary display of black soldiers in the battlefields, the vigorous advocacy of the Radicals, and the necessity of the war itself all made the war go beyond its basic aim of maintaining the Union, and drove the war's moral aim of advancing liberty and equality to the fore. In the view of Republicans, blacks' status had changed from persons to citizens. On November 29, 1862, Attorney General Edward Bates declared that all native-born free blacks were citizens of the United States, overruling the previous decision of Chief Justice Roger B. Taney in *Dred Scott* in 1854 that no black was a citizen. Bates's decision symbolized that Republican authorities had made a great step forward on the issue of whether blacks were citizens. In the meantime, Bates emphasized the narrow sense of citizenship. Although native-born white infants and women were citizens, he pointed out, they possessed few rights generally associated with that status. Bates also noticed that even those who were sold into servitude as a punishment for crime retained their citizenship. Then he came to this conclusion:

> In my opinion, the Constitution uses the word citizen only to express the political quality of the individual in his relation to the nation; to declare that he is a member of the body politic, and bound to it by the reciprocal obligation of allegiance on the one side and protection on the other.[612]

Obviously, the black franchise was excluded by the federal judicial institution.

More and more Republicans, however, theoretically approved of black suffrage, and this change was clearly shown in the discussions of the bill for the organization of the Montana Territory in the Thirty-eighth Congress in 1864. While the House of Representatives limited the suffrage to white male inhabitants, Senator Morton S. Wilkinson of Minnesota moved to enfranchise "every free male citizen and those who have declared their intention to become such," and got his bill passed by a vote of 29 to 8 on the Senate floor. Even in the House of Representatives, there were still fifty-four Republicans who supported the Wilkinson bill, and only twenty who voted against it.[613] At the state level, the election results in the last stage of the Civil War were even more heartening. Black suffrage had attracted 43 percent of the vote in Connecticut, 45 percent in Minnesota, and 47 percent in Wisconsin.[614] Since almost all Democrats were opposed to black suffrage, most Republicans were undoubtedly positive on this issue. The Republican majority eventually failed in their efforts, because there was a conservative minority within the party who had formed an effective alliance with Democrats, and black suffrage had little chance to pass so long as the alliance remained solid. By the end of 1865, therefore, among mainstream Republicans unanimity emerged on the issue of black suffrage and the indispensability of black citizenship.

Superseding the antebellum problem of slavery, the civil right issue in the meantime gradually became the symbol of Republican unity. Hopelessly disagreeing on the tariff, financial reform, and governmental aids to commerce,[615] Republicans were unwilling to make more concessions in their moral principles and especially in the aspect of black citizenship, lest the minor issues should disintegrate their political alignment. Moral promise had become the lifeblood of the Republican party. To the Radicals, the party was not only a political organization, but also a moral instrument based on antislavery and civil right principles. "The strength of the Republican party," Senator Samuel C. Pomeroy insisted, "consists in its adherence to principle, and to that embodiment of its principles, equality of rights among men. Without that there would be no motive to sustain the party, and the party would not be worth sustaining."[616] Without the moral mainstay, the party would have been, as one radical said, "*Hamlet* with Hamlet left out."[617]

Although Republicans had reached their saturation point on the civil right problem, there still remained an obvious obstacle to Reconstruction: how to surmount the limitation of federalism and guarantee black civil rights. In a sense, the crux of Reconstruction was how to achieve a perfect balance between the aim of unity and morality, blacks' due rights and Constitutional order. To maintain the party, Republicans had to overcome the obstacle of their former adherence to state rights and find a point for penetration.

The nearer to the antebellum days, the more persistent the sense of federalism. Although Republicans did not maintain that states had supreme sovereignty, they did cherish a strong sense of state rights, which was embodied in their arguments about slavery and black status. No mainstream politician advocated that the federal government had authority to abolish slavery in the existing states. On the contrary, the increase in federal power was even harmful to the antislavery movement in the free states, if the strong proslavery forces in federal government were taken into account. The basic view of Republicans was that federal citizenship was only the appendage of state citizenship, and it was the states that had the supreme power to decide whether their people were citizens. When Congress passed the Fugitive Slave Act of 1850, Northern states soon adopted the "personal liberty laws" to obstruct the return of fugitive slaves. The confrontation between the legislatures and Congress approached its climax in *Ableman v. Booth*. Although Chief Justice Taney of the U.S. Supreme Court ultimately overturned the decision of the Wisconsin Supreme Court, which tried to invalidate the Fugitive Slave Act by issuing a writ of *habeas corpus* ordering Booth, the accused, be released from federal custody, this case illustrated Republicans' intense apprehension about federal assistance to combat slavery. More inauspicious was the decision in *Dred Scott*, which asserted that Congress had no authority to nullify slavery in a territory. As Lincoln pointed out in his debates with Stephen Douglas, Republicans worried that the next step of the Court would be to allow Southerners to bring their slaves into the free states and in fact change Northern states into slaveholding states.[618] The main divergence with Taney, Lincoln stressed, lay in his denying the states' power to confer citizenship on former slaves rather than the view on whether free blacks were citizens.[619] As a matter of fact, Lincoln was driven to deny that blacks should be citizens, lest he be charged with advocating racial equality. Lincoln's defense of black rights, therefore, was based on federalism instead of racial equality.

With the secession of the Southern states and the outbreak of the war, the strength of the Republican party in federal authorities greatly increased, and its state-centered concept of citizenship was no longer in step with the new circumstances. The decision of Attorney General Bates in 1862 reflected this change. Citizenship, he declared, was solely a matter of federal law and all citizens of the United States were also citizens of their respective states.[620] Yet to declare the precedence of federal citizenship was one thing, and how to define its related rights and how to protect them by federal authorities was another. Until the end of the war, almost all Republicans were unwilling to give up the state-centered federal system. The Civil War was mainly considered as an event to restore the states' former status, and the expansion of federal power to be temporary. Once peace came, normalcy must be reestablished, and the federal and state governments must stay in their respective places. On December 20, 1865, Lyman Trumbull of Illinois expressed the point that the sovereignty of the national entity was divided between the two kinds of governments:

> The States are sovereign as to their reserved rights; but the rights they surrendered up to the Federal Government do not now belong to the States. [It was agreed that the Constitution] should be the supreme law of the land, any law or constitution of [any] State notwithstanding. You have surrendered up that power, and you have no power to absolve yourselves from that allegiance.[621]

The development of the situation in 1865 made the concept of state-centered citizenship less attractive. The ex-Confederates' return to power, the increase in the number of Southern seats, and the persecution of freedmen and Unionists by Southern authorities all intensified Republicans' anxiety over the revival of former slaveholders and the fate of freedmen, and the question whether or not the federal authorities had power to explain and protect civil rights became critical. Republicans unavoidably found themselves in disagreement.

One solution to this problem came from the Radicals. Concerning the legality of federal coercive power over the Southern states, they argued that Southern states need territory status. Having no right to secede from the Union, according to these theories, Southern states had reduced themselves to the position of territories because of their attempt to secede. Therefore, the federal government might directly control the occupied states, and at the same time reserve the autonomy of loyal states. Since the process of accepting a territory as a state was solely supervised by Congress, the occupied states could not restore their former position until the conditions set by Congress were satisfied. Charles Sumner, for example, posed the concept of "state suicide." While having illegitimately seceded, the Southern states had lost their attributes of being states and had now become territories subject to congressional authority. Thaddeus Stevens, on the other hand, adopted the theory of "conquered provinces," as if the war had been waged against a foreign power. By their secession, he argued, the Southern states had rejected the Constitution and had no right to claim its protection. Congress might act with regard to the people and territory of the South as it saw fit; as rebels they had no "standing" in court.[622]

As regards the imposition of compulsory conditions, some Radicals invoked several authoritative sources. As early as 1852, Sumner hailed the Declaration of Independence as that "Great Character of our country" embodying "in immoral words, those primal truths to which our country pledged itself with baptismal vows as a Nation."[623] After the war, he still appealed for reforming the South by resorting to the Declaration:

> I insist the Declaration is of equal and co-ordinate authority with the Constitution itself. Show me any words in the Constitution applicable to human rights, and I invoke at once the great truths of the *Declaration* as the absolute guide in determining their meaning.[624]

The Radicals also found favorable grounds in the Preamble to the Constitution, regarding it as the bridge by which the Declaration was integrated into the Constitution as well as an authoritative statement of national purpose as important as the Declaration itself. To Timothy D. Farrar, George Hoar, Legrand Perce, Joel Tiffany and others, the Preamble not only made the Declaration become the principles of the Constitution, but it was also a power-granting clause and an "indefinable reservoir of power," which might "secure the blessings of liberty and promote the general welfare by prohibiting the State from doing what is inconsistent with civil liberty, and compelling them to do what is essential to its maintenance."[625]

An even more persuasive instrument was the guarantee clause of the Constitution that specified maintenance of "a republican form of government." Initially intended as a device against the revival of monarchy within the American boundaries, this clause was ambiguous and its broadness easily led to diverse interpretations. Since the 1820s, this clause was used by Abolitionists as a weapon, who claimed that human bondage was inconsistent with "a republican form of government." By linking it directly with the Declaration of Independence and with Madison's majority definition of republicanism in *Federalist 39*. Abolitionists made a powerful argument that Congress had authority to abolish slavery in the existing states.[626] Aware that it might be used as a reason for federal intervention in civil rights, the Radicals now took hold of this sharp sword without the slightest hesitation. This was "the jewel of the Constitution," declared Illinois Senator Richard Yates, and Sumner praised it as "a sleeping giant, never until this recent war awakened, but now it comes forward with a giant's power. There is no clause in the Constitution like it. There is no other clause that gives to Congress such supreme power over the states." Since the republican form of government was not clearcut, "the time has come," Sumner stressed, "to fix a meaning on these words."[627]

The mainstream Republicans, however, were much more cautious about the binding force of federalism than the Radicals were. While the Radicals' demonstrations had not convinced the majority of Republicans, the latter did not intend to simply accept the former Confederate states. Against this background, Richard Henry Dana, a Republican lawyer from Boston, advanced the most persuasive theory of "grasp of war." Based on the widespread notion that the national government had temporarily expanded power during wartime, Dana asserted that only the federal government had the authority to decide when the war ended. As long as the wartime state had not been renounced, the Southern states remained in a condition of suspended animation, with Congress having the right to determine the terms on which their full status might be resumed. Until the terms were satisfied, the federal coercive power could not be withdrawn from the relevant states. As Dana put it, "The conquering party may hold the other in the grasp of war until it has secured whatever it has a right to acquire."[628] According to this theory, Republicans could draw a clear line between the former Confederate states and the loyal states; it could both provide grounds for the temporarily expanded federal power and restore the restrictions of the Constitution in normal times.

In 1865 and 1866, more and more Republicans regarded black suffrage as the key to the Reconstruction problem. Not only radical organs such as the *National Anti-Slavery Standard* and *New York Tribune*, but also the moderate periodicals, including *Harper's Weekly*, the *Nation*, and the *Germantown Telegraph*, favored this position. Even those who opposed black suffrage more often based their arguments on federalism rather than civil rights principles. The *New York Times*, for example, admitted that black suffrage was desirable, but the structure of federalism did not allow such federal interference on this subject.[629] The supporters of black suffrage, however, maintained that this action could guarantee blacks' fundamental rights without touching traditional federalism. If the revised state constitutions could protect blacks' franchise and other rights, there would be no necessity for the federal government to intervene in the former Confederate states after their admission to the Union, for the freedmen might defend themselves by this political weapon. "The ballot," Radical Senator Richard Yates announced, "will finish the negro question, it will settle everything connected with this question. We need no vast expenditures, we need no standing army. Sir, the ballot is the freedmen's Moses."[630] Therefore, black suffrage was not only considered as a moral problem, but also the key to the restrictions of federalism. In a sense, black suffrage was regarded as a conservative solution to the Reconstruction dilemma. Luckily enough, the political pattern in Congress favored this philosophy. The election of 1864 substantially increased the size of the Republican majority: in both the Senate and the House of Representatives, Republicans held two-thirds of the membership. United, they could easily pass any bill they chose. Conditions were ripe for black suffrage.

Even so, black suffrage was still restricted by a third factor. To politicians, whether black suffrage could be listed on the agenda still depended on practical political considerations. To retain their control over Congress and future presidential elections, almost all Republicans hoped to build up a force in the South that sympathized with the Republican party. What made Republicans extremely anxious was that Southern delegates to Congress and the Electoral College would greatly increase in their number, because the black population was no longer counted at the rate of three-fifths. Without any precondition imposed, the former Confederates would arrogantly penetrate into Washington as victors. If black suffrage was carried out, many Republicans believed, the Southern leadership would be regenerated, and the Republican party would exceed its regional limits and develop into a national party, with the whole country firmly controlled in its hands. "*Do not let the power pass away*," Alexander K. McKilure insisted. "If necessary let suffrage go, & confiscation also if thereby you can save the rest."[631]

At the initial stage, however, Republicans felt little pressing political necessity to adopt black suffrage. They generally hoped that Johnson's moderate Reconstruction plan would win Southerners' favor and build up a force sympathetic to their party, and that black rights would be appropriately protected by white Southerners themselves. *Harper's Weekly* was confident that Johnson was only "feeling his way," that he did "not assume to dictate in any least degree to Congress." Senator Lot M. Morrill of Maine believed that "still it is only an experiment. Let him try it."[632] Although some persons began to deride Johnson's "experiment," only a minority entirely gave up their confidence in him, until the Thirty-ninth Congress was summoned. Both moderates and conservatives hoped that the conflict between the president and the Congress could be avoided. An important fact was that the moderates' support for the president would rule out the danger that the president and the conservatives might drop out of the party. This split of party would be disastrous, for it meant that the Republican party would face an alignment of former Confederates, Democrats in the North, and dissenters within the Republican party, with the president as their leader. Thus, the moderates now seeking cooperation with the president had to first win over the conservatives; to make concessions to the moral pressure within the party meanwhile, they also needed flexible attitudes on the part of the president lest the party fall apart.

As soon as Congress convened, the moderates began to carry out their program. Using a brilliant tactic in the process of roll call, they shelved Southern delegates' assumption of their seats, and chose a Joint Committee on Reconstruction chaired by a conservative Republican leader of the Senate, William Pitt Fessenden of Maine. On January 12, 1866, Lyman Trumbull, a very moderate Republican senator from Illinois, submitted to the Senate the Freedmen's Bureau Bill, which extended the life of the Freedmen's Bureau and slightly expanded its power.

Asserting that this bill was unconstitutional, the Democrats immediately launched an offensive against the Republicans. They were particularly intolerant of the two sections that provided that "In any state or district in which the ordinary course of judicial proceedings has been interrupted by the rebellion," military authorities would ensure that blacks' civil rights were protected. While the Democrats criticized that these provisions had violated states' rights, Republicans generally perceived it as a moderate Reconstruction proposal. They either argued in favor of its legality on condition of war powers or invoked the enforcement clause of the Thirteenth Amendment to defend its authority. On January 25, the Freedmen's Bureau Bill passed the Senate by a 37 to 10 margin. Frustrating the Radicals' hope of adding provisions on land confiscation and public education, moderates also easily passed the bill on the House floor on February 6.

President Johnson was very annoyed. Since the Republicans refused to accept the Southern delegates, he became increasingly impatient. Firmly believing that the Democrats would support him without reservation, and that there would be a large number of Conservatives to follow him in the Republic party, Johnson flatly vetoed this bill. On the one hand, he asserted that Congress had no power to pass this measure, and any bill would be invalid without the attendance of Southern delegates; on the other hand, he implied that his Reconstruction plan was final and supreme:

> The Constitution imperatively declares, in connection with taxation, that each State *shall* have at least one Representative. It also provided that the Senate of the United States *shall* be composed of two Senators from each State. At the time, however, of the consideration and the passing of this bill there was no Senator or Representative in Congress from the eleven States which are to be mainly affected by its provision. I would not interfere with the unquestionable right of Congress to judge, each House for itself, "of the elections, returns, and qualifications of its own members"; but that authority can not be constructed as including the right to shut out in time of peace any State from the representation to which it is entitled by the Constitution.[633]

Therefore, Johnson, the president elected by Northern voters, issued a challenge to the authority of Congress on the most fundamental issue.

The president's veto caused Republicans to fall into temporary confusion. Eight conservative Republican Senators withdrew their support for the bill, including Doolittle, Stewart, James Dixon of Connecticut, Edwin D. Morgan of New York, Daniel S. Norton of Minnesota, Peter Van Winkle, Waitman T. Willey of West Virginia, and Edgar Cowan of

Pennsylvania. The vote in the Senate was 30 to 18, two votes short of the two-thirds majority necessary to override the veto. Thus, the first attempt of the Thirty-ninth Congress to protect civil rights ended in failure. The result illustrated that the support of the conservatives was critical and that any attempt to override a presidential veto must have their approval.

While the Freedmen's Bureau bill was brewing, moderate Republicans also sought Conservatives' endorsement of a Constitutional amendment that would redistribute the House seats to dispel their serious misgivings about the expansion of Southern power. In early 1866, however, any Constitutional amendment enfranchising blacks could not gain the support of the conservatives. The only practical choice was to reduce the representation of the states that denied black suffrage. One motion was that representation be based on the number of voters in each state. Yet this proposal would change the power balance among the Northern states as well as between the North and the South. Because women had no franchise, New England, whose ratio of men to women had decreased, was rather dissatisfied with this arrangement.[634] Many Republicans worried that it would intensify Southern unhappiness with the disenfranchisement of the former Confederates and encourage the states to improperly extend the suffrage to aliens and children. So the Joint Committee revised the proposal. Representation was still based on population, but the number of representatives of the states that did not enfranchise blacks would be reduced accordingly. On January 31, the Joint Committee proposal passed without difficulty in the House, with only twelve Republicans opposed. Among the dissenters there were both conservative and Radical Republicans. While the conservatives and the Democrats insisted that it was unnecessary to amend the Constitution, the Radicals complained that this proposal would imply acquiescence in the states' right to disfranchise blacks. Thinking that it was purely on the basis of pragmatism and just was a "constitutional recognition of an Oligarch, Aristocracy, Caste and Monopoly, founded on color," Charles Sumner, the defender of the Radical position in the Senate, fiercely attacked this proposal.[635] With four other Radical senators, Sumner voted against this proposal on March 9. Although their position helped to throttle the amendment, the whole vote would still have been short of the two-thirds majority even if they had voted in favor of it. In such a critical moment, not only was the strategy of the moderates crucial, but the conservatives' attitude towards President Johnson was key. Unexpectedly, the president's veto of the civil rights bill drove a wedge between him and some conservatives.

The civil rights bill was also advanced by Lyman Trumbull, and its final form was reached after many revisions. For the first time, this bill defined citizenship and delimited the range of civil rights:

> All persons born in the United States and not subject to any foreign power, excluding Indians not taxed, are hereby declared to be citizens of the United States; and such citizens, of every race and color, without regard to any previous condition of slavery or involuntary servitude, except as a punishment for crime whereof the party shall have been duly convicted, shall have the same right, in every State and Territory in the United States, to make and enforce contracts, to sue, be parties, and give evidence, to inherit, purchase, lease, sell, hold, and equal benefit of all laws and proceedings for the security of person and property, as is enjoyed by white citizens.[636]

The civil rights listed in the first section of the bill could be divided into two classes. One included the economic rights to participate in a free labor–based society, the other embraced the right to equal protection by government, and particularly right of due process. Those were the basic principles that Republicans could not yield.

As for the federalism involved in the civil rights bill, many Republicans were looking before they leap. Compared with the Freedmen's Bureau bill, the civil rights bill was national rather than regional, and permanent rather than temporary. So it could not be justified by the war power theory. Did the federal government have the authority to define citizenship? Could it provide some appropriate protection for its citizens? Invoking the enforcement clause of the Thirteenth Amendment and congressional power to provide a uniform rule of naturalization, Trumbull answered affirmatively. Although the second clause of Article III of the Constitution applied only to cases in which citizens of one state were sojourning in another state, Trumbull argued, it clearly implied that Congress possessed authority to require states to bestow basic civil rights on all inhabitants.[637] On the other hand, James F. Wilson, chairman of the House Judicial Committee, claimed that this clause not only prevented a state from depriving other states' citizens of basic rights, but also applied to a state's relationship to its own citizens. Since there was no enforcement provision in this clause, Wilson meaningfully adopted Justice Story's *proslavery* opinion that Congress had power to implement Section 3 of Article III by adopting appropriate legislation such as the Fugitive Slave Act.[638] Thus, playing into the hands of Republicans, the former proslavery judgment was now used to prove the supremacy of the relationship between citizens and the federal government.

Section one and section two of the civil rights bill embodied the above-mentioned position, stipulating that any civil and criminal cases "affecting persons who are denied or cannot enforce in the court or judicial tribunals of the State or locality where they may be any of the rights secured to them" might be removed to the proper district or circuit court of the United States.[639] Whether this bill "embodied a profound change in federal-state relations," however, still needs scrutinizing.[640] First, this bill was directed against the discriminatory public policies of states rather than personal discrimination. Second, if the states abided by the requirement, according to William Stewart, the federal law would become "a nullity" and have "no operation."[641] Many Republicans believed that Trumbull had devised an ingenious instrument to retain state rights while he forced the states to grant all citizens equality before the law. As a persistent deterrent, the federal government would interfere only in case of the states' defaulting their due responsibilities instead of directly protecting fundamental civil rights. Federalism was considerably altered, but its basic structure did not change.

Although Trumbull's argument had not convinced all Republicans, most of them still felt a great necessity to protect freedmen's rights and at the same time avoid the disastrous fate of the Freedmen's Bureau bill. Almost unanimously, the Republicans passed the civil rights bill in Congress. On March 27, President Johnson resolutely vetoed the bill. Instead of criticizing the details of the bill, Johnson again insisted that the existing Congress possessed no authority to pass any civil rights legislation, thereby leaving no conciliatory margin. More obviously relying on whites' racist feelings, he now raised the sensitive topic of intermarriage, and claimed that "the distinction of race and color is, by the bill, made to operate in favor of the colored and against the white race."[642]

The president's tough stand estranged him from the Republicans who originally hoped to cooperate with him. To them, blacks' fundamental rights as citizens could not be compromised. Conservative Senator Edwin D. Morgan had made the "most earnest efforts with Mr. Fessenden and with the President to have a compromise bill agreed upon and passed." Had the president not objected to the "principle and pointed out the defects of the details, the Senate would have amended and passed the bill without any break or serious trouble, as we all know that the second section was objectionable. But the first could not and would not give up."[643] Because Johnson refused to make any concession, Morgan eventually joined the ranks opposing the president. Since there would be little or no benefit if their fundamental creeds were abandoned, Republicans decided to take a firm position even at the cost of presidential leadership. On June 6, the civil rights bill passed the Senate by a narrow margin of two-thirds votes; on June 9, it was also approved on the House floor. The civil rights bill immediately became a law.

The clash over the Freedmen's Bureau and the civil rights bill made the Republicans thoroughly break with the president. Consequently, the Republican party was not only confronted with a group of hostile former Confederates in the South, but also with a campaign that could end Republican ascendancy in the impending middle election of Congress in the North. Worrying about the fate of his party, Henry L. Dawes, a moderate representative from Massachusetts, said pessimistically that "the war has begun which can end only in general in ruin of the party."[644] Republicans were eager to reach agreement and fought the election on a distinct platform different from that of the President. Only the civil rights bill, however, was insufficient, and itself might be easily overthrown by a new Congress. Under the circumstances, the Fourteenth Amendment was born.

Despite their willingness to guarantee the basic rights of blacks, most Republicans were not ready to sacrifice the support of wavering Republicans and adopt the Radicals' suggestion to lower the Southern states into territories and bestow impartial or universal suffrage on blacks. Regardless of the pressure from the Radicals, Republicans set about implementing the moderate plan they had sought from the beginning. The paramount consideration was to gain the two-thirds majority in Congress.

As a result of the attempt to maintain party unity, the Fourteenth Amendment was obviously motivated by both ideals and expedience. Section one consisted of two parts. One part defined the citizenship and promised to protect civil "privileges" and "immunities"; another part concerning due process and equal protection under the law was applicable to noncitizens as well as citizens. Since it was stated in universal words, blacks were not mentioned specifically. Section two proposed that "Representatives shall be apportioned among the several States according to their respective numbers, counting the whole number of persons in each states, excluding Indians not taxed."[645] The original terms about black suffrage were deleted, because some important Republicans did not wish to conduct an election campaign on such a basis.[646] As a compromise agreement, this section stipulated that the number of representatives should be reduced in proportion to the number of disfranchised male citizens. Although it could preclude Southerners from enjoying total representation if they disfranchised blacks, this section left them some leeway to limit the vote on the basis of race. Wendall Philips, a radical Abolitionist, denounced it as a "fatal and total surrender."[647] The conservatives, on the other hand, strongly objected to the third section that prohibited former Confederates from official tenure unless Congress removed such disability by a vote of two-thirds of both House and Senate. There was much dispute over the amendment among Republicans, but in the end they had made the necessary concessions. On June 13, the House accepted the Senate's position and, without a Democrat in favor of it or a Republican opposed to it, approved the amendment.[648]

Did the Fourteenth Amendment fundamentally change the structure of federalism? The Republican party and the Democrat party each stuck to its own version. The focus of debates was the first section. Expressing the Republicans' view, John Bingham said that "this amendment takes from no State any right that ever pertained to it." Democrat George S. Shanklin, on the other hand, asserted that "the first section of this proposed amendment to the Constitution is to strike down States' rights and invest all power in the national government."[649] In reviewing these contrasting opinions, it is necessary to take account of the complicated composition of the Republican party. Since any possibility of excessively expansive judicial interpretation would lead to a split in the Republican party, the alteration of federalism could not go too far.[650] This section merely outlined the status of citizens and noncitizens and placed both under federal protection. Of those rights mentioned, the right of due process had been partially adopted by the Thirteenth Amendment; the citizenship and the "privileges and immunities" thereof just reaffirmed the principles of the civil rights bill. Thus, Thaddeus Stevens noted that it was "partially true" that the amendment "secures the same things" as the civil rights bill,[651] and the federal government was allowed to regulate the states' actions only when they had adopted discriminatory public policies. Bingham stated this pure state-action theory: "National law must protest the privileges and immunities of all the citizens as well as aliens in the Republic. It must prevent any state from abridging or denying the inborn rights of every person in its jurisdiction."[652] Hence the writers of the Fourteenth Amendment did not intent to drastically alter federalism. The amendment simply empowered an existing national instrument, the Supreme Court, to supervise the public policy of each state rather than setting up a separate institution to defend civil rights. The new supervising function of the Supreme Court, admittedly, did not exist before, and this change was permanent.

The Radicals regarded this amendment as an essential precondition of Southern states' restoration. They still pinned their hopes on the federal protection of black suffrage. Henry M. Turner, a black minister and political organizer, reported that "several Congressmen tell me, 'the negro must vote,' but the issue must be avoided now so as 'to keep up a two thirds power in Congress.'" [653] Yet the majority of Republicans considered it the last requirement. Having ratified the Fourteenth Amendment before the adjournment of Congress in July, Tennessee quickly regained its right to representation, by which the Republicans sent out a signal to the South that their policy was limited. As the moderate Republican organ the *Nation* declared, "The South has now an opportunity to choose its own destiny." [654]

In the campaign of 1866, the ally of the South, Democrats in the North, unexpectedly suffered a crushing defeat; even so the Southern states still clung tenaciously to their course and refused to ratify the amendment. Neither could they accept reduced Southern power in national government nor expanded federal authority over the states. Although the amendment did not allow the federal government to involve itself directly in state suffrage, white Southerners worried that it might be the thin end of the wedge for black suffrage. The punitive intention of the disfranchisement clause and the change of Southern power structure it might effect also greatly repelled them. Some accommodationists had devised the "North Carolina Plan," but it only attracted a few supporters. [655]

The Republican victory in the election stimulated the vitality of the second session of the Thirty-ninth Congress. Being confident of support from their constituencies, Republicans were much more determined to seek their moral goal. At the same time, the most conservative Republicans, such as Senator James Doolittle of Wisconsin, Senator James Dixon of Connecticut, and the cabinet members Montgomery Blair and Gideon Wells, had openly come over to the side of the president and no longer exerted positive influence on the decisions of the party. Thus, the Thirty-ninth Congress was more radical than ever before. If Southerners could not voluntarily ratify the Fourteenth Amendment, a substitute must be found that might compel Southerners to accept the conditions set by Congress, without drastically altering the structure of federalism. The only feasible and the simplest plan was to put the South under temporary military occupation, enfranchise blacks, and finally approve the amendment through the hands of Unionists. Senator John Sherman of Ohio regrettably felt the narrow room for maneuver: "If they do not accept [the amend-ment], then what is left to us? We have either got to be ruled by these people or we have got to rule them."[656]

Hence the moderate leader James G. Blaine devised a plan for military occupation, the "Blaine amendment," requiring that the ex-Confederate states ratify the Fourteenth Amendment as a starting point for their restora-tion and additionally modify their constitutions to place the vote in the hands of "all male citizens of the United States without regard to race, color or previous condition of servitude."[657] The Radicals, however, still complained at its insufficiency. As George W. Julian recalled, the Radicals "warned the country, and foretold that no theories of democracy could avail unless adequately supported by a healthy and intelligent public opin-ion."[658] Expecting further economic and social changes, they were unwill-ing to definitely promise the rapid restoration of the Southern states. In the House, Radicals hindered the Blaine amendment from passing; but on the Senate floor, moderates transformed the Blaine amendment into a bill that won a comforting victory. To break the deadlock, however, the moderates had to make some concessions. As the price for Radical support, the added clause declared that the state governments established by Johnson were only provisional and, if necessary, could be disbanded by the military com-manders, and that the Southerners disqualified by the Fourteenth Amend-ment should not be eligible for any office under the state governments.[659] Johnson vetoed the bill, only to find himself overridden again by Congress. On March 2, 1867, the Reconstruction Act became law.

Thus, to include suffrage among the indispensable civil rights and implement these rights by the federal government became key in the Re-construction dilemma. Such being the case, the Fourteenth Amendment and the Reconstruction Act only required Southerners to "pass judgment on the governments that would rule them, rather than simply have them imposed from outside."[660] Nor had the Republicans created special agen-cies institutionally committed to defending black rights. As a result, the duty of supervising the local administration of the law mainly fell to the overworked Justice Department. Naturally, Republicans did their utmost to prove the moderation of these measures. As Carl Schurz put it later,

> Far from desiring centralization repugnant to the genius of the country,
> it is in the distinct interest of local self-government and legitimate state
> rights that we urge these propositions, and nothing can be more certain
> that this is the only way in which a dangerous centralization of power
> in the hands of our general government can be prevented.[661]

Radicals were not yet satisfied. They pressed further their demand for a statute that would insure impartial suffrage throughout the nation, asserting that the guarantee clause and the enforcement provision of the Thirteenth Amendment had provided Congress with the necessary authority. In this regard Charles Sumner and Henry Wilson were the most persistent and clamorous advocates of the Radical position.[662] On the other hand, some suggested that ratification of the Fourteenth Amendment would give Congress the necessary authority.[663] The moderates, however, refused to accept these explanations. Trumbull insisted that "even to do a right thing in a wrong way is often fraught with greater danger than to leave the thing undone," and that "to allow [Congress] to exercise powers not granted would be to make [the legislators] masters instead of the servants of the people, and such a representative government would be little better than despotism."[664] When Sumner submitted his universal suffrage bill to the Senate in July 1867, fifteen Republicans joined with Democrats in refusing to consider the bill.

The reason that the moderates and the conservatives objected to statutory regulation of suffrage was not that they did not approve of the principle of impartial suffrage, but that such a statute meant that Congress possessed the flexible authority to define the "republic form." On the contrary, they firmly believed the rightness of impartial suffrage, and many sincerely regarded the Democrats' return to power as a disaster for the nation. In some cases, they sought for impartial suffrage even at the risk of losing more white votes.[665] Edmund G. Ross of Kansas voiced the common sentiments of Republicans: "The first great and sufficient reason why the negro should be admitted to the right of suffrage in all the States is that it is right."[666] How to find a workable solution? Since the right to vote was neither considered a necessary concomitant of citizenship or a natural right connected with freedom, Republicans could not have recourse to the Fourteenth or Thirteenth Amendment. This problem, the moderate and conservative Republicans believed, could be solely resolved by another amendment. To them, the Constitutional amendment regulating the states' suffrage might more or less encroach on states' rights, but it could clearly define the relationship between the states and the federal government and thereby maintain the necessary balance.

Another consideration also influenced Republicans' decision. The statute might be annulled by Congress, overthrown by judicial decision, or ignored by Southern states after their restoration.[667] Only a Constitutional amendment could guarantee security. Even before the election of

1868, for example, the *Nation* had expressed the fear that white Southerners would disfranchise blacks after their readmission to the Union.[668]

On March 7, 1867, John Henderson proposed a Constitutional amendment that would prohibit racial discrimination on the suffrage issue. Not being eager to carry out this program, however, the moderates confined their agenda mainly to improving the Reconstruction Act, perhaps because they thought that the time was not yet ripe for another amendment. In the following state elections in the fall of 1867, the party suffered a setback, and many attributed it to Republican sponsorship of black suffrage.[669] In early 1868, Johnson's impeachment became another focus for Republican attention. The president narrowly escaped from the charge by a margin of one vote. In the presidential election of 1868, the wishes of the conservatives affected the nomination of the Republican candidate for the presidency, and moderate Republican candidate Ulysses S. Grant promised the earliest restoration of normalcy. with control of the presidency, Republicans wanted to resolve the problem of suffrage and end Reconstruction. Oliver Morton of Indiana made this point very clearly:

> The Democratic party for more than twenty years has lived upon the negro question. It has been its daily food, and if the negro question shall now be withdrawn from politics the Democracy, as a party, will literally starve to death. This constitutional amendment will forever withdraw the subject from politics, and will strike down that prejudice to which the Democratic party has appealed for years.[670]

At the same time, taking advantage of their temporary ascendancy in Congress, Republicans also hoped to eliminate the problem of the party's treating Northern and Southern blacks in different ways. Frederick A. Sawyer, a senator from the recently reconstructed state of South Carolina, complained that "we have for two years been subjected to the charge that the Republican party of the northern States put the negro on one platform in the loyal States and upon another platform in the lately disloyal States."[671]

In the third session of the Fortieth Congress, the Radicals were pressing for a suffrage statute, but both the moderates and the Democrats doubted the Constitutional authority for Congress to regulate suffrage without a Constitutional amendment. Proposed by Congressman Samuel Shellabarger, a Constitutional amendment of universal suffrage was also defeated. The remaining choice was the relatively conservative suffrage proposal that would prohibit discrimination based on race, color, or previous condition of servitude. As to blacks' right to hold office, most Republicans did not oppose it in theory, but they would rather sacrifice it to gain the necessary majority votes. Once blacks were securely enfranchised, they argued, the office-holding problem would look after itself. Based on the consideration of federalism, the moderates compelled the Radicals to give up the open-ended Constitutional view of federal power. Even so, a number of Radicals still refused to cooperate.[672] On February 26,1868, the Fifteenth Amendment was passed in Congress.

Undoubtedly, the intrinsic forces driving the situation forward included Republicans' consideration for power. The politicians obviously believed that it was not sensible to merely rely on morality itself to propel individuals forward. Even Sumner himself conceded with forthrightness that "it was on this ground, rather than principle, that I relied most."[673] Public moral feelings, however, were also a strong force, while the commitment to civil rights had in fact become the lifeblood of Republican interests. What the politicians could do was to command more or less flexibility under this prerequisite. Furthermore, while Republicans sought their party's interests, they also believed in the rightness of their cause As Bernard A. Weisberger put it, "This is a high order of abstraction! Yet it was fundamentally American."[674] The rightness of their cause was not only embodied in their beliefs in fundamental rights, but also in their devotion to federalism. Even the Radicals had never intended to violate Constitutional principles. To them, the true Constitution was the one in harmony with the civil rights principle. Sumner even declared that "anything for Human Rights is constitutional" and that "there can be no State Rights against Human Rights."[675] But this extreme Constitutional view had never prevailed in the whole process of amending the Constitution. It was the moderates that had shaped Reconstruction policy, which was further tempered by the balancing power of the conservatives. The frequent Constitutional debates themselves were enough to demonstrate their respect for the Constitution. At least subjectively, the draftsmen of the Reconstruction amendments had no intention of changing federalism drastically. The revolutionary nature was only limited to the aspect that an insufficiently represented Congress willfully drew up the amendments and then forced them through the national legislature, which, just as Lincoln published the Emancipation Proclamation, represented the continuation of war power.

Thus, the balance between the states and the federal government had been readjusted, but there was no fundamental revolution of federalism.

The objective of the adjustment was to find a proper intersection between federalism and states' rights, between the practical aim of the war and its moral aim, and between political expediency and ideals. Thanks to this adjustment, the controversial issue of citizenship had been settled once and for all in the American political system. State-centered citizenship was superseded by the dual citizenship shared by both the states and the nation, and African Americans were integrated into the mainstream of American society as one of "all men" in the Declaration of Independence and "we, the people of the United States" in the Preamble, but the operational system between the states and the federal government had not been greatly altered. To the black person, that was a great stride. Yet he was not regarded as a particular favorite, different from others, but as an ordinary element of the whole society. In theory, the amendments to the Constitution removed the obstacles to blacks' integration into the main body politic, and eliminated racial discrimination from public policy. When tackling the civil right problem, the draftsmen of the Reconstruction amendments did not intend to create a revolution that would transform the existing system. They only hoped to include blacks in the present system, and only a limited, conservative revolution had taken place within the original democratic framework.

In a deeper sense, the Reconstruction amendments theoretically expanded the original principle of the Constitution, excluded exceptions, and harmonized the Constitutional principle with practice. In the view of the neoabolitionists, however, the "Reconstruction Constitution" departed from the original Constitution in two basic aspects. Firstly, as did the old Abolitionists, they thought that the original Constitution contained no principle of equality and clearly excluded blacks from the main body politic of America because of its recognition and protection of slavery. Secondly, the liberty embodied in the Constitution was in reality a defective concept of possessive individualism that allowed humans to be considered property. The Reconstruction amendments, on the other hand, incarnated a sounder idea of liberty and further introduced the concept of equality. Thus, as a matter of fact, a new Constitution was born. In *University of California Regents v. Bakke*, Justice Thurgood Marshall expressed this opinion.[676]

Yet this Constitutional view was not convincing as it seemed to be. Property was a natural right recognized by the Constitution, but it received no special emphasis, nor was it elevated to a position of political priority.[677] Just as Locke's political philosophy contained the duality inherent in a liberal doctrine often conflating human rights with property rights,[678] the Constitution also embodied this ambiguity, without clearly defining the dividing line between the two. On the one hand, the draftsmen of the Constitution emphasized the protection of private property; on the other hand, they also committed themselves to championing human rights. Arguing that it was unnecessary to include the Bill of Rights in the Constitution, Alexander Hamilton wrote, "The Constitution is itself, in every rational sense, and to every useful purpose, a bill of rights." "Here, in strictness, the people surrender nothing."[679] Having their eyes on the future, the draftsmen of the Constitution placed their hopes on the death of slavery, and were unwilling to integrate it into the national law as an eternal system. The tendency to recognize human rights was obvious. As James Madison put it, it would be "wrong to admit in the Constitution the idea that there could be property in man."[680] Seen from the circumstances at that time, the North was finishing its task of abolishing slavery, while the South was apologizing over and again for the presence of the peculiar institution, which was generally regarded as an evil. The wording used by the draftsmen of the Constitution showed their moral uneasiness at the presence of slavery. So there was no word about slavery in the Constitution. Although they had to tolerate it as a temporary phenomenon, the founding fathers had no intention of recognizing slavery in theory. Evidence that whites were somewhat tolerant of black rights was that free blacks possessed the right to vote in all the original states except for South Carolina and Georgia at the time of enacting the Constitution.[681] Since the principles observed by the government were always higher than its practice, Frederick Douglass inferred, the fact itself that there was no word admitting slavery in the Constitution was convincing evidence that the Constitution had not established slavery.[682] The Constitution avoided explicitly recognizing slavery, which meant that the people in this land could not justify the legality of humans as property on the grounds of the fundamental law. The Constitution mainly had in mind long-term interests of the people; the liberty established by it began in individuality and ended in common choice and public welfare. Self-interest had been fully taken into account, but it must be balanced in a republic form and in harmony with positive moral purpose. Since the Constitution had not definitely clarified the potential conflicts between human rights and humans as property, and since it contained the third-fifths ratio caused by the political compromise, the Constitution left enough leeway to be explained as a proslavery document that included the concept of possessive individualism. Thus, there arose the Fugitive Slave Act, the *Dred Scott* decision;

and the extreme words of William Lloyd Garrison, the Abolitionist, who condemned the Constitution as "your covenant with Death" and "your agreement with Hell" and declared that "the Constitution which subjects them to hopeless bondage, is one that we cannot swear to support!"[683] Having eliminated the ambiguity caused by the presence of slavery, the Reconstruction amendments gave prominence to the human rights principles in the Declaration of Independence, and clearly recognized the universal significance of liberty. Once the Thirteenth Amendment was no longer enough to bear the heavy burden of protecting civil rights, the Republicans brought forth the Fourteenth Amendment; when the Fourteenth amendment could not guarantee the impartial suffrage of citizens, they again passed the Fifteenth Amendment. Without interrupting the continuity of tradition, the Republicans had not undertaken a radical revolution in reforming the original meaning of liberty or shaking the federal system itself, although the right to vote had gone beyond the fundamental category of civil rights; yet at the same time it was a conservative revolution that extended the Constitutional liberty monopolized by whites to another race, that included blacks in the former democratic and federal frameworks and established a new racial democracy, and that integrated democratic theory with democratic practice. In a sense, the presence of African Americans stimulated the expansion of American democracy. Willis J. King put this point succinctly: "One of the significant contributions made by the Negro to American life has been the development and extension of the American idea of Democracy."[684]

HOPE AND BURDEN: CONGRESSIONAL RECONSTRUCTION AND BLACK POWER

By means of the Reconstruction Act of March 1867, Congress finally decided to let Southern blacks protect themselves through the ballot. Although it had neither devised any economic and social reform plan necessary for the success of this program, nor had it carried out any trial period that might alleviate white resistance, Congress did provide Southern blacks with an opportunity and the exterior driving force that might bring about further changes by requiring that Southern states should adopt new constitutions conforming with Reconstruction policy. A new era seething with excitement began.

Under the Reconstruction Act, the Southern states were divided into five military districts. The commander of each district was empowered to protect life and peace, supervise the process of reorganization, and replace officials who hindered Reconstruction procedure. Such being the case, the military occupation was relatively moderate, and the soldiers dispatched to the ten states were no more than twenty thousand, of whom some saw service on the Texas frontier. New Orleans and Richmond had each 1,000 men, but no other places had 500 and many counties saw very few or none.[685] Of the commanders chosen by Johnson, only Philip H. Sheridan of the fifth district vigorously supported the Republican party and discharged many officials from their posts. The president, however, soon replaced him with General Winfield S. Hancock, who declared that the military authorities would be subordinate to the civil government.[686] Other commanders were unwilling to interfere in civil affairs. Thus, the state and local governments established by Johnson were at least temporarily unimpaired. Most openly discriminatory laws were revised or annulled, but the civil courts were still manipulated by local influential whites, and only the cases obviously discriminating against blacks and Unionists were overthrown. As for the media through which Southern whites wantonly vilified Reconstruction policy, the military authorities left it alone. E. Q. C. Ord of the fourth district, for example, once arrested William T. McCardle, editor of the *Vicksburg Times*, and James Dugan, editor of the *Vicksburg Republican* for "disturbing the public peace." Each was freed upon the payment of a one thousand dollar peace bond, but General Gillem, Ord's successor, simply returned the money.[687] Compared with the hard line of Southern governments towards blacks and Unionists, the military "dictatorship" over Southern states was much more generous.

The most imperative task for the army was to register voters according to the Reconstruction Act. It needed first to decide which persons had voluntarily assisted the Confederacy, but how to determine the ranks of the officials and the degrees to which they had served the Confederacy was left to the registration committee of each county, which was generally composed of military officers, the Bureau's agents, and local Unionists. Consequently, most former Confederate officials were temporarily disfranchised.

For blacks, the practice of the universal norms of conduct in politics and the opening of public power stimulated their desire to integrate fully into American mainstream society. In principle, they were due not only equal protection under the law and the right to participate in the labor market, but also could share political power and take part in making the rules of the political game. Although the change came swiftly and violently, blacks soon considered it a natural thing and the prelude to being complete Americans. As an Alabama black convention insisted, "We claim exactly *the same rights, privileges and immunities as are enjoyed by white men.* We asked nothing more and will be content with nothing less. The law no longer knows white nor black, but simply men."[688] Certainly, these demands did not mean the utter abandonment of racial identity. As Du Bois put it, Reconstruction allowed the African Americans to "attain self-conscious manhood" by merging "his double self into a truer and better self."[689] Yet the emphasis on racial identity was overwhelmed by the desire for assimilation. Martin R. Delany, the South Carolina organizer, found it "dangerous to go into the country and speak of color in any manner whatever."[690]

The enthusiasm for politics aroused among blacks also had other dynamic sources. In a society like America that relied on voters to directly control public affairs but had little tradition of independent and neutral administration, according to Gunnar Myrdal, the ballot was of much importance for the daily welfare of blacks.[691] As a result, each group must have a voice in the government, otherwise they would be in a very difficult predicament. In the era of Reconstruction, therefore, blacks understandably placed emphasis on their right to vote. Although they were in general lacking in political experience, blacks could at least understand their interests. "The only salvation for us besides the power of the Government," asserted Virginia freedmen, "is in the *possession of the ballot.* Give us this, and we will protect ourselves."[692] Many blacks believed that they might achieve other practical aims through the ballot. When the land dream was nearly shattered, the bestowal of suffrage revived their expectations. In December 1867, many freedmen refused to sign labor contracts for the coming year in the hope of getting a patch of land. Here and there hearsay about confiscation was spread. The discussion of land distribution, reported an official of the American Missionary Association from North Carolina, "has much greater prominence here than our friends at the North seem to be aware."[693]

At the same time, the political mobilization of the African American community was launched on a grand and spectacular scale. Political lecture meetings swept across the whole black belt. To participate in all sorts of political activities, many blacks put aside their work. Because too many black laborers attended the Republican state convention, Richmond's tobacco factories had to close on August 1, 1867.[694] Black institutions such as churches and schools were politicized. One black minister said: "Politics got in our midst and our revival or religious work for a while began to wane."[695] "You never saw a people more excited on the subject of politics than are the negroes of the south," one plantation manager said in describing the excitement of the black community. "They are perfectly wild."[696]

Beating the drum for the Republican party, the Union League played a large part in the mobilization of the African American community. Initially established in wartime Philadelphia, this flag-waving organization defined its purpose as fidelity to the Union. With the advent of Congressional Reconstruction, it spread rapidly through the whole South.[697] Although its meetings, pledges, and duties were secret, the league made its member list public and openly organized mass demonstrations, party rallies, and support activities. Because of its energetic support for black interests, almost all black voters joined the Union League or similar organizations by the end of 1867.

The main function of the Union League was to guide blacks to devote themselves to the Republican party. Centering on lectures made by party leaders and candidates, its activities also included debates about current events. This political training brought freedmen out of their secluded lives, helped them overcome their ignorance, and channeled their feelings to the support for the Union. In York County, South Carolina, for example, the League "frequently read and discussed" the Black Codes to remind them of the injustice in the days of Presidential Reconstruction.[698] The Union League, however, did not create a movement by itself, but merely added fuel to the existing flames. The freedmen themselves, as Michael W. Fitzgerald noted, were far from passive, for they had the social network and embryonic organizations as well as resentment on which the League built.[699]

In a lively atmosphere, black leadership was built up. Many were free blacks, including Oscar J. Dunn, who once held the lieutenant governorship of Louisiana between 1868 and 1871. Quite a few possessed the experiences of Union Army servicemen like Alfred Wright, the Republican organizer of South Carolina, and Calvin Rogers, a police officer in Florida. Some came from the North, often possessing more educational qualifications than their Southern counterparts. Others were descendants of Underground Railroad travelers returning home.[700] The Radical Reconstruction provided these Northern blacks possessing talents and ambitions with a good opportunity to render service to their race. As long as Reconstruction seemed hopeful, the migration to the South would continue. As a consequence, Reconstruction changed considerably the goals that many blacks strove for in life. Plunging their energy and creative ability into political affairs, many found their element in a new activity.[701]

Because there were few free blacks in the black belt, political mobilization proved to be somewhat difficult there, and their leaders often came from the ex-slaves who had been simply "nobodies." Many were ministers, teachers, or craftsmen. In fact, the largest number of local leaders appeared to have been artisans. James T. Alston, who had "a stronger influence over the minds of the colored men in Macon county" than any other persons, was an Alabama shoemaker.[702] Whatever their professions might be, the talents of these ex-slaves bore witness to the potential creativity long suppressed in an enslaved race.

In the process of political mobilization, blacks' political power gradually emerged. Despite their illiteracy and deficiency in economic resources, blacks possessed the vote and their own leaders, which meant they were enjoying some bargaining power. Neither white Republicans nor Southern conservatives could afford to ignore this fact. Admittedly, there were still some issues that could easily lead to inner splits. Consciously or unconsciously, free blacks drew a line between themselves and ex-slaves, and within the ranks of free blacks there was also a tendency towards classification according to the lightness of color. While free blacks acquiring leadership were mainly interested in civil rights, freedmen mainly concerned themselves with economic issues and especially the ownership of land. Within the black community, moderate blacks and those who stood for an eye for eye were also involved in conflict. Men like Sydenham Porter of Alabama, who advised his fellow blacks to avoid politics, "go to work, and cherish good and kind feelings toward our old friends,"[703] were confronted with frowns and anger from their people. The number of black Democrats, however, was very small. Some conservatives had once imagined that freedmen would regard themselves as their best friends and vote for the candidates according to their exhortation, but this hope fell through before the hard fact that blacks supported Republicans almost without exception and constituted the firm majority of the Southern Republican party. Blacks still could not calmly regard the vote as a simple act of exercising their right, but as the defiance of white supremacy and the cardinal issue of right or wrong. Therefore, "the loss of suffrage" was "the loss of freedom."[704] Just as Republicans could not allow the civil rights problem to split their party, blacks could not afford to bypass the racial issue, which was closely connected with the fundamental interests of their race. The crux of the problem still lay in whites' racial consciousness and their need for domination. Blacks had to maintain racial solidarity to maintain their new position.

Therefore, black power was conditioned by their own issues as well as whites' racial feelings. Their allies, the white Republicans, similarly embodied this character.

The Republican party did not exist at all in the antebellum South, because it was regarded as a subversive organization. It was black suffrage that made it take shape in this former paradise of slaveowners. As for the sources of its power, the Republican party was entrenched in two centers: the plantation belt, where blacks made up the majority of the total population, and the white counties, where black population was of little consequence.[705] The Unionists who joined the Republican party primarily lived in the Appalachia and Ozark mountain districts, where slavery had not thrived, and white yeomen were long discontent with the planters' domination in Southern politics.[706] Mostly concentrated in eastern Tennessee, white Republicans mustered a following in Virginia, North Carolina, Georgia, Arkansas, and Texas. Elsewhere native white Republicans were rare. In the whole South, the native whites who voted for the Republican party were perhaps no more than one-fifth of white voters. As far as the Piedmont region of South Carolina was concerned, white Republicans generally constituted one-quarter or one-third of the white voters.[707] The antagonism between white Republicans and Southern conservatives was so intense that the latter castigated them as "scalawags," which meant the dregs of Southern society. In fact, however, scalawags differed barely from other whites in their morality and ability. Among them there were elite members as well as lower class members, and opportunists as well as sincere men. Some were antebellum distinguished leaders or descendants of famous families. The five most influential Republican figures of Alabama, for example, were all lawyers and had held public office before converting to the Republican party, and three of them suffered heavy losses because of emancipation. Most scalawag leaders in Alabama, according to Woolfolk, were lawyers having college education, and "many were members of outstanding families and some were men of considerable property."[708] Even among the Arkansas Republicans, who were famous for their "nobody" origins, there were also former Confederate senior officials and congressmen like John M. Bradly and Oliver P. Synder.[709] On the other end of the spectrum, the Republican party was mainly composed of the poor. The statistics given by Allen Trelease showed that scalawags were most powerful in the white counties of the South, where the yeomen were concentrated. By analyzing the constitutional conventions of 1867–1869, Thomas Alexander also reached the same conclusion that the Radicals were relatively poor and in the lower social positions.[710] The scalawags, a Tennessee conservative said, were the "party paying no taxes, riding poor horses, wearing dirty shirts, and having no use for soap."[711]

With the poor as their main support, scalawags could lay their racism aside and temporarily unite with blacks in the hope of changing the South, though they were more conservative than white Northerners on racial issues. As dissenters of the South, many scalawags were sincere believers of Jacksonian democracy, being long discontented with the nondemocratic characters of state politics such as property qualifications for public office and the representation allotment partial towards the plantation belt. Even before Congress required the ex-Confederates to be disfranchised, the Unionists of Tennessee took it as the basis of election. They also desired the Republican party to reform unfair taxation, distribute land, and promote economic equality. The idea of confiscation, according to a Union officer in South Carolina, "was received with more favor by this caste than by the negroes."[712] Scalawags, however, were not interested in blacks' rights and interests, and their cooperation with blacks was at best based on political expediency. One Tennessee scalawag clearly confessed that "the great aim of the radical politicians of Tennessee of all classes is to exclude as many white conservatives from voting as possible and to control the negro vote."[713]

Primarily composed of the upper circles, the former Whigs joined the Republican party mainly because of their antebellum Unionism rather than their approval of racial equality. As one Nashville editor said, the Whigs of Tennessee "were never reconciled to the faith of the faithful. They regard the Democratic party as author of all their troubles, and hold the very name of Democracy as a synonym of disaster and defeat."[714] Having analyzed the Republicans of North Carolina, James L. Lancaster pointed out that although "Whiggery and relative poverty are strong in the scalawags" profile, it is obvious that disaffection towards the Confederacy, especially support for the native peace movement of 1863–1864, was the principle catalyst in making Republicans of native whites."[715] Seeking to place the South on a broader base for economic development, the Whigs also appreciated the industrious and commercial policy of the Republican party. Antebellum "ideas and feelings," claimed Thomas Settle of North Carolina, must be buried "a thousand fathoms deep. Yankees and Yankee notions are just what we want in this country. We want their intelligence, their energy and enterprise."[716] On the racial issue, their goal in joining the Republican party was to control blacks. Moved by these practical considerations, James L. Alcorn, later on the scalawag governor of Mississippi, became a Republican. In his view, to fiercely resist Radical Reconstruction was of no avail; the best way of avoiding Radical Reconstruction was to make blacks become their "friends" rather than clamor outside the party. By means of black support, the conservatives might have the party well in hand and channel the implementation of Reconstruction policy into their scheme. To achieve the aim of white domination, he proposed to "vote with the negro, discuss politics with them, sit, if need be, in counsel with him, and form a platform acceptable to both [races], and pluck our common liberty and prosperity from the jaws of inevitable ruin."[717] As long as blacks played a secondary role, Alcorn would remain in the Republican party. Once they were no longer willing to act as political vassals, however, Alcorn would disembark from the Republican boat and return the Democratic party.

Another group of Republicans, whose number was very small but whose influence was relatively strong, was denounced as "carpetbaggers." They were described as the avaricious foreign invaders who came to the South with empty pockets but returned home after ransacking the South. In reality, however, far from being mediocre persons in Northern society, most carpetbaggers had a middle-class background. Quite a few had been lawyers, businessmen, editors, or teachers, and others were veterans of the Union Army or Freedmen's Bureau agents. Attracted by the prospect of commercial success and cheap land, most came to the South for permanent residence, and their motives scarcely differed from those of the Western migration. Nearly all came before 1867, when their political future was not bright. A few stepped on Southern land with a dream of changing the South and helping the freedmen. Yet by 1867, many plunged their energies into politics because of the launch of Radical Reconstruction. To men like Albert T. Morgan, the cotton failure in 1866 was an important factor, and later on they found politics a more easily exploited commodity than cotton plantations.[718] Coming from Illinois, Joseph P. Newshanm became involved in politics purely because he was the only lawyer in his community, while the newly established Republican party was badly in need of candidates. Still others engaged in the party's affairs on the basis of their good impressions on freedmen as Bureau agents. Although some persons had practical or ideal aims, many more carpetbaggers combined the two. They had both the desire for personal gain and the commitment to "substitute the civilization of freedom for that of slavery," believing that Northern investment and political participation would be a double-edged sword shaping the "unprogressive" South.[719]

The carpetbaggers' commitment to reforming the South formed the political basis on which they allied themselves with blacks. Generally speaking, carpetbaggers advocated the aims of democratizing and modernizing the South, including the civil rights legislation, the public school system, and the construction of railroads. Many sympathized with blacks' desire for land, though they did not support the radical measure of confiscation. Lands, Alabama carpetbagger C. W. Dustan declared, "cannot be owned without being earned, and they cannot be earned without labor."[720] Since carpetbaggers were more willing to satisfy blacks' expectation than scalawags, they initially played an important role not proportionate to their number in the process of organizing the Republican party and launching Reconstruction in the black community. By and large, they were more influential in the deep South than in the upper South, and more powerful in the black belt than in the white counties. Just because they primarily represented the interests of the constituency in the black belt, carpetbaggers had a major share of Reconstruction offices, particularly in Florida, South Carolina, and Louisiana, while their number in any Southern state was no more than 2 percent of the total population.

The carpetbaggers' commitment to black rights, however, was limited. Like scalawags, they hoped to manipulate the black vote, and the promise of civil rights was a necessary concession to blacks. At the same time, they tried to establish a biracial party with a broader basis, casting aside the racial line in politics. They were unwilling to advocate any more radical measures lest more whites be estranged, especially taking into account that their families lived in unpleasant surroundings full of animosity.[721] Furthermore, to those who had concealed racism, though they could condescend to connect themselves with the fate of blacks, they would never accept blacks' dominant role for practical and ideological reasons. Realizing that blacks had little room to maneuver in choosing a party, carpetbaggers could go their own way to a considerable extent, despite powerful pressure from blacks.

Thus, conditioned by inner splits and outside opposition, blacks had to accept a secondary position in the political coalition. Certainly, the most restrictive factor on black power was still the animosity of Southern whites. In a sense, the restraints on blacks within the Republican coalition was also a result of outside hostile forces. In such a situation, blacks had to watch their step lest whites react violently. Ironically, on the one hand, black votes formed the basis of Republican power; on the other hand, they were also a potential menace to its further growth. In other words, while their votes were enough to place the Republican party in power, blacks might push ahead with their own determination; as long as their experience and ambition were not noticeable, and as long as blacks were willing to restrict themselves, the negative effect of black power would never fully counteract the consolidating force of the party, and blacks could even gain some sympathy from local whites. Once blacks displayed too much initiative and were linked with the so-called "Reconstruction evil," the tolerant basis for black power would be reduced. This dilemma of black power would be continuously illustrated in the development of Reconstruction.

The first postbellum elections began at the end of 1867, and only in Texas were they postponed to February of the following year. The first problem to be settled by the voters was whether it was necessary to call constitutional conventions. If the answer was affirmative, the voters would at the same time elect their delegates to the conventions. Since Congress required a majority of registered voters rather than those casting their votes to determine the proceedings, Democrats tried to thwart the opening of the constitutional conventions by refusing to vote. Due to the disfranchisement of most ex-Confederates and given the majority of blacks and Unionists, however, every state endorsed the convening of a constitutional convention. Because of the Democratic boycott, Republicans in each state retained adequate and sometimes overwhelming majority in representation. The Democrats' first step proved contrary to their wishes, and black voters demonstrated more powerful strength than expected.

The elected Republican delegates to the conventions reflected the social components of the first biracial party. About one-sixth were carpetbaggers. Since most of them were elected from the black belt, their ascendancy indirectly embodied black power. Well-educated, confidently ambitious, and rather youthful, carpetbaggers generally chaired the main committees and formulated the key provisions of the new constitutions.[722] As far as their number was concerned, however, scalawags constituted the largest group among the delegates, especially in North Carolina, Georgia, Arkansas, Alabama, and Texas. Although some scalawags had an Establishment background, most were upcountry farmers and professionals. Since their power had little relation to black votes, scalawags' attitudes towards racial issues reflected the natural tendencies of the native whites. Their views, however, varied with regions and individual experiences, and now and again sharply conflicted with each other.

Of the 1,000 delegates to the conventions, 265 were African Americans. Taking into account the fact that this was the freedmen's first foray into politics, this figure was relatively appropriate. In Louisiana and South Carolina, blacks outnumbered white delegates, and in Florida they made up nearly 40 percent of the total. Yet they only amounted to some 20 percent in Alabama, Georgia, Mississippi, and Virginia, and 10 percent in Arkansas, North Carolina, and Texas.[723] The largest occupational groups were ministers, artisans, farmers, and teachers, and only a tiny number were agricultural laborers. Most states only had a few black delegates of free origins, with the only exceptions being South Carolina and Louisiana. In these two states, free blacks formed a majority and played a key part in the conventions. In other states, where black delegates were mostly ex-slaves, there were indeed a handful of active roles for them, but their influence was out of proportion to their number. All the same, they still could quite keenly judge the political situation and constitutional affairs. Except for their differences over disfranchisement and the economic program, black delegates were able to keep in step on the civil rights issues.

By and large, because of blacks' direct assistance and indirect influence (mainly through carpetbaggers), the delegates in each state designed the most democratic constitutions in Southern history. All the constitutions had removed racial distinctions from their provisions and guaranteed blacks' equal civil rights. The Florida constitution even provided Seminole Indians with two representatives in the state legislature. To reduce the power of the Democratic party, each state disfranchised the ex-Confederates to some degree. Primarily mirroring the determination of the upcountry delegates, the limitation at last resulted in injury to the impartial image Republicans tried to create. Generally favorable to democracy and progress, the political structure was also readjusted at the same time. In Virginia and the Carolinas, the former allotment of representation to the detriment of white counties was now changed.[724] In North Carolina, the upcountry disgust at the undemocratic structure of the state and the relative security of the biracial coalition made the convention create what Henry Wilson called "the most republican constitution in the land."[725] Under pressure from the scalawags, admittedly, some states set about restricting black power. In Georgia, for example, not only was the representation unfavorable to the black belt, but the new constitution did not mention blacks' right to hold office. In general, however, the new legislative apportionment more closely reflected the population than before. In addition, some states like Mississippi abolished the property restrictions on office-holding, and many increased the numbers of elected officials, so that the people could more directly control the government;[726] by the same token, the local governments were granted more independence and responsibility.[727] Yet in Louisiana, Florida, and Mississippi, the governors were vested with stronger patronage. In Mississippi, for instance, the tenure of governorship was prolonged from two to four years, and, significantly, the governor might appoint militia officers and all judges above the rank of Justice of the Peace.[728] The power of the governor was obviously expanded. These measures were a critical factor in the establishment of a statewide Republican political machine. These developments exposed the Republican dilemma between enhancing the government by the people and promoting the party's power, and between advancing blacks' civil rights and maintaining the power balance within the party, in which, naturally, blacks were not always the beneficiaries in every respect.

Also important were the constitutional provisions about social affairs, which remarkably elevated the groups usually ignored by law and tradition. Assuming responsibility for taking care of those who had no kith and kin and could not support themselves, many states for the first time set up mental homes, hospitals, and asylums. Women's guardianship over their children, their separate property rights, and even the right to divorce were recognized, while their children were legally protected from abuse. A more important measure was the public school system supported by taxation in each state. In the past, none of the Southern states had a sound public system, let alone acceptance of black students. As a consequence, there arose the question of interracial or separate schools. The white delegates, including white Republicans, were so strongly opposed to racially mixed schools that any demand for this measure would virtually lead to the cancellation of black schools. Paying attention to the very opportunity for education, however, most blacks in fact only liked the separate but equal schools, and only a few educated delegates yearned for the biracial ones. Yet all blacks opposed any provision to clearly stipulate racial segregation, thinking that it would make them lose the bargaining power to force whites to provide equal facilities. Thus, Reconstruction governments made themselves the originators of the "separate but equal" principle. Temporarily accepted by both races, however, this de facto segregation was a positive negation of the former exclusive policy, and differed in principle from the de jure imposition of the "separate but equal" cliché at the end of the century.[729] Similarly, black delegates put emphasis on equal access to vehicles and other public accommodations, but carpetbaggers and scalawags disagreed with each other. Consequently, most conventions evaded this question. Only Louisiana definitely required equal treatment in transport, and in this regard South Carolina and Mississippi ambiguously prohibited "distinction" on the basis of color.[730] On the whole, the provisions about social affairs were somewhat improved, indicating that the settlement of black issues might promote the progress of the whole society and benefit the general welfare.

On economic matters, the keynote of the constitutional conventions was to promote Southern modernization and economic democracy. Nonetheless the motive power was mainly provided by carpetbaggers, while blacks and upcountry scalawags were more cautious and indecisive. Most states permitted extensive public funds to aid railroads and other ventures, but some states like Mississippi, Arkansas, Texas, and Virginia made it more difficult for the governments to assist private enterprises. In Alabama, for instance, Daniel Bingham suggested that railroads receiving state aid should be levied a special tax. This proposal won extensive support from upcountry scalawags and blacks, only to be frustrated by a coalition of carpetbaggers, conservatives, and black belt scalawags.[731] The discord showed that the policy of industrialization still met with the strong resistance of Jacksoniaism. The constitutional conventions, however, were rather successful in establishing a system of taxation conforming to the modern standard. Most states reduced the amount of the poll tax and added a general property tax, which meant the state revenues mainly rest on land taxation. In the hope of breaking up the large estates, some blacks and scalawags tried to imposed a special tax on uncultivated land, but this demand was only realized in Virginia. Nor did the conventions enact the necessary provision that would help freedmen to acquire their homesteads. Instead they only tried to consolidate the existing yeoman economy through debtor relief. Alabama, Georgia, and Mississippi all passed resolutions suspending the collection of debts, and each state increased the amount of property exempted for seizure in case of bankruptcy.[732] A measure favorable to laborers was that some states provided them or merchants with the priority of liens on crops. On the other hand, some states still allowed the existence of the convict lease system, a menace always to the poor. In sum, the conventions did not go too far in helping the poor of the two races, and ex-slaves had not been granted the opportunity to acquire land. Just as Republicans were reluctant to provide blacks with preferential treatment on political issues, the heart of their economic policy was to establish an impersonal market system, avoiding class legislation as far as possible; in the meantime, the aim of the market economy also conflicted with the idea of self-sufficiency. Restricted by these factors, Republicans were hard put to provide a more substantial basis for their biracial coalition; blacks were given limited legal assistance, with few economic aids being provided that would consolidate their political liberty.

According to the requirement of Congress, the new constitutions had to be sanctioned by the majority of all registered voters. In Alabama, however, the constitution only won sufficient support from a majority of actual voters because of the Democrats' boycott. As a countermeasure, Congress passed a new act, accepting the legality of the majority of actual votes. By the spring of 1868, most states had recognized the new constitutions. At the same time, the elections of the legislatures have also finished. The new legislatures soon sanctioned the Fourteenth Amendment and submitted the state constitutions to Congress. By individually passing a series of acts, Congress one by one restored Southern states' status. Only four states' acceptance was postponed. In Mississippi, Virginia, and Texas, the disagreement on the clause of disfranchisement brought about a serious constitutional crisis. Subsequently permitted to vote separately on the clause, they were eventually accepted in 1870. Trouble for Georgia arose after its restoration. Finding a loophole that the constitution made no explanation regarding blacks' right to hold public office, a coalition of Democrats and conservative Republicans in this state expelled twenty-seven black legislators. Congress immediately resumed military control. Until the black legislators were accepted, the Georgia delegates had not been allowed to sit in the national legislature. This capricious process in the case of Georgia again demonstrated that black power was far from tolerated. Only the pressure of the bayonet made local whites grudgingly consent to it.

The Republicans won a majority of seats in the legislature of each state, and the administrative posts at different ranks fell into their hands, too. Democrats ridiculed this election result as "black and tan" domination, but in fact the positions shared by blacks were still not in proportion to their population. During Reconstruction, sixteen blacks sat in the House of Representatives, of whom only three served in the Forty-first Congress (1869–1871).[733] Only Mississippi elected black senators; Hiram Revels was the first. As a North Carolina–born minister and educator, Revels served in the U.S. Senate in 1870. In 1875, just before the Democrats captured Mississippi, Blanche K. Bruce, a mulatto planter of this state, was elected to the Senate, where he served a full term until 1881.[734] No black congressman became a leader in Congress, but each had credibility.

At the highest ranks of state government, blacks were not fully represented either. In North Carolina, Texas, Alabama, and Virginia, none held a key post during Reconstruction. In Tennessee, blacks and carpetbaggers were almost entirely excluded. Jonathan C. Gibbs, the Philadelphia-born missionary and educator, was the only black to win a major office in Florida. Even in Mississippi, Louisiana, and South Carolina, where blacks exerted a great influence, whites all but controlled statewide positions in the early stages. During Reconstruction, there were eighteen blacks in all that served as lieutenant governor, treasurer, superintendent of education, or secretary of state, of whom P. B. S. Pinchback, the lieutenant governor of Louisiana, temporarily succeeded Henry C. Warmoth as governor in December 1872. These posts, however, were mostly symbolic, and the real power was kept in whites' hands, with the exception of four black superintendents of education, who exercised real influence on the new school system.[735]

In each state legislature, blacks had their own positions, though their number was initially underrepresented. In Mississippi, Alabama, and Louisiana, the portions shared by blacks were relatively considerable. With the advance of Reconstruction, their numbers increased. Nevertheless, only in the lower house of South Carolina did blacks make up a majority, dominate its key committees, and in 1872 begin to elect black speakers.[736] "Sambo," reported a Northern journalist in 1873, "is already his own leader in the Legislature. The speaker is black, the Clerk is black, the doorkeepers are black, the little pages are black."[737]

Local officials had more direct influence on blacks' daily lives. Justices of the peace were generally in charge of most civil cases and minor criminal offenses, while county commissioners fixed tax rates, directed local appropriations, and extended poor relief, and the sheriff executed the law, selected trial jurors, and carried out foreclosures and public sales of land. Before the war and during Presidential Reconstruction, all these offices were controlled by whites, whereas Radical Reconstruction changed the phenomenon of the white monopoly in public employment. No state lacked its black officials. Florida, Georgia, and Alabama saw the least, while South Carolina, Louisiana, and Mississippi had the most. Some black officials, including Pierre Landry of Donaldson, Louisiana, and Robert H. Wood of Natchez, once assumed the mayoralties. Washington also elected two black aldermen in 1868. Blacks constituted one third in Nashville's council, and at times made up a majority in Little Rock.[738] Reconstruction brought few changes to the Southern court system.[739] Most judges were still white, but black justices of the peace were no longer rare in many cities. Nevertheless they did not deal with cases involving whites. On the controversial issue of black jurors, the ban against them also began to crumble under Radical Reconstruction. Black jurors even constituted one-half of the jury of Davis Bend.[740] In the Nashville court, blacks also gained a foothold.[741] Tallahassee, Little Rock, Atlanta, Vicksburg, Montgomery, and other cities employed a large number of black police.[742] By 1870, hundreds of blacks were serving as city policemen and rural constables, and in Montgomery and Vicksburg comprised half the police forces.[743] Eventually, blacks shared the office of sheriff, whose power was strongest at the local level. In Louisiana, for example, nineteen occupied the position, and in Mississippi fifteen.[744]

Generally speaking, whites manipulated the Republican party's statewide political machine. Restricted by their inexperience, blacks' share of offices was usually underrepresented. Nevertheless the main reason rested on the structure of the Republican party. Having few subsistence means of support, many party leaders reluctantly made room for blacks, because they themselves needed a comfortable livelihood. Another important factor was that the Republican party hoped to establish their legitimacy among the white race and rid itself of the reputation of being a black party. Accordingly, blacks mostly won appointments in places where the population of their race was preponderant. Most officials were still local whites, many of them former Whigs. This situation was particularly typical at the local level.[745] Even in such places as Arkansas, Florida, and Louisiana, where Northerners controlled the governorship, the influence of carpetbaggers gradually fell into decline.[746]

Within the Republican party, blacks also realized their dilemma. When the political "loaves and fishes" were divided up, many blacks patiently stood aside lest internal discord heighten or embarrass the party. Georgia blacks "went from door to door in the 'negro belt'" looking for qualified white Republican candidates, while James H. Harris, the North Carolina black leader, declined a congressional nomination for fear that it "would damage the party at the North."[747] Without fail, not all blacks exercised so great restraint, and some demanded a fair share of public office from the beginning. In South Carolina, for example, the Northern-born blacks stressed that they must be "admitted to a full participation in the control of affairs," and, regardless of white opposition, put their leader Benjamin F. Randolph at the head of the state Republican committee in 1868.[748] As time went on, blacks had more and more confidence in themselves and began to make more and more requests for their share of offices. Fully making using of whites' contention within the party, blacks lost no time in putting the weight of the balance of power on their side. On the whole, in each state there were two contending fractions, which centered on the patronage of federal office and the governorship. Both sides promised blacks the earth, and now and then blacks reaped a profit. Because blacks held the balance of power and could gain advantages from both sides, many blacks were unexpectedly elected in Mississippi in 1873.[749] In other cases, including Texas, white Republican leaders endlessly vied with each other because of regional splits. The dissenting groups then made more promises to black voters, and the Establishment could no longer count on black support if they did not treat blacks fairly.[750] Hence some enclaves of black political power were established in the plantation districts of Mississippi, Louisiana, and South Carolina. In Beaufort, South Carolina, the mayor, police force, and magistrates were all black, and the distinguished ex-slave Robert Small controlled its local politics. "Here the revolution penetrated to the quick," reported Edward King in 1873.[751] Having gone through the continuous trials of political struggle, freedmen at the same time gradually came to the fore in the movement, and rural Baptist exhorters began to outnumber urban-based preachers, though they seldom enjoyed political ascendancy.[752]

Reflecting improvement in blacks' ability, the increase in the share of offices represented the consolidation of black power; yet the advantage brought by factional struggles in turn gave an ironic twist to black power itself. On the one hand, the balance of power elected some blacks less fit for these offices; on the other hand, "black domination" was so exaggerated that the conservatives began to close their rift and strike back vigorously. Frustrated by their failure to attract more white voters, disunity among the Republicans was intensified. Thus, the Republican party was doomed just at the time when black power grew in strength.

Assuredly, there were some positive factors that might counteract the negative effect of black power. The change in whites' attitude to blacks was just one of the most heartening results. Within the Republican party, the coalition between scalawags and blacks was not of their own accord from the start. With the increase in their contacts with blacks, however, some scalawags gradually watered down their former racial prejudice. Having never been friendly towards black suffrage, an Alabama scalawag changed his mind after March 1867 and said that scalawags must "look this Negro question directly in the face " and do justice to their new "unwelcome allies."[753] Perhaps a crucial factor was the improvement in blacks' conduct and quality. Having observed the process of blacks' participation in politics, even the opponents of the Republican party found that they must look at the ex-slaves with new eyes. One Democrat wrote in his diary after election day of 1867: "I must say that Fletcher McNeil (negro) behaved pretty well. Must praise him some for his good conduct."[754] The enforcement of racial justice and the appearance of black power made blacks more responsible and more moral than in slavery.

Consequently, blacks' improvement would inevitably dissolve whites' inveterate prejudice bit by bit. On the other side, the simple fact that blacks had some power at their command forced some whites to accept the accomplished fact. As a Mississippi newspaper put it, "We are led to this course, not through choice, but by the stern logic of events."[755] Based on external pressure and internal change, some whites eventually accepted black rights and launched the New Departure movement.

Carrying out a series of laws, the Republican regimes mainly based on black votes gradually improved blacks' environment. Laws similar to the civil rights bill were enacted in many states. Georgia and Arkansas required equal treatment on public conveyances; Texas in 1871 prohibited the state's railroads from "making any distinction in the carrying of passengers"; and two years later Mississippi, Louisiana, and Florida imposed fines and imprisonment on railroads, steamboats, inns, and theaters denying "full and equal rights" to any citizens.[756] On the whole, however, blacks were still generally seated in the secondary cars, and only in parks, streetcars, and playgrounds were there mixed examples as well as segregated ones.[757]

The most delicate factor in Southern race relations was racial intermarriage. The civil rights bill of 1866 did not prohibit private discrimination respecting the right to marry, but at the same time it did not allow the states to prevent racial intermarriage "under color of law."[758] Yet in reality some states still retained their former clauses about miscegenation, while other states relaxed restrictions.[759] Thus, Reconstruction saw a few cases of intermarriage not allowed in slavery, a famous one of which took place in Mississippi. A. T. Morgan, a formerly affluent planter from Ohio and now a state senator, married a young mulatto teacher who had come down from New York, thereby creating a great sensation.[760]

The most conspicuous achievement of the Reconstruction governments was perhaps the Southern public school system. By 1872, there were 1,500 schools in Texas, with a majority of the state's children registering for courses. The enrollment in Mississippi, Florida, and South Carolina made up about half the children of the two races.[761] Taught by

3,068 teachers, 123,035 students attended 2,776 schools in South Carolina in 1876, while Florida had 28,444 pupils in this year.[762] In many aspects, however, educational progress was very slow. The classrooms were often old and shabby, the educational levels of the teachers were irregular, and the ideas of local autonomy and low taxation made it difficult for many schools to make ends meet. Generally speaking, black schools had worse facilities and less qualified teachers, especially in the rural areas. In most cities, however, the enrollment of black children was never lower than that of their white counterparts, showing that blacks' enthusiasm for learning was steadily increasing.[763] In addition to elementary schools, Reconstruction governments also expanded the institutions for higher learning. Some existing universities like South Carolina University were now opened to both races, but more numerous were the newly established separate black or white universities. Named after the governor, Alcorn University, the sole university supported by state funds in Mississippi, was established in 1871, with a black board of trustees controlling its affairs.[764] Built in 1874, Alabama State University was also a state-supported university open to blacks. Yet most black institutions, including Fisk University, Shaw Institute, Meharry Medical College, and Clark University, were subsidized by churches.[765]

As in the educational sphere, economic legislation reflected the expansion of states' public functions and a change in their attributes. Regarding labor relations, Southern states redefined vagrancy and reduced the criminal scope. When apprentices were adopted, parental consent was required; offenders who could not pay their fines were no longer hired in large numbers; the number of capital offenders was greatly reduced; and the penalties for theft were alleviated. Southern states also provided laborers with a preferential lien upon crops, and required that dismissed laborers be paid for work already done. South Carolina even secured laborers' wages from attachment for debt, and laborers could ask a disinterested party to oversee the division of crops. A black legislator from Florida commented that "nowhere is a law that allows a man to get what he works for." On the other hand, planters poured out endless grievances. As a white put it, "under the laws of most of the Southern States, ample protection is afforded to tenants and very little to landlords."[766]

In the long run, the economic strategies of Reconstruction governments had a more profound influence on blacks' lives. Considered as a lever of economic growth, railroads had become the second largest project in expenditure next to the public school system. The federal government generously granted land to the long-distance railroad investors, while the states provided them with enormous funds by issuing public bonds, and the local governments directly sold the railroad shares. By 1879, the national and state subsidies had spurred the building of 7,000 miles of new railroads.[767] To encourage industrial and commercial development, some states considerably reduced the profit tax. In Mississippi, for example, the legislature passed a measure in 1872 that allowed tax refunds for manufacturing firms showing a profit of less than 4 percent.[768] Some Republican governments still allowed the convict lease system, so that their allies could obtain cheap laborers. Inevitably, this mercantilism counteracted the Republican image as the spokesman of the poor. All the same, economic development gave blacks more employment opportunities. Where the work was not done by black convicts, the jobs were relatively steady and well paid. Since railroad construction needed a large quantity of unskilled labor, many blacks were employed here as brakemen and firemen. Collieries, iron mines, and tobacco factories equally depended on blacks.[769] A few wealthy blacks also shared in the economic projects. Despite their small numbers and minor economic importance, the black bourgeoisie was now faintly visible in cities, visible mainly in running groceries, restaurants, funeral parlors, and so forth. Benefiting from the segregated situation of black residences, their steady development betokened that a black middle class was taking shape.[770] The continuity of mercantilism would structurally readjust black issues, because the progress of black civil rights in the end depended on the "new blacks" in a free labor–based system and the transfer of political power from the rural and land cliques to the businessmen and middle classes within cities.[771]

The existence of black power and Republican governments considerably affected the daily lives of blacks. Not only did the law itself treat blacks more equally than ever before, its enforcement became fairer. In the courts, whites sometimes were confronted with black magistrates, black Justices of the Peace, and racially integrated juries. Considered it "the severest blow I have felt," a white lawyer found himself compelled to address blacks as "gentlemen of the jury."[772] Just because the law became fairer, blacks increasingly had recourse to the law and the authorities. In many cases, Republican officials found themselves overburdened with great expectations. When he served as Justice of the Peace, John R. Lynch recalled, freedmen had "magnified" his office "far beyond its importance."[773] Regarding labor relations, many officials tried to guarantee an equal share of jobs on municipal works to blacks. In Louisiana, for example, the state government employed blacks, whites, and Chinese to repair the levees, providing them with the same wage.[774] The vagrancy laws became mere formalities, and laborers were not forced to sign labor contracts. Correspondingly, planters complained that it was impossible to get convictions in contract disputes. "There is a vagrant law on our state books," commented an Alabama newspaper in 1870, "but it is a dead letter because those who are charged with enforcement are indebted to the vagrant vote for their offices."[775] As a result, the phenomenon of labor withdrawal was encouraged, and in turn the labor shortage enhanced blacks' bargaining power. In destroying the labor monopoly and establishing fairer labor relations, Radical Reconstruction promoted an agricultural change more in conformity with market norms, and eliminated some artificially imposed obstacles to market principles and the universal norms of conduct. In this process, blacks were a beneficiary of general progress.

NOTES

604. Robert W. Johannsen, ed., *The Lincoln-Douglass Debates of 1853*. New York: Knopf, 1965, p. 19.

605. Earl M. Maltz, *Civil Rights, the Constitution, and Congress, 1863–1869*. Lawrence: University Press of Kansas, 1990, p. 4.

606. Paul Finkelman, "Rehearsal for Reconstruction," in Eric Anderson and Alfred A. Moss, Jr., eds., *The Facts of Reconstruction: Essays in Honor of John Hope Franklin*. Baton Rouge: Louisiana State University Press, 1991, pp. 13–15.

607. August Meyer and Elliot Rudiwick, *From Plantation to Ghetto*. New York: Hill and Wang, 1970, p. 76.

608. C. Vann Woodward, *The Strange Career of Jim Crow*. New York: Oxford University Press, 1968, p. 18; Finkelman, *op. cit.,* p. 26.

609. John Hope Franklin, *From Slavery to Freedom: A History of Negro Americans*. New York: Knopf, 1947, p. 236.

610. Maltz, *op. cit.,* p. 1.

611. Finkelman, *op. cit.,* p. 25.

612. Maltz, *op. cit.,* p. 8.

613. *ibid.,* pp. 8–10.

614. Eric Foner, *Reconstruction: America's Unfinished Revolution, 1863–1877*. New York: Harper & Row, 1988, p. 223.

615. Stanley Coben, "North Businessmen and Radical Reconstruction," in Robert D. Marcus and David Burner, eds., *The American Scene*. New York: Harper & Row, 1971.

616. Michael Les Benedict, *The Fruits of Victory: Alternatives in Restoring the Union, 1865–1877.* New York: University Press of America, p. 19.

617. Kenneth M. Stampp, *The Era of Reconstruction, 1865–1877.* New York: Knopf, 1965, p. 100.

618. Johannsen, *op. cit.,* p. 19.

619. *ibid.,* p. 196.

620. Maltz, *op. cit.,* pp. 7–8.

621. *ibid.,* p. 31.

622. Foner, *op. cit.,* p. 232; Raymond G. Gettell, *History of American Political Thought.* New York: The Century Co., 1928, p. 377.

623. S. G. F. Spackman, "Beyond the Federal Consensus," in Rhodri Jeffreys-Jones and Bruce Collins, eds., *The Growth of Federal Power in American History.* Edinburgh: Edinburgh University Press, 1983, p. 53.

624. *ibid.,* pp. 53–54.

625. *ibid.,* pp. 54–55.

626. *ibid.,* p. 56.

627. Maltz, *op. cit.,* p. 133; Foner, *op. cit.,* p. 232.

628. Benedict, *op. cit.,* p. 102.

629. Maltz, *op. cit.,* pp. 36–37.

630. Foner, *op. cit.,* p. 278.

631. Benedict, *op. cit.,* p. 21.

632. Stampp, *op. cit.,* p. 85.

633. Benedict, *op. cit.,* pp. 107–108.

634. W. E. B. Du Bois, *Black Reconstruction in America, 1860–1880.* Cleveland: World Publications, 1964, p. 287.

635. Maltz, *op. cit.,* p. 51.

636. Benedict, *op. cit.,* p. 105.

637. Maltz, *op. cit.,* p. 63.

638. *ibid.,* p. 64.

639. Benedict, *op. cit.,* p. 105.

640. Foner, *op. cit.,* p. 244.

641. Maltz, *op. cit.,* p. 77.

642. LaWanda Cox and John H. Cox, *Politics, Principles, and Prejudice, 1865–1866.* New York: Oxford University Press, 1963, p. 213.

643. *ibid.,* p. 201.

644. *ibid.,* p. 172.

645. Benedict, *op. cit.,* p. 112.

646. Maltz, *op. cit.,* pp. 89, 91.

647. Foner, *op. cit.,* p. 255.

648. *ibid.,* p. 254.

649. Maltz, *op. cit.,* p. 93.

650. *ibid.,* p. 92.

651. *ibid.,* p. 93.

652. *ibid.,* p. 105.

653. Foner, *op. cit.,* p. 261.

654. Benedict, *op. cit.,* p. 30.

655. Michael Perman, *Reunion without Compromise: The South and Reconstruction.* Cambridge, England: Cambridge University Press, 1973, pp. 260–265.

656. Allen W. Trelease, *Reconstruction: The Great Experiment.* New York: Harper & Row, 1971, p. 74.

657. Maltz, *op. cit.,* p. 129.

658. George W. Julian, *Recollections, 1840–1872.* Chicago: Aldine, 1884, p. 305.

659. Benedict, *op. cit.,* p. 115.

660. Foner, *op. cit.,* p. 278.

661. Benedict, *op. cit.,* p. 34.

662. Spackman, *op. cit.,* p. 56; Maltz, *op. cit.,* p. 132.

663. Maltz, *op. cit.,* p. 133.

664. Maltz, *op. cit.,* p. 133.

665. LaWanda Cox and John H. Cox, "Negro Suffrage and Republican Politics: The Problem of Motivation in Reconstruction Historiography," in Allen Weinstein, ed., *Origins of Modern America.* New York: Random House, 1970, p. 42.

666. ibid., p. 143.

667. LaWanda Cox and John H. Cox, *op. cit.,* p. 42.

668. Maltz, *op. cit.,* p. 143.

669. Cox, *op. cit.,* p. 51.

670. Maltz, *op. cit.,* p. 144.

671. *ibid.,* p. 142.

672. *ibid.,* p. 155.

673. Cox, *op. cit.,* p. 53.

674. Herman Belz, "The Constitution and Reconstruction," in Eric Anderson and Alfred A. Moss, Jr., eds., *The Facts of Reconstruction: Essays in Honor of John Hope Franklin.* Baton Rouge: Louisiana State University Press, 1991, p. 199.

675. Maltz, *op. cit.,* p. 147.

676. Belz, op. cit., p. 211.

677. James H. Hutson, "The Constitution: An Economic Document?" in Leonard W. Levy and Dennis J. Mahoney, eds., *The Framing and Ratification of the Constitution.* New York: Harper & Row, 1987, pp. 259–270.

678. C. B. Macpherson, *The Political Theory of Possessive Individualism: Hobbes to Locke.* New York: Cambridge University Press, 1962.

679. *The Federalist*, quoted from Herbert W. Schneider, *A History of American Philosophy.* New York: Columbia University Press, 1963, p. 44.

680. Don E. Fehrenbacher, *The Dred Scott Case: Its Significance in American Law and Politics.* New York: Oxford University Press, 1978, p. 21; Belz, *op. cit.,* p. 215.

681. Gilbert T. Stephenson, *Race Distinctions in American Law,* 1910, p. 284; Gunnar Myrdal, *An American Dilemma: The Negro Problem and Modern Democracy,* Vol. I. New York: Random House, 1962, p. 429.

682. Waldo E. Martin, Jr., *The Mind of Frederick Douglass.* Chapel Hill: University of North Carolina Press, 1984, p. 37.

683. George M. Fredrickson, ed., *William Lloyd Garrison.* Englewood Cliffs: Prentice-Hall, 1968, pp. 53, 143.

684. Leoland D. Baldwin, ed., *Ideas in Action: Documentary and Interpretive Readings in American History.* Vol. I. Pittsburgh and New York: American Book Company, 1968, p. 58.

685. Trelease, *op. cit.,* p. 101.

686. Foner, *op. cit.,* p. 307.

687. James T. Currie, *Enclave: Vicksburg and Her Plantations, 1863–1870.* Oxford: University Press of Mississippi, 1980, p. 196.

688. Foner, *op. cit.,* p. 288.

689. Robert Cruden, *The Negro in Reconstruction.* Englewood Cliffs: Prentice-Hall, 1969, p. 93.

690. Foner, *op. cit.,* p. 288.

691. Myrdal, *op. cit.,* pp. 432–437.

692. Leon F. Litwack, *Been in the Storm So Long.* New York: Knopf, 1979, p. 531.

693. Foner, *op. cit.,* p. 290.

694. Edward Magdol, *A Right to the Land: Essays on the Freedmen's Community.* Westport, CT: Greenwood, 1977, p. 42.

695. Foner, *op. cit.,* p. 282.

696. *ibid.,* p. 283.

697. Allen W. Trelease, *White Terror: The Ku Klux Klan Conspiracy and Southern Reconstruction.* New York: Harper & Row, 1971.

698. S. B. Hall, *A Shell in the Radical Camp,* quoted from Foner, *op. cit.,* p. 283.

699. Michael W. Fitzgerald, *The Union League Movement in the Deep South,* reviewed by *American Historical Review,* Vol. 96, 1991, p. 265.

700. Cruden, *op. cit.,* p. 95.

701. Foner, *op. cit.,* p. 286.

702. *ibid.,* p. 287.

703. Cruden, *op. cit.,* p. 291.

704. Foner, *op. cit.,* p. 291.

705. Allen Trelease, "Who Were the Scalawags?" in Edwin C. Rozwenc, ed., *Reconstruction in the South.* Lexington, MA: D. C. Heath, 1972, pp. 119–144.

706. Trelease, *Reconstruction,* p. 107.

707. Paul D. Escott, "White Republicanism and Ku Klux Klan Terror: The North Carolina Piedmont During Reconstruction," in J. J. Crow, P. D. Escott, and C. L. Flynn, Jr., eds., *Race, Class, and Politics in Southern History.* Baton Rouge: Louisiana State University Press, 1989, p. 10.

708. Carl N. Degler, *The Other South: Southern Dissenters in the Nineteenth Century.* Baton Rouge: Harper & Row, 1974, p. 200.

709. *ibid.,* p. 200.

710. *ibid.,* pp. 195–197.

711. *ibid.,* p. 210.

712. Stampp, *op. cit.,* p. 163.

713. Degler, *op. cit.,* p. 205.

714. *ibid..,* p. 205.

715. Escott, *op. cit.,* p. 26.

716. Foner, *op. cit.,* p. 299.

717. Trelease, *op. cit.,* p. 127.

718. Currie, *op. cit.,* p. 156.

719. William C. Harris, "The Creed of Carpetbaggers: The Case of Mississippi," *Journal of Southern History,* May, 1974, p. 199.

720. Foner, *op. cit.,* p. 296.

721. Ruth Currie-McDaniel, "The Wives of the Carpetbaggers," in J. J. Crow, P. D. Escott, and C. L. Flynn, Jr., eds., *op. cit.,* p. 35.

722. Foner, *op. cit.,* p. 317.

723. *ibid.,* p. 318.

724. Stampp, *op. cit.,* p. 172.

725. Foner, *op. cit.,* p. 322.

726. W. E. B. Du Bois, "Reconstruction and Its Benefits," in Robert, D. Marcus, ed., *The American Scene: Varieties of American History.* New York: Appleton-Century-Crofts, 1974, p. 410.

727. Trelease, *op. cit.,* p. 116.

728. William Harris, "The Reconstruction of the Commonwealth," in Richard A. Melemore, *A History of Mississippi.* Jackson: University Press of Mississippi, 1973, p. 564.

729. Howard N. Rabinowitz, *Race Relations in the Urban South, 1865–1890.* New York: Oxford University Press, 1978, pp. 165, 132; Degler, *op. cit.,* p. 244.

730. Foner, *op. cit.,* p. 321.

731. *ibid.,* p. 325.

732. Benedict, *op. cit.,* p. 40.

733. Foner, *op. cit.,* p. 352.

734. Trelease, *op. cit.,* p. 122.

735. Foner, *op. cit.,* p. 354.

736. Stampp, *op. cit.,* p. 167.

737. Foner, *op. cit.,* p. 354.

738. *ibid.,* p. 355.

739. Trelease, *op. cit.,* p. 133.

740. Rabinowitz, *op. cit.,* p. 38.

741. *ibid.,* p. 37.

742. *ibid.,* p. 41.

743. Foner, *op. cit.,* p. 362.

744. *ibid.,* p. 356.

745. Trelease, *op. cit.,* p. 126.

746. Degler, *op. cit.,* p. 194.

747. Foner, *op. cit.,* p. 351.

748. *ibid.,* p. 351.

749. David G. Sansing, "Congressional Reconstruction," in Melemore, *op. cit.,* p. 584.

750. Carl Moneyhon, *Republicanism in Reconstruction Texas.* Austin: University of Texas Press, 1980, p. 196.

751. Edward King, *The Southern States of North America,* quoted from Foner, *op. cit.,* p. 357.

752. Foner, *op. cit.,* p. 358.

753. Degler, *op. cit.,* p. 233.

754. *ibid.,* p. 237.

755. Thomas B. Alexander, "Persistent Wiggery in Mississippi Reconstruction: The *Hinds County Gazette,*" quoted from Foner, *op. cit.,* p. 417.

756. Foner, *op. cit.,* p. 370.

757. Trelease, *op. cit.,* p. 134.

758. Maltz, *op. cit.,* p. 76.

759. Vernon Lane Wharton, *The Negro in Mississippi.* New York: Harper & Row, 1965, p. 150.

760. *ibid.,* p. 228.

761. Foner, *op. cit.,* p. 366.

762. W. E. B. Du Bois, *Black Reconstruction in America, 1860–1880.* Cleveland: World Publications, 1964, pp. 650, 655.

763. Rabinowitz, *op. cit.,* p. 179.

764. John K. Bettersworth, "The Reawakening of Society and Cultural Life, 1865–1890," in Melemore, *op. cit.,* p. 626.

765. Rabinowitz, *op. cit.,* p. 163.

766. Foner, *op. cit.,* p. 373.

767. Cruden, *op. cit.,* p. 109.

768. Sansing, *op. cit.,* p. 578.

769. Cruden, *op. cit.,* p. 110.

770. Meier, and Rudiwick, *op. cit.,* p. 199.

771. Jack M. Bloom, *Class, Race, and the Civil Rights Movement.* Bloomington and Indianapolis: Indiana University Press, 1987, pp. 2, 13.

772. Katherine W. Springs, *The Squires of Springfield,* quoted from Foner, *op. cit.,* p. 363.

773. John H. Franklin, *Reminiscence of an Active Life: Autobiography of John Roy Lynch.* Chicago: University of Chicago Press, 1970, pp. 60–64.

774. Foner, *op. cit.,* p. 362.

775. *ibid.,* p. 363.

CHAPTER 5

The Withering of
the New Democracy

RAMPANT RACISM

"I believe," historian Leland D. Baldwin said, "that democracy operates by seeking successive compromises in order to maintain a balance among constantly shifting alliances of social interests; and that these compromises are expressed in laws which are supreme and can be changed only by the will of the people."[776] One of the most important changes in the period of Reconstruction—the bestowal of black civil rights and suffrage—had allowed blacks to enter into reasonable competition in the political game, by which a crucial step was made towards new racial democracy and the universal norms of conduct in politics. The breakthrough in social changes, however, arose not out of grassroots demand, but from external coercive power, whose action itself posed a serious legal problem. More gravely, having brought about the appearance of black power, these measures incurred radical resistance from Southern whites, who did not recognize blacks' membership in the political game and did not spare any effort to expel blacks out of the competition. Consequently, the lofty experiment of the new democracy was at last reduced to a wizened skeleton of law. The other side of whites' souls—the native whites' desire for conquest—and their social interests were the biggest burden for black power.

To planters, blacks enfranchisement meant that laborers became more uncontrollable. While emancipation itself had raised the question of readjusting labor relations, Reconstruction governments made the legal means of labor control impractical. The coercive means habitually practiced in the production of the staple crop were now illegal, and the cooperative relations between employer and employee were mandated by law. Planters had to compete against each other to attract laborers, and the price of labor became increasingly expensive. The former rich labor supply now seemed to be vanishing. To counteract the bargaining power of laborers, planters tried to increase the labor supply by promoting immigration. But these attempts failed.[777]

If these changes were not enough to provoke planters, the economic policies of Reconstruction authorities, of which the most controversial was the tax issue, added fuel to the flames. Because of the increasing amount of Republican governmental expenditure, property taxes were four times higher in 1870 than 1860 throughout the South.[778] Having long been accustomed to low tax rates, Southern whites believed that this policy violated their cherished principles. Furthermore, the tax distribution, according to them, was deliberately designed to discriminate against planters, because the Republican regimes placed most of the burden for state revenues on real and personal property rather than on cotton or privilege and license taxes.[779] Since Republicans were holding the power, planters also lost their influence on property assessment, and their land was often assessed at more than its practical value for tax purposes. A harsh fact was that the benefit of the taxation was not proportionate to the corresponding contribution of taxpayers, for the public school system and other public facilities were more advantageous to the poor of both races. In addition, a large number of officials elected by blacks and scalawags enjoyed salaries provided by taxpayers and were in charge of the expenditure of taxes. Thus, believing savageness had superseded civilization, the former elite was particularly enraged by the tax policy. As early as the colonial period, the idea of "no taxation without representation" had once made the colonists sever relations with Great Britain, and now this tradition provided conservatives with a sharp weapon. Holding that "when computed according to wealth, it was a more oppressive taxation, in all probability, than has ever been bore before or since in the United States," they bitterly denounced the so-called "class legislation."[780] In some states, conservatives organized Taxpayers' Conventions, whose platforms bitterly protested against the extravagance and corruption of Reconstruction governments. While their leaders were men of "wealth, virtue and intelligence," the complaints about rising taxes cut across class lines. In many areas, even a few dollars' tax might invite hostility and anger. Asked if his tax of four dollars on 100 acres of land seemed excessive, a farmer responded resolutely: "It appears so, sir, to what it was formerly, next to nothing."[781] After studying the situation in Mississippi, William C. Harris pointed out the sensitivity of tax policy. The failure of Republicans, he believed, was rooted in their fiscal policy. They failed to distribute taxes equitably, refused to go beyond the property tax, and could not eliminate embezzlement. "Perhaps more than any other reason," concluded Harris, "including the endemic race issue and the emotionalism generated by Reconstruction politics, the problem of finance proved the undoing of the Republican dream."[782]

To a large extent favored by Reconstruction governments, the merchant class tended to support Republicans with all their strength. Corporation laws were now on the statute books, and enterprises enjoyed preferential taxes and public aid. To accumulate construction funds, each state vied with each other to issue a large amount of public bonds. The convict lease system was also ready to provide them with steady cheap labor. Under the "gospel of prosperity" of the Reconstruction governments, the South supported large-scale construction of railroads and other projects. At the same time, supply merchants moved into Southern rural areas and exerted the vital function of financial medium.[783] Their influence was so large that even the planters, who previously had exerted the greatest influence in their communities, now had to change their lifestyle and joined the ranks of the merchant class, who increasingly expanding their regional monopoly. These two groups gradually merged to create a new commercial, bourgeois class.[784]

The mercantilism of the Reconstruction governments initially did win some white supporters. The two parties even cooperated with each other on state subsidization and railroad construction. In Edgefield County, Alabama, Democrats put aside their racism to ally themselves with black officials in an effort to attract a railroad, while Charleston's Board of Trade did not hesitate to lobby black legislators for public aid to the Blue Ridge Railroad.[785] But Republicans had never procured widespread white support through their development platform. Many merchants adopted a reserved attitude towards the tax policy favorable to the poor. More disappointing was the increase in state debt, much of which existed only on paper, without any state resources as its guarantee. If anything went wrong, it was the merchants and planters that would be assessed the taxes necessary to pay it off.[786] Because of the encroachment of corruption, such a situation deteriorated. Bribes might encourage state officials to sign more public bonds than the legislature could recognize. After the sale of public bonds, the surplus then lined these officials' pockets. In Louisiana, for example, Henry C. Warmoth established a system of "exacting tribute" from railroads and left the governorship a wealthy man.[787] Undoubtedly, the ubiquity of corruption and debt-riddenness made the investment environments go from bad to worse. Even in places where there was no large-scale embezzlement, businessmen who were not direct beneficiaries also might be easily angered. In Alabama, for instance, friendly legislation won for the Republicans the support of V. K. Stevenson and his railroad corporation, but the management of its rival, the Louisiana and Nashville, was alienated.[788] In addition, the instability of Southern politics increased the risk of investment. It was very dangerous to affiliate with a government stuck labeled as being under "black domination." In North Carolina, for instance, Kemp P. Battle and William J. Hawkins all remained firm conservatives despite the favors they received from the Republican government.[789] Thus, the prevailing "social discord," commented New York diarist George Templeton Strong, made the South "the last region on earth in which a Northern or European capitalist [would] invest a dollar."[790]

The farmers were also courted by the Reconstruction governments. Republicans represented a hope for change in places where they were in power. Clearly, most scalawags were poor whites strongly longing to raise their position. As reformers and inheritors of Jacksonianism, they were likely to transcend racism in order to fulfill practical interests. In the Piedmont counties in North Carolina, where the white population were predominant, they formed a firm biracial coalition with blacks, which in some cases remained through the rest of the nineteenth century into the twentieth century.[791] In fact, the potential challenge to the existing political and economic order issued by the poor of both races during Reconstruction was always a rankling anxiety for conservatives. Yet there were still many inharmonious factors that would impede possible cooperation between the two poor groups. The psychological obstacles persistently remained strong, either out of whites' self-consciousness or out of their mutual animosity.[792] In economics, the competition between black and white laborers once caused the Klan to drive blacks out of the white counties.[793] More frustratingly, the politics of livelihood also circumscribed the poor whites' tenure of office.[794] At the same time, Republican policies had not formed a solid link between the party's popularity and the interests of its ordinary members. On the one hand, the shift of the tax burden from cotton sales and license fees to real property put a load on farmers and drove many away from the party;[795] on the other hand, Republican mercantilism considerably conflicted with the yeoman economy. When the credit monopoly of rural merchants had begun to encroach their independent status, farmers and artisans in the upcountry areas feared railroads would further subordinate their self-sufficient society to the tyranny of the marketplace.[796] As historian Otto Olsen observed, the endless divergence between farmers, who constituted the backbone of white Republicans, and merchants or former Whigs, who generally played a leading role in local politics, precluded the party from achieving a program that would have consolidated its position.[797] In local communities where scalawags preponderated, Republicanism exerted considerable influence on Southern poor whites, but carpetbaggers who achieved state or federal offices had not satisfied their appetite for reform.[798] Therefore, there arose a great deal of friction between poor whites and other groups within the party.

While internal contradictions eroded the basis of the Republican position, Reconstruction regimes also divided white society. Under the great pressure of Reconstruction, white society began to disintegrate. Increasingly, whites fell away from one another, turned their fidelity to local, sometimes isolated organizations, and retreated from loyalty to ideals and institutions to loyalty to individuals.[799] In such a situation, conservatives gradually found that there would be no cement holding their society together except for racism. Although upper-class elements mainly concerned themselves with restoring their own influence, they knew that their object could not be achieved unless the interests of most whites were satisfied. Since their former tactic of controlling poor whites through the manipulation of blacks no longer worked, conservatives now acted in the opposite way, seeking a coalition with poor whites and then consolidating their social control in the campaign for white supremacy.

The Democratic press played an important role in the campaign to promote white unification. Many reports were full of allegations and slanders, which, just because they "served a good end" in discrediting Reconstruction regimes, were adopted even when editors themselves did not believe them. The Radicals, they alarmingly predicted, would create a "mongrel" race in the South, while white people would be "in the hands of camp-followers, horse-holders, cooks, bottle-washers, and thieves."[800] The freedom of the press was greatly misused by the desperate white Southerners.

The racial feelings that conservatives exploited had a widespread social basis. No matter how hard the Republican party worked to win Southern whites' favor, it was after all the party that had emancipated blacks and approved of racial equality. While emancipation gave rise to whites' dread of social change, Radical Reconstruction intensified their anxiety over social security because it deprived whites of the legal means by which the racial control system had been built. To conservatives, who were accustomed to blacks' staying in their lowest class, this was an inconceivable and disintegrating world. Because they could no longer do as they pleased towards blacks, conservatives deeply felt humiliated. In their eyes, the devil had been released from the bottle, and their urgent goal was to put an end to the further spread of the Reconstruction evil. To a large extent, Reconstruction exposed the deep character flaw of Southern whites and polarized the South along racial lines.

The most troublesome annoyance for conservatives was the enfranchisement of blacks. This measure destroyed the former power structure in the South, driving them into an unfamiliar and unsafe world. Believing blacks were unfit to vote, much less hold office, they were outraged by the appearance of freedmen at the polls en masse. According to Woodward, "Here was the Federalist beast who would turn every garden into a pigsty. Here was old John Adams' shiftless and improvident Demos, pawn of demagogues and plutocrats and menace to all order. Here in the flesh was Hamilton's 'turbulent and changing' mass who 'seldom judge or determine right.' "[801] Many years later, Adelbert Ames, Mississippi's last Radical governor, recalled what an injury the enfranchisement was to conservatives. As they said, an "unjust and tyrannical power had filled their state with mourning, beggared them, freed their slaves and as a last insult and injury made the ex-slave a political equal."[802] The Union League, which played an important role in mobilizing black support, was regarded as a dangerous organization. After it helped the Republican party win elections, Democrats with one voice denounced its subversiveness and were determined to wipe out its existence at any cost. In fact, the activities of the League to a large extent gave rise to the appearance of white vigilantism. The hostility was so great that Republicans themselves disbanded this organization after the Presidential election of 1868.[803] Conservatives also bitterly decried scalawags and carpetbaggers, whose presence was not only a mark of their loss of control, but also symbolized the danger of losing the principle of white supremacy. As a matter of fact, a revolutionary aspect of Reconstruction was the open relations that occurred between the two races in the course of organizing the Republican party. In North Carolina, for instance, black and white met "upon the same floor on the same footing and cooperated together in the most cordial and harmonious manner."[804] In the conservatives' view, only the humblest whites would join blacks in their capacity as servants waiting on a master. Concerning the Radicals' policy portending racial equality, conservatives were even more resentful. It was considered the supreme sin of Reconstruction.[805] Any laws enacted for that purpose would

> have no binding force or moral sanction, and will be disregarded and declared null and void as soon as the inalienable rights of people are again recognized. No privilege can be secured to the negro to which his white neighbors do not consent, and if he attempts to enforce privileges on the strength of carpetbag authority he will simply destroy his claims of future peace, and heap up wrath against the day of wrath.[806]

Demonstrating the serious differences of legal opinion between the South and the North, the rebellious attitudes of conservatives raised the problem of the legitimacy of the Reconstruction regimes. Inheriting the classical concept of natural law from Greek and Roman culture, Americans held that in the natural and social order there was a "higher law" above all sorts of man-made laws. Although it was not necessarily fulfilled by worldly authorities, the divine or natural law was the moral source of man-made laws and had a supreme binding force on men. In the first century B.C., Cicero gave an famous summary of "the higher law."

> True law is right reason in agreement with Nature; it is of universal application, unchanging and everlasting; it summons to duty by its commands, and averts from wrongdoing by its prohibitions. We cannot be freed from its obligations by Senate or People, and we need not look outside ourselves for an expounder or interpreter of it. And there will not be different laws at Rome and at Athens, or different laws now and in the future, but one eternal and unchangeable law will be valid for all nations and for all times, and there will be one master and one ruler, that is, God, over us all, for He is the author of this law, its promulgator, and its enforcing judge.[807]

The reverence for "the higher law" and the innermost mission to carry out its commandments constituted one driving force of Western democracy. When the early representative bodies emerged as indispensable political institutions, they did not conceive of themselves as "legislatures" in the modern sense, but pretended only to state the law that already "existed." The American Revolution strengthened the tradition about "the higher law," with the idea of natural law gaining high popularity. The ordinary laws were nothing but an emanation of the natural law or an

concrete expression of the abstract moral principle. As Ralph H. Gabriel
put it, "A peculiarity of American democracy had been from the beginning that it put its faith in a higher law rather than in the changing will of
the people."[808] On the one hand, the laws gained holiness because of the
sanction of the moral principle; on the other hand, every citizen might
decide whether the laws were just according to his own scrutiny. This
contradiction brought about Americans' duality of both reverence and
contempt for man-made laws. If he felt injustice, a man would not think
he had the duty to observe them. Thoreau even declared that the best
government was no government at all, and that when men were fully developed they would need none. When his conscience clashed with the
laws, the latter must yield. No government, he said, had any "right over
any person and property but what I concede to it."[809] Another example
was the frontier tradition of personal law enforcement, which was sometimes called lawlessness. Perhaps the most important example was the
regional disputes and the difference of legal opinions between the North
and the South caused by slavery. The North insisted that the Constitution
had changed with changing times and that its words must be taken in
broad meaning; to defend their interests and check the expansion of
Northern power, the South insisted on the Constitution's supremacy in its
original literal meaning, while the state laws restraining Southerners
themselves were not so valued, because slavery was "degrading the law
by putting the authority of the master above it," and the presence of slavery had made them "haughty and jealous of their liberties, and so impatient of restraint that they could hardly bear the thought of being
controlled by any superior power."[810] The North appealed for the broad
teachings of Scripture, including brotherly love, the Golden Rule, and
the equality of all men before God; the South replied that in Holy Writ
many passages explicitly sanctioned the existence of slavery and that it
was misleading to set up another standard of conduct, no matter how
plausible, contrary to the literal teachings of the Bible. While the North
emphasized the propriety of practicing moral principles through social
reforms, the South kept a jealous eye on their customs and way of life.
It was their "the higher law," because it embodied the truth of God. As
one white declared, "We owe an obligation to the laws, but we owe a
higher one to the communities in which we live, and if the former be per-
verted to destroy the latter, it is patriotism to disregard them."[811]

In the period of Reconstruction, conservatives felt that the laws were
distorted and that their former way of life was menaced. Stubbornly, they
believed in the perfection of Southern life, in which both blacks and

whites should be in their "proper places" and coexist peacefully. This position was summarized by Senator Carter Glass as follows: "White supremacy is too precious a thing to surrender for the sake of a theoretical justice that would let a brutish African deem himself the equal of white men and women in Dixie."[812] Rather naturally, a Southern white thought that he belonged to the community he lived in as well as himself. Community feeling required that he be courageous, resolute, and skilled at horsemanship and firearms. Any provocation towards himself, his family, or his community would stimulate him to put his life at risk and fight it out. Any enemy appearing within was even more dangerous than one from the outside, as evidenced in the way in which scalawags were treated. "The Northern people have no idea of the animosity which exists against Union men in the South," a Virginia Republican wrote. "I am a Virginian, and I have no blood relations who are not Southern men and I assure you upon my honor there is a worse feeling in Virginia today than there is in March of 1861."[813] To conservatives, the devotion to racial order was a powerful weapon to defeat their opponents.

Furthermore, Southern whites felt imposed by a tyranny of law. Not only were the civil rights laws themselves made without a Southern voice, but enforcement was under the pressure of the bayonet. Although the commanders generally adopted a moderate policy, occupation itself was a most disgusting fact. No matter how justifiable it might be, the presence of military supervision over civil authorities had always been anathema, not only to white Southerners, but to all Americans. In the 1760s, the colonists so abominated the use of British troops to enforce parliamentary legislation that they staged a mass protest that culminated in the Boston Massacre. When the army again administered Massachusetts under the Intolerable Acts, the Founding Fathers felt compelled to list them in the Declaration of Independence as the main reason for American Revolution.[814] The suspicion about the army overstepping its boundaries was also embodied in the Articles of Confederation, which entrusted the duty of defense to the militia, and the Constitution, which put military power under the strict control of the president elected by the people. Having exerted a leadership influence since colonial times, the Southern states now groaned under the presence of federal soldiers. No matter that Southern whites accepted the failure of the war, what they had anticipated was only to give up the right to secession and accept emancipation, and never had they imagined experiencing such a reconstruction. To free themselves from this "colonial rule" and restore the "real" laws, Southern whites were determined to cast aside any laws imposed by the

Republicans, "to defy the reconstructed State Government, to treat them with contempt, and show that they have no real existence."[815]

Although conservatives all agreed on the need to overthrow the Reconstruction regimes, to reduce black power, and to reshape the Southern legal system, they differed considerably on strategy. Reluctantly accepting blacks' right to vote as a fait accompli, a minority were willing to have their eyes on the future, cast aside the Reconstruction issue, take vigorous action to enter into election contests, cultivate their legality in the eyes of Northerners and blacks, and thereby achieve their aim of "home rule" in the end. Having observed that the black population only made up a minority in the whole South except for two or three states, and that the Republican triumph was based on a biracial coalition, they believed that the Republican party could be defeated by splitting up either one of its allies. Rather than resort to racism as most conservatives did, they placed hope on the conversion of black voters. Compared with scalawags, they assumed, landless blacks could not dispense with their support. Thus, it was necessary to make blacks understand that they had been fooled by others. In addition, their secure social position also mitigated their fear of black power. Out of these considerations, they quenched their racial feelings, at least outwardly. Their standpoint was later on embodied in the talks of two leading Southern statesmen, L. Q. C. Lamar and Wade Hampton, in a symposium. Lamar said:

1. That the disfranchisement of the negro is a political impossibility under any circumstances short of revolution.
2. That the ballot in the hands of the negro, however its exercise may have been embarrassed and diminished by what he considers, erroneously, a general southern policy, has been to that race a means of defense and an element of progress.

Hampton pointed out:

Whatever may have been the policy of conferring the right of voting upon the negro, ignorant and incompetent as he was to comprehend the high responsibility thrust upon him, and whatever may have been the reasons which dictated this dangerous experiment, the deed has been done and is irrevocable. It is now the part of true statesmanship to give it as far as possible that direction which will be most beneficial or least hurtful to the body politic.[816]

Therefore, some conservatives accepted the black vote for practical reasons. The dilemma Reconstruction had put them in was that to make blacks and Northerners accept their legality, conservatives must first concede, even if hypocritically, the legality of Reconstruction. Black suffrage was temporarily tolerated as a necessary means to the end of white domination. Since the election of 1868, Lamar himself admitted, Democratic nominations and platforms had been designed primarily with the aim of "secur[ing] the sanction and favor" of the national government.[817] As early as 1867, the conservatives in Tennessee had endorsed blacks' officeholding before the white Radicals in power accepted the principle; some conservatives in Virginia support black suffrage so enthusiastically that they were accused by some Radicals of being Negrophiles.[818] In 1870, the "New Departure" reached its zenith throughout the South. Democrats participated in elections in most Southern states and sometimes nominated blacks as candidates for junior offices. Benjamin H. Hill of Georgia, an uncompromising opponent of black suffrage in 1867, now declared his willingness to recognize blacks' right to the "free, full, and unrestricted enjoyment" of the ballot. Louisiana Democrats also cast aside the rhetoric of race. As the party's state convention announced, "our platform is retrenchment and reform."[819]

The independent campaigns of the Democratic party to attract black votes were unsuccessful almost without exception. Many Democrats realized the impossibility of success at the end of 1868. Where Democrats were a hopeless minority, they sometimes made use of the differences within the Republican party and supported the conservative faction. In Virginia, Democratic leader William Mahone, who promised to "gracefully acquiesce in accomplished facts" by "acknowledging [blacks'] legal status," became a designer of a "new movement" that brought together Democrats and moderate Republicans in supporting the same scheme. In 1869, the coalition successfully elected Gilbert C. Walker, a moderate Republican, to the governorship, and at the same time controlled the legislature. Virginia thus became the only Southern state to avoid the experience of Radical Reconstruction.[820] In Missouri, Democrats followed a similar strategy in cooperating with the Republicans who approved repeal of anti-Confederate political restrictions.[821] In Tennessee, it was the Republican party that first launched the coalition. In 1869, Democrats helped elect a conservative Republican, De Witt Senator, as governor of Tennessee, bringing Reconstruction to a close in this first reconstructed state.[822] In Mississippi, South Carolina, and Texas, however, the coalitions of Democrats and Republicans resulted in failure.[823]

In general, the New Departure had little success in winning over blacks. Only a few well-to-do blacks such as Gilbert Myers of Mississippi, who identified his personal interests with whites', followed this movement.[824] Democrats even converted some black Republican leaders, of whom the most famous was Hiram Revels.[825] Yet most blacks remained indifferent to the appeals from conservatives. As scalawags were isolated in the white race, blacks who followed Democrats were often regarded as traitors of their race. To blacks, voting was not a simple political act, but involved whether or not they denied the legality of Democratic domination. Blacks were very clear that the tacit Democratic goal was to maintain white supremacy and social control. Even when the North was still glaring at their every action, the Tennessee conservatives who came to power passed without any hesitation a series of measures to restrict hunting and fishing, repeal the former lien law, and impose a heavy poll tax.[826] Even if Democrats could cast aside their goal of racial supremacy, in their economic program blacks could only serve as agricultural laborers, and planters would restore their monopoly on labor and freely fix the price of this special kind of commodity. Unwilling to remain eternal inferior laborers, blacks regarded the Republican party as their only hope. In addition, although the New Departure tried to avoid the racial issue, the mission of racial supremacy was not limited to the level of tacit understanding. Like Hampton, most Democratic politicians who spoke to blacks would immediately resort to race demagoguery when bidding for the votes of lower-class whites.[827] Blacks were indeed invited to join the ranks of Democrats, but they were seated in segregated places, and their nominations were mostly symbolic.[828] Therefore, blacks on the whole firmly rallied around the Republican party.

Even when the movement reached its high point, the New Departure had not drawn much support from Democrats. A large number of the party still refused to recognize the legality of Reconstruction regimes and black power. To most Democrats, their moral object was their social interests. As Northern whites promoted civil rights, they also embodied the perfect combination of value rationality and instrumental rationality when defending their racial position. Thus, even when they resorted to extreme means to overthrow Reconstruction, Southern whites still typically demonstrated their American disposition and their devotion to "the higher law." Consoling themselves with its ultimate aim, many initially took a wait-and-see attitude towards the New Departure. When it became clear that blacks refused to cooperate, however, they immediately became enraged and condemned blacks for ignorantly throwing themselves into the arms of the Republican party like "senseless live-stock."[829] To restore white domination and overthrow the "illegal" Reconstruction regimes, Southern whites were determined to spare no means. The new situation promoted the escalation of violence, and the movement that aimed to conquer another race soon reached a new stage.

Although violence appeared as early as emancipation, it was not so strongly politicized in this initial period. In this transitional period, the character of violence gradually developed from personal acts into organized ones. As Reconstruction proceeded, secret terrorist organizations such as the Knights of the White Camellia, the White Brotherhood, the Pale Faces, and the '76 Association became active, of which the most notorious was the Ku Klux Klan.

Sponsored by six Confederate veterans, the Ku Klux Klan was set up in Tennessee in 1866. To attract attention, they gave it an odd name. *Ku Klan* was borrowed from the Greek *kluox*, which meant "ring," "band," or "gang." Added to rhyme with the former words, *Klan* was originally a superfluous word.[830] Its organization was also mysterious. The local Klan units were called dens; these were organized into provinces; the provinces into dominations; the dominations into realms; and the whole into an empire, "the Invisible Empire of the South." Members of the dens were called ghouls, and the den chief was called a cyclops. Superior to them were grand dragons, furies, hydras, titans, and night-hawks. At the top of the tree were a grand wizard and ten genii.[831] Dressing in white robes and hoods, the Klansmen held secret rites and recreational activities, and later on entertained themselves by making fun of blacks. Acting as ghosts, burning crosses, giving out warning letters, or placing small coffins in front of blacks' houses, were all done to try to intimidate blacks. Sometimes they made raids on sleeping blacks at night, imposing the lash and other punishments on them.

These intimidation tactics were soon used to restore whites' dominant position in both the private and public spheres. Undoubtedly, the overriding goal was to consolidate white racial domination. In some whites' eyes, the most urgent necessity was to foster their spirit of solidarity and vigilance and to check blacks' growing independence. Other whites regarded the Klan as an instrument to punish black "crime," a function which the Republican authorities allegedly could not or would not perform. Even when they conceded that the courts were ready to do so, many whites were still reluctant to abandon the ready method of violence or intimidation, for fear of directly recognizing the Reconstruction regimes. "I suppose," an Alabamian said, "these men who belong to this

organization do not wish to take the trouble of having the matter investigated in court when they can attend to it so easily."[832] More usually, violence was directed against the alleged "impudent negroes," those who
were unwilling to observe racial etiquette as demanded under slavery.
After he was whipped, a North Carolina black described how the Klansmen "told me the law, their law, that whenever I met a white person, no
matter who he was, whether he was poor or rich, I was to take off my
hat."[833] Any black who did not speak respectfully to whites, did not
yield the sidewalk to white passers by, or dressed in a distinctive style
might provoke white anger, and those most certain to suffer mistreat-
ment were interracial couples in which the males were black. As a
Southern white observed, "In the aftermath of Civil War the motto of
those who rode with the Ku Klux Klan was the protection of Southern
womanhood." "I have always understood that a Negro who touch a white
woman must die."[834]

   At the same time, to maintain white employers' authority, to reduce
the competitive power of labor, and to maintain labor discipline was another objective the Klan assiduously strove for. According to Stagg,
where problems of labor control and land tenure were most acute, the
Klan was most rampant, especially in the upcountry areas. The Klan arose
to compel black renters to labor on "acceptable" terms.[835] Although his
argument does not mention the general power relationship, Stagg did
point out a real origin of violence, "labor troubles," because the economic relations between white and black formed an important basis for
their general relations. When the new Republican governments began to
make and enforce laws regulating labor after 1868, the labor problem
was politicized. Soon violence became widespread, with its goal to take
the place of the vanishing personal authority of the master and legal control of the white authorities. An Alabama scalawag reported that the Klan
became active just because employers felt unable to "control the labor
through the courts" and made up their mind to "compel them to do by
fear what they were unable to make them do by law."[836] In the black belt,
now and again the upper class opposed the Klan, because its violence
was detrimental to labor and investment. If laborers were not well disciplined, however, they did not hesitate to use it, not even sparing poor
whites. "The bands," a Republican editor wrote, "are having a great
effect, in inspiring a nameless *terror* among Negroes, poor whites, and
even others."[837] An important aim of the Klan violence was to make the
Reconstruction laws dead letters and compel blacks to forever belong
to a docile labor class. Any attempt to change an employer, to take an

employer to court, or to resist the superintendence of an employer would incur unexpected misfortune, whereas blacks who achieved a modicum of economic success were especially "offensive," because the Klansmen "do not like to see the negro go ahead."[838]

The Klan was also used for political purposes. Nevertheless, its political nature was broad, with white domination in every aspect of Southern life, including politics, its aim. In reality, the Klan became an instrument serving the interests of the Democratic party. Because it was very rare for blacks to occupy the leadership position even at the high point of Reconstruction, the substantial issue was to what extent whites would dominate or which whites would dominate. Generally speaking, a good many carpetbaggers gained state or federal offices, whereas scalawags dominated at the local level.[839] In some states such as Texas, scalawags composed a majority of the Republican infrastructure and manipulated the state.[840] In such a situation, the Klan provided a ready-made instrument for the dissenters who were determined to break up the biracial coalition and boost whites' morale through their tactics. By violence or intimation, the Klansmen compelled blacks either to vote for Democrats or to stay away from politics. Since there was no secret ballot at that time, blacks who exercised their civil rights were very vulnerable to attack.[841] Alabama freedmen George Moor related how, in 1869, Klansmen came to his home, administered a whipping, wounded a neighbor, and "ravished a young girl who was visiting my wife." "The cause of this treatment, they said, was that we voted the radical ticket."[842] In many cases, violence was directed against local black leaders. "The object of it," reported Emanuel Fortune, driven from Jackson County, Florida, by the Klan, "is to kill out the leading men of the Republican party."[843] Although most victims left behind no historical records, the existence of black leaders did represent a challenge to the old racial order. It was estimated that about one-tenth of the black delegates to the constitutional conventions became the victims of violence during Reconstruction.[844] After brutal whippings, numeral local leaders had to make their getaway. Unquestionably, white Republicans, the other mainstay of the Republican party, could not escape the harassment of the Klan either. A Mississippi Republican said: "a great many white men who would vote the republican ticket never say anything about it publicly [and] are afraid of the odium, the denunciation, the persecution, the deprivation of patronage, and the loss of social position."[845] The danger from the nightriding Klan was so serious that "quite a large number of respectable [Republican] farmers [did] not sle[ep] in the houses any time."[846]

Before the early 1870s, however, the Klan had not played a decisive role in the "Redemption" of the South. In this regard, Otto Olsen held that the Klan's ability to establish "Conservative political control" was "somewhat uncertain," and that its appearance was only a manifestation of political and social dysfunction rather than a premeditated political maneuver.[847] Seen from an evolutionary angle, this view did reflect social reality in the early period of Reconstruction. The Klan was after all a grassroots movement, strongly characterized by its local and personal color. Just because of its spontaneousness and lack of strict leadership, the Klan could evolve into a widespread movement and in the end overstepped control of itself. When Klan leaders realized this trend, they tried, unsuccessfully, to disband the organization.[848] Even when its object was directly aimed at politics, the Klan's actions were still secret and not well coordinated. Concerning its early political effect, George C. Rable keenly observed that, although the Klan might have weakened Republican voting strength in many areas and spread a sense of fear, its "lack of organization beyond the local level made it a weak instrument to attack Republican state governments."[849] On the other hand, although some blacks were intimidated and showed their cowardice, many displayed great valor on election days. Sometimes "the blacks rather invited a contest, saying they were willing to go out into an open field and 'fight it out.' "[850] And the Klan's resort to violence and threat was not necessarily effective in intimidating white Republicans. In Blount County, Alabama, for instance, Union Army veterans organized "the anti-Ku Klux," which put an end to Klan violence there.[851]

By the early 1870s, most Southern states were still under Republican control. These states can be classified into two groups. In one group, including Florida, Arkansas, and Missouri, there was an insufficient black voting bloc, and the party in power was divided into two competitive factions and confronted with an equally divided opposition. In such a situation, the Democrats were confident that their party would sweep the South sooner or later, once they had organized themselves well. To some extent, Republican victories in these states were linked with the disfranchisement of the former Confederates and the indifference of some white voters. Once this basis was reduced, the Democratic party might be irresistible. The Klan's activities in these states were not so much to seal off blacks' political space as to rally whites' own forces. Blacks were only their external target, and the central contest was to enhance the morale of white voters and punish dissenters. The other group, including Alabama, Mississippi, Georgia, and North Carolina, was mainly distributed over the deep South. Here black voters were in the overwhelming majority, the Republican party could retain their power with little or no support from white voters, and there seemed to be no possible means to end Republican rule through normal political proceedings. In these states, the failure of the New Departure and the political nature of the conflict for survival compelled Democrats to find any necessary solutions. Under the circumstances, the Klan's violence encouraged the Democrats and made itself a necessary prerequisite for their success. The link between the Democrats and the Klansmen became close.

From the beginning, both the New Departure and the "white line" party leaders spoke of the "good" the Klan achieved despite their discontent with its "excesses." Some even denied the existence of the organization, dismissing reports of violence as a result of personal grudges or the Republican "slander mill."[852] Others tried to defend the atrocities by portraying the victims as criminals. Still others justified this organization as a result of the growth of the Union League. "The one really new ingredient of regulator activity after 1867," Allen W. Trelease pointed out, "was political opposition to the Radicals."

> And so far as the Klan loomed larger than the earlier vigilante groups, this was undoubtedly the reason. Only now did upper-class elements and Conservative political leaders take much interest in the idea. In many places some took over Klan leadership, at least temporarily. The Klan became in effect a terrorist arm of the Democratic party, whether the party leaders as a whole liked it or not.[853]

The new function of the Klan, however, became prominent only from the 1870s onwards, especially after the general election of 1872, when Democrats were eager to find a new strategy for seizing power. At this stage, the nature of violence changed considerably. Intimidation and violence were carried out in the open by organized bands. The violence was not only directed against individuals but inflicted on Republican institutions such as schools, courthouses, jails, militia units, and mass meetings. Although federal intervention nominally disbanded the Klan, it did not mean the end of organized violence, because the federal government only imposed penalties on persons who "shall *conspire together,* or *go in disguise* for the purpose of depriving any person or any class of equal privileges or immunities under the laws,"(italics mine).[854] In a sense, this measure only brought violence out into the open. By 1872–1873, secret terrorist organizations had disappeared, and in their stead appeared new bands who called themselves Rifle Companies, Red Shirts, or other such names, threatening Republicans through both secret and public methods.[855] Violence also received encouragement from the Democratic party leadership at the highest level, was channeled into the well-devised goals of the party, and gave prominence to the racial color of political conflicts. In the end, the Democratic party took over the Klan's role.[856] A typical example was the terrorist plan invented by Mississippi Democrats in 1875, "the Mississippi plan" or the "shotgun policy." This kind of violence was especially serious in Mississippi, Alabama, Louisiana, and South Carolina.

Although they were determined to seize power by whatever means, Democrats took note of their own legality even when they committed violence. In most cases, they suspended violent action several weeks before election days. If they found that mere intimidation could keep Republicans far from the ballot boxes and that economic sanctions were enough to be effective, Democrats were content with the exercise of these moderate means. The "oligarchy in the rebel ranks," complained an Alabama scalawag, "held the bread-basket before the hungry gaze of the voters, both white and colored, and said to hundreds and thousands of them vote if you dare and the earth be your bed and stones be your bread."[857] The use of these tactics was not only to avoid Northern doubt about the legality of future Democratic regimes and any basis for intervention, but also was the manifestation of the traditional politicians' emphasis on form as much as outcome. So it was not strange that the purposes of the Klan were flaunted as to "protect the weak, the innocent, and the defenseless" and to "protect and defend the Constitution of the United States."[858] And conservatives argued that they had not fully given up their democratic faith. They jealously guarded it lest it would be "abused" by others. The comment of James McPherson pointed out the conservative form of this movement. If this process had to be interpreted as either "redemption or counterrevolution," he said, the former term could more accurately describe the whole episode.[859]

The characteristics of the violent activities at the second stage demonstrated that the racial problem was at the core of Reconstruction politics. In the South, the two parties increasingly followed racial lines, with the Republican party having evolved into an organization primarily based on blacks and carpetbaggers. Violence had destroyed the local bases of the Republican party and put the rank and file into chaos. "They have no leaders up there, no leaders," lamented a freedmen of Union County, South Carolina.[860] In a time when political activities were carried out mainly through oral messages and personal contacts, the disappearance of local leaders was a severe blow to black ambitions. As examples who started at the bottom and worked their way up at the top, black leaders represented the hope of their race. Their murder or exile had a depressing impact upon their communities. No party, commented Adelbert Ames, could see hundreds of its "best and most reliable workers" murdered and still "retain its vigor."[861] Under the constant threat of violence, black suffrage proved to be a fragile weapon for the Republican party.

The Democrats' resolution to introduce racial violence aggravated the internal discord of the Republican party. Unmoved by local Republicans' appeals for help, Alabama Governor William H. Smith denied the gravity of violence and stressed that local authorities bore the primary responsibility for law enforcement. As a result, his credibility was eroded among the black masses, and the influence of his rival, Senator George Spencer, was on the increase.[862] Even in states where state militias could be used, the consequences were still complicated and dangerous. In Alabama, although the constitution had not empowered the governor to proclaim martial law, William W. Holden declared in 1870 that Alamance and Laswell were in open rebellion and dispatched Colonel George W. Kirk to the two counties. This action repelled many white Republicans, who were afraid of any foreign intervention in local affairs, and provided a rallying point for Democrats, who launched an all-out attack against the so-called "Kirk-Holden war" and clamored for the personal safety of the mobs. In August, Democrats gained an overwhelming victory in the legislative election. In the fall of that year, the new legislature successfully impeached Holden, who became the first governor expelled by impeachment in American history.[863]

At the same time, internal unity among whites were greatly consolidated. In some locations, black votes decreased dramatically. In Nachitoches Parish, Louisiana, for example, the vote was 2,800 Democratic, no Republican in 1878.[864] But according to Michael Perman, the statewide Republican counts did not decline conspicuously. In Mississippi, for instance, Republicans cast 70,462 votes for state treasurer in 1873; two years later, in the white supremacy campaign of 1875, the total was 67,171, while in thirty-five of the state's seventy-two counties, the Republican vote even increased slightly.[865] The failure of Republicans at this stage was to a large extent attributable to the participation of previously apathetic white voters and the scalawags' transference of their allegiance. In Alabama, for example, the white-supremacy tactics increased Democratic votes by 26,000.[866] The new tactics not only punctured blacks' confidence, but also consolidated the white line and shortened the psychological distance between whites. In this campaign, the white elite tried to add fuel to the flames and then placed the whole campaign into their own hands. In this sense, racial demagogy was indeed a unique skill of the white upper class.

The use of violence in the South made the new racial democracy an abnormal phenomenon. To overthrow the previous coercive racial relations and carry out the universal norms of conduct in politics, the North forced the new democracy on white Southerners and brought about a legal crisis; this coercive action was in turn resisted by whites' tenacious disobedience, and Reconstruction laws were thoroughly shorn of their sanctity. While Southern violence aroused white citizens' community emotions and sense of responsibility, it also encouraged their contempt for Reconstruction laws and exacerbated the conflict between the laws of minorities and those of majorities. In Southern election history, the "Redemption" and its aftermath was the period in which fraudulence was most epidemic. The aim of fraudulence was to retain white supremacy and elite domination. The crux of the problem was that Southern whites did not accept the new rules of the political game formulated by the North and did not recognize blacks' position as political opponents. This fact, regrettably, was totally incompatible with the basis of democracy: the principle of seeking *successive compromises*. What the whites wanted was simply conquest, to score a resounding triumph over another race and, at most, to add some sentimental condiments of humanism to the harsh oppression. Overwhelmed by unruly, primitive forces, these circumstances made Reconstruction politics go far beyond the competitive nature of a reasonable political game. In the antebellum South, Democrats and Whigs had once vied keenly with each other, but the contest had never become so white-hot. "It is terrible to see the extent to which all classes go in their determination to win," one Northern observer wrote home. "Conscience offers no restraint. Nothing is so common as the resort to perjury, unless it is violence. In short, I do not know whom to believe."[867] Both blacks and whites regarded the contest as a life-and-death struggle and a cardinal issue of right and wrong. Neither of them could afford to lose. The dominant Southern whites must bear responsibility for this situation. There is no reason to doubt their moral enthusiasm, which was a glorious American tradition, even among Southern whites, and a fundamental element of Southern community feelings. Its quintessence was embodied in John Adams' letter to encourage John Quincy Adams (1782).

> Your studies, I doubt not, you pursue, because I know you to be a studious youth; but, above all, preserve a sacred regard to your own honor and reputation. Your morals are worth all the sciences. Your conscience is the minister plenipotentiary of God Almighty in your breast. See to it that this minister never negotiates in vain. Attend to him in opposition to all the courts in the world.[868]

Concerning blacks, however, what whites lacked was not the moral courage to defend their own compatriots, but moral self-restraint towards another race, whereas the two kinds of self-cultivation were the balance wheels upon which democracy depended.[869] To whites, the comment of Robert P. Warren was penetrating. "Nor are all social problems best solved by an abstract commitment to virtue. Ethics should be, indeed, the measure of politics, but there is an ethic that demands scrutiny of motive, context, and consequences, particularly the consequences to others."[870]

RADICALISM ON THE WANE

For national Republican leaders, the years after 1869 were a time of irresolution. Confronted with the political and social crisis caused by rampant Southern racism, they were trapped again between federalism and civil rights and between the protection of their Southern allies and the end of Reconstruction. The changing situation and Republicans' consideration of their own interests were vital to the policy-making process.

The problem was complicated by Republicans' promise, made too precipitately during the general election of 1868, that the war issues had been finally settled. According to Dana's theory, Reconstruction legislation was just a temporary phenomenon in the unusual postbellum state, and it was enforced only because Southern states were caught up in the "grasp of war." Most Republicans conceded that the unusual power of the national government would come to a close with the restoration of the Southern states. Now that the Southern states had met all sorts of preconditions made by Northerners and returned to their due places in the federal system, would the Northern constituencies permit raising the old issue again? Would they tolerate new legislation to support the feeble Southern Republican regimes?

One indication as to the changing situation was that radicalism as a powerful source of social reform was experiencing a turning point. Considering it a triumphal conclusion of four decades of agitation on behalf of the ex-slaves, most reformers hailed the passage of the Fifteenth

Amendment. "Nothing in all history," rejoiced William Lloyd Garrison, equaled "this wonderful, quiet, sudden transformation of four millions of human beings from the auction-block to the ballot-box."[871] As a result, many institutions aiding the freedmen were disbanded in the early 1870s. In March 1870, the American Anti-Slavery Society put an end to its activities, and its mission, members believed, was now completed. Although some Radicals doubted the reliability of black freedom, most reformers believed that the freedmen need not depend on their receiving the nation's "special sympathy." The freedmen, Thomas W. Higgison stressed, "should not continue to be kept wards of the nation."[872]

Some organizations, to be sure, were still persisting with their work. Although they did not lose sight of the ultimate goal of black equality, their focal point had transferred from the advocacy of equal rights legislation to the "preparation" of freedmen for the rights and responsibilities of citizenship. In 1875, the American Missionary Association declared that Reconstruction laws had destroyed the "superstructure" of slavery but had left the "foundation" intact. The foundation was the "antagonism of races, the ignorance of the black, and the prejudices of the whites" which were "embedded in the *minds and hearts* of men" and "can only be overcome by education."[873] Frustrated by Reconstruction's incapacity to free the freedmen from the bondage of "ignorance and degradation" imposed by slavery, Richard Rust, the executive secretary of the Freedmen's Aid Society, wrote in 1877 that it was impossible to expect a people wore down by "centuries of heathenish and oppression" to "come forth clothed with all the qualification of citizenship. Christian education, the development of heart and intellect, the education which our schools impart, is the only hope of this unfortunate people."[874]

The transition from immediatism to gradualism in the theories of racial progress reflected the widespread propagation of social Darwinism in ideological circles. As the powerful driving force of social reform, radicalism was firmly rooted in the complicated interplay of intellectual, moral, and religious forces, including the Enlightenment's concept of natural rights and its optimism stressing the environment, Transcendentalism's notion that human beings were primarily good and capable of limitless advancement and perfection, and evangelical Christianity's belief in the immediate expiation of individual and social sins by conversion to God's truth. From the 1830s onwards, the surging reform waves, with their emphasis on immediate social change produced by the purposeful action of men working in harmony with God's will, had a profound impact on the ideological substructure of Abolitionism. In a sense,

Radical Reconstruction was a legislative outcome of radicalism. By the 1870s, however, the Darwinian concept of biological evolution was extensively applied to the observation and study of social problems. The whole society was regarded as a gradually evolving organism, whose change could not be attained overnight by men's conscious legislation, but could develop slowly only through the hands of natural or mysterious forces beyond the control of men. Man's subjective efforts, to be sure, were not entirely useless, but their positive role was only embodied in his strict deference to evolutionary laws. Therefore, "The wise radical is content to wait and slowly to build up when the work of pulling down is properly over."[875] "It seems to me," wrote Abram W. Stevens, a former radical reformer, "that the great gospel of the nineteenth century is the discovery of Evolution." "We see that everything does not depend upon us alone, to make society what it should be, that Nature works even while we are asleep." Once we understand the true meaning of evolution, "we become, not content with evil, but patient with it," and any social change "hastened or brought about by violent means is, so far as true progress concerned, a *stumble*, not a step."[876] As to the work of promoting racial progress, people increasingly believed that education and Christian faith were more effective than law or the bayonet.

At the same time, the influence of Radicals in the Republican party decreased, and their leadership strength became weaker and weaker. When the party was organized in the 1850s, many reformers, including antislavery crusaders, regarded it as an instrument of moral reform and joined its ranks. Under their pressure, the Republican party wrote the antislavery goal into its platform in 1864. Despite their minority position, their presence itself could well explain the distinctiveness of the party. According to Stampp, they were "the custodians of its conscience."[877] After the war, many Radicals considered Reconstruction as the final lap of utopian reforms in the nineteenth century. Partly because of their persistence, the Republican party in principle expanded its negation of slavery and began to carry out its commitment to political equality. By the end of the 1860s, however, many Radical leaders had died or retired. Thaddeus Stevens, the Radical leader in the House, died in August 1868, and his death put many white Southerners in good heart. Soon Joshua K. Giddings, Edwin M. Stanton, and Salmon P. Chase followed in Stevens' footsteps. Even Charles Sumner, who still retained his seat in the Senate, lost his influence and died in 1874.[878]

The decline of radicalism indicated that the time was almost past when the Republican party acted as an instrument of moral reform. Once the party accomplished its task of abolishing slavery and wrote civil rights into the Constitution, idealism aroused by the war was for the most part spent, and the party became less propulsive and more bureaucratic. Since the party's strength was to a large extent based on its moral goal, the faintness of its moral color would inevitably expose the importance of other issues. A new political era had dawned, declared the Radical Boston *Commonwealth*. "A party cannot be maintained on past traditions. It must move on to new conquests."[879] The vigorous upsurge of the liberal Republican movement reflected this new tendency.

Primarily based in the intelligentsia, the liberal Republicans emerged from the dissent groups within the party. During the war and the early years of Reconstruction, those reformers, who professed to be "the best men," had been firmly supporters of the antislavery movement, providing a theoretical foundation and practical political support for Reconstruction legislation.[880] Yet once Reconstruction policy took shape, these "former advocates of strong measures against the South turned their fire on those attempting to carry out the strong measure."[881] In fact, it was these men that redefined the word "reform," replacing its goal of eliminating racial inequality from American life with that of purifying the existing political system. By 1870, they had become clearly hostile to much of the leadership of the Republican party and launched the movement already known as "liberal Republicanism."

These new reformers believed that there existed, like the natural laws in the universe, invariable laws of economics and politics in human affairs. Firmly rooted in the intrinsic nature of everything, these laws were beyond human interference, though they could be somewhat perceived by man's reason and science. As clergyman-economist Lyman Atwater put it, "Legislation cannot alter the laws of nature, of man, of political economics."[882] Thus, "the higher law" behind political, economic, and social phenomena formed the core of these reformers' innermost beliefs.

Perhaps in no area were reformers more certain that scientific truth had been discovered than in economics. While Amasa Walker called it the "science of wealth," Edwin L. Godkin termed it "a real science." The heart of this science was the laissez-faire of classic liberalism, the "let-alone principle," as the financial writer Simon Newcomb put it.[883] The axioms of the reformers' "financial science," free trade, the law of supply and demand, and the gold standard, all derived from this general principle. These, according to reformers, were not only pure economic issues, but also serious moral ones. As Godkin asserted, "any honest man" could understand financial questions "because they are also, and equally, moral questions."[884] The laissez-faire theory was perceived as a commitment to liberty, namely, to the "right of every man to employ his own efforts for the gratification of his own wants."[885] Imposing high prices on the mass of consumers, tariff protection was only in the interests of capital and labor in a special sector, and it violated the individuals' liberty by depriving them of their opportunities to produce or buy products at the lowest cost. Greenback inflation, on the other hand, would lead to "dishonesty, corruption, repudiation," "gamblings, coundrelism, and effrontery," not to mention "the diffusion of a taste for luxury, dissipation, and excess."[886] All the dangers lay in the enactment of "special" or "class" legislation by governmental coercive power in the interests of one group at the expense of others. Even if the state action was on behalf of a group hardly able to protect itself, such intervention also shared dangerous antilibertarian tendencies. In fact, Edward Atkinson equated protection to communism. "The two ideas are identical in principle," he maintained, because "protection attempts to enforce an inequitable distribution of our annual product," while communism always "invokes the forces of law under the mistaken idea that a more equitable division may be had."[887] Thus, the principle of limited government was gaining great respect. "The Government," declared Godkin, "must get out of the 'protective' business and the 'subsidy' business and the 'improvement' and 'development' business. It cannot touch them without breeding corruption."[888]

When touching on black issues, the laissez-faire principle gave new political meaning to them. The Founding Fathers had fought a bloody war against the English king, who used state power to levy monopolistic exaction from the rest of society. Holding high the banner of populism, Jackson resisted the exploitation of the common people by the "privileged group." The same monopolistic power had been used by the slaveowners to expropriate labor from blacks; therefore, "the highest right of property is the right to freely exchange it for other property," a reformer declared. "Any system of laws which denies or restricts this right for the purpose of subserving private or class interests, reaffirms the principle of slavery."[889] Based on this notion of "equal right," Republicans had waged a unprecedented war against the privileged interests of the slavocracy. Once the majority rule of the Radical Republicans had been established, however, the menace to liberty no longer came from above, but originated from the bottom masses, the "dangerous classes." Poisoned by propaganda, they charged, the ignorant voters were eventually playing into the hands of the shameless politicians. The reformers railed at scalawags and carpetbaggers, who "control the politics of the State through the control which they have obtained over the colored man."[890] As a result, a massive system of "class legislation" was taking shape. To support improvement programs and public facilities and pay them bloated salaries of officials, Southern Reconstruction governments, which were elected by penniless blacks, recklessly taxed whites for the benefit of some people at the expense of the others. This Tammany Hall–like corruption was no more than "organized communism and destruction of property under the guise of taxation."[891] In addition, the liberal reformers pessimistically found that most Radical leaders of the party, including Thaddeus Stevens, Benjamin F. Butler, William D. Kelly, Benjamin F. Wade, and Zachariah Chandler, approved of high tariffs and greenback inflation. Undoubtedly, the link between governmental activism and class legislation further strengthened the reformers' weariness of Radical Reconstruction.

The liberal reformers insisted on social order and harmony. To them, democracy was not the process in which the will of majority was translated into action. It was instead "the art by which the teachings of social science are put into practice." Since "Truth is not settled by majorities," legislators must at any moment bear in mind the "laws of social order and well-being" and apply the "commercial principle" to the solution of urban affairs.[892] The highest allegiance, they thought, should be owed to liberty and civilization, and to these ends the suffrage was just a means remaining to be tested. Having retreated from their former position on civil rights, liberal reformers now approved of educational and property qualifications for voting and advocated the reform of civil servants to eliminate the maladies of party politics and place the power into the hands of an intellectual and moral elite. The "great problem of every system of Government," Henry Adams affirmed, "has been to place administration and legislation in the hands of the best men," those with "the loftiest developments of moral and intellectual education."[893] Although elitism "clash[ed] with our fundamental principle that one man is as good as another," and there seemed to be no leeway to escape this dilemma, most liberal reformers did not hesitate, like Adams, to embrace elitism. "The tendency among thoughtful men," reported a New York newspaper in 1869, "is towards a restriction of the right of suffrage considerably inside its present limits."[894]

The liberal Republican movement, fundamentally speaking, was a power struggle, a struggle in which Republicans excluded from the policy-making core tried to established their own leadership status. Almost all reformers, including Lyman Trumbull and George W. Julian, were pushed aside by the party's new leadership.[895] Eager to deprive the Radicals of the vehicle by which they could gain ascendancy in the party, reformers called on people to cast aside the civil rights issues and eliminate the "Negro question" from politics. "Let the reconstruction matters be once settled," Edward Atkinson insisted, "and the fight between Protection and Free Trade will be upon us, and Free-Trade views will win."[896] In their opinion, the moral issues of slavery had secured the Radical Republicans' leadership, whereas the new questions of finance, taxation, and administrative reform applied the truths of social science, in which they were particularly skilled.

Without fail, reformers were increasingly disappointed with the freedmen. "They are an easy, worthless race," lamented Horace Greeley, "taking no thought for the morrow, and your course aggravated their weakness."[897] The "blackest" legislators, Godkin asserted, were the worst offenders, and South Carolina freedmen enjoyed an overall "average of intelligence but slightly above the level of animals."[898] On the question of blacks' ability, reformers gradually exposed their white racism. On the whole, however, reformers were not so much dissatisfied with the black race itself as blacks' incompetence, and they did not intend to completely restrict blacks' political rights. What frustrated them was "a large portion of the most active and intelligent people [remain] under political disability." At the same time, Southern misgovernment was aggravated by placing "the control of affairs in the hands of the more ignorant classes." Thus, they advised putting aside "the question of color" and placing confidence in the region's "natural leaders."[899]

Initially, reformers put their trust in Grant. If they could obtain support from the President, their aim would be to a large extent realized. After their hope was shattered, the liberal reformers decided to drop out of the orthodox camp of the party and offered Horace Greeley, the founder of the *New York Tribune,* as the candidate for the Presidency in 1872. Although they acquired support from Democrats, the liberal reformers still suffered a crushing defeat. All the same, radicalism gradually lost its attraction to the Republican rank and file because of the powerful offensive launched by the liberal Republican-Democratic opposition. As the war and Reconstruction issues in the 1860s had pushed established Republican leaders towards radicalism, the situation in the 1870s drove many to conservatism. Despite its outward support for black suffrage, the Republican party, which plagiarized its platform from the liberal reformers in the presidential election, greatly blunted its radicalism and was forced on the defensive. Especially after the party was soundly defeated at the middle elections of 1874, more and more Republicans emphasized the new issues. In short, the battle of the liberal Republican movement marked the end of the old "moral politics."

Ironically, the pro-Grant professional politicians had weakened Reconstruction policy as vigorously as liberal reformers did. Since Grant's coming to power, the old leadership was gradually replaced by the "Stalwarts" of the party, who simply regarded government as a means of seeking gain rather than an instrument of moral reform. By dividing up the spoils of office, they had institutionalized the party. By every possible means, the party bosses tried to create whatever majority the party needed in every election. The enormous cost of elections and the vast sums handled by officials caused the party to wallow in the mire with businessmen seeking governmental aid, producing unprecedented scandals in the Gilded Age. "Like all parties that have an undisturbed power for a long time," wrote Senator James W. Grimes, the Republican party "has become corrupt, and I believe it is today the most corrupt and debauched political party that has ever existed."[900] The civil rights issues were the lubricating oil for this huge political machine. By waving the "blood shirt," for instance, ex-General John A. Logan in one county of Illinois "elected a *one-legged* soldier for County Treasure, a *one-armed* soldier for circuit clerk, and a good soldier for County judge."[901] As realists, they were not as easily swayed by moral enthusiasm as liberal reformers were, but calmly watched over practical interests. So long as the civil rights issues could not be transcended by other ones and continued to act as the ties of the party, and so long as the Stalwarts found that black votes remained effective in maintaining their Southern allies, they would pay continuous attention to the fate of Southern Republicans. While they remained committed to what had been accomplished, the Stalwarts in Congress even added new requirements to the process of restoration in 1870, prohibiting all possible amendments that would abridge the right to vote and hold office or deny citizens access to education.[902] But this measure was not so much an aggressive attack as a pose to ward off blows. In other words, in the orthodox Republican camp the commitment to civil rights had degenerated from a moral crusade into an inertial political force.

While the Republican party was afflicted with disunity because of the deterioration in its moral power, its rival, the Democratic party, tried to enhance its legitimacy by stressing new issues such as tariffs, administrative reform, and governmental aid to private enterprise. In the Democratic rhetoric and platform, the term "nigger" was replaced by "negro" or "colored person" to express its determination to abandon racial politics. Peter B. Sweeney of New York's Tammany Hall called on Democrats to drop "the negro agitation," which enabled their enemies to "carry away many votes" by identifying themselves with equality and progress. Most Democrats, including Ohio Democrat Clement Valladigham, the notorious Copperhead, approved of this new policy. Despite their strong opposition to any federal enforcement effort, Democrats declared they were willing to accept "the *Constitution* as it stands *now*." When the liberal Republican movement was gathering momentum, Democrats felt that they had found a golden opportunity to defeat Republicans and leave behind the shadows of war. Although they were embarrassed and found it difficult to support a man who had attacked them on civil rights questions in the past, Democrats agreed to Greeley as their candidate for President and accepted the Liberal platform as their own. Whether Greeley won or lost, asserted the *World*, was irrelevant; the most important thing was that his nomination had "cut the party loose from the dead issues of an effete past."[903]

The "New Departure" of Northern Democrats blurred the target which the Republican party had long attacked. As the famous philosopher John Dewey put it, "a man does not fire as soon as he sees the target; instead he erects it so as to shoot more effectively and meaningfully."[904] The Democratic party's abandonment of racial politics, at least outwardly, changed the Republican wolf-cry into a tilt at windmills. The Northern public might still only half believe in Democrats' commitment, but once Republican faults became intolerable, they gave their confidence to the Democratic party. When depression spread over the whole country, the Democratic party seized is chance and carried most seats in the House in 1875. As the first failure of the Republican party in national elections since the Civil War, this election result indicated that Northern voters were no longer as wary of the Democratic party as before. It was then that Republican politicians concluded that the public had been bored with the "wore-out cry of 'southern outrages'" and were reminded that the Civil War had not been waged primarily to free blacks, who were not "the end and aim of all our effort."[905]

By the early 1870s, the former Confederates controlled Georgia, Tennessee, North Carolina, West Virginia, and Missouri through their cooperation with moderate Republicans or by means of violence. Other Southern Republican governments were also in a very precarious state. Menaced by violence, Southern Republicans sent numerous letters to

Washington for help. Yet with the decline of antislavery idealism and the growing indifference to racial politics in the North, Republican authorities were left with little leeway to protect civil rights and Southern Reconstruction regimes. To make matters worse, the federal government was now staggering in a morass of Constitutional conservatism and administrative inefficiency.

Conditioned by federalism, specialized machinery for enforcing laws had not been created during Reconstruction. The life of the Freedmen's Bureau was extended out of need, but it ended in 1869 nevertheless. The federal government then lost an instrument of directly dealing with Southern social and economic affairs and protecting black civil rights. The Union Army still exerted some supervisory duties, but the law-enforcement work had been handed over to the civil authorities, and the management of cases concerning Reconstruction laws had to rely on an overburdened federal judicial system. Previously, the Supreme Court proved reluctant to be involved in Reconstruction controversies. During the 1870s, however, it gradually emasculated the Reconstruction amendments to cater to the shifting atmosphere of Northern opinion.

The Court decision in the *Slaughterhouse* cases explains best the issue. While concluding that the Fourteenth Amendment was intended primarily to enlarge the rights of ex-slaves, Justice Samuel F. Miller insisted that the amendment only protected the relevant federal rights, access to ports and navigable waterways, the ability to run for federal office, travel to the seat of government, and be protected on the high seas and abroad. Obviously, the rights listed here by Miller were of little importance to freedmen. Most of the tangible rights of citizens, according to Miller, were "left to the state governments for security and protection," whereas the federal government had "nothing to do" with them.[906] In fact, Miller's delineation of federal rights had declared most clauses of the Enforcement Acts of 1870 and 1871 to be invalid.

In 1875, a Missouri woman sued in a case brought before the Supreme Court, claiming her rights under the Fourteenth Amendment were violated by state laws. The Court ruled that the right to vote derived from state, not national, citizenship, and was properly subject to state control, because "the Constitution of the United States does not confer the right of suffrage upon any one."[907]

More dismaying was the 1876 decision in *U.S. v. Cruikshank*. Indictments were brought under the Enforcement Act of 1870, alleging a conspiracy conducted by Louisiana whites to attack a black meeting and deprive the victims of their civil rights. On the ground that the legislation was not authorized by the Fourteenth Amendment, the Court rejected this case. It went on to declare that the Reconstruction amendments only empowered the federal government to prohibit violations of black rights by states, whereas "That duty [to protect the basic rights of citizens] was originally assumed by the state; and it still remains there."[908]

Meanwhile, Republicans in Congress were seeking opportunities to consolidate their position, but they were hesitating over whether to retreat from Reconstruction. Even as they hoped to seize "cohesive power" over the war and Reconstruction issues, most were reluctant to intervene in state affairs to rescue their Southern allies. After the collapse of the Brownlow government, Tennessee Republicans appealed for a second period of military rule in this state, only to find Congress "heartily sick of this reconstruction legislation" and "much averse to interfering in any way."[909] Cooperating with conservative Republicans, Georgia conservatives ejected black legislators in 1868. Congress, after wavering for more than one year, put the state back under military control, and Grant instructed General Alfred H. Terry to restore the black legislators and expel ex-Confederates who could not take the Test Oath. This, however, was the only case in which Congress tried to enforce military intervention.[910] Republicans were very uneasy about the possible impairment of the federal structure. Such an effort to "usurp unauthorized power," Lyman Trumbull warned, would hang "like a millstone around the neck of the party."[911]

Just as the stubbornness of Johnson and his Southern governments had provoked Congress into adhering to radicalism, the endless Klan-type violence at last drove the congressional Republicans to overcome their non-intervention stand. "If that is the only alternative," John Sherman declared, "I am willing to again appeal to the power of the nation to crush, as we once before have done, this organized civil war."[912] After a long period of hesitation, Republican leaders made up their mind to offer direct federal protection to their Southern companions. After the Fifteenth Amendment was sanctioned in 1870, the first Enforcement Act was adopted by Congress in March of that year, forbidding state officials to discriminate among voters on the basis of race and empowering the President to appoint election supervisors, who might bring before federal courts the cases of election fraud and intimidation of voters, and the conspiracies to prevent citizens from exercising their Constitutional rights. But this act was not enough to defend blacks against the Klan's violence. In fact, it proved difficult for federal district courts to obtain any testimony against the alleged Klansmen because of their popularity among the white masses.[913] Even when witnesses were available, juries would shrink from any conviction. As a Republican leader observed, if "any one of these men is on the jury, you cannot convict."[914] Because of the noncompliance of white citizens, the Enforcement Act was paralyzed.

The invalidation of the Enforcement Act again gave prominence to the problem of legitimacy. As always refusing to recognize the Reconstruction laws and regimes, whites did not regard the atrocities committed on blacks as crimes. That was the root of the troubles. "If a white man kills a colored man in any of the counties of this State," signed a Florida sheriff, "you cannot convict him."[915] Led by Benjamin Butler, desperate Radicals were determined to combat poison with poison, trying to put forward a stringent Reconstruction bill. Their attempt, however, was thwarted by moderate Republican leaders such as Garfield, Blaine, and Bingham. To alleviate the anxiety of Southern Republicans, who asked the President over and over for military aid, Grant personally came to the Congress on March 1871 to encourage congressional action. At last the conservative Republicans became a bit more flexible, and a second act, the Ku Klux Klan Act, was proposed. The proposed bill for the first time designated certain ordinary crimes, like murder and assault, as offenses punishable under federal law. If states failed to protect their citizens, amounting to denial of the "equal protection of the laws" granted by the Fourteenth Amendment, the President could use military force, declare martial law, and suspend the privilege of habeas corpus to provide protection.

Already bothered because they were being compelled to legislate in states no longer in "the grasp of war," conservative Republicans insisted that Congress could only punish discriminations in state laws, and that it had never been authorized to enact a code against these personal acts. Conceding that the Fourteenth Amendment permitted the national legislature to punish violations of civil rights by individuals, more moderate Republicans stressed that Congress must act in a limited way and could not one by one enact codes against those concrete crimes such as murder and whipping. Otherwise, they admonished, there would appear a set of national criminal codes. In addition, it was emphasized that federal authorities could punish crimes against civil rights only when states failed to act effectively. "The destruction or serious crippling of the principle of local Government," Garfield warned, "would be as fatal to liberty as secession would have been fatal to the Union."[916]

Based on this Constitutional conservatism, the original bill had to be modified. The list of ordinary crimes was deleted; the discussion of the sections about martial law and habeas corpus was postponed to the end of the next session of Congress; and the president's use of the state militias against the Klan was no longer specified.[917] As a result of this modification, the Ku Klux Klan Act of April 1871 did not symbolize a new radicalism in Washington. It was only a minimum measure Republicans could take when confronted with widespread violence. Republicans generally hoped that it would exert deterrent pressure, under which the states themselves would be forced to protect civil rights, or acts of violence would automatically disappear. All the same, this act pushed Republicans to the brink of Constitutional change because it unprecedentedly put private criminal acts directly under federal jurisdiction. "The Radical laws to enforce the Fifteenth or Fourteenth Amendment," announced California Democratic Senator Eugene Casserly, "are unconstitutional clearly so far as they deal with *individuals* and not with *states*. This is the rock which is to wreck these scoundrel bills."[918]

Because of the states' feebleness, the main responsibility for suppressing violence fell upon the federal government. The newly established Department of Justice and an array of federal marshals and district attorneys were responsible for this, and the army was used only as a last resort. Despite his reluctance, Grant was finally forced to carry out the Enforcement Acts, dispatching troops to South Carolina. In Georgia and North Carolina, where conservatives had already regained power, the threat of federal intervention ended the existence of the Klan. Although this result did not mean the end of organized terrorism, the Enforcement Acts compelled Southern whites to acquiesce, at least outwardly, in the mandatory order. "The law on the side of freedmen," Frederick Douglass would later comment, "is of great advantage only where there is power to make that law respected."[919] If the word *durable* is added before the word *power*, he would be more correct.

The adoption of the Enforcement Acts, however, was only a temporary phenomenon. Republicans soon realized that it was just to defer making a decision on whether to protect their Southern allies or retreat from Reconstruction. Even before the 1872 election, Republicans tried to placate Southern whites by refusing to extend the period in which the President might suspend *habeas corpus* or announce martial law under the Ku Klux Klan Act. In the meantime, Congress passed the Amnesty Act in May 1872, restoring most ex-Confederates' right to hold office proscribed by the Fourteenth Amendment. Having been criticized in the election for pushing the nation into the abyss of "centralization" and military dictatorship, the mainstream Republicans had to make concessions to the liberal elements within the party, who thought reform was more important than the fate of the "corrupt" Reconstruction regimes. After the exposure of the Mobile scandal, pressure became stronger. Checked by many sides, the President became more hesitate to enforce the Ku Klux Klan Act. His attorney general instructed district attorneys to press "pending prosecutions only as far as may appear to be necessary to preserve the public peace and prevent future violation of the law."[920] The indecision of the administrative and judicial authorities caused historian William Gillette to conclude that the lawmakers "preferred to write new laws rather than to oversee the proper enforcement of existing laws."[921] In 1872, the government dropped 203 of the 225 cases pending in Tennessee. In the next year, U.S. attorneys dropped about half the cases that had been pending at the beginning of that year. By 1874, they dropped almost all the rest.[922]

The Panic of 1873 was so disastrous that it was only secondary to the Great Depression of the 1930s. In the winter of that year, cities from Boston to Chicago saw many massive demonstrations demanding the delivery of public relief and an increase in public projects. In rural areas, poverty-stricken farmers flooded into the Granges, crying for greenback inflation and governmental regulation over railroads and land speculations. The surging labor and farmer upheaval now raised another controversial problem about equality, that is, whether Republicans could transcend their commitment to equality before the law and the freedom of participating in the labor market, be prepared for the question of unequal distribution of economic resources, and further intervene in the labor market to react to these "class requests." To a few radical Republicans, the two kinds of equality were identical. "The laboring people of this nation," declared Indiana Congressman John P. Shanks, "think to day that they are subjected unjustly to capital. If they are correct, it is the duty of Congress to redeem them from that thralldom."[923] To most Republicans, however, labor's demands would violate the law of supply and demand, the gold standard, the golden rule of free contract, as well as the principle of limited government. All these proved too much for both Democrats attacking Reconstruction policy and Republicans retreating from the idea of an activist state.

The conservative atmosphere caused by the depression soon pervaded the politics of the nation. To the urban middle and upper classes, the former European ghost of communism now began to wander the American mainland and menace the existence of American democracy. Propertied citizens found themselves more and more sympathetic with

Southern whites, who had never changed their idea that laborers "ought to be slaves."[924] As one Northerner said, "there was reason to believe" that the attitude towards "the labor question" and the "general view of society and government" held by the Southern "old ruling class" were now "substantially shared by a large class in the North."[925] Being made up of Northern "men of business and property" on one side and the black "humble and defenseless millions of the south" on the other,[926] the Republican party was very sensitive to the labor question. It was difficult for the party to behave as supporters of free labor in the South while repressing labor upheavals in the North. At the end of Reconstruction, the urban middle and upper classes were increasingly impatient with the labor movement. In the Great Strike of 1877, for example, they joined with municipal authorities and veterans' organizations to form "citizen militias" that did battle with strikers.[927] The Republican party, which was composed more and more of rich men, gradually took a hard-line on the labor question. Sharing common interests regarding the labor question, the Northern middle and upper classes now had a pressing sense of cooperating with the Southern elite. The class basis of national reconciliation had taken shape.

Because the federal government was reluctant to play an active role, Southern racial violence at this time was again on the offensive. Under the attack of Southern whites, Reconstruction governments collapsed one after another. In some states, racial violence evolved into an open civil war. The most deteriorated state was Louisiana, where the Republican government was on its last legs despite federal intervention and a backup force equal to half the state's population. In the controversial election of 1872, Senator William P. Kellogg, the Republican candidate for the governorship, and his Democrat opponent, John McEnery, both claimed to be the winner. By January 1873, there were two state governments and legislatures in New Orleans, both appealing to the president for recognition as the legal government. Grant reluctantly recognized the Republican regime, but he notified Kellogg that "any compromise that will suit all parties in Louisiana will suit the President."[928] Hence Kellogg tried to conciliate his opponents by offering appointments to local offices and reforming the state's finances, but McEnery refused to make any concession. Enraged by federal intervention, the Democrats were determined to seize the state government by force. In March 1873, they organized their own militia, which, unsuccessfully, attempted to take over the New Orleans police stations. The Colfax Massacre subsequently occurred, and even the arrival of federal troops could not restore order.

In 1874, the situation deteriorated with the organization of the armed "White League," which openly launched "a war of races."[929] In September, a mob again laid siege to the New Orleans police stations. Having left over fifty people dead, the police and the black state militia surrendered. The mob then proclaimed McEnery the true governor of the state. Responding to Kellogg's desperate pleas, Grant instructed the local federal garrison to suppress the rebellion after a delay of two days. Kellogg was thereafter reinstated. In the fall election, however, the White League created another controversial result by intimidation. Once again the federal military garrison was activated. "I have deplored the necessity," lamented Grant, "which seemed to make it my duty under the Constitution and laws to direct such interference. I have always refused except where it seemed to be my imperative duty to act in such a manner. I have repeatedly and earnestly entreated the people of the South to live together in peace."[930]

The rampant violence placed Republicans in a dilemma. If the authorities adopted an interventionist policy, liberal reformers and Democrats would gain strength because the people were "tired out with these annual autumnal outbreaks in the South."[931] The spectacle of soldiers "marching into the Halland expelling members at the point of the bayonet" aroused unheard of Northern criticism.[932] In the South, the intervention of the army was even more corrosive. It proved that tough measures could only bring about more opposition and could not permanently maintain the feeble Reconstruction regimes. If they acquiesced in Southern violence, however, the remaining Reconstruction regimes would soon break down. Since their position was consolidated and their power reigned supreme in the West by the 1870s,[933] Republicans concluded that Southern regimes were not worth maintaining by military force. In the presidential campaign of 1876, Republicans applied a strategy of lip service. On the one hand, they were still talking about Southern rebellion to win over voters who were disturbed by Southern violence; on the other hand, they did not take it seriously and make any real effort to interfere in the South. Their energies were concentrated on the North and in fact surrendered Southern states submissively to their opponents. When violence was spreading through South Carolina, Florida, Louisiana, and other states, Grant only signed a perfunctory proclamation condemning its excess. As a result of this noninterference strategy, violence and intimidation became more epidemic, and the election results were disputed; in turn, terrorism and the electoral crisis accelerated the federal government's steps to abandon Reconstruction. Believing that the Reconstruction regimes were already beyond redemption,

Rutherford B. Hayes, the Republican candidate for the presidency, envisaged the possibility of reshaping the basis of Southern Republicanism. Even William D. Kelley, for three decades a leading Radical, now advised Hayes that the party must rely on the "Old Whigs or Union" elements as its Southern mainstay. Hayes himself expressed that he held "precisely" this view. "I believe," he remarked, "and I have always believed, that the intelligence of any country ought to govern it."[934]

It was against this background that Republicans finalized a political deal with Democrats at the cost of black interests. Of the 369 electoral votes, Samuel J. Tilden, the Democratic candidate, carried 184, whereas Hayes won 165. The remaining 20 were controversial. Nineteen of the 20 came from terrorism-stricken Louisiana, Florida, and South Carolina, where both parties claimed victory and were involved in armed opposition. The remaining one was from Oregon, where Hayes had been approved, but Democrats asserted the right to replace one Republican voter in the Electoral College. To break the deadlock, Hayes promised that once elected, Republicans would rule out the possibility of interfering in Southern affairs, which meant their acquiescence to the Democrats taking over Louisiana, Florida, and South Carolina. He was also prepared to provide Democrats with fair appointments and allocate funds to aid Southern development. To uproot black power and dispense with foreign control, Southern Democrats were more concerned with the restoration of "home rule." Despite the strong opposition of their Northern allies, in the end they accepted the verdict of the congressional joint committee. As a result, Hayes was elected by a margin of one vote. Beset with local and national pressures, the surviving Southern Reconstruction regimes soon broke down completely.

The compromise of 1876 fully demonstrated the limit of Northern idealism. For over one decade after the Civil War, the object of defending black rights had played a vital role in preserving Republican unity and public sympathy. Only when the party in power found its interests in harmony with civil rights, however, had the Constitution been revised. Once the ideals of racial democracy were incarnated into law, the idealism lost its momentum. With the dissipation of idealism and the consolidation of whites' self-consciousness, Reconstruction at last reached its turning point. The regrettable historical ending showed that the driving forces of the new racial democracy mainly came from Northern people and their idealism, and that Reconstruction was basically a white reform, whose trend was not completely controlled by blacks themselves. Just as their freedom and civil rights were procured through whites' quarrels, blacks now lost some rights because of whites' conciliation. The Reconstruction amendments and other laws were still on the statute books, but their implications became increasingly narrow, and their enforcement increasingly perfunctory. The new racial democracy was gradually castrated. The postwar amendments, a Southern newspaper declared, "may stand forever; but we intend to make them dead letters on the statute-book."[935] Piercing as it is, this voice clearly sent people a message that regarding black issues there were factors more important than laws, that is, whites' self-consciousness and their interests.

NOTES

776. Leland Baldwin, *Ideas in Action: Documentary and Interpretive Readings in American History.* New York: American Book Company, 1968, p. 49.

777. Michael Les Benedict, *The Fruits of Victory: Alternatives in Restoring the Union.* New York: University Press of America, 1986, p. 46.

778. Jack M. Bloom, *Class, Race and the Civil Rights Movement.* Indianapolis: Indiana University Press, 1987, p. 21.

779. Vernon Lane Wharton, *The Negro in Mississippi.* New York: Harper & Row, 1965, p. 178.

780. C. Van Woodward, *Origins of the New South, 1877–1913.* Baton Rouge: Louisiana State University Press, 1971, p. 58.

781. Eric Foner, Reconstruction: America's Unfinished Revolution, 1863–1877. New York: Harper & Row, 1988, p. 416.

782. William C. Harris, *The Day of Carpetbaggers: Republican Reconstruction in Mississippi.* Baton Rouge: Louisiana State University Press, 1979, p. 333.

783. Roger L. Ransom and Richard Sutch, *One Kind of Freedom: The Economic Consequences of Emancipation.* New York: Cambridge University Press, 1977, p. 121.

784. Bloom, *op. cit.,* p. 42.

785. Foner, *op. cit.,* p. 381.

786. Benedict, *op. cit.,* p. 42.

787. Foner, *op. cit.,* pp. 384–385.

788. Benedict, *op. cit.,* p. 43.

789. *ibid.,* p. 44.

790. Foner, *op. cit.,* p. 391.

791. Paul D. Escott, "White Republicanism and Ku Klux Klan Terror: The North Carolina Piedmont During Reconstruction," in J. J. Crow, P. D. Escott, and

C. L. Flynn, Jr., eds., *Race, Class and Politics in Southern History.* Baton Rouge: Louisiana State University Press, 1989, p. 34.

792. Wharton, *op. cit.,* p. 216; Kenneth M. Stampp, *The Era of Reconstruction, 1865–1877,* New York: Knopf, p. 196.

793. Bloom, *op. cit.,* p. 32.

794. Lawrence N. Powell, "The Politics of Livelihood: Carpetbaggers in the Deep South," in J. Morgan Kousser and James M. McPerson, eds., *Region, Race, and Reconstruction.* New York: Oxford University Press, 1982, pp. 318–319.

795. Mills Thornton, "Fiscal Policy and the Failure of Reconstruction in the Lower South," in Kousser and McPerson eds., *op. cit.,* pp. 371, 381.

796. Foner, *op. cit.,* p. 382.

797. Otto Olsen, "Reconsidering the Scalawags," *Civil War History,* 1966, p. 318.

798. Carl H. Moneyhon, "The Failure of Southern Republicanism, 1867–1876," in Eric Anderson and Alfred N. Moss, Jr., eds., *The Facts of Reconstruction: Essays in Honor of John Hope Franklin.* Baton Rouge: Louisiana State University Press, 1991, pp. 117–118.

799. Joel Williamson, *The Crucible of Race: Black-White Relations in the American South Since Emancipation.* New York: Oxford University Press, 1965, pp. 80–81.

800. Allen W. Trelease, *White Terror: The Ku Klux Klan Conspiracy and Southern Reconstruction.* New York: Harper & Row, 1971.

801. C. Vann Woodward, *The Burden of Southern History.* Baton Rouge: Louisiana State University Press, 1993, p. 100.

802. Stampp, *op. cit.,* p. 199.

803. Trelease, *op. cit.*

804. Carl N. Degler, *The Other South: Southern Dissenters in the Nineteenth Century.* New York: Oxford University Press, 1974, p. 238.

805. Francis B. Simkins, "The Ku Klux Klan in South Carolina, 1868–1871," *Journal of Negro History,* 1927, p. 629.

806. Trelease, *op. cit.,* p. 31.

807. J. W. Harris, *Legal Philosophies,* London: Butterworths, 1980, pp. 7–8.

808. Ralph H. Gabriel, *The Course of American Democratic Thought.* New York: The Ronald Press, 1940, p. 406.

809. Thoreau, *Civil Disobedience.* Boston: Ticknor, 1849, p. 280.

810. Charles S. Sydnor, "The Southerner and the Laws," in George Brown Tindall, ed., *The Pursuit of Southern History: Presidential Addresses of the Southern Historical Association, 1935–1963.* Baton Rouge: Louisiana State University Press, 1964, pp. 66–67.

811. David R. Weber, *Civil Disobedience in America: A Documentary History.* Ithaca: Cornell University Press, 1978, p. 22.

812. Gunnar Myrdal, *An American Dilemma: The Negro Problem and Modern Democracy.* Vol. I. New York: Random House, 1962, p. 1314.

813. Degler, *op. cit.,* p. 255.

814. William L. Richter, *The Army in Texas During Reconstruction, 1865– 1870.* College Station: Texas A & M University Press, 1987, p. 4.

815. Foner, *op. cit.,* p. 444.

816. Myrdal, *op. cit.,* pp. 1312–1313.

817. James H. Stone, *L. Q. C. Lamar's Letters to Edward Donaldson Clark, 1868–1885,* quoted from Foner, *op. cit.,* p. 415.

818. Degler, *op. cit.,* p. 239.

819. Foner, *op. cit.,* p. 415.

820. Jack P. Maddex, Jr., *The Virginia Conservatives, 1869–1879.* Chapel Hill: University of North Carolina Press, 1970, pp. 66–82.

821. Benedict, *op. cit.,* p. 54.

822. Allen W. Trelease, *Reconstruction: The Great Experiment.* New York: Harper & Row, 1971, p. 151.

823. W. C. Harris, *op. cit.,* pp. 219–237; Foner, *op. cit.,* p. 414.

824. Robert Cruden, *The Negro in Mississippi.* Englewood Cliffs: Prentice-Hall, p. 147.

825. Trelease, *op. cit.,* p. 123.

826. Foner, *op. cit.,* p. 423.

827. Stampp, *op. cit.,* p. 197.

828. Trelease, *op. cit.,* p. 150.

829. Francis B. Simkins and Robert H. Woody, *South Carolina During Reconstruction.* Chapel Hill: University of North Carolina Press, 1932, p. 80.

830. Trelease, *White Terror,* p. 4.

831. Stampp, *op. cit.,* p. 199.

832. Trelease, *op. cit.,* p. 71.

833. Foner, *op. cit.,* p. 430.

834. Rollin Chambliss, *What Negro Newspapers of Georgia Say about Some Social Problems,* quoted from Myrdal, *op. cit.,* p. 1194.

835. J. C. A. Stagg, "The Problem of Klan Violence: The South Carolina Up-Country, 1868–1871," *Journal of American Studies,* 1974.

836. Foner, *op. cit.,* p. 428.

837. Bloom, *op. cit.,* p. 32.

838. Foner, *op. cit.,* p. 429.

839. Carl H. Moneyhon, "The Failure of Southern Republicanism, 1867– 1876," in Eric Anderson and Alfred A. Moss, Jr., *op. cit.,* p. 117.

840. Richter, *op. cit.,* p. 190.

841. Degler, *op. cit.,* p. 255.

842. Foner, *op. cit.,* p. 427.

843. *ibid.,* p. 426.

844. Richard L. Hume "Negro Delegates to the State Constitution Convention of 1867–1869," in Rabinowitz, ed., *Southern Black Leaders,* p.146.

845. Degler, *op. cit.,* p. 255.

846. Escott, *op. cit.,* p. 30.

847. Otto Olsen, "The Ku Klux Klan: A Study in Reconstruction Politics and Propaganda," *North Carolina Historical Review,* 1962.

848. Stampp, *op. cit.,* p. 200.

849. George Rable, *But There Was No Peace: The Role of Violence in the Politics of Reconstruction.* Athens: University of Georgia Press, 1984, p. 111.

850. Foner, *op. cit.,* p. 435.

851. *ibid.,* p. 435.

852. *ibid.,* p. 434.

853. Trelease, *op. cit.,* p. 71.

854. Stampp, *op. cit.,* p. 200; Benedict, *op. cit.,* p. 131.

855. I. A. Newby, *The South: A History.* New York: Holt, Rinehart, and Winston, 1978, p. 272.

856. Benedict, *op. cit.,* p. 59.

857. Stampp, *op. cit.,* p. 204.

858. *ibid.,* p. 200.

859. James M. McPerson, "Redemption or Counterrevolution? The South in the 1870s," *Reviews in American History,* Vol. 13, 1985, pp. 545–550.

860. Foner, *op. cit.,* p. 442.

861. *ibid.,* p. 442.

862. *ibid.,* p. 439.

863. Trelease, *Reconstruction,* p. 172.

864. Bloom, *op. cit.,* p. 33.

865. Michael Perman, "Counter Revolution: The Role of Violence in Southern Redemption," in Anderson and Moss, eds., *op. cit.,* pp. 133–134.

866. Walter Fleming, *Civil War and Reconstruction in Alabama.* New York: Scribner's, 1905, p. 795.

867. Lew Wallace, *Lew Wallace: An Autobiography.* Vol. II. New York: Random House, 1945, p. 901.

868. David R. Weber, *Civil War Disobedience in America: A Documentary History.* Ithaca: Cornell University Press, 1978, p. 33.

869. Baldwin, *op. cit.,* pp. 49, 51.

870. Robert Penn Warren, *The Legacy of the Civil War.* New York: Knopf, 1961, p. 31.

871. Foner, *op. cit.,* p. 448.

872. *ibid.,* p. 449.

873. James McPerson, "The Antislavery Legacy: From Reconstruction to the NAACP," in Berton J. Berstein, ed, *Towards a Past: Dissenting Essays in American History.* New York: Random House, 1969. p. 141.

874. *ibid.,* p.142.

875. Michael Les Benedict, "Reform Republicans and the Retreat from Reconstruction," in Anderson and Moss, eds., *op. cit.,* p. 70.

876. McPerson, *op. cit.,* p. 138.

877. Stampp, *op. cit.,* p. 100.

878. *ibid.,* p. 189.

879. Foner, *op. cit.,* p. 449.

880. George Fredrickson, *The Inner Civil War: Northern Intellectuals and the Crisis of the Union.* New York: Harper & Row, 1965, pp. 113–129.

881. John Hope Franklin, *Reconstruction: After the Civil War.* Chicago: Scott, Foresman, 1965, p. 198.

882. Sidney Fine, *Laissez Faire and General Welfare State: A Study of Conflict in American Thought, 1865–1879.* Ann Arbor: University of Michigan Press, 1956, p. 123.

883. Benedict, *op. cit.,* p. 57.

884. Irwin Unger, *The Greenback Era, A Social and Political History of American Finance, 1865–1879.* Princeton, NJ: Princeton University Press, 1964, p. 121.

885. Benedict, *op. cit.,* p.57.

886. Foner, *op. cit.,* p. 489; Francis Bowen, *American Political Economy,* quoted from Benedict, *op. cit.,* p. 62.

887. Edward Atkinson, "The Inefficiency of Economic Legislation," quoted from Benedict, *op. cit.,* p. 58.

888. Richard L. McCormic, "The Discovery That 'Business Corrupt Politics': A Reappraisal of the Origins of Progressivism," quoted from Foner, *op. cit.,* p. 489.

889. Benedict, *op. cit.,* p. 58.

890. *ibid.,* p. 75.

891. *ibid.,* p. 59.

892. *ibid.,* p. 60.

893. *ibid.,* pp. 60–61.

894. Foner, *op. cit.,* p. 493.

895. *ibid.,* p. 500.

896. Benedict, *op. cit.,* p. 73.

897. Foner, *op. cit.,* p. 503.

898. *ibid.,* p. 526.

899. *ibid.,* p. 499.

900. Stampp, *op. cit.,* p. 190.

901. Foner, *op. cit.,* p. 485

902. *ibid.,* p. 452.

903. *ibid.,* p. 506.

904. John Dewey, *Human Nature and Conduct.* New York: Scribner's, 1922, p. 226. Translated from the Chinese edition.

905. Stampp, *op. cit.,* p. 209.

906. Foner, *op. cit.,* p. 529.

907. Cruden, *op. cit.,* p. 140.

908. *ibid.,* p. 141.

909. Foner, *op. cit.,* p. 453.

910. Benedict, *The Fruits of Victory: Alternatives in Restoring the Union, 1867–1877,* p. 55.

911. Foner, *op. cit.,* p. 454.

912. *ibid.,* p. 454.

913. Degler, *op. cit.,* p. 250.

914. Foner, *op. cit.,* pp. 434–435.

915. ibid., p. 435.

916. Benedict, *op. cit.,* p. 58.

917. *ibid.,* p. 132.

918. Foner, *op. cit.,* p. 455.

919. Frederick Douglass, *Life and Times of Frederick Douglass.* New York: Collier Books, 1962, p. 377.

920. Benedict, *op. cit.,* p. 62.

921. William Gillette, *Retreat from Reconstruction, 1869–1879.* Baton Rouge: Louisiana State University Press, 1968, pp. 363–380.

922. Benedict, *op. cit.,* p. 62.

923. Foner, *op. cit.,* p. 483.

924. Foner, *op. cit.,* p. 525.

925. *ibid.,* p. 525.

926. Willard H. Smith, *Schugler, Colfax: The Changing Fortunes of a Political Idol,* quoted from Foner, *op. cit.,* p. 563.

927. Foner, *op. cit.,* p. 584.

928. Benedict, *op. cit.,* p. 67.

929. Foner, *op. cit.,* p. 550.
930. Benedict, *op. cit.,* 69.
931. Stampp, *op. cit.,* p. 210.
932. Foner, *op. cit.,* p. 554.
933. Stampp, *op. cit.,* pp. 211–212.
934. Foner, *op. cit.,* p. 577.
935. *ibid.,* p. 590.

CHAPTER 6

The Heritage of Reconstruction

THE SOLIDIFICATION OF IDEOLOGY: "REDEMPTION" AND SOUTHERN CONSERVATISM

What disappointed Rutherford B. Hayes was that after the compromise of 1877, former Whigs did not lead the rebellious Southern Republicans as he expected, but remained in the Democratic party to seek their own political power. Like other Democrats, they called themselves "Redeemers," implying their unparalleled feat of crushing black power and removing foreign, i.e., federal, control. Others, however, called them Bourbons after the royal family of France, which allegedly had learned nothing and forgotten nothing at its restoration. With the Bourbons' rise to power, Southern oligarchy was now reviving. It was indeed a bad beginning.

As Irish pointed out, "The elementary determinant in Southern politics is an intense Negro phobia that has scarcely abated since Reconstruction."[936] After the compromise of 1877, black equality as a national issue gradually lost its importance. In the South, however, whites still turned pale at the mere mention of Reconstruction, and black equality was still the foremost factor to unite whites. Forming the unbreakable basis for social and political conduct, the ideology of racism, once firmly rooted in slavery, now became institutionalized. In fear of Reconstruction, any other issues that might split the white alignment were temporarily put aside. Even Southern liberals, who often criticized the domination of the conservatives, expressed their condemnation of the "tyranny" of Reconstruction. As the turn-of-the-century was considered the "nadir of the Negro," Reconstruction was regarded as the "nadir of the Southern white" and the most miserable chapter in Southern history, sharply engraved on whites' memories. "It was the lasting damage to the mind, spirit, and culture of the South that made it so devastating," Henry Savage once mentioned. "Reconstruction broke the South's spirit, planted hampering prejudices and frustrating hates, and paralyzed its will to move forward with the nation and the world."[937] In fact, the common memories of Reconstruction became the symbol of regional loyalty, skillfully used by conservatives to perform social control functions. Henry W. Grady, the great Southern orator in the post-Reconstruction period, pointed out that "The whites understand that the slightest division on their part will revive these desperate days. So that the whites have agreed everywhere to sink their differences on moral and economic issues, and present solid unbroken ranks to this alien and dangerous element. This once done, the rest is easy." Because of their ignorance, blacks themselves were not worth fearing. "The fear is that this vast swarm of ignorant, purchasable and credulous voters will be compacted and controlled by desperate and unscrupulous white men, and made to hold the balance of power wherever the whites are divided."[938] Thus, depending on their emphasis on racial difference and Southern tradition, the political means of conservatives appeared to have a romantic flavor that ignored practical issues. "The fact is that the present Democratic party in Virginia was formed without any reference to economic questions," declared the leading spokesman of that party. "In other States it may be different," wrote the editor of Mississippi's most influential newspaper, the *Weekly Clarion*, "in this State for some time to come there is but one issue. All know what it is."[939]

The problem of "white superiority vs. Negro domination," which occupied the central place in Southern political affairs, had long retarded social reforms and affected whites' progress as well as blacks' liberty. While the social movements striving for women's rights, collectively bargaining rights, labor legislation, and children's welfare swept across other regions of the country, the South was still suspicion-ridden and indecisive. In the 1880s, Southern liberalism criticized the root of Southern backwardness but was confined to the university campuses or other academic institutions, without the active participation of the masses. "Who among us has not seen now the presence of the Negro has molded our political history since emancipation?" asked the liberal Southern author, Willis D. Weatherford. "We have been slow to pass laws for compulsory school attendance, lest we tie ourselves to the task of classical education of the Negro. We are slow enough about extending the suffrage, lest the colored man should become too influential. No major political issue has faced the South in the last hundred years that has not been decided largely in the light of the presence of the Negro."[940]

Thus, the memories of Reconstruction and black equality were effectively utilized by conservatives to defend the one-party system. In the South, there once existed an imperfect two-party system before the 1830s, but the two parties merged into one in the crisis of secession; at the beginning of Reconstruction, there was a golden opportunity for the Whig party to revive, but Radical Reconstruction buried this possibility. Even the rise of populists did not introduce an effective opposition system into the South. If the structure of the Democratic party had been democratic, the situation might have been mitigated. The problem was that the Democratic party was not democratic. In one way or the other, the party system in the nineteenth century was far from mature and had a strong personal touch, which was typically embodied in the Bourbon regimes. After Reconstruction, the Democratic party strengthened its central state electoral machines. All questions, including the selection of candidates and the adoption of party platforms, were decided by a few politicians in the "ring." The key man in the Democratic organization of Virginia, for example, was the county chairman in charge of the electoral board. The electoral board in turn appointed election judges and clerks. Through these "election officials and the use of money and local pressure," the county chairman "was able to see that only his men were chosen as treasurer, sheriff, clerk of court, commissioner of revenue, member of the legislature, and supervisors." Thus it can be concluded that "the county chairman and his immediate assistants determined who would be chosen to every office in the county."[941] The expanding power of party bosses was further reinforced by the changing political structure. Finding that the Republican constitution of 1868 was advantageous to them, Bourbons in Florida successfully resisted all its possible alteration for eight years after Redemption. The constitution empowered the governor to appoint in each county the tax collector and assessor, treasurer, surveyor, superintendent of schools, county commissioner, sheriff, clerk of court, county judge, and Justice of the Peace. In Louisiana, the governor also had "an inordinate appointive power."[942] By hook or by crook, Bourbons had actually restored the antebellum oligarchy of local governments.

More serious was the erosion of the democratic process. Having controlled the electoral machine built in Reconstruction, Democrats discovered that they could reduce black voting power and manipulate election results by deceitful tricks. Electoral frauds then became wide-spread, especially in the black belt. In the whole South, gerrymanders were elaborately devised for the benefits of the Democratic party. "I have nothing to conceal in the matters," admitted a leader of Tennessee frankly. "One main object was to redistrict the state that for the next ten years not a Republican can be elected to the Legislature. I believe in the laws of revenge. The radicals disfranchised us, and now we intend to disfranchise them."[943] Georgia severely restricted black voting by an unfair poll tax requirement, a measure plotted by Robert Toombs, who professed his aim "to face thirty years of war to get rid of negro suffrage in the South."[944] In North Carolina, the legislature immediately passed a county-government act providing that the legislature itself appoint local officials, with "every principle of local self-government" being roughly violated.[945] To create election results favorable to Democrats, tricks of every hue were invented. The comments of Paul H. Buck are worth quoting:

> Polling places were set up at points remote from colored communities. Ferries between the black districts and voting booths went "out of repair" on election day. Grim-visaged white men carrying arms sauntered through the street or stood near the polling booths. In districts where the blacks greatly outnumbered the whites, election officials permitted members of the superior race to "stuff the ballot box," and manipulated the count without fear of censure. Fantastic gerrymanders were devised to nullify Negro strength. The payment of poll taxes, striking at the Negro's poverty and carelessness in preserving receipts, was made a requirement for voting. Some states confused the ignorant by enacting multiple ballot box laws which required the voter to place correctly his votes for various candidates in eight or more separate boxes. The bolder members of the colored race met threats of violence, and, in a diminishing number of instances, physical punishment. When the black man succeeded in passing through this maze of restrictions and cast his vote there was no assurance that it would be counted. Highly centralized election codes vested arbitrary powers in the election boards, and these powers were used to complete the elimination of the Negro vote.[946]

These games, however, were not strictly confined to predominantly black areas. In order to restore the oligarchy, the upper class sometimes used these means to deal with poor whites. The complicated voting registrations and qualifications, for example, also could be adopted for whites having the same economic and educational capabilities as blacks. They were particularly disadvantageous to tenants, who were relatively mobile and not accustomed to carrying certificates, because legislation required that registration be fulfilled several months before the election.

Thus, contempt for the democratic process permeated Southern politics. "A strong man struggling upward under the consciousness of submergence and suffocation strikes right and left with little thought of either principal or policy."[947] To achieve their aims, Southern whites spared no trouble and consequently encouraged these unfair tactics. In the long run, a much harder effort proved necessary to eliminate them from Southern politics.

Along with this process was the decline of democratic faith in the South. While the Northern idealism revealed its limitations in the failure of Reconstruction, democratic tenets in the South, following the precedent of the 1830s, continued to wane because of the experience of Reconstruction and the consolidation of whites' self-consciousness. Southern whites were not only sensitive to any possible social changes, but also kept a wary eye on the motive force behind them, namely American traditional beliefs in the universal norms of conduct. Black suffrage, Joseph Le Conte asserted, was regarded by all thoughtful men as the greatest crime ever committed by any nation.[948] The Richmond *Dispatch* thought that "every step towards pure democracy in the state has increased the depravity in the political arena."[949] Like liberal Republicans in the North, they were full of suspicions about majority rule and anxious to replace it with an elitism which, unfortunately, was entangled with racism. The "best Government in the world," the Richmond *State* warned, was the "rule of the best people." "All men may aspire to the highest ranks in their caste, and each class may continue to improve its condition."[950] It went without saying that whites must control public affairs, since "they own the property. They have the intelligence. Theirs is the responsibility. For these reasons they are entitled to control. Beyond these reasons is a racial one. They are the superior race, and will not and cannot submit to the domination of an inferior race."[951] Thus, where the principle of equality was accepted, there was an equal emphasis on racial differences. In other words, the original universal principle now was definitely prescribed with an exception. George W. Cable, a Southern liberal writer, criticized that conservatives first made a pretense to equality and freedom, and then took control with the promise of "pure government first, free government afterward." But it had proved a "twin fallacy" and a complete "delusion," for they had neither produced any free or pure government, nor had they enhanced the democratic atmosphere.[952]

That is not to say that Southern whites had fully abandoned their democratic faith. They simply were bound by racism. It was for this reason that the fraudulent practices placed them in a dilemma. "One consequence of realistic racial conflict," Joseph S. Himes commented, "then, is to bring the core values of the society into sharp focus and national attention."[953] On the one hand, they adopted illegal means by reason of racial domination; on the other hand, they were disturbed by their immoral methods. As Mississippi Judge J. J. Chrisman stated, no one would deliberately choose to perpetuate these acts, unless one was "a moral idiot."[954] William L. Royall admitted that "the elections in Virginia became a farce. We got rid of negro government but we got in place of it a government resting upon fraud and chicanery."[955] This embarrassing position would continually perplex Southern whites and rack their consciences. Later this dilemma became the main spiritual impetus for Southern progressivism: in fact, the contradictory mood would fully demonstrate its moral energy in the near future.

THE AFTERGLOW OF RECONSTRUCTION

While Southern whites restored their domination over local affairs, black civil rights began its process of continuous retrogression, and there arose a de facto resurgence of the double standard in the political sphere. The domination of Southern whites, however, had not immediately arrested all social changes and racial conflicts. The hopeful sparks ignited by Reconstruction dimmed after the compromise of 1877, but they did not go out. In this unstable period, black power was in general developing in a pessimistic direction, but it was still secured to some extent in some isolated areas such as the eastern counties of North Carolina, low counties of South Carolina, and black belts of Texas.[956] Even in the districts where conservatives retained control, the demands for depriving blacks of their civil rights were not very popular. Blacks retained their right to vote and continuously held state and federal office. North Carolina, for example, elected fifty-two black legislators of the lower house between 1876 and 1894, forty-seven blacks held office in South Carolina between 1878 and 1902, and every session of the Congress had at least one black member from the South between 1869 and 1901.

In addition to pressure from the North and the obstruction posed by the Constitution, this result can be attributed to the fact that Southern conservatives renewed their paternalism after they felt secure. So long as blacks stayed in their "place" and remained patient with their submissive status, or extra-legal methods could guarantee their domination, Conservatives would not go too far lest the situation get out of control. Lamar, one of the most distinguished politicians in the period of Redemption, thought that the acceptance of black votes might consolidate national compromise and reduce the possibility of federal intervention.[957] A more practical reason was that conservatives not only depended on black labor, but also might use black votes to deal with discontented whites and split the Republican alignment. On the other side, the necessity of safety drove some helpless blacks to turn to their former masters. Thus, a reciprocal alliance was grudgingly formed. To cover up their real motives, conservatives always made noises about their "duties." Thomas G. Jones, a conservatives leader in Alabama, expressed this noble philosophy of his class: "The Negro race is under us. He is in our power. We are his custodians. We should extend to him, as far as possible, all the civil rights that will fit him to be a decent and self respecting, law-abiding and intelligent citizen. If we do not lift them up, they will drag us down."[958] For this reason, conservatives adopted the dual tactic of both organizing black Democrats and threatening black Republicans or dissenting Democrats.[959]

The black vote, however, also might be used by conservatives' opponents. One opposition was the Republican party. Where the party had not been routed, blacks still loyally voted for it, regardless of its "lily white" policy by which Republicans tried to draw support from white voters. But the vitality of the Republican party had been sapped, and it was difficult to rally its forces. To Southern whites, it was after all the humiliating symbol of the failure of war, "foreign" interference, and black equality. Even when the white camp was fractured, dissenters were still reluctant to join the Republican party, but instead organized independent opposition factions. In most cases, it was they, rather than Republicans, that sent a ray of hope that would break up the solid front of Southern politics. In this period, perhaps the greatest importance of the presence of the Republican party was not the threat posed by the party itself, but the fact that it stimulated the rise of other opposition forces.

The Readjuster movement in Virginia successfully fulfilled this challenging mission. Since this state had not truly experienced any radical Reconstruction, the fear of change was not as great as in of other states.

In addition, since blacks only made up 40 percent of the total population, the danger of "Negro domination" seemed an illusion. When conservatives refused to reduce state debts, William Mahone, the former Confederate general, led impoverished farmers and launched a third-party movement to require that the state debts be readjusted. To avoid a crushing defeat, the Readjusters had to invite blacks to join their ranks. Belonging to the poor class, blacks and white yeomen were often faced with the same economic problems and both were exploited by Conservatives. Based on this reality instead of their sympathy for blacks, Readjusters decided to form another biracial coalition and compromise with blacks. For the common cause of mitigating state debts, they jointly charged the lines of the Bourbons and were overwhelmingly successful in 1879 and 1881. Thus, chinks appeared in the Southern oligarchy which dimmed the afterglow of Reconstruction. Its theoretical significance was that it tested the possibility that class consciousness might transcend racial consciousness in a multiracial society and that the solid Southern ideology might be broken someday. "The precursor of a break up in the solid South," a Louisianaian said, speaking of Mahone in glowing colors, "proclaims the political emancipation of the Southern people." Lincoln had freed the slaves, but had not freed whites from the tyranny of oligarchy. Thus, "Mahone has appeared to finish the work of Abraham Lincoln."[960] To blacks, the important fact was "that the Readjuster party has done more in the brief year of power towards liberalizing public sentiment, abolishing caste legislation, restoring the poor man his rights than the Republican party has been able to do in all the years of its existence in the South."[961] Mahone's victories, a Boston newspaper also observed, demonstrated that "the enfranchisement of the colored man had at last been made real in one of the lately rebellious states."[962]

One result of the Readjuster rebellion was that Southern whites, blacks, and Republicans managed to cooperate harmoniously in a common movement. As a black editor put it, Mahoneism had constructed "the acceptable middle ground between impracticable Radicalism and intolerant Bourbonism, on which any patriot willing to sacrifice small personal prejudices and resentments for the peace and prosperity of his County or Section, can honestly and honorably stand."[963] But Mahone did not confine himself to stressing the benefit of racial cooperation. The racial philosophy he expounded was a mixture of the old paternalism and liberalism, whose keynote was interdependence. Since the colored man "is an essential factor in and to our labor system," and was essential to Virginia's "fields of industry as the machinery of New England is to her factories," Mahone thought it was necessary "to make the colored man feel his identification with us, and to stimulate in him the feeling of contentment by wise and generous care and consideration that here may be prevented the calamity to the South of a heavy emigration of the colored people."[964] White men must restrict themselves, because "the hand of God all mighty was against [us] for the sin of Slavery," and a similar retribution, he was sure, awaited those who "oppress the lowly, the weak of his creation."[965] He warned that "the time must come, or our civilization fails, when men will cease to condemn the work of the creator by refusing to crusade against the weak and lowley [sic] because his skin is black."[966] As to blacks, "the colored man is entitled to all the rights that properly belong to him, but his place is not at the extreme front yet."[967] "Our colored people must now realize that to preserve their liberties they must let us lead. They must not over burthen us. Prejudices are still to be consulted. Time will subdue them but we must be wise not fight them even with reason nothing [against] them avails."[968]

While Mahoneism was tinted with the romantic color of extra-realism, populism in the 1890s gave free rein to realism in racial relations. Unlike Republicans, who posed as the custodians of blacks' freedom, or conservatives, who condescended to adopt hypocritical paternalism, populists only simply carried forward the realism practiced by the Readjusters without their liberalism. The characteristics of populism were clarity of ideology, consistency of their outward show and inner thoughts, and blunt realism based on mutual need and class interests. Tom Watson, the foremost leader of the Populist party, summarized it as follows: "gratitude may fail, so may sympathy and friendship and generosity and patriotism; but in the long run, self interest *always* controls."[969] He stressed that "the accident of color can make no difference in the interest of farmers, croppers, and laborers," and that only "the identity of interest" placed "the colored tenant in the same boat with the white tenant, the colored laborer with the white laborer."[970] Upon this basis, Watson asserted that "the People's party will settle the question. First, by enacting the Australian ballot system. Second, by offering to white and black a rallying point which is free from the odium of former discords and strife. Third, by presenting a platform immensely beneficial to both races and injurious to neither. Fourth, by making it to the interest of both races to act together for the success of the platform."[971]

Through the biracial alliance of the lower classes, populists, as the Readjusters had done, breached the Bourbons' racial order, seriously threatened the rigid one-party system, and enabled the appearance of an effective opposition mechanism in the South. While the Readjuster movement was confined to one state, the storm of populists swept across the whole South. It is worth mentioning that the "fusion politics" created by populists and Republicans in North Carolina brought the state a "second Reconstruction" and successfully brought about the second party shift since the Readjuster movement.[972] As former Democrats, populists had no intention of introducing a challenge into the sphere of racial relations, but the momentum of the movement had transcended their subjective limitation. In the Populist party, blacks were absorbed into the most important campaign committees instead of receiving symbolic nominations. Their seats in juries were ensured by the populist justices of the peace, and there was "misterization." Against the background of the nineteenth century, these acts challenged racial etiquette, especially taking into account that the achievements had been provided by whites of their own accord. In the opinion of Henry D. Lloyd, Southern populists had given the "negro of the South a political fellowship which they have never obtained, not even from their saviors, the Republicans."[973] The *Nation* also optimistically stated that "the lively bidding for negro votes by the rival white parties in the recent contest over prohibition in Atlanta is only one of a number of signs that the color line in politics is vanishing throughout the South."[974] The widespread failure to transform a politics of race into a politics of class, however, reflected how strong the racial barriers were that a biracial politics had to overcome.[975] The success of the rebellious movements was at most temporary and local and was immediately drowned by a strong wave of racism. The comments of a Readjuster were also applicable to the populist movement: "No party can ever succeed in Virginia that accepts issue on the color line. Why, I can scarcely tell, but a Virginia sovereign is more afraid of a negro voter than the devil is of holy water."[976] The populist principle that "self-interest always controls" was reasonable to some extent, but only took into account economic and political interests, ignoring the serious psychological obstacle of race. The latter could be equally transformed into a powerful force. Their failure to do so was the root of the populist failure.

Spreading like wildfire, the rebellious movement scared the aristocrats. Conservatives were enraged, not only because the dissenting Democrats dared challenge the one-party system, but also because of the danger that Republicans and blacks might come to power and bring centrifugal forces into the South and humiliation to all whites. Although conservatives provided paternalistic protection to appease blacks obedient to them, they were astonished at the extent of the populist success. As in the period of Reconstruction, they played the same old trick, agitating for racial feelings, shouted about the danger of "niggar domination," and appealed for white unity. "The man blessed with a white cuticle," declared one Virginia Democrat in 1892, "is false if he does not in this emergency cooperate with the Democratic party. As my father used to say, 'deserters since the war are worse than deserters during the war!'"[977]

Borrowing some ideas from the opposition platform, conservatives at the same time extensively applied the usual methods of violent intimidation and fraud. Under the conservative counterattack, the opposition movement dispersed, the fragile basis of the alliance crumbled, and populism's biracial cooperation collapsed like a house of cards. So long as the vote was fairly counted, almost every populist leader defended black suffrage, but Conservatives' tricks dashed their hopes. Even Watson himself changed his stand and began to oppose black suffrage. In the conflict between Bourbons and dissenting Democrats, whites again broadcast the opinion that whites would never dare diverge on the real political and economic issues if blacks were active in politics.[978] Others stressed that corruption would permeate through politics if blacks were bribed and threatened by white politicians, and only by excluding blacks could the populist credos be realized. In the meantime, conservatives also worried about the indefinite results created by black votes, hoping to include as many common whites as possible in the disenfranchising process. Hence both vied with each other to exclude blacks from politics.[979] In the end, Southern whites made compromises at the cost of black political participation. As a result, populism was engulfed in waves of racism. Racism then united the two political forces. Southern whites began their common cause, the progressive movement, and dissolved their divergence through white primaries.[980] On that account, Edgar G. Murphy thought of "the conscious unity of race" as "the broader ground of the two democracies," and believed that despite all its limitations, it was "better as a basis of democratic reorganization than the distinction of wealth, of trade, of property, of family, or class."[981] With the withdrawal of the last federal garrison,[982] the mass violence as a means of racial control reached its summit in 1892. In that year, 162 blacks and 69 whites were cruelly killed. Thereafter the number declined, though for the next twelve years, from 1893 to 1904, an average of more than a hundred blacks a year were lynched.[983] The use of cruel means, including lynching and burning, reflected the eruption of whites' sadism and desire for conquest. Through the poll tax, literacy tests, and white primaries, one state after another circuitously disenfranchised blacks.[984] The de facto segregation begun during Reconstruction now also began was institutionalized and expanded. In almost every social field, mandatory segregation was put into effect. As Woodward put it, "in bulk and detail as well as in effectiveness of enforcement the segregation codes were comparable with the black codes of the old regime."[985] Blacks were firmly fettered by the four ropes of mass violence, disenfranchisement, segregation, and economic compulsion. Ironically, the new "democracy" of whites was closely related to racism. While whites achieved their "progress," blacks slid down into their dark "nadir."

Following these developments, a ruthless racism rolled and foamed in the political and social waves at the turn of century. Racist books came forth one after another, including Charles Carroll's *The Negro a Beast; or In the Image of God* (1900), William P. Calhoun's *The Caucasian and the Negro in the United States* (1902), William B. Smith's *The Color Line: A Brief in Behalf of the Unborn* (1905), and Robert W. Shufeldt's *The Negro, A Menace to American Civilization* (1907). The motion picture *Birth of a Nation* was issued, too. Even the social scientific circles who praised themselves for impartiality tried to be the first to join in the racist chorus. Under the heading "Negro," the prestigious *Encyclopedia Brittanica* of 1903 stated that

> Weight of brain, as indicating cranial capacity, 35 ounces (highest gorilla 20, average European 45); thick epidermis emitting a peculiar rancid odour, compared to that of a buck goat; cranial sutures which close much earlier in the Negro than in other races. To this premature ossification of the skull, preventing all further development of the brain, many pathologists have attributed the inherent mental inferiority of the blacks, an inferiority which is even more marked than their physical differences. Nearly all observers admit that the Negro child is on the whole quite as intelligent as those of other human varieties, but that on arriving at puberty all further progress seems to be arrested. We must necessarily suppose that the development of the Negro and white proceeds on different lines. It is more correct to say of the Negro that he is nonmoral than immoral. All the social institutions are at the same low level, and seem to have made no perceptible advance except under the stimulus of foreign influences.[986]

In politics, racism had become a necessary tool used by party candidates to enable them to seize power. James Kimble Vardaman, who campaigned for the governorship of Mississippi in 1900, asserted that the black was a "lazy, lying, lustful animal which no conceivable amount of training can transform into a tolerable citizen." One did not inquire into the justice of killing predatory animals. "We do not stop when we see a wolf," he said boldly, "to find if it will kill sheep before disposing of it, but assume that it will." Therefore, "We would be justified in slaughtering every Ethiopian on the earth to preserve unsullied the honor of one Caucasian home."[987] Completely distorting the conquest versus anticonquest nature of conflict between whites and blacks, Vardaman bluntly expressed whites' self-consciousness and their intent to retain their dominant position and social interests. While pursuing their deserved rights, blacks were considered to be threats and were menaced. Such a situation exposed the radical nature of the conflict between whites and blacks as well as the intensity of whites' panic. In the bloody struggle for survival, blacks suffered many temporary setbacks.

THE NEW ECONOMIC DEPENDENCE

As their civil rights were steadily eroded in the unfavorable Southern environment, blacks also slid to the bottom of the South's rigid economic system, and the color-blind market principles established in Reconstruction were lost almost completely.

With the sharecropping system as the main mode of production in agriculture, the credit system in the South experienced a revival beginning in the 1870s. Unable to satisfy the needs of scattered customers, the former commercial agents mainly in contact with planters were now replaced with scattered rural storekeepers. To obtain cotton liens, these small furnishing merchants provided food and credits for both planters and sharecroppers and transported the cotton to the Northern market after harvest. Soon these merchants gained a regional monopoly, whose influence extended far beyond the economic sphere. The storekeeper, according to Thomas Clark, "was all things to his community. His store was the hub of the local source, recreational center, public forum, and news exchange."[988] In the initial stage, the rise of furnishing merchants reduced planters' power and their influence on labor and land. Because of shortage of funds, planters had to sign bills between their sharecroppers and merchants, and, consequently, might suffer heavy losses caused by crop failure or sharecroppers' overdrafts. As Michael Schwartz said, "A man could start up as a rich planter with a large plantation and thousands of dollars but end up impoverished if he was forced to countersign his tenants' liens."[989] When planters and their descendants entered the commercial sphere, and when supply merchants invested their profits in land, however, the monopolized credit power blended with the land power. By the end of this century, a new type of merchant-landowner or landowner-merchant gradually occupied a dominant position in the Southern rural districts.[990]

Sharecropping gradually became a synonym for economic exploitation or debt peonage. Due to regional monopoly and shortage of funds, the interest rates of the goods purchased on credit were generally as high as 50 percent. Henry Grady reported that "the cotton farmer has to pay the usurious percentage charged by his merchant broker, which is never less than 30 percent, and frequently runs up to 70 percent."[991] Since cotton was a money crop, whose market network was well organized, the furnishing merchants put great pressure on farmers to plant cotton. The overreliance on cotton in turn compelled farmers to purchase food on credit. In either case it was advantageous to furnishing merchants and not to farmers. Consequently, as cotton prices declined during the 1870s, there was an abnormal overreliance on cotton.[992] A resident of North Carolina complained that "The landlord and merchants who furnish supplies on time won't let [the tenants] sow much grain. They want cotton; and having to buy on time, they have to do as the merchant or landlord says, and the result is, they do not often pay out, and when they do they have nothing left. We shall soon be swallowed up by the commission merchants and guano men. It is cotton! cotton! cotton! Buy everything and make cotton pay for it."[993] Because of control over merchants' credit, farmers and tenants could not support themselves, and were caught up in the endless vicious circle of undue cotton-planting and short-term debt. Crops were mortgaged for supplies even before they were planted. Yet some cunning merchants sometimes raised cotton prices lest their customers escape the excessive debt. They "offer this bonus to induce the rascally inclined customer to pay his debts."[994]

Nevertheless the furnishing merchants did not accumulate enough funds from agriculture to become engines of local prosperity. Since farmers remained in debt and poverty, these merchants could not share the benefit of agricultural increase, either. Despite the tremendous interest rates, the profits were not as great as might be imagined, for contracts were often broken and the supervisory costs were high. According to the census of 1880, 48 percent of the storekeepers could not net more than five thousand dollars, and only 7.3 percent managed to obtain over fifty thousand. Owing to the poor demand caused by poverty, the profits acquired were neither invested in industrial projects nor returned to the furnishing stores, but were often used to buy land or securities.[995] Since most furnishing merchants' funds directly or indirectly came from the North, their growing influence epitomized the deepening dependent status of the Southern economy. As the economy in the North and the West made giant strides, the South remained sluggish. As a rural area, the South lost its self-sufficiency in grain and had to import foods from other regions.[996] While the annual rate of gross national product was 3.95 percent between 1874 and 1884, the annual rate of grain production in the South was only 1.32 percent.[997] The South stagnated in poverty.

As W. W. Jones, the statistician of North Carolina, put it in the annual report of 1887, "More evils have come to the farmers of the States on account of the mortgage and lien bond system than from any other, and indeed from every other source. It was proved a worse curse to North Carolina than droughts, floods, cyclones, storms, rust, caterpillars, and every other evil that attends the farmer."[998] Locked in the shackles of the lien system, farmers had to sell at low prices and buy at high prices. "The mortgage system," sighed a farmer of North Carolina, "is working its deadly way into the county, and making sad havoc where its tempting offers are at once entered into. Alas! one never gets out from its magic embrace until he dies out or is sold out."[999] The independent position of white farmers was now unstable, and from the census of 1870 onward, white sharecroppers outnumbered their black counterparts; by 1900, 36 percent of all white farmers were tenants and sharecroppers, although this ratio was lower than that of blacks. The famous writer W. J. Cash keenly commented that

> For here was an end for these people of the independence and self-sufficiency, the freedom from direct exploitation and servitude, which had been so primary for the preservation and growth of the old frontier individualism, for the suppression of class feeling, and the binding of the South into its extraordinary unity of purpose and outlook. The relation of master and man, patron and client, was pouring over into the taboo confines of white men.[1000]

Black sharecroppers were in a condition more miserable than their white counterparts. Clearly, they were under extralegal compulsion and discrimination as well as normal economic compulsion. As for crop management, blacks had little voice in making decisions, being under the supervision of landlords or merchants. They naturally wished to improve productivity, only to find most of the increased earnings went into others' hands. If they sought training or education, the skills could not ensure them a higher reward. Even if employers had no prejudice, they were still unwilling to break the usual practice and give outstanding black laborers higher payment. If blacks tried to improve their position in the South, they met all sorts of obstacles. Not only did illiteracy and the shortage of information prevent them from understanding employment opportunities in other regions, but the lack of skills and expensive traveling fares held them back. If they had successfully overcome all the obstacles, racially discriminatory policies would act as a final barrier. If they tried to leave the South, blacks still in debt were regarded as criminals. Those who enticed black laborers from their jobs were fined or met with violence.[1001] A railroad emigration agent testified that

> I know of several counties not a hundred miles from Atlanta where its more than a man's life is worth to go in to get Negroes to move to some other state. There are farmers that would not hesitate to shoot their brother were he to come from Mississippi to get 'his niggers,' as he calls them, even though he has no contract with them. I know personally numbers of Negro men who have moved West, and after accumulating a little, return to get a brother, sister or an old father or mother and they were compelled to return without them, their lives being imperiled.[1002]

Thus, in the backward economic system of the South, blacks had to dampen their enterprising spirit and remain in the lowest place, eking out a meager existence and being bored to tears.

As Eric Foner put it, "partly because of Redeemer rule, the South emerged as a peculiar hybrid and impoverished colonial economy integrated into the national capitalist marketplace yet with its own distinctive system of repressive labor relations."[1003] The economic changes brought by the restoring of "home rule" were mainly advantageous to the commercialized upper class, and, in labor–capital relations, the scales of power began to incline towards the latter. Some measures, including the new lien laws giving a landlord the preceding claim to his crop share over a merchant's claim to his supplies, admittedly involved the readjustment of power within the upper class.[1004] The independent merchants were driven out of former slaveholding areas, too.[1005] More measures, however, were to consolidate control over laborers, especially blacks. The vagrancy laws were revived, allowing the arrest of virtually any black without a job; the "sunset" measures prohibited the nighttime sale of farm products; the "antienticement" laws made it criminal to offer employ-ment to an individual already under contract by "decoying," "persuad-ing," or "enticing" him.[1006] Mississippi's "pig law" defined the theft of any cattle or swine worth over ten dollars as grand larceny punishable by five years in jail.[1007] Since 1872, the court decisions of Georgia a defined sharecropper not as a "partner," but as a wage laborer owning "only a right to go on the land to plant, work, and gather the crop."[1008] If blacks tried to go on strike, their leaders were soon arrested, and the strike crushed.[1009] All these measures served the dual purpose of maintaining white supremacy and obtaining a docile and cheap labor source. The convict lease system is worth mentioning here. Under the reign of the Bourbons, this disgraceful practice originating in the period of military occupation and Presidential Reconstruction was extended and system-atized.[1010] Within two months of Redemption, South Carolina's legis-lature eagerly authorized the hiring out of virtually every convict in the state, and Florida simply dismantled its penitentiary.[1011] In the imple-mentation process, cases of cruel treatment were not rare. In 1884, for example, there was a sensational one involving the shipment through Vicksburg of a squad of eighteen half-naked convicts, showing "signs of cruel goaders and tortures, their fingers and toes frostbitten."[1012] Under the oppressive labor and economic systems, black laborers lapsed into an abyss of suffering, and Republicans were not far from the truth when they charged that "the courts of law are employed to reenslave the colored race."[1013]

Southern industry was born with maladies similar to those of the agricultural system. As in agriculture, almost all industries in the South depended on cheap laborers or leased convicts. Since laborers only had a meager income, it was necessary for all members of a family to earn their keep.[1014] Workshops were organized like a plantation; workers' lodging-houses were similar to the slave quarters on the antebellum plantations; mess sections provided an advance on board; and there were also schools and churches controlled by the company. This was in sharp contrast to the impersonal division of labor in the North.[1015] Analogous to the mo-nopoly of the furnishing merchants, local industries excluded foreign investment in new projects lest the competition for labor be intensified. In the Gulf states, for example, planters almost fully blocked the intro-duction of industrial projects.[1016] Following racial lines, the labor class was split into two parts, and blacks generally did the most strenuous or dirtiest work. In the eastern cotton states, employment opportunities in the textile industry were almost monopolized by white labor. Blacks were employed only in the mines, iron furnaces, and tobacco factories in the upper South.[1017] Because of a weak home market and the regional monopoly, the rise of factories had not rooted out the sources of Southern poverty. Following the pace of national development, the South only could hobble along and present "a miserable landscape dotted only by a few rich enclaves that cast little or no light upon the poverty surrounding them."[1018] If white labor scraped along in dimness, blacks struggled for survival in the darkness.

Bourbons, however, could not hold back all social changes. Blacks could at least enjoy family autonomy on farms and move from one plantation to another. Laws themselves could not ensure that black laborers were under full control; it was impossible for employers to restore their former absolute authority; and the relationship between employee and employer was primarily based on contract. In the post-Reconstruction South, therefore, the withdrawal of labor continued, and whites still complained about the labor shortage. This fact reflected blacks' silent protest against the oppressive economic system. In the stagnate system of the South, blacks' greatest hope perhaps rested on continuous commercial changes and the emergence of mass emigration. As for internal changes, the fusion of planters and merchants gradually transformed the old power pattern centering on land into a plural structure revolving around capital and technology, in which mobile and professional laborers rather than fixed and unskilled workers succeeded. Mentioning the progressive function of commercial changes for racial relations, the *Boston Transcript* rejoiced that the South was becoming a "peaceful, law-respecting, industrious" section "devoted to business first and politics afterwards. The freedman will share in this general improvement." Having reformed Southern ideals, this tendency made the fashion in the 1880s different from that in slavery times. "Work and money," the *Transcript* said, "have brought into vogue new ideals, new tests and new ambitions in Southern society. Capital is, after all, the greatest agent of civilization."[1019] External changes were exhibited in transportation development in local rural areas, particularly the transportation revolution induced by the invention of the automobile, the revolution of the postal service at the end of this century, the cotton failure caused by the rampant boll weevil, the decrease in foreign immigrants caused by the First World War, and the increasing waves of emigration surging towards Northern cities.[1020] The development of industry and commerce in the North outpaced the fragile and backward economic system of the South, and the social structure built on it began to shake loose, too. In this period, a new black generation was growing up, and, particularly in cities, the conflict between blacks and police intensified.[1021] When the old economic system could no longer ensure that blacks stayed in their "place," Southern states set about passing segregation laws. Violent attacks by whites demonstrated that the social order they strove to maintain now encountered a stern challenge.

THE CASTING OF BLACK SOULS

In the fierce struggle to restore home rule and black subordination, conservatives won battle after battle and, with these accomplished, rapidly consolidated their overall control. For blacks, the important fact was that they not only returned to a social system characterized by oligarchy and economic exploitation but were trapped again in a society following the color line. Thus, they belonged to a discriminated, or even conquered, class as well as a poor, powerless class. Because of the difficulties created by racism, class solidarity proved ineffective, possible friends became enemies, and the driving force of change was cut off, as the populist movement had clearly shown. In these gloomy conditions, those the bare-handed and isolated blacks confronted were not only the white upper class commanding most resources but also their white lower class counterparts trying to maintain white supremacy. Given these circumstances, what course would blacks follow?

For many blacks, the failure of Reconstruction and rampant racism shook their confidence in seeking for their self-meaning in the mainstream culture. This had been their sole pursuit in the Reconstruction era when American idealism was broadly carried out. With the recession of the universal ideals as the foundation of their assimilation in the white world, blacks doubted whether they could take root in this land, although they were still unwilling to give up on this goal.

The resurgence of overseas emigration reflected their pessimism. Shortly after the Bourbons came to power, black delegates and letters to the American Colonization Society increased. Henry Adams, the former Louisiana political organizer, claimed in 1877 to have enrolled over 60,000 "hard laboring people" eager to leave the South. "This is a horrible part of the country," he wrote to this society, "and our race can not get money for our labor. It is impossible for us to live with these slaveholders of the South and enjoy the right as they enjoy it."[1022] Emigration to Africa, however, was obviously impractical. Thus more blacks transferred their attention to other districts in the United States. In the late 1870s, Mississippi blacks proposed to move to New Mexico or Arizona, and North Carolina blacks hoped to build a black paradise in Nebraska. Yet the greatest interest centered on Kansas, which became the destination of tens of thousands of refugees from "oppression and bondage."[1023] Ironically, even when they tried to escape from whites physically, blacks still stressed the universal ideals inherited from whites and their citizenship as the "colored Americans."

But even the domestic colonization proved illusive, and blacks had to strive for survival in the white world. Being forced to withdraw their offensive against the external world, blacks now shifted their attention to self-preservation. Among black leaders, a tendency to deemphasize political participation was growing. When the constitutional convention of South Carolina was convened in 1895, even black delegates supported the proposal for literary or property limitations on suffrage, provided that they were equally applicable to both races.[1024] When the political door closed, most black leaders limited their ambition to the economic sphere, advocating independence and racial consolidation because the development of the black economy and racial progress depended on blacks' purchasing their own goods and services. If blacks found economic success and gained the middle-class status, they believed, whites would look at blacks with new eyes, and the wall of discrimination would collapse.[1025]

Reacting to whites' racial policies, the characteristics of black leadership changed. In the Bourbon period, the new constituents of black leadership reflected a growing black middle class. Previously composed mainly of preachers, they were gradually replaced by capitalists or professionals who had received higher education. The improvement in their numbers, however, did not mean that they could exert any proportional influence.[1026] Compared with their former insistence on civil rights in Reconstruction, black leaders now had to obtain favors from white individuals.[1027] The source of their influence to a large extent depended on their personal relations with the white elite rather than their political mobilization in black communities. Conversely, a feudalizing tendency was introduced into their relations with lower class blacks. To face the harsh, outer reality, inner disciplines were greatly strengthened. Blacks were admonished to act properly, remain loyal, believe in God, and work hard. Their leaders worked with whites to reduce tensions, ask for white assistance, and provide benefits and protection for their followers.[1028] Consequently, an arbitrary power that might astonish whites was formed within black communities.

The concentration of power among black leaders was not merely to satisfy their desire for power, but to ensure for the existence of the whole race. In the face of an external world beset with dangers, they had to pay attention above all to their self-image, wear a modest mask, and create a safe environment. They were not only overcautious of whites, but also suspected the motives of other blacks. As some Jews informed against or framed their compatriots under Hitler's terror, black factions were caught up in endless inner warfare. Any misjudgment might trigger total failure. "Awful as were the quick death in lynchings, murders, and riots and the slower deaths of the convict lease system," Williamson observed, "these probably accounted for only a few of the vast number of victims. The great truth is that most blacks died by black hands."[1029] In the life-and-death struggle that did not allow losing even one battle, black leaders resorted to Machiavellism.

For blacks, the continuous existence of racism confused the meaning of their daily lives. Unable to withstand the heavy spiritual burden, many were bogged down in despair and self-condemnation, drifted with the tide, or indulged themselves in perplexity and depression. As an Episcopal priest who had experienced a very successful career, H. A. Parris still felt that he could not rid himself of a sense of "miserable failure." No matter how vigorously he tried to join the white world, Parris found that the white world was still a long distance off. At the same time, Parris estranged himself from the black community because of his intimacy with white culture, and at last he lamented that "There is much of prejudice among colored people." In this conflict, "I have gone mostly alone, trying to keep step outwardly with the world as I find it; but inwardly rebellious & weary & protestant and lonely."[1030] To some mulattos whose skin colors were similar to whites, "passing" physically from the black world seemed the most convenient shortcut to shake off racist pressure.[1031] Their number, however, was limited, and it was difficult for them to "pass" in a time of strong racism.[1032] To those who could not "pass," flaunting their intimacy with the white world seemed to raise their status and soothed their injured and self-abased souls. Charles N. Hunter of North Carolina, for instance, made a boast that "My brother and I were reared at the fireside of one of the grandest families of this state. I feel convinced that the Southern Negro has no better friend than the Southern white man once owned them, lived in close contact with him, and whose children were raised by negroes."[1033]

Many blacks retreated to an "Ivory tower" and avoided contact with whites as far as possible. But racist pressure was always present, however, so this strategy was difficult and, consequently, very rare.[1034] A popular means to alleviate anxiety was to extricate oneself from the external word through religion. To evade the harsh reality they faced, blacks sought their hopes in the spiritual world. Sometimes comparing themselves with Jews, blacks tried to find the road to salvation in their experiences. The freedmen, a Montgomery black convention declared shortly after the Democrats' 1874 victory in Alabama, might be compelled "to repeat the history of the Israelites," and "seek new homes beyond the reign and rule of Pharaoh."[1035] The increasingly sentimental feature of black religion reflected their daily agonies. The Christian doctrine that "The last shall be first, and the first shall be last" gave them comfort. In a colored church in rural Mississippi, a sermon told "the story of a rich woman who lived in a big house and had no time for God. When she went to Heaven she was give an old shanty in which to live and she exclaimed: 'Why that's the shanty my cook used to live in!' The cook, who on earth had given all her time to God, was now living in a big house in Heaven, very much like the one in which her former mistress used to live."[1036] Believing that they were much finer Christians than their white counterparts, blacks then dreamed of pleasure or superiority, which might act as compensation for their psychological wounds in real life.[1037]

The desire to escape from the external world, however, did not indicate that blacks had fully accepted their unequal reality. On the contrary, blacks had never convinced themselves of the justness and legality of the social order in which they were compelled to live. "When a white criminal is pursued and arrested," the *Constitution* complained, "we never hear of the white people surrounding the officers of the law and attempting a rescue. But the conditions are all changed when the criminal is a negro. The moment that a negro steals, or robs, or commits some other crime, his person seems to become sacred in the eyes of his race, and he is harbored, protected and deified."[1038] Although they seemed to be docile outwardly, it was in fact a camouflage for their real feelings. As Charles S. Johnson said, "Outward submissiveness and respect may thus be, as often as not, a mask behind which these youth conceal their attitude. George Cator is an example of this behavior. He has learned to flatter as a means of preserving his estimate of himself. 'When I'm around them, I act like they are more than I am. I don't think they are, but they do. I hear people say that's the best way to act.'"[1039] Sometimes discontented blacks shifted their anger onto other blacks and made the latter the scapegoat. At the appropriate time, however, the potential discontent might be directly vented on whites, just as blacks did when besieging white police. But direct revolt generally took place in the North, where white attitudes were more tolerant, and black strength was more concentrated. In the South, blacks could only adopt the tactics of mouse against cat. "We have no enemy in our front," declared Lucius Q. C. Lamar, the leader of the New Departure in Mississippi. "But the negroes are almost as well disciplined in their silence and inactivity as they were before in their aggressiveness."[1040]

The fluctuation in the destinies of Frederick Douglass, Booker T. Washington, and W. E. B. Du Bois reflected the changing situation in which blacks lived. Douglass lived in the days of moral giants, days when idealism was all the rage. As a product of his time, Douglass plunged himself into the fierce struggle for black liberation. Like a mettlesome lion, he kept on fighting in spite of all setbacks; his method was to insist upon black rights, resort to the force of moral jurisdiction, and speak highly of the Golden Rule, the Declaration of Independence, and the Constitution. In his eyes, the black cause had no limits, and its object was to fully assimilate his race into a mainstream society in which color itself was no impediment. "I am of those," he declared to the American Anti-Slavery Society in 1863,

> who believe that the work of the American Anti-Slavery Society will not have been completed until the black men of the South, and the black men of the North, shall have been admitted, fully and completely, into the body politic of America. A mightier work than the abolition of slavery now looms up before the Abolitionist. This society was organized, if I remember rightly, for two distinct objects: one was the emancipation of the slave, and the other the elevation of the colored people. When we have taken the chains off the slaves, as I believe we shall do, we shall find a harder resistance to the second purpose of this great association than we have found even upon slavery itself.[1041]

In the period of Reconstruction, he was reckoned among the most famous black leaders. But with decreasing enthusiasm for assimilation, his influence continuously reduced. Upon his marriage to a white woman in 1884, it virtually evaporated.[1042]

Fighting his way out of the fierce rivalries with iron hands, Booker T. Washington, the "Wizard of Tuskegee" and the final despot of the black kingdom, lived in the time emphasizing black inferiority and white supremacy. Compared with Douglass, Washington no longer emphasized principles, but provided a practical expedient applicable to present needs; instead of advocating divine rights, Washington temporarily retreated from the object of complete equality, although this object still lingered in his mind. As a realist, "to gain the sympathy and cooperation of the various elements comprising the white South was Mr. Washington's first task."[1043] What he first insisted on was safety, and at the same time he was ready to act in the inglorious role of collaborator. In the compromise of Atlanta, he attempted to build a fort of safety for his race, exchange principles for racial tolerance, substitute gradualism in racial progress for former aggressive and radical adventures, and, under the banner of mutual racial confidence, found a winding path leading to racial survival and eventual realization of black civil rights. In fact, what he ceded were the things blacks had lost, namely overall political participation and racial mixture in public facilities. Although overtly Washington touched the importance of civil rights only lightly, covertly he was a tough defender of black interests and deeply involved in political affairs to prevent disfranchisement and other forms of discrimination.[1044] Meier's conclusion is correct: "The picture that emerges from Washington's own correspondence is distinctly at variance with the ingratiating mask he presented to the world."[1045] Because of the conflicting personality showed by Washington, it was more appropriate to describe him as "a warrior wearing a mask" than to criticize him one who capitulated.

It was, however, still dangerous for *content* to be drowned by *form*, which might at last replace the former. In fact, accommodationism had not stopped racism. On the contrary, it was considered by radical whites as the obvious proof of black cowardice and weakness. Thus, the challenge for Du Bois was to demonstrate the value of blacks' existence. Du Bois previously attempted to fight a guerrilla war in the South, only to find that his support was in the North. His mission was not to resort to any expedient, but to devise a blueprint for the black future. "In actuality," according to Rudiwick, "he was the College Professor of Niagara, giving lectures here, writing papers there, and expecting all the while that his 'students' would carry his ideas far and wide.'"[1046] In *The Souls of Black Folk* of 1903, Du Bois condemned Washington for giving in and tolerating racial castes. While Washington counted on the economic success of the black masses, Du Bois pinned his hopes on the elite leadership, i.e., "the Talented Tenth." While Washington emphasized harmony, Du Bois preferred protest. But both were nationalists in a broad sense. Even though Washington himself was not a radical nationalist, as some historians believe, he had, in reality, built the economic basis and given a fundamental impetus to black nationalism.[1047] In the meantime, Du Bois aimed at providing a spiritual basis for nationalism. Like Douglass, Du Bois, who "was brought up in the primary democracy of a New

England village,"[1048] restored interest in "principles."[1049] As to the ultimate object of assimilation, however, he differed from Washington as well as Douglass. His aim was a limited assimilation. In the ideal societies of Douglass and Washington, color was of no practical significance. But for Du Bois, "black is beautiful," and it was the key to salvation.[1050] Before him, no black leader had said that they were a people different from whites. But according to Du Bois's interpretation, every people was imbued by God at creation with a distinct genius. Throughout its life each people struggled to realize its special nature. Black people in America, so recently out of slavery, were at a point of "absolute division" with the white race,[1051] and only then came to the threshold of self-understanding. Yet with the unyielding struggle, and with black self-help and the accumulation of "physical power,"[1052] the true nature of black souls would become increasingly evident. On this basis, blacks would at last find themselves in close harmony with the Creator, and presumably, through Him, with all else. Ridiculing blacks who imitated whites, Du Bois emphasized that both races would make their respective contributions in American culture. Perfect assimilation did not rest on "whitening" themselves, but in seeking the significance of blackness itself. The radical and time-transcending nature of his thought led to his attempt at self-segregation in the 1930s and inevitable conflicts with the NAACP (National Association for the Advancement of Colored People). In the 1960s, however, the slogans of "black souls," "black beauty," and "black power" greatly moved the black public.[1053]

NOTES

936. Maria D. Irish, "The Southern One-Party System and National Politics," *The Journal of Politics*, February 1942, p. 80.

937. I. A. Newby, *The South: A History*. New York: Holt, Rinehart & Winston, 1978, p. 275.

938. Henry W. Grady, *The New South*, quoted from Gunnar Myrdal, *An American Dilemma: Negro Problem and Modern Democracy*, Vol. I. New York: Random House, 1962, pp. 453–454.

939. C. Vann Woodward, *Origins of the New South, 1877–1913*. Baton Rouge: Louisiana State university Press, 1971, p. 51.

940. Willis D. Weatherford and Charles S. Johnson, *Race Relations*, quoted from Myrdal, *op. cit.*, p. 1310.

941. Allen W. Moger, "The Origin of the Democratic Machine in Virginia," *Journal of Southern History*, quoted from Woodward, *op. cit.*, p. 52.

942. Woodward, *op. cit.*, pp. 54–55.

943. Philip M. Hamar, ed., *Tennessee: A History, 1673–1932.* Vol. II, New York: Scribner's, p. 676.

944. William Y. Thompson, *Robert Toombs of Georgia,* quoted from Eric Foner, *Reconstruction: America's Unfinished Revolution, 1863–1877,* p. 591.

945. J. G. de R. Hamilton, *North Carolina Since 1860,* quoted from Woodward, *op. cit.,* p. 54.

946. Paul H. Buck, *The Road to Reunion, 1865–1900,* quoted from Myrdal, *op. cit.,* p. 450.

947. Edgar Murphy, *The Basis of Ascendancy,* quoted from Myrdal, *op. cit.,* p. 450.

948. William D. Armes, ed., *The Autobiography of Joseph le Conte.* New York: McClure, 1903, pp. 238–239.

949. Richmond *Dispatch,* August 2, 1877, quoted from Woodward, *op. cit.,* p. 53.

950. Richmond *State,* October 7, 1881, quoted from Woodward, *op. cit.,* p. 53.

951. Henry W. Grady, *The New South,* quoted from Myrdal, *op. cit.,* p. 454.

952. George W. Cable, *The Southern Struggle for Pure Government: An Address.* Boston: Ticknor & Fields, 1890, pp. 15–19.

953. Joseph S. Himes, "The Functions of Racial Conflict," in Norval D. Glenn, and Charles M. Bonjean, eds., *Blacks in the United States.* San Francisco: Chandler Publishing, 1969, p. 475.

954. Jackson *Clarion-Ledger,* September 11, 1890, quoted from Woodward, *op. cit.,* p. 58.

955. William L. Royall, *Some Reminiscences.* New York: Macmillan, 1909, pp. 201–202.

956. Paul D. Escott, "White Republicanism and Ku Klux Klan Terror," in Jeffrey J. Crow, P. D. Escott, and Charles L. Flynn, eds., *Race, Class, and Politics in Southern History.* Baton Rouge: Louisiana State University Press, 1989, p. 34; Eric Foner, *Reconstruction: America's Unfinished Revolution, 1863–1877,* New York: Harper & Row, 1988, p. 591.

957. Revels, "Rednecks and Racial Integrity," in Richard A. Melmore, ed., *A History of Mississippi.* Vol. I. Jackson: University Press of Mississippi, 1973, p. 616.

958. C. Vann Woodward, *The Strange Career of the Jim Crow.* New York: Oxford University Press, 1968, p. 49.

959. Jack M. Bloom, *Class, Race, and the Civil Rights Movement.* Indianapolis: Bobbs-Merrill, 1987, p. 36.

960. Carl N. Degler, *The Other South: Southern Dissenters in the Nineteenth Century.* New York: Oxford University Press, 1974, p. 286.

961. *ibid.,* p. 279.

962. Boston *Traveler,* March 15, 1881, quoted from Degler, *op. cit.,* p. 281.

963. Degler, *op. cit.,* p. 285.

964. *ibid.,* pp. 306, 309.

965. *ibid.,* p. 308.

966. *ibid.,* p. 308.

967. *ibid.,* p. 311.

968. *ibid.,* p. 310.

969. Thomas E. Watson, "The Negro Question in the South," quoted from Woodward, *op. cit.,* p. 61; Degler, *op. cit.,* p. 353.

970. Woodward, *op. cit.,* p. 63.

971. *ibid.,* p. 61.

972. Foner, *op. cit.,* p. 592.

973. Woodward, *op. cit.,* p. 64.

974. James M. McPerson, "The Antislavery Legacy: From Reconstruction to the NAACP," in Barton J. Bernstein, ed., *Towards a New Past: Dissenting Essays in American History.* New York: Random House, 1968, p.143.

975. Paul Horton, "Testing the Limits of Class Politics in Postbellum Alabama: Agrarian Radicalism in Lawrence County," *Journal of Southern History,* February 1991, p. 83.

976. Degler, *op. cit.,* p. 300.

977. William D. Sheldon, *Populism in the Old Dominion: Virginia Farm Politics, 1885–1900.* Princeton, NJ: Princeton University Press, 1935, pp. 87–88.

978. Revels, *op. cit.,* p. 618.

979. Thomas F. Gossett, *Race: The History of an Idea in America.* Dallas, TX: Southern Methodist University Press, 1963, p. 265.

980. Bloom, *op. cit.,* p. 50.

981. Woodward, *op. cit.,* pp. 91–92.

982. Gossett, *op. cit.,* p. 265.

983. *ibid.,* p. 269.

984. Allen W. Trelease, *Reconstruction: The Great Experiment.* New York: Harper & Row, 1971, p. 199.

985. Woodward, *op. cit.,* p. 7.

986. *Encyclopedia Brittanica,* quoted from Bloom, *op. cit.,* p. 45.

987. Albert D. Kirwan, *Revolt of the Rednecks in Mississippi Politics: 1876–1925.* Lexington: University of Kentucky, 1951, pp. 146–147.

988. Roger L. Ransom and Richard Sutch, *One Kind of Freedom: The Economic Consequences of Emancipation.* New York: Cambridge University Press, 1977, p. 126.

989. Michael Schwartz, *Radical Protest and Social Structure*. New York: Ronald Press, 1976, p. 59.

990. Ransom and Sutch, *op. cit.*, pp. 146–148

991. Henry Grady, "Cotton and Its Kingdom," quoted from Ransom and Sutch, *op. cit.*, p. 128.

992. Eric Foner, *Reconstruction: America's Unfinished Revolution, 1863–1877*. New York: Harper & Row, 1988.

993. Ransom and Sutch, *op. cit.*, p. 161.

994. *ibid.*, p. 163.

995. *ibid.*, p. 138.

996. *ibid.*, p. 156.

997. *Historical Statistics of the United States*. Washington, DC, 1960, Series F-4, p. 139.

998. Ransom and Sutch, *op. cit.*, p. 149.

999. *ibid.*, p. 163.

1000. W. J. Cash, *The Mind of the South*. New York: Knopf, 1941, p. 158.

1001. Vernon Lane Wharton, *The Negro in Mississippi*. New York: Harper & Row, 1965, p. 95.

1002. Bloom, *op. cit.*, p. 27.

1003. Foner, *op. cit.*, p. 596.

1004. *ibid.*, p. 594.

1005. Bloom, *op. cit.*, p. 25.

1006. Foner, *op. cit.*, p. 593.

1007. Revels, *op. cit.*, p. 612.

1008. Foner, *op. cit.*, p. 594.

1009. Bloom, *op. cit.*, p. 34.

1010. Wharton, *op. cit.*, p. 238.

1011. Foner, *op. cit.*, p. 594.

1012. David G. Sansing, "Congressional Reconstruction," in Melemore, ed., *op. cit.*, p. 631.

1013. Foner, *op. cit.*, p. 594.

1014. Woodward, *Origins of the New South*, p. 2.

1015. Bloom, *op. cit.*, p. 57; Cash, *op. cit.*, p. 205.

1016. Bloom, *op. cit.*, p. 57.

1017. Foner, *op. cit.*, p. 597.

1018. Robert L. Brandfon, *Cotton Kingdom of the New South*, quoted from Foner, *op. cit.*, p. 597.

1019. McPerson, *op. cit.*, p. 144.

1020. Ransom and Sutch, *op. cit.*, p. 197.

1021. Howard N. Rabinowitz, *Race Relation in the Urban South, 1865–1890*. New York: Oxford University Press, 1978, p. 336.

1022. Foner, *op. cit.*, p. 599.

1023. *ibid.*, p. 600.

1024. August Meier and Elliot Rudiwick, *From Plantation to Ghetto.* New York: Hill and Wang, 1970, p. 194.

1025. *ibid.*, p. 195.

1026. Foner, *op. cit.*, p. 591.

1027. Hortense Powdermaker, "The Channeling of Negro Aggression by the Cultural Process," in August Meier and Elliot Rudiwick, eds., *The Making of Black America,* Vol. I. New York: Random House, 1969, p. 97.

1028. Rabinowitz, *op. cit.*, p. 257.

1029. Joel Wiliamson, *The Crucible of Race: Black-White Relations in the American South Since Emancipation.* New York: Oxford University Press, 1984, p. 58.

1030. *ibid.*, p. 69.

1031. Myrdal, *op. cit.*, pp. 129–130.

1032. Joel Williamson, *New People: Miscegenation and Mulattos in the United States.* New York: Harper & Row, 1980, p. 107.

1033. J. Williamson, *The Crucible of Race,* p. 68.

1034. Powdermaker, *op. cit.*, p. 98.

1035. Foner, *op. cit.*, p. 600.

1036. Hortense Powdermaker, *After Freedom.* New York: Viking Press, 1939, p. 243.

1037. Powdermaker, "The Channeling of Negro Aggression," p. 102.

1038. Rabinowitz, *op. cit.*, pp. 337–338.

1039. Charles S. Johnson, *Growing Up in the Black Belt,* quoted from Hortense Powdermaker, *op. cit.*, p. 100.

1040. Foner, *op. cit.*, p. 601.

1041. Meier and Rudiwick, *From Plantation to Ghetto,* p. 148.

1042. Williamson, *op. cit.*, p. 70.

1043. W. E. B. Du Bois, *The Souls of Black Folk.* New York: McClure, 1969, p. 80.

1044. August Meier, "Towards a Reinterpretation of Booker T. Washington," in Meier and Rudiwick, eds., *The Making of Black America*, Vol. I., pp. 126, 130.

1045. *ibid.*, p. 130.

1046. Rudiwick, "The Niagara Movement," in Meier and Rudiwick, eds., *op. cit.*, p. 148.

1047. Robert L. Allen, *American Blacks in Awakening.* Chinese edition. Shanghai, 1976, p. 100.

1048. Du Bois, "Dusk of Down," in Edward Spargo, ed., *Selections from the Black Press.* Providence: University of Rhode Island Press, 1970, p. 14.

1049. Rudiwick, *op. cit.,* p. 132; McPerson, *op. cit.,* p. 149.

1050. Arvin F. Poussaint, "The Souls of Black Folk: A Critique," in Du Bois, *The Souls of Black Folk,* p. 268.

1051. Nathan Hare, "Du Bois: An Appreciation," in Du Bois, *op. cit.,* p. 310.

1052. *ibid.,* p. 311.

1053. Williamson, *op. cit.,* pp. 73–78.

Conclusion

There was no "Negro problem," Albion W. Tourge, a former North Carolina Judge, commented in the period of Bourbons, but rather a "white" one, since "the hate, the oppression, the injustice, are all on our side."[1054] Although he pointed out the main reasons for black problems in white society, and his moral valor might evoke respect among modern audiences, Tourge only mentioned one part of the issue. More accurately speaking, whites' ideals and actions, including the moral power embodied in the words of Tourge himself, were both the main source of black problems and the main impetus to their solution.

Indeed, problems faced by blacks were whites' creations. Driven by self-interest, the fusion of whites' self-consciousness and their desire for conquest led to the prevalence of racism and formed the ideological basis for discrimination against blacks, which was institutionalized in the political, economic, and social systems. Because of the contradiction between racism and idealism and the conflicts of interest behind them, blacks had to make a difficult choice between freedom and safety and wavered between complete assimilation and black self-consciousness, giving rise to their unreconcilable "two souls" and the legal deadlock between whites and blacks. Due to the presence of racism, the universal ideals of liberty and equality encountered a huge obstacle, democratic theory was divorced from its practice, and American democracy was faced with both challenges and ordeals. Due to racism, blacks' peculiar status in political, economic, and social systems was fixed. On account of the lingering ghost of racism, racial conflicts and tensions became the unchanging melody of history, and the racial problem became "the central theme of South history,"[1055] or, according to Barbara J. Fields, "the central theme of America."[1056] When Reconstruction began, racism had become an integral part of white convictions and formed the basis for political and social behavior; it was much more deep-rooted in the South. Emancipation and Reconstruction released whites' extremism, derived from their feelings of insecurity, but did not provide sufficient power or resources for blacks to resist this oppressive force. Reconstruction was radical in terms of incurring sentimental polarization and whites' antagonism; yet as regards its protective role in black rights, it seemed overcautious by virtue of the limitations of federalism and whites' idealism. This does not mean that Reconstruction had no effect on reforming whites' racial notions. The "New Departure" and, afterward, populism indicated that whites might make the first step in accepting black rights. The strength of racism, however, was in general consolidated and solidified by the Reconstruction experience.

To emphasize the importance of racism is not to deny the significance of political oppression or economic exploitation. The issue of conquest in the former factor was, after all, the substance of black problems, and the latter a decisive element of black problems as class problems. Without the factor of racism, however, black issues would be immediately transformed into the issues of human rights, of the poor, or of labor, etc., and the social strata of blacks would to a large extent depend on their postnatal qualities and competitive ability. Black problems were, first, racial ones. Another factor to be reckoned with was that racism itself was one of the driving forces of political oppression and economic exploitation. Without racism, blacks would not be forever fixed in the lowest place in society, but would show a tendency to pluralism. The two factors of political oppression and economic exploitation were not unimportant, but their significance rested on how they consolidated racism and how they were entangled with racism. Perhaps the complicated nature of black problems was that political oppression and economic exploitation could not get rid of the racial factor. The starting point of studying black problems, therefore, is to analyze how the racial factor has created the peculiarity of blacks' status in the larger society.

In addition to racism emanating from whites' self-consciousness, in whites' minds there was still idealism derived from their democratic beliefs. This idealism in the core values connected with the Covenant of Grace and white mission, and later on the equally important intellectual factor was added to it. The inevitable result was the admiration of and devotion to "the higher law," among which was the natural law or the rational law. The tendency to seek perfection and salvation held a central place in American culture and in fact laid the foundation of the American moral system. American universal creeds such as liberty and equality were in reality the natural extension of the tendency towards perfection. Based on their moral beliefs, American whites explored their ideal kingdom from the beginning. Having experienced a series of conflicts, the embryo of modern democracy gradually took shape. As Max Weber commented, the relationship between a religion advocating salvation of souls and its social structure was forever strained. He generalized an important aspect of American faiths. Among these conflicts, race was one of the main focuses. Since their self-consciousness had permeated, affected, or twisted idealism in different ways and to different extents, whites became antagonistic to each other on racial issues. The most troublesome problem was slavery, which drew a dividing line between districts and parties. During the Reconstruction era, the North forced the South to carry out the new democracy and arbitrarily exported its own values. This action was in fact a radical expression of the aforementioned conflicts. While white's idealism constituted the spiritual impetus to the new racial democracy, the presence of whites' self-consciousness restricted the extent to which the new democracy was performed. As a result, the presence of black people served as a touchstone for the sincerity of American democratic faiths. As Alain Leroy Locke put it, "the slow, consistently steady rise of the Negro's status since emancipation in 1863 has served as a base-level fulcrum for new freedom and wider foundations for American democracy. The Negro's progression from chattel to freedom, to legal citizenship, to increasing equality of rights and opportunities, to accepted neighbor and compatriot represents a dramatic testament to democracy's positive and dynamic character."[1057] The cultural framework of whites, within which blacks themselves could pursue both the universal ideals and the significance of particularism, formed the basis on which black issues were solved step by step. Further, the solutions to black problems began at the time when whites clashed with each other. Since the driving forces behind solutions to black issues originated from the strength of whites' moral evaluation and sympathy, Reconstruction was firstly a white one, and only secondly a black one. The efforts of blacks themselves were not unimportant, but their significance depended on the extent to which blacks forced whites to fulfill their promises. Since the external impetus mainly came from whites, we may see that the splits among whites often provided opportunities for solutions to black issues, and, when their rifts on racial issues were closed, black problems were ignored again. The solutions to black issues, however, perhaps still depend on white unity on a new basis of idealism.

When emphasizing moral forces and moral conflicts, we naturally cannot deny the powerful strength of the political and economic interests behind them. Morality is not a static entity completely separated from the outside world, but is closely related to practical interests. Practical interests cause social conflicts which present an outward appearance of moral conflicts. In the Reconstruction era, the dividing lines of moral conflicts were drawn in this way. It must be pointed out, however, that the moral division was not merely a trivial auxiliary, but actually constituted one part of the whole conflict, had its own operational rules, and now and then rose to be the central focus. Another problem to be considered is whether Republicans were hypocritical when advocating civil rights. Although they devoted much attention to the interests of reality and even concealed their real goals, the reformers did not have to become hypocrites whose deeds did not match their words. Not only had the freedom to believe in truths given them sufficient opportunities to express their consciences, but also these beliefs in harmony with practical interests convinced them of the rightness of seeking their own interests. Quite a few even could transcend the barrier of self-interest and enter the selfless realm of morality. When the motives of Republicans are investigated, these factors need to be particularly taken into account; white supremacists often thought that what they defended was "the lofty moral principles," too.

In the conflict between whites' self-consciousness and idealism, Reconstruction left a political heritage. Although it was not so successful in reforming white thought, Reconstruction marked the beginning of the period of challenging racial conquest and erected legal barriers against racism. Racial discrimination had to bypass these obstacles and advanced by a roundabout route. Even the legalization of segregation had to be labeled "separate but equal"; when disfranchising blacks, whites had to emphasize that this act was not against any "race, color, or any previous condition of slavery or involuntary servitude," but against ignorance and irresponsibility. While traditional federalism had restricted the radical extent of Reconstruction, the new federalism, having whisking off the dust that covered the meaning of liberty in the Constitution created by the slavery problem, equally restricted the extreme extent of racism. The attack from racists, in fact, verified that the defense against racial subjugation was no longer impregnable. Having at least erected the principle that one person's self-identity should not violate others' rights, the legal framework of the new democracy restricted racism to some extent. When people repeatedly stressed that racial differences could not be regarded as the basis for disfranchisement, it is difficult to say that whites would not be imperceptibly affected by this atmosphere. When blacks accumulated strength and took the offensive again, what they relied on was the legal shell of the new racial democracy that Reconstruction had left. Reconstruction had after all provided a fulcrum for the civil rights movement in the 1960s. Carrying forward the unfinished cause of Reconstruction, the "second Reconstruction" made the racial democracy bored through by racism full-grown.

In the economic sphere, Reconstruction tried to break up the power monopoly of the planter class in the labor market, put blacks into a color-blind and free labor–based society, bring labor and capital into a mutually cooperative contractual relationship, and place them on the same starting line for competition. Other than that, Reconstruction did very little. It not only allowed the landholding structure to maintain its previous condition, but also added another coercive commercial power, monopoly on credit, to the old economic forces. While poor whites were also faced with the same problems, the extra-legal compulsion to control the labor market made the fate of blacks more miserable. Confronted with coercive extra-legal force, Reconstruction was incapable of action. In the aspect of building a mature system for free market, therefore, Reconstruction also met with defeat. Nevertheless, it at least started the new system and integrated the South into a national market, in which positive forces were continuously pounding at the backward system of the South, and the economic foundation for the success of the black cause was gradually established.

Regarding race relations, Reconstruction had in fact posed a question that addressed how a dominant race treated a weak one. Instead of advocating absolute triumph and conquest of one race over another, Reconstruction tried to put whites and blacks into equal positions of holding continuous dialogs with each other, i.e., to admit the latter's fundamental rights to participate in mainstream society, despite how "childish" they were considered as a race. Instead of unconditionally emphasizing harmony between the two races, Reconstruction tried to introduce racial justice and universal norms of conduct into race relations, keep a balance between change and stability, and place race relations on a broader foundation. Instead of surrounding and suppressing all difficult factors, which proved impractical even in the time of slavery and did not conform to their long-term common interests, Reconstruction tried to channel racial frictions into a legal system and ensure confrontations remain reasonable.

Seen from this angle, black issues were mainly civil rights issues. The speed at which Reconstruction fulfilled its aim rather than the aim itself was radical. The reason was that Reconstruction hurriedly did so before whites voluntarily accepted blacks' opponent status in the political game. Without these changes, however, how and when could whites accept blacks' competitive status? The real crux of the problem was that racism had put black issues into an endless tangled deadlock. Without elevating the position of blacks, racial justice and the universal norms of conduct would have no substance, reality would contradict the universal principle of democracy, and warfare between the races would not be eliminated. Yet to accept blacks' competitive status might intensify antagonism between the two races and even threaten democracy itself. Because racism was still rampant, it proved scarcely possible to reach a suitable intersection between universal fairness and racial harmony. It was, perhaps, the moral height achieved by Reconstruction rather than its achievement itself that is worth marveling at. In its heroic attempt to break the impasse of discrimination against blacks, Reconstruction manifested an admirable American image of pursuing a perfect society towards this world. This spiritual temperament was not only helpful to resolving black issues, but proved to be whites' foundation for self-salvation and self-transcendence, indicating the extent to which the white civilization could reach.

While whites bore the main responsibility for the solution to as well as the emergence of discrimination against blacks, blacks had their own obligations for political, economic, and spiritual Reconstruction, especially when they had sufficient opportunities to seek their liberties. In fact, black awakening and the sense of responsibility constituted an important facet to blacks' problems. Under the oppression of slavery, blacks naturally related corporal punishment and physical pains to labor itself, their enterprising spirit was inhibited, and the double nature of morality was also an evil consequence of the peculiar system. When blacks strode across the threshold of freedom, the inveterate inertia of old harmful habits was deliberately exaggerated by white racists. While we criticize whites' avoidance of their responsibility, blacks should not ignore their own responsibility for self-improvement and the determination to transform the damaging factors. Thus, blacks themselves faced a tremendous challenge. Especially when their basic rights were guaranteed, the main responsibilities for black issues were then shifted onto the shoulders of blacks themselves. Difficult as it might be, the self-reconstruction of their own qualities could not be shirked by virtue of the existence of racism.

At the same time, it should be admitted that Reconstruction played a part in promoting blacks' progress. Taking into account their limited strength and understanding, the positive results achieved by blacks in Reconstruction were fairly impressive. They could sue and be sued, their due process right was observed, and they also had the right to vote. Despite eventually being disenfranchised, blacks accumulated their experiences in political participation, built up their leadership, and showed considerable understanding of politics. "Altogether," wrote Vernon Wharton, "as government goes, that supplied by the Negro and white Republicans in Mississippi between 1870 and 1876 was not a bad government."[1058] Compared with political participation, their achievements in the economic and social spheres were even more substantial and durable. Public education became an important aspect in their lives. They could enjoy more liberties in arranging their labor, and it was impossible for whites to absolutely control the labor system as before. They also acquired considerable autonomy in family, church, and other social institutions. All these achievements enabled blacks to gather strength. Reconstruction, admittedly, produced little effect in changing blacks' political and economic dependence. Even when Reconstruction was at its height, blacks still played a subordinate role, and color itself was the bottleneck preventing them from making greater success. Nonetheless, Reconstruction marked the beginning of challenging harsh realities. In the long run, black awakening formed the basic solution to the problems facing blacks.

Thus, black issues display their exceedingly difficult nature. In the period of Reconstruction, they were complicated by other problems, including the paradox between elitism and majority rule, the paradox between majority rule and minority interests, and the paradox between federalism and the coercive power caused by the war. No wonder that Reconstruction policies led to so many disputes. Because of its complicated character, Reconstruction provides a window with a wide field of vision for studying black issues.

The experience of Southern Reconstruction tells us that the solution to black issues may be found through two basic plans:

- The deterrent force plan, or the hard plan. So long as racism exists, and so long as whites carry out their desire for conquest, the solution to black issues must rely on a powerful backup force; in other words, blacks must "speak moderately, yet with a stick in hand." To blacks, therefore, to accumulate their political, economic, and moral strength is fundamental and long-term work. On the one hand, blacks should actively strive for their due rights (not privileges or whatever affirmative plan) and wage a reasonable, temperate struggle; on the other hand, blacks should not wait quietly for the advent of a savior and let slip opportunities for self-development under existing conditions, but it is necessary for them to set about elevating their subculture. Here the words of Stokely Carmichael have inspirational significance: "The concept of Black Power rests on a fundamental premise: Before a group can enter the open society, it must close ranks. By this we mean that group solidarity is necessary before a group can operate effectively from a bargaining position of strength in a pluralistic society."[1059] The definition of black power should be more general nevertheless. The balance between the solid strength of a discriminated group and the dominant group does not have to be exactly equal, but there must be a clear demarcation line of justice. Thus, black power must be used with restraint. In other words, if racism vanishes, or the existence of whites' self-consciousness does not form an obstacle to concrete problems, black issues should be treated as nonracial problems. The Populist practice of class politics has some value as a starting point for action. On the prerequisite of seeking reasonable goals, the use of black power should particularly pay attention to retrograde racism (black extremism); otherwise, negative influences might arise.

• The moral reform plan, or the soft plan. Whites need to release themselves from internal dread, suspicions, hate, and other ill feelings, enhance their moral self-restraint, introduce universal justice and the golden rule into racial relations, foster a tolerant spirit in the mainstream culture, respect others, and, at least, prevent self-consciousness from depriving others of their due rights. To blacks, it is important to foster their self-esteem, overcome any inferiority complex, mold healthy black souls, increase their qualities, reform their self-images, and do constructive works. Unquestionably, it does not mean that they should abandon their respective racial identity, for that proposal is contrary to human nature. In fact, excessive sensitivity to racism now has become a social problem in America. In a society like America where many races are in constant contact with one another, the best way is not to eliminate cultural or traditional characters of each race, but to foster and protect their respective healthy self-consciousness, namely, positive "white souls" or "black souls."

Compared to the hard plan, the soft plan is a high-level plan, and only after all sorts of black rights are guaranteed is it possible to be fully implemented. Once the universal norms of conduct are carried out, and equal civil rights are given to blacks and also recognized by whites, the racial conquered state might be transformed into "reasonable governance" or "joint sovereignty," and the nature of black issues would be softened. These hopes, gratifyingly, have to a large extent become reality since the civil rights movement of the 1960s. Thereafter the significance of the soft plan is coming to fruition. If it is completely performed, the fundamental crux of black issues would be solved, the two races would constantly hold dialogues in a pluralistic framework, and racial harmony would be fully realized. Although the toxicity of discrimination is much less strong, to be sure, its thorough elimination seems much more complicated than the bestowal of civil rights. On the one hand, we suggest that we do not have to be too preoccupied by the existence of racial self-consciousness, for personal discrimination is of minor importance when the universal norms of conduct have been established in public policy; on the other hand, since racial self-consciousness is after all a vital source of visible or invisible discrimination in public policy and private affairs, we give our best wishes as follows:

> But let justice roll down like waters,
>   and righteousness like an ever-flowing stream.

NOTES

1054. Otto H. Olsen, *Carpetbaggers: The Life of Albion Winegar Tourge,* quoted from Eric Foner, *Reconstruction: America's Unfinished Revolution, 1863–1877.* New York: Harper & Row, 1988, p. 606.

1055. Ulrich B. Phillips, "The Central Theme of Southern History," *American Historical Review,* October 1928, pp. 30–43.

1056. Babara J. Fields, "Theology and Race in American History," quoted from J. Morgan Kousser and James M. McPerson, eds., *Region, Race, and Reconstruction: Essays in Honor of C. Vann Woodward.* New York: Oxford University Press, 1982, p. 143.

1057. Alain Locke, "The Negro: A Proud Collaborator in the Advance of American Democracy," in Leland D. Baldwin, *Ideas in Action: Documentary and Interpretive Readings in American History,* Vol. I. New York: Random House, 1971, p. 58.

1058. Quoted from C. Vann Woodward, *The Burden of Southern History.* Baton Rouge: Louisiana State University Press, 1993, p. 102.

1059. Stokely Carmichael and Charles V. Hamilton, *Black Power.* New York: Random House, 1967, p. 44.

Bibliography

Allen, James S. *Reconstruction: The Battle for Democracy.* New York: International, 1937.

Anderson, Eric, and Moss, Alfred A. Jr. *The Fact of Reconstruction.* Baton Rouge: Louisiana State University Press, 1991.

Bailey, Thomas A. *The American Spirit: United States History as Seen by Contemporaries.* Lexington, MA: D. C. Heath, 1973.

Bailyn, Bernard, et al. *The Great Republic.* Boston: Little, Brown, 1977.

Baldwin, Leland D., ed. *The Flavor of the Past: Readings in American Social and Political Portraiture.* New York: American Book, 1968.

———. *Ideas in Action: Documentary and Interpretive Readings in American History.* New York: American Book, 1968.

Baltzell, E. Digby. *Puritan Boston and Quaker Philadelphia: Two Protestant Ethics and the Spirit of Class Authority and Leadership.* New York: Free Press, 1979.

Benedict, Michael Les. *The Fruits of Victory: Alternatives in Restoring the Union, 1865–1877.* Washington, DC: University Press of America, 1986.

Bergerson, Paul H. *The Papers of Anderson Johnson.* Vol. 8. Knoxville: University of Tennessee Press, 1989.

Bernstein, Barton J., ed. *Towards a New Past: Dissenting Essays in American History.* New York: Random House, 1968.

Bloom, Jack M. *Class, Race, and the Civil Rights Movement.* Indianapolis: Indiana University Press, 1987.

Boorstin, Daniel J. *The Americans: The Colonial Experience.* New York: Random House, 1958.

Carlisle, Rodney P. *Prologue to Liberation: A History of Black People in America.* New Brunswick, NJ: Rutgers University, 1972.

Cash, W. J. *The Mind of the South.* New York: Knopf, 1941.

Cox, La Wanda, and John H. *Politics, Principles, and Prejudice, 1865–1866.* New York: Free Press, 1963.

Crouch, Barry A. *The Freedmen's Bureau and Black Texans.* Austin: University of Texas Press, 1992.

Crow, J. J., Escott, P. D., and Flynn, C. L. Jr., eds. *Race, Class and Politics in Southern History.* Baton Rouge: Louisiana State University Press, 1989.

Cruden, Robert, *The Negro in Reconstruction.* Englewood Cliffs: Prentice-Hall, 1969.

Currie, James T. *Enclave: Vicksburg and Her Plantations, 1863–1870.* Jackson: University Press of Mississippi, 1980.

Degler, Carl N. *The Other South: Southern Dissenters in the Nineteen Century.* New York: Harper & Row, 1974.

Du Bois, W. E. B. *Black Reconstruction in America, 1860–1880.* Cleveland: World Publishing Company, 1964.

———. *The Souls of Black Folk.* New York: McClure, 1969.

Foner, Eric. *Reconstruction: America's Unfinished Revolution, 1863–1877.* New York: Harper & Row, 1988.

Frank, Tibor, ed. *The Origins and Originality of American Culture.* Budapest, 1984.

Fredrickson, George M., ed. *William Lloyd Garrison.* Englewood Cliffs: Prentice-Hall, 1968.

Fromm, Erich. *Escape from Freedom.* New York: Farrar & Rinehart, 1942.

Gabriel, Ralph H. *The Course of American Democratic Thought: An Intellectual History Since 1815.* New York: Ronald Press, 1940.

Gettell, Raymond G. *History of American Political Thought.* New York: Century, 1928.

Gispen, Kees, ed. *What Made the South Different.* Jackson: University Press of Mississippi, 1990.

Glenn, Norval D., and Bonjean Charles M., eds. *Blacks in the United States.* San Francisco: Chandler Publishing, 1969.

Gossett, Thomas F. *Race: The History of an Idea in America.* Dallas, TX: Southern Methodist University Press, 1963.

Grantham, Dewey W. *The Democratic South: The Economic and Social Revolution in the South Interpreted in the Light of History.* New York: Harper & Row, 1972.

Grob, Gerald N., and Billias, George A. *Interpretations of American History: Patterns and Perspectives.* New York: Free Press, 1972.

Handlin, Oscar. *Race and Nationality in American Life*. New York: Doubleday, 1957.

Harris, William C. *The Day of Carpetbaggers: Republican Reconstruction in Mississippi*. Baton Rouge: Louisiana University Press, 1979.

Harris, William H. *The Harder We Run: Black Workers Since the Civil War*. New York: Oxford University Press, 1982.

Hudson, Winthrop S. *Religion in America: An Historical Account of the Development of American Religious Life*. New York: Macmillan, 1981.

Hyman, Harold M. *Into Slavery: Racial Decisions in the Virginia Colony*. New York: J. B. Lippincott, 1976.

Isaacs, Harold R. *The New World of Negro Americans*. New York: Viking Press, 1963.

Jeffrey-Jones, Rhodri, ed. *The Growth of Federal Power in American History*. Edinburgh: Scottish Academic Press, 1983.

Jordan, Winthrop D. *The White Men's Burden: Historical Origins of Racism in the United States*. New York: Oxford University Press, 1974.

Katz, Stanley N., ed. *Colonial America: Essays in Politics and Social Development*. Boston: D. C. Heath, 1969.

———. *New Perspectives on the American Past, 1607 to 1877*. Boston: Little, Brown, 1971.

Kern, Meyers C. *Sources of the American Republic: A Documentary History of Politics, Society, and Thought*. Glenview, IL: Scott, Foresman, 1967.

Kolchin, Peter. *American Slavery*. New York: The Penguin Group, 1993.

Kousser, J. Morgan, and McPherson, James M. *Region, Race, and Reconstruction*. New York: Oxford University Press, 1982.

Kusmer, Kenneth L. *The Civil War and Reconstruction*. New York: Garland Publishing, 1991.

Laski Harold J. *The American Democracy: A Commentary and an Interpretation*. New York: Viking Press, 1948.

Litwack, Leon F. *Been in the Storm So Long*. New York: Random House, 1979.

Macleod, Duncan J. *Slavery, Race and the American Reconstruction*. Cambridge: Cambridge University Press, 1974.

Maltz, Earl M. *Civil Rights, the Constitution, and Congress, 1863–1869*. Lawrence: University Press of Kansas, 1990.

Marcus, Robert D., and Burner, David, eds. *The American Scene: Varieties of American History*. New York: Appleton-Century-Crofts, 1974.

Martin James K., ed. *Interpreting Colonial America: Selected Readings*. New York: Dodd, Mead, 1973.

McFarland, C. K. *Readings in Intellectual History*. New York: Holt, Rinehart & Winston, 1970.

McKitrick, Eric L., ed. *Slavery Defended: The View of the Old South.* Englewood Cliffs: Prentice-Hall, 1963.

Meier, August, and Rudiwick, Elliott. *From Plantation to Ghetto.* New York: Hill and Wang, 1970.

———. *The Making of Black America.* Vol. I. New York: Atheneum, 1973.

Melemore, Richard A., ed. *A History of Mississippi.* Vol. I. Jackson: University Press of Mississippi, 1973.

Messner, Gerald, ed. *Another View: To Be Black in America.* New York: Harcourt, Brace & World, 1970.

Meyers, Marwin, and Pole, J. R., eds. *The Meanings of American History: Interpretations of Events, Ideas, and Institutions.* Glenview, IL: Scott, Foresman, 1971.

Montgomery, William. *Under Their Own Vine and Fig Tree: The African Church in the South, 1865–1900.* Baton Rouge: Louisiana State University Press, 1993.

Mouseley, James G. *A Cultural History of Religion in America.* Westport, CT: Greenwood, 1981.

Myrdal, Gunnar. *An American Dilemma: Negro Problem and Modern Democracy.* Vol. I. New York: Random House, 1962.

Newby, I. A. *The South: A History.* New York: Holt, Rinehart and Winston, 1978.

Ostrander, Gilman. *The Rights of Man in America, 1606–1861.* Columbia: University of Missouri Press, 1969.

Parrington, Vernon L. *Main Currents in American Thought.* New York, Random House, 1954.

Perry, Ralph B. *Puritanism and Democracy.* New York: Vanguard Press, 1944.

Piersen, William D. *Black Legacy: America's Hidden Heritage.* Amherst: University of Massachusetts Press, 1993.

Quit, Howard N. *Main Problems in America History.* Homewood, IL: Dorsey Press, 1978.

Rabinowitz, Howard N. *Race Relation in the Urban South, 1865–1890.* New York: Oxford University Press, 1978.

Ransom, Roger L., and Sutch, Richard. *One Kind of Freedom: The Economic Consequences of Emancipation.* New York: Cambridge University Press, 1977.

Reid, John Phillip. *The Concept of Liberty in the Age of the American Revolution.* Chicago: University of Chicago Press, 1988.

Reuter, Edward Byron. *The Mulatto in the United States.* New York: Negro University Press, 1969.

Richter, William L. *The Army in Texas During Reconstruction, 1865–1870.* College Station: Texas A & M University Press, 1987.

Robinson, Ronald, Gallagher, John, and Denny, Alice. *Africa and the Victorians.* New York: Macmillan, 1961.

Schneider, Herbert W. *A History of American Philosophy.* New York: Columbia University Press, 1963.

Schneider, Seth M., and Edelstein, Tilden G., eds. *The Black Americans: Interpretive Readings.* New York: Random House, 1971.

Smith, Gerald B. *Social Idealism and the Changing Theology: A Study of the Ethical Aspect of Christian Doctrine.* New York: Harper & Brothers, 1913.

Spargo, Edward. *Selections from the Black Press.* Providence, RI: Jamestown Publishers, 1970.

Stampp, Kenneth M. *The Era of Reconstruction.* New York: Knopf, 1965.

Steinfield, Melvin, ed. *Our Racist Presidents: From Washington to Nixon.* California: Consensus Publishers, 1972.

Thomas, Emory M. *The Confederacy as a Revolutionary Experience.* Englewood Cliffs: Prentice-Hall, 1971.

Tindall, George B., ed. *The Pursuit of Southern History: Presidential Addresses of the Southern Historical Association, 1935–1963.* Baton Rouge: Louisiana State University Press, 1964.

Trelease, Allen W. *Reconstruction: The Great Experiment.* New York: Harper & Row, 1971.

————. White Terror: *The Ku Klux Klan Conspiracy and Southern Reconstruction.* New York: Oxford University Press, 1971.

Unger, Irwin, Brody, David, and Goodman, Paul, eds. *The American Past: A Social Record.* Waltham, MA: D. C. Heath, 1971.

Ward, F. Champion, et al., eds. *The People Shall Judge: Readings in the Formation of American Policy.* Vol. I. Chicago: University of Chicago Press, 1949.

Weber, David R. *Civil Disobedience in America: A Documentary History.* Ithaca: Cornell University Press, 1978.

Weber, Max. *The Protestant Ethic and the Spirit of Capitalism.* New York: Scribner's, 1958.

Weinstein, Allen, ed. *Origins of Modern America.* New York: Random House, 1970.

Wharton, Vernon Lane. *The Negro in Mississippi.* New York: Harper & Row, 1965.

Williamson, Joel. *The Crucible of Race: Black-White Relations in the American South Since Emancipation.* New York: Oxford University Press, 1984.

————. *New People: Miscegenation and Mulattos in the United States.* New York: Free Press, 1980.

Woodhouse, A. S. P. *Puritanism and Liberty.* London: Peel and Sons, 1938.

Woodward, C. Vann. *The Burden of Southern History*. Baton Rouge: Louisiana State University Press, 1993.

————. *Origins of the New South, 1877–1913*. Baton Rouge: Louisiana State University Press, 1971.

————. *The Strange Career of Jim Crow*. New York: Oxford University Press, 1968.

Index